Mallorca

Damien Simonis
Sarah Andrews

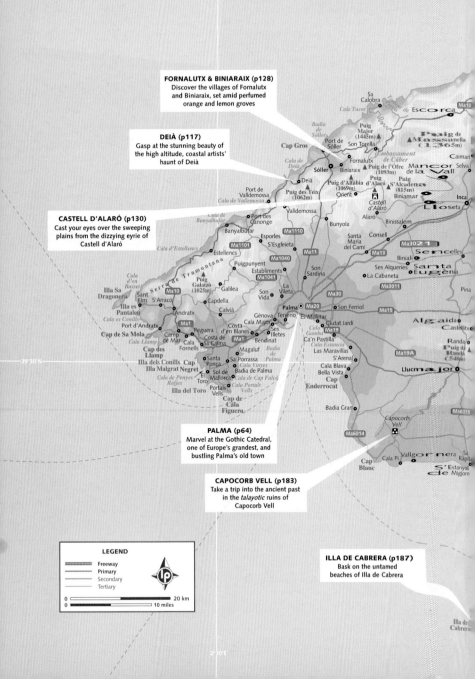

FORNALUTX & BINIARAIX (p128)
Discover the villages of Fornalutx and Biniaraix, set amid perfumed orange and lemon groves

DEIÀ (p117)
Gasp at the stunning beauty of the high altitude, coastal artists' haunt of Deià

CASTELL D'ALARÓ (p130)
Cast your eyes over the sweeping plains from the dizzying eyrie of Castell d'Alaró

PALMA (p64)
Marvel at the Gothic Catedral, one of Europe's grandest, and bustling Palma's old town

CAPOCORB VELL (p183)
Take a trip into the ancient past in the *talayotic* ruins of Capocorb Vell

ILLA DE CABRERA (p187)
Bask on the untamed beaches of Illa de Cabrera

LEGEND

▭▭▭▭	Freeway
────	Primary
────	Secondary
────	Tertiary

0 ⊢──────⊣ 20 km
0 ⊢──────⊣ 10 miles

POLLENÇA (p134)
Climb the pilgrim steps of Calvari in the perky northern town of Pollença

PARC NATURAL DE S'ALBUFERA (p148)
Join twitchers for a spot of bird-watching in the Parc Natural de S'Albufera wetlands

ELS CALDERERS (p162)
Inspect the Mallorquin nobles' grand old way of rural life at Els Calderers *possessió*

COVES DEL DRAC (p177)
Explore the Coves del Drac, Mallorca's most spectacular stalactite and stalagmite show

ELEVATION

	1000m
	700m
	500m
	300m
	200m
	100m
	0

MEDITERRANEAN SEA

On the Road

DAMIEN SIMONIS Coordinating Author

On a sweltering August day, I found myself within sniffing distance of the sea on the edge of pretty Alcúdia, rambling the Roman ruins of ancient Pol·lentia (p142). At this 1st century AD theatre, at the height of the Pax Romana, local citizens would settle down for a little theatre or spillage of gladiatorial blood. Did the Romans go sunbathing at the nearby beaches? Perhaps not. Either way, the passage of civilisations through the island's history adds a fascinating dimension to the traveller's discovery of Mallorca. Although not a great deal remains of this once thriving provincial town, there is enough to fuel the time traveller's imagination.

SARAH ANDREWS

It was a breezy, cloudy afternoon when I decided to visit Artà's Santuari de Sant Salvador (p167), which turned out to be the perfect time to visit. The walk up was cool enough to be enjoyable, and the view from the top of the fortress was amazing. Those low, dark clouds made the landscape so much more dramatic than it would have been on a perfectly sunny day. I spent way more time than I'd planned to at the Santuari, just soaking in the view and writing in my notebook.

See full author bios page 224

INTRODUCING MALLORCA

Majestic limestone cliffs plunge into the topaz depths of the Mediterranean. Vast plains carpeted with almonds, carobs, olives and vineyards stretch across the interior. Yachts drop anchor in the translucent waters of hidden inlets. Lonely hermitages and castles stand sentinel on isolated hills. While seaside revellers let rip in the beach resorts around Palma, others explore that city's ochre-tinged medieval heart or check out of the hurly-burly by trekking the Serra de Tramuntana mountains or relaxing in centuries-old manor houses turned rural hotels. The facets of this island jewel sparkle for everyone.

Natural Highs

From Palma to Cap de Formentor, there's no shortage of extraordinary coastal lookout points from which to gaze out over the twinkling Mediterranean. The views are at their most startling along the Serra de Tramuntana. But jutting out of the plains of central Mallorca are strangely isolated castle- and monastery-topped heights that afford equally breathtaking feasts for the eyes.

❶ Castell d'Alaró

For centuries, Muslim and Christian warriors controlled a proud and impregnable fortress high above the town of Alaró (p130). Today the steep drive or climb on foot is rewarded not only with a snack bar and the possibility of sleeping over, but also by extraordinary views in all directions, including to Palma.

❷ Santuari de Sant Salvador & Castell de Santueri

Only separated by a few kilometres as the crow flies, this monastery and castle (p164) compete to offer vast panoramas of the island's southeast. The castle ruins in particular watch over the waters from whence countless pirate assaults no doubt came. From Santuari de Sant Salvador the sea seems more distant, but you can gaze over the plains of central Mallorca to the west and the inland side of the Serra de Tramuntana to the north.

❸ Santuari de la Mare de Déu des Puig

Overshadowing nearby Pollença, this hilltop hermitage (p135), where you can sleep in former hermits' cells, requires a breathless climb but rewards you with breathtaking views over the Pollença and Alcúdia bays.

❹ Talaia d'Albercuix

Built as early-warning 'radar' against Moorish pirates, this watchtower (at 380m one of the highest points on the jagged Formentor peninsula, p141) brings only pleasure today to those who come to contemplate the grandeur of the Med and Mallorca.

❺ Torre des Verger

Vertigo sufferers beware! This *talayot* (watchtower) hovers at cliff's edge atop the limestone walls of the Serra de Tramuntana outside Banyalbufar (p112). On a clear night you should be able to see across to the lights of Barcelona.

Take the plunge

The sparkling waters of the Mediterranean exert an almost mesmerising power over Mallorca's visitors. Small wonder that most stay on the coast! Some just rejoice in splashing around in the generally translucent sea. Others like more vigorous activity and there's plenty on offer, from plumbing the depths in scuba gear to sailing in search of hidden coves or sea kayaking.

❶ Dropping Anchor in Cala Figuera (Formentor)

Sailing along part of the coast (or around the island) allows you to see Mallorca in a different way, and makes reaching some beautiful coves much easier! Except in bad weather, you'll always find a few craft anchored in the long, turquoise inlet of Cala Figuera (p190) near Cap de Formentor.

❷ Cala de Deià

Of the tiny inlets along the forbidding western stretch of the Serra de Tramuntana, Cala de Deià (p118), down from one of the island's prettiest towns, is the most enticing. Its transparent emerald water and pebbly beach are backed by two summer eateries.

❸ Diving off Illa de Cabrera

Surprisingly for the Mediterranean, there's still life in Mallorca's waters. Good dive spots abound but the protected nature reserve of Illa de Cabrera (p187) is best for marine flora and fauna.

❹ Portals Vells

A half-hour drive from Palma, the picture-perfect sandy cove beaches of Portals Vells (p106) are a sliver of heaven. At Cala Portals Vells especially, it is hard to stay out of the turquoise water.

❺ Sea Kayaking around Cap de Formentor

Those with iron in their arms and a lust for sea salt in their lungs can brave the waves off Cap de Formentor in sea kayaks. Excursions leave from Port de Pollença (p139). For the less experienced, a fortifying paddle around the bay is satisfying.

3

Local Flavours

Many standard Spanish dishes have been fully absorbed into local culinary culture but Mallorca is richly endowed with its own specialities, and the pleasure doesn't stop at your plate. The palate will also be tickled by some fine island wines, whose quality has skyrocketed in recent years. Limited production in two main areas (around Binissalem and the Pla i Llevant area in the southeast) means that many of these wines can be hard to find outside Mallorca, so try them on home ground in restaurants and at the wineries themselves! For more on local wine, see p47.

2

❶ Cellers of Inca

Inca (p155) may not be Mallorca's prettiest town, but at its centre beats the heart of tradition in a handful of *cellers* (former wine cellars) that operate as restaurants. Grand 18th-century barrels of oak and olive line the walls and hearty Mallorcan dishes form the fare.

❷ José Luis Ferrer

One of the best known names in Binissalem (p154) wine, this big winery on the edge of that town is one of a few on the island that runs tours. Witness the processes of turning grapes into the most pleasant of drinks.

❸ Ensaïmades

If you are to try just one of the many local pastries on the island, do not leave out this feather-light whirl topped with a puff of icing sugar. It is perfect with your morning *café con leche* (coffee and milk).

❹ Pa amb Oli

The standard traditional snack in Mallorca is *pa amb oli* (literally 'bread with oil'). Generally served warm with a little garlic and perhaps some tomato rubbed in, it comes with ham and other cold meats, a little salad and olives on the side.

❺ Dirty Rice

It may sound awful but *arros brut* (dirty rice) is the island's signature dish, a hearty rice extravaganza. This soupy dish made with pork, rabbit and vegetables is a genuine local alternative to the ubiquitous Valencian paella and a tasty way to go native.

❻ Lovely Lechona

Also known as *porcella* (in Catalan), there's nothing quite like suckling pig when it's done well. An island favourite, you are best advised to hunt around for it in the interior, and as far off the tourist trail as possible.

¡Fiesta!

Mallorquins love a *festa* (or *fiesta*). Throughout the year patron saints' days in the island's towns provide the excuse for indulging in centuries-old celebrations. Highlights include *correfoc* (fire-running), traditional folk dancing by *cossiers*, colourful processions (such as Corpus Christi), the re-staging of Muslim pirate raids that ended in victory for the home side and more. For more on local festivals, see p20.

Author Tip

In summer especially, Mallorquins happily follow the *festa* fun from one town to another. Find out from the tourist what's on in which towns during your stay. Most town *festes* are generally accompanied by much eating, drinking and conviviality in the streets and bars.

❶ Moros i Cristians

Brandishing wooden scimitars and war paint, hordes of (locals dressed up as) Moors invade the streets and squares of Pollença in the early evening of 2 August (p137). Blunderbusses blast, drums roll and villagers fight back with rods and pitchforks. The *mesclat* (a local liquor) flows, but not as much as the night before, when Pollença is synonymous with party!

❷ Festes de la Verema

Binissalem's wine harvest festival (aka Festa d'es Vermar, p154) lasts nine days at the tail end of September. It attracts visitors from all over the island for processions, folk dancing, craft markets, exhibitions and lots of local tipples. It culminates with a big public dinner for the townsfolk, at which you will see huge pans full of *fideus de vermar*, a hearty noodle dish.

Contents

Regional Map Contents

Northern
Mallorca
p134

Western
Mallorca
p106

The Interior
p153

Eastern
Mallorca
p166

Palma
pp66-7

Southern
Mallorca
p183

Destination Mallorca

To Mallorquins, it is Sa Roqueta (Little Rock), to the Romans it was Balearis Major. Mallorca is not only the biggest, but also the most varied and spectacular of the four main isles that make up the Balearic Islands (Illes Balears in Mallorquin, Islas Baleares in Spanish).

Tourism since the mid-1950s and the accompanying massive development have turned the island's values on their head. In half a century a largely rural backwater has been transformed into one of Spain's richest regions. Coastal land that until then had been considered worthless was suddenly a gold mine. Agricultural land has come to be seen as a dead weight.

In a process known as *balearización*, swathes of the coast have been disfigured forever by thoughtless construction. All too often builders and the authorities have cheerfully ignored regulations limiting construction. Backhanders are part of daily life in municipal and regional politics and this corruption goes largely unpunished. The Andratx scandal is the exception that proves the rule.

Many Mallorquins (who admit to being a conservative lot) fear that policies that don't favour development could lose them tourist euros. A canny bunch, they have become world leaders in major hotel chains. In 2007 an international conference on the Caribbean hospitality industry was held in...Palma.

The massive arrival of mainland Spaniards and Europeans, buying up property across Mallorca, has pushed housing prices beyond the reach of many locals and unleashed debate on island identity. Some fear that local culture and language are being swept aside.

The bulk of visitors to the island remain blissfully ignorant of all this. Many, stuck in package-holiday enclaves, remain equally unaware of the island's varied and captivating beauty.

From bayside Palma, with one of the world's greatest Gothic cathedrals and a fascinating medieval centre, to the four corners of the Part Forana (Part Outside, ie the rest of the island), Mallorca presents a kaleidoscope of natural and artificial attractions. The mighty Serra de Tramuntana mountain range along the northwest coast is a highlight. Atop its vertigo-inducing cliffs is strung a series of compact villages, each with its own tiny pebble beach, which has attracted curious outsiders for centuries. The area around Sóller, where the mountains draw inland from the sea, is a golden valley crammed with sweet-smelling citrus orchards. In the interior, cream and ochre towns are scattered like dice over a gaming table. The reddish plains are dotted with castles, ancient sites and hilltop hermitages.

Tourism made farming unviable for most and much agricultural land lies abandoned. In an ironic twist, tourism is now perhaps coming to the rescue, as farms increasingly turn to rural accommodation formulas to keep their core activities alive. Environmentalists fight a constant battle to turn the tide of thought and to brake development. They have scored successes down the years, including the creation and improvement of several natural parks. Ever practical, a measure of the environmental debate centres on trying not to kill the goose that lays the golden egg.

FAST FACTS

Population: 790,760

Area: 3620 sq km

GDP (Balearic Islands): €24.4 billion

GDP per head (Balearic Islands): €24,460

GDP growth (Balearic Islands): 3.5%

Unemployment rate (Balearic Islands): 6.5%

Average life expectancy: 80.5 years

Highest point in Mallorca: Puig Major de Son Torrella 1445m

Number of Michelin-rated restaurants in Mallorca: 48 (six have stars)

Number of air passengers through Mallorca's airport (2006): 22,408,230

Getting Started

Mallorca is a case of good things coming in small packages. Although largely perceived as a summer-only, sun-and-fun destination, there is much more to the place. The mountain trails of the Serra de Tramuntana can be walked throughout most of the year, and cyclists will also enjoy the back inland roads. Diving, sailing, sea kayaking and other sports are attractions for the sport-minded (see p60). The growing network of quality rural hotels makes for peaceful country holidays at any time of the year and Palma offers everything from culture to shopping for the short-break city-stopper. Many of the island's resorts are geared to families, so bringing the kids isn't a problem. Everyone from toddlers to clubbers is catered for.

WHEN TO GO

Mallorca can be considered a year-round destination. Want to be in the thick of the summer heat and action? Then July to mid-September (high season) is for you. The coastal resorts largely shut down from November to March but country hotels and the like are open most of the year.

Touring the countryside is pleasant any time of year. Spring (April to mid-June) is generally the best. September is also good but can get rain. In winter, city breaks in Palma and country stays, especially in the plains towns (watch for the almond blossoms), make for a great escape. There's a good chance you'll find crisp sunny weather, except in the Serra de Tramuntana, which is often cold and wet and where snow falls as low as 1000m (although it rarely lasts long).

See Climate Charts (p197) for more information.

Mallorca's rich calendar of traditional festivals and cultural activities (see p20) should also be taken into account.

COSTS & MONEY

Your biggest costs in Mallorca will probably be accommodation and food. For a family holiday of a week or two, the best value will come from self-catering apartments or villas, allowing you to prepare your own meals. Car hire is cheap by general European standards and distances are moderate.

Backpackers sticking to the cheapest hotels (not always easy because in many locations there are few dirt-cheap options), sandwiches and the occasional simple meal can reckon on spending around €50 a day. Solo travellers are penalised, as single rooms generally cost at least two-thirds the price of a double.

A couple staying in a typical rural hotel, eating out and touring by car each day should expect to pay from €120 to €150 a day each. Opting for a sandwich at lunch helps rein in the expense.

TRAVELLING SUSTAINABLY

Feelings can run high in Mallorca on ecology issues and sustainable development (see p56).

GOOD THINGS SOMETIMES COME IN PACKAGES

Package tours need not simply mean a week holed up in some high-rise apartment on the holiday coast. Various companies provide alternative package offers to Mallorca for those who want to get to know the island without any of the hassle. See p204 for a list of operators offering anything from wine tours to bird-watching holidays, generally of a week's duration. Operators for more standard packages include **Try Holidays** (www.tryholidays.co.uk), **Thomson** (www.thomson.co.uk) and **Ibertours** (www.ibertours.com.au).

FIND A VILLA

You can rent self-catering apartments and villas all over the island. There is no shortage of agencies and websites offering such accommodation. A typical two-bed apartment, perhaps in a complex with its own pool, can cost around UK£700 to £800 in August, and drop to less than half that in winter. An apartment sleeping six will typically cost around UK£1000 in August. Generally, rental is for a week at a time. Some places to try:

- **Cottages 4 You** (☎ 0870 078 2100; www.cottages4you.co.uk)
- **Fincaservice** (www.fincaservice.de, in German)
- **James Villas** (☎ 0870 055 5118; www.jamesvillas.co.uk)
- **Landmark** (www.landmark-gmbh.de)
- **Mallorca Farmhouses** (☎ 0845 800 8080; www.mfh.co.uk)
- **Owners Direct** (www.ownersdirect.co.uk)
- **Villaparade** (☎ 0870 062 6040; www.villaparade.co.uk)
- **Villa Retreats** (☎ 0870 013 3979; www.villaretreats.com)
- **Vintage** (☎ 0845 344 0457; www.vintagetravel.co.uk)

In 2004 the non-profit Fundació pel Desenvolupament Sostenible de les Illes Balears (Sustainable Development Foundation for the Balearic Islands) was set up. It introduced the **Targeta Verda** (Green Card; ☎ 902 929928; www.targetaverda.com) in 2005. Anyone can buy the card (€10) from hotels, airline desks, newspaper stands and post offices. It entitles holders to discounts at many sights, restaurants and shops throughout the Balearic Islands.

Proceeds go to environmental protection and sustainable projects. The most important of these so far has been the improvement of infrastructure and protection at the Parc Natural de S'Albufera (p148), at a cost of around €1 million.

A motorised vehicle is definitely advantageous for getting to some parts of the island but some judicious choices can give drivers, their vehicles and the atmosphere a rest. You can cover some of the ground easily with local transport. Trains run from Palma to a series of inland towns (plus the popular Palma–Sóller run) and, in summer especially, buses cover most destinations. Mallorca is ideal for cycling too.

You are what you eat! Seeking out better restaurants that use fresh island products or shopping at the produce markets is a way of contributing to your wellbeing and the local economy. The restaurants in this guide have been selected with the quality of their cooking, and hence the use of good products, in mind. Foodies with an interest in local products (wine, olive oil and traditional foodstuffs), food and wine touring routes across the island, and recipes should check out **Illes Balears Qualitat** (www.illesbalearsqualitat.org).

Being an island, Mallorca is sensitive to water use, so reining in those long showers is good for everyone!

Just as walkers should tread softly and leave no refuse behind them, so divers should be careful not to disturb the seabed, coral and marine life. Boaters should not drop anchor in areas where poseidon grass grows on the seabed, as they will tear up this sea flora. Look for a sandy bottom.

In Palma you'll see strange copper-toned receptacles for separated refuse all over the town centre. Containers for separated refuse to aid recycling are also liberally scattered around, making it possible to dispose of paper, plastic and glass items separately for recycling. And if locals and visitors used these and the standard bins all the time, maybe the city of Palma would not need to expend so much water on street cleaning!

HOW MUCH?

El País newspaper €1

Admission to dance clubs €10-20

Cocktail €6-8

Palma city bus ride €1.10

Taxi from airport to central Palma €15-18

YOUR CARBON TRAIL

Your travel leaves a carbon trail whether you fly, drive or take the train. Take a trip from London to Palma as an example: taking the train as far as Barcelona and then a ferry will emit 97kg of carbon (per person). Substituting the rail portion with a car will increase this to 320kg (this halves if two travel together) and flying direct will emit 189kg, the negative effect of which is multiplied due to emissions being pumped into the upper atmosphere. Calculations are not simple: precise figures for trains depend on speed (high-speed rail works out equivalent to flying), where the power comes from and whether your train is diesel or electric. While there are no easy answers, taking fewer long-distance trips and staying longer reduces your footprint and means longer, more relaxing holidays for you. Where you can't reduce your carbon think about offsetting your emissions.

TRAVEL LITERATURE

The earliest written accounts of Mallorca come from the Roman chronicler Plinius the Elder. Northern European travellers, especially from France, began writing on the island in the 18th century.

For a light-hearted, contemporary foreigner's view of Mallorca, Peter Kerr has managed to monopolise many a visitor's attention with his series of four chortlers based on his family's attempts over three years to run an orange farm. *Snowball Oranges, Mañana Mañana, Viva Mallorca* and *A Basketful of Snowflakes* follow the seasons and tribulations of rural life, in which the author becomes a master at relaxation. They offer a lively diversion, possibly more therapeutic on a rainy day in London than on location. The last in the series, *From Paella to Porridge*, sees the Kerrs returning to their native Scotland, where Peter turns his hand to fiction.

Tuning Up At Dawn, by Robert Graves' son, Tomás, is full of subtle wit and joy. The book looks at Mallorca (and Spain) since the Civil War, especially the music world in which he was caught up. Graves also writes at length of the Deià expat crowd and its links with the UK music world. His *Bread and Oil: Majorcan Culture's Last Stand*, takes a broader look at contemporary Mallorca.

The French novelist George Sand (actually Amandine-Aurore-Lucille Dupin), a feisty writer, traveller and lover, landed in Mallorca with her then partner, the Polish composer Frédéric Chopin, and two children in 1838–39. She later wrote of their somewhat disastrous stay in *Un Hiver à Mallorque* (A Winter in Mallorca), causing much vexation among Mallorquins, about whom she was not altogether complimentary.

Gordon West's *Jogging Around Mallorca* (1929) remains one of the wittiest and most enjoyable accounts of the trials and tribulations of getting around Mallorca (jogging in those days meant touring!).

The easiest access to 19th-century writing on Mallorca comes through *British Travellers in Mallorca in the Nineteenth Century*, edited by Brian J Dendle and Shelby Thacker. Eight different accounts show all manner of ways of seeing the island. Some thought the roads good, while others found the lower classes rather cheeky.

Charles W Wood's *Letters From Mallorca*, composed in two trips in 1886 and 1887, offers a largely idyllic view, at times owing more to fantasy than research. Getting hold of an illustrated edition makes all the difference.

'Getting hold of an illustrated edition makes all the difference'

INTERNET RESOURCES

The following sites will get you started on a virtual research tour of the island.

a2z Mallorca (www.a2zmallorca.com) General site with lots of links to anything from the Mallorca Yellow Pages in English to a selection of island legends.

TOP 10   MALLORCA

PLACES TO BASE YOURSELF

For such a small island, Mallorca is teeming with landscape and hideaways. Weekenders can base themselves in the medieval heart of Palma, while those in search of peace might opt for pleasant towns like Pollença or Artà, or a seaside or country location.

- Fornalutx (p128)
- Pollença (p134)
- Palma (p64)
- Sant Elm (p110)
- Artà (p167)

- Deià (p117)
- Sóller (p119)
- Cala Figuera (p190)
- Cala d'Or (p192)
- Cala Sant Vicenç (p138)

RURAL HOTELS

The Mallorcan countryside was once the island's main source of richness. Ignored by many beach-seekers, it is peppered with beautifully restored, often centuries-old country mansions converted into stylish places to stay. They range from the tastefully simple to the sublimely luxurious.

- Finca Son Brull, Pollença (p137)
- Muleta de Ca S'Hereu (p126)
- Finca Son Palou (p129)
- Sa Torre (p154)
- Es Castell (p158)

- Agroturisme Monnàber Vell (p158)
- Hotel León de Sineu (p159)
- Scott's (p154)
- Cases de Son Barbassa (p170)
- Hotel Sant Salvador (p169)

BEACHES & COVES

From narrow hidden inlets to the occasional broad, dune-backed strand, the Mallorcan coastline presents innumerable options for those thirsting for the Med's sparkling waters. While some get fairly crowded in mid-summer, others remain surprisingly little visited on all but weekends.

- Platja de Formentor (p142)
- Cala Mondragó (p191)
- Portals Vells (p106)
- Cala Figuera (p190)
- Cala Llombards (p190)

- Platja des Trenc (p187)
- Cala Sant Vicenç (p138)
- Cala de Deià (p118)
- Cala Torta (p170)
- Platja de Sa Canova (p150)

abc-mallorca.com (www.abcmallorca.com) A business and leisure guide with hotels, restaurants, properties for sale, events and classifieds.
Consell de Mallorca (www.conselldemallorca.net) The island's government website, with information on tourism, history and upcoming events.
Infomallorca.net (www.infomallorca.net) Mallorca's official island-wide tourist office website.
Lonely Planet (www.lonelyplanet.com) Travellers' tips, links to other sites and the valuable Thorn Tree forum.
MallorcaWeb (www.mallorcaweb.com) A search engine with articles, upcoming events, listings, village-by-village information and more.
www.mallorca.web (www.mallorca.com) A general site with all sorts of information.

A Year in Mallorca

Hardly a Mallorcan town can resist putting on a show at least once a year in honour of its patron saint. Many indulge in several annual events. Some go on for a week or more, with concerts, parades, traditional dancing, feasting and, often enough, not a little drinking. Palma's calendar, with traditional events, concert cycles of all musical genres, fashion shows and fairs, is busy year-round. There's rarely a dull moment on the island.

SPRING

Spring is the time to come for wild flowers around the island, and bird-watching in the Parc Natural de S'Albufera (p148), when you can see migratory species at home with the resident fauna.

MARCH
Semana Santa (Easter Week) usually falls some time in March or April and is the occasion for colourful processions around the island. In Palma the most impressive are those on Holy Thursday evening (p86). North, in Pollença, the **Davallament** (bringing down, p135) is a Good Friday procession in which the body of Christ is symbolically paraded down the steps of Calvari. It is one of the most moving of the island's Easter celebrations. Over in Montuïri, locals celebrate **S'Encuentro** (p161) on Easter Sunday.

APRIL
The world comes to Palma (p85) for five days in April for the **Festival Mundial de Danses Folklòriques** (www.worldfolkdance.com), with folk dancers performing in central Palma's streets and squares. **MUST** (www.dissenymallorca.com) is a three-day fashion fest held around central Palma.

MAY
The **Festival Internacional de Teatre de Teresetes** (www.festivalteresetesmallorca.com) brings puppet companies from around the world for about two weeks to Palma and towns around the island.

Sineu stages the annual **Sa Fira** (p159), one of Mallorca's biggest produce markets, on the first Sunday of May.

On the second weekend of May, Sóller stages one of the island's most colourful traditional festivals. The high point of **Es Firó** (p121) is a re-enactment of a pirate assault on the town.

One of Palma's most important religious celebrations, **Corpus Christi** (p86), falls on the Thursday of the ninth week after Easter. The weeks leading up to it are marked by concerts in the city's baroque courtyards.

SUMMER

The island's towns move into top gear in summer. Annual patron saints' festivals, in which religious tradition mixes with good old-fashioned pagan partying, are the excuse for many a knees-up. Mallorquins happily traverse the island to get to their favourite *festes*.

On a more restrained note, various concert cycles fill the warm night air. Palma's Castell del Bellver hosts the **Estiu de Cultura** (www.palmademallorca.es), a series of musical events through July and August ranging from classical to jazz. In Pollença, the Sant Domingo cloister is the stage for concerts during the **Festival de Pollença** (www.festivalpollenca.org). Outside Deià on the Serra de Tramuntana coast, the Son Marroig mansion hosts the **Festival Internacional de Deià** (www.soundpost.org), a series of light classical concerts.

JUNE
All over the Catalan-speaking lands, the feast day of St John (24 June) is preceded the night before by fiery partying on the **Nit de Sant Joan** (p86). In Palma this is one of the year's big events, with *correfocs* (fire running), concerts and partying on the beaches until dawn. Other towns also celebrate, including Deià, Muro, Sant Joan, Mancor de la Vall and Son Servera.

Port d'Alcúdia holds the **Festival de Sant Pere** (p146) in honour of its patron saint, St Peter, on 29 June.

JULY
Many coastal towns stage processions on 16 July for the **Festa de la Verge del Carme** (p155

and p173), the patron saint of fishers and sailors. Curiously, the inland hamlet of Ruberts also celebrates.

Cossiers do traditional dances in the streets of Algaida for the **Festa de Sant Jaume** (25 July, p160).

On 28 July Valldemossa celebrates the **Festa de la Beata** (p116), in honour of its saintly daughter, Santa Catalina Thomàs.

Santa Maria del Camí puts on its party clothes for three weeks in July to celebrate the **Festes de Santa Margalida** (p153).

AUGUST

One of the most colourful festivals and intense moments of partying, culminating in a staged battle between townsfolk and invading Moorish pirates, takes place in Pollença on the first two days of August during the week-long **Festes de la Patrona** (p135).

Four days later the focus shifts to Artà (p167) for the **Festa de Sant Salvador**.

On 16 August, Alaró celebrates the feast day of **Sant Roc** and dances by *cossiers*.

August can be a musical month in Mallorca. Classical music performances are held in Valldemossa's Cartoixa for the **Festival Chopin** (p116; www.festivalchopin.com), and jazz comes to Sa Pobla for the annual **Mallorca Jazz Festival** (p160; www.jazzinmallorca.com).

The **Festa de Sant Bartomeu**, patron saint of Montuïri, falls on 24 August. The main event is the traditional dancing by the *cossiers* on the 23rd and 24th.

AUTUMN

September remains a busy month in Mallorca's towns, but thereafter things begin to slow down. Autumn is a good time for catching migrating birds in the Parc Natural de S'Albufera (p148).

SEPTEMBER

The small town of Santa Margalida in the eastern plains of Mallorca springs into action for the **Festa de Santa Catalina Thomàs**, with a colourful procession at 9pm on 2 September.

One week later Santa Ponça commemorates the Christian conquest of the island with a re-enactment of the landing of Jaume I on the beach as the focal point of the **Festes del Rei Jaume I**.

Mallorca's wine centres celebrate the annual grape harvest with the **Festes de la Verema** (aka Festa d'es Vermar, p154). Binissalem's celebrations are the best known and grandest, stretching over the last nine days of September.

September is a key month for contemporary art lovers in Palma, which stages **Art Cologne**, **Jam Art Mallorca** and **Nit de l'Art** (p86).

OCTOBER

Alcúdia's big annual event is the **Fira d'Alcúdia** (p144), on the first weekend of October, which combines a produce market with traditional dancing, music and parades.

NOVEMBER

Inca bursts into life on **Dijous Bo** (Good Thursday, p157), the third Thursday of November.

WINTER

Throughout the island, but especially in and around Palma, a rich calendar of concerts and other events are promoted as part of **Hivern a Mallorca** (Winter in Mallorca). Information is available from the tourist offices by mid-autumn each year.

DECEMBER

On the second Sunday in December, the town of Sineu holds the **Fira de Sant Tomás** (p159), which features the annual *matanza* (pig slaughter).

THE LONG MARCH

At midnight on the first Saturday of August, a flood of folk (around 15,000) leaves Palma to walk the 48km to the Monestir de Lluc. The quickest arrive around 6am. It all started in July 1974, when a soda-water bottle exploded in the hands of the six-year-old daughter of Tolo Güell in a bar in Palma. Fortunately nothing happened to her and Tolo's pals all agreed it was a miracle. And so they decided to walk to Lluc to give thanks to the Virgin Mary the next day. This became a regular event (especially when the same daughter later contracted leukaemia, from which she died) that has since developed into a social and sporting expression of, as Mr Güell put it, 'Mallorquindad' (Mallorcanness).

JANUARY

Almond trees blossom, especially from mid-January to mid-February. The best place to plunge into these cotton-bud-white forests are the south and central western areas of the interior, particularly around Bunyola, Santa Maria del Camí, Sencelles, Lloseta, Selva, Manacor and Sant Llorenç. Rose-coloured late blooms can be espied as late as March. The flowers are traditionally used to produce an almond-based perfume *(flor d'ametler)*.

The **Festes de Sant Antoni Abat** (17 January) are greeted the previous night with huge pyres in towns across central Mallorca. On the day of the festival itself, parading farm animals get a blessing (St Anthony being their patron saint). This feast day (which has pagan Roman origins) is celebrated with particular gusto in Sa Pobla (p160), but you can catch celebrations in many other towns including Algaida, Artà, Costitx, Maria de la Salut, Montuïri, Petra, Porreres, Santanyí and Sant Joan. The night of 16 January is the liveliest, with concerts, public barbecues, drinking, dancing, prancing demons, pyres and fireworks. In Algaida, the 16th also happens to see the **Festes de Sant Honorat**, at which traditional dances by *cossiers* please a local audience. The night before the festival,

> **YEAR-ROUND ART**
>
> **La Artevisita** (www.laartevisita.com) is a curious initiative linking you to local and foreign artists across the island. Through their website you can create itineraries to visit the artists involved (and buy their works). Twice a year, usually in April and October, La Artevisita organises two week-long joint exhibitions at different points on the island.

townsfolk light pyres in Algaida's church square.

Palma holds the **Festa de Sant Sebastiá** (19 to 20 January, p85) in honour of its patron, St Sebastian. It is marked with concerts, pyres in the streets and fireworks.

FEBRUARY

Dates change each year, but the high point of February (and sometimes March) is Carnaval. Towns all over the island celebrate. In Palma a children's procession, **Sa Rueta**, is followed by the grown-ups' version, **Sa Rua** (p85), which is the biggest Carnaval procession on the island.

A rather more odd approach to this pre-Lent feast is Llubí's **Festa del Siurell** (p158), held on the Saturday before the Tuesday of Carnaval.

History

Mallorca's position in the western Mediterranean has made it a key piece in the machinations of the powerful on occasion, but it has rarely been at the heart of great European affairs. Still, the island has known its share of invasion, war, prosperity and hunger. Together with mainland Spain (with which it has shared its history since the Middle Ages) it is one of the few parts of Europe to have experienced a long and prosperous period of Muslim rule. Mass tourism since the 1960s has yanked the island from centuries of provincial doldrums and propelled it to newfound wealth and somewhat forced cosmopolitanism.

THE TALAYOTIC PERIOD

The Balearic Islands were separated from the Spanish continent eight million years ago. They were inhabited by a variety of animal life that carried on in splendid isolation until around 9000 to 10,000 years ago, until the first groups of Epipaleolithic people set out from the Spanish coast in rudimentary vessels and bumped into Mallorca.

The earliest signs of human presence on the island date to around 7200 BC. In the following 6000 years the population, made up of disparate groups or tribes, largely lived in caves or other natural shelters as hunter-gatherers. About 2000 BC they started building megalithic funerary monuments, such as Son Bauló (p149), but the island was certainly not at the epicentre of advanced ancient civilisation. In Egypt they were creating the pyramids at this time.

Things were shaken up with the arrival of warrior tribes in Mallorca and Menorca around 1200 BC, probably from Asia Minor, which overwhelmed the local populace. They are known today as the Talayotic people, because of the buildings and villages they left behind. The *talayots* (watchtowers) are their call sign to posterity. The circular (and sometimes square-based or ship's hull-shaped) stone edifices are testimony to an organised and hierarchical society. The most common were the circular *talayots*, which could reach a height of 6m and had two floors. Their purpose is a matter of conjecture. Were they symbolic of the power of local chieftains, or burial places for them? Were they used for storage or defence? Were they religious sites? There were at least 200 *talayotic* villages across the island, the most important in the south and southeast. Simple ceramics, along with artefacts in bronze (swords, axes, necklaces), have been found on these sites.

The ancients knew Mallorca and Menorca as the Gymnesias Islands, from a word meaning 'naked' (it appears that at least some of the islanders got about with a minimum of covering). Talayotic society seems to have been

For a comprehensive history of the ancient, pre-Roman world in Mallorca, Spanish readers should look no further than *Guía Arqueológica de Mallorca*, by Javier Arambau, Carlos Garrido and Vicenç Sastre.

7200 BC	c 2200 BC	c 1200 BC
Archaeologists believe the first human settlements in Mallorca date from around 7200 BC, based on carbon-dated findings in the southwest of the island in the Cova de Canet, a cave near Esporles.	After some eight million years of blissfully untroubled existence, the *Myotragus balearicus*, a rather ugly endemic species of dwarf antelope, becomes extinct, presumably as the result of unfettered hunting by a growing human population.	Warrior tribes invade Mallorca, Menorca, Corsica and Sardinia. Those in Mallorca and Menorca are known today as the Talayotic people because of the stone towers they built.

divided into a ruling elite, a broad subsistence farming underclass and slaves. It is not known if they had a written language.

Contact with the outside world came through Greek and Phoenician traders. The Carthaginians attempted to establish a foothold in Mallorca but failed. They did, however, enrol Mallorquins as mercenaries. Balearic men were gifted with slingshots (which it is said they learned to use with deadly accuracy as children). These Mallorquin and Menorcan slingshot warriors (*foners* in Catalan) called themselves Balears (possibly derived from an ancient Greek word meaning 'to throw'), and so their island homes also came to be known as the Balearics. These men weren't averse to payment (in kind, because the use of money was banned in their society) and developed a reputation as slings for hire. In Carthaginian armies, they would launch salvos of 4cm to 6cm oval-shaped projectiles on the enemy before the infantry went in. They also carried daggers or short swords for hand-to-hand combat but wore virtually no protection. They were present in the Carthaginian victory over the Greeks in Sicily in the 5th century BC and again in the Punic Wars against Rome.

With the Romans established in Spain and Carthage soundly defeated at the end of the Second Punic War, Mallorca's chiefs sent peace emissaries to Rome. In an act of uncommon ruthlessness, the Romans completely destroyed Carthage in 146 BC in the Third (and last) Punic War. Undisputed masters of the western Mediterranean, the Romans might well have ignored Mallorca and Menorca, had the two islands not acquired an irritating reputation as bases for piracy against imperial merchant ships. Rome could not permit this.

ROMANS, VANDALS & BYZANTINES

When the Roman Consul Quintus Cecilius Metelus approached the shores of Mallorca in 123 BC, possibly around Platja des Trenc in the south, he did not come unprepared. Knowing that the island warriors were capable of slinging heavy stones at his ships' waterline and sinking them, he had come up with a novel idea. Using heavy skins and leather, he effectively invented the first armoured vessels. Stunned by their incapacity to inflict serious damage, the Mallorquin warriors fled inland before the advance of Metelus' men. Within two years the island had been pacified.

Metelus had 3000 settlers brought over from mainland Iberia and founded two military camps in the usual Roman style (with the intersecting main streets of the *decumanus* and *cardus maximus*). Known as Palmeria or Palma and Pol·lentia, they soon developed into Mallorca's main towns. Pol·lentia, neatly situated between the two northeast bays of Pollença and Alcúdia, was the senior of the two.

At the same time as Pol·lentia was embellished with fine buildings, temples, a theatre and more (Pol·lentia has Mallorca's most extensive Roman remains, see p142), some Roman citizens opted for the rural life and built grand

c 500 BC	123 BC	AD 426
Phoenician traders install themselves around the coast, extending their influence over the island's inhabitants (especially in the use of ceramics and changes in social structure). Balearic warriors serve as mercenaries in Carthaginian armies.	On the pretext of needing to end Balearic piracy, the Roman general Quintus Cecilius Metelus, later dubbed Balearicus, storms ashore and in a short time takes control of Mallorca and Menorca.	Raids on Mallorca by the Vandals, central European barbarian tribes that had raped and pillaged their way across Europe to Spain and North Africa, lead to the destruction and abandonment of the Roman city of Pol·lentia.

DISCOVERING ANCIENT MALLORCA

It is remarkable how many ancient, pre-Roman sites are scattered about Mallorca, many quite abandoned. A handful are fenced in and enjoy a minimum of protection, many are barely iden-tifiable, overgrown, on private property and hard to reach, but some of these major sites can be freely visited:

- Ses Païsses (p167)
- Capocorb Vell (p183)
- Son Servera (p174)
- S'Hospitalet Vell (p178)
- Els Antigors (p188)

- Son Fornés (p161)
- the Necròpolis de Son Real (p149)
- Es Figueral Son Real (p149)
- the Talayot de Son Serra (p150)
- the Coves de L'Alzineret (p138)

---

country villas. Nothing much of them remains today but it is tempting to see them as the precursor to the Arab *alqueries* and Mallorcan *possessions*.

The indigenous population slowly adopted the Roman language and customs but continued to live in its own villages. Plinius the Elder reported that Mallorcan wine was as good as in Italy, and the island's wheat and snails were also appreciated.

The tranquillity of the islands was disturbed during the civil strife in Republican Rome in the 3rd century AD. The fighting in Italy spread to the rest of Rome's territories, as did an economic crisis that might have sparked revolts that seem to have severely hurt Pol·lentia.

Archaeological evidence, such as the remains of the 5th-century early Christian basilica at Son Peretó (p163), shows that Christianity had arrived in the island by the 4th century AD. By then storm clouds were gathering, and in the 5th century they broke as barbarian tribes launched assaults on the Roman Empire. The Balearic Islands felt the scourge of the Vandals (an East Germanic tribe that plundered their way into Roman territory) in 426. Forty years later, having crashed across Spain to establish their base in North Africa, they returned to take the islands.

The Vandals got their comeuppance when Byzantine Emperor Justinian decided to try to rebuild the Roman Empire. His tireless general, Belisarius, vanquished the Vandals in North Africa in 533 and the following year took the Balearic Islands. The Byzantine Empire was basically the rump of Rome, with its capital in Constantinople (modern Istanbul). It could not pull off Justinian's ambitious dream. After his death in 565, Byzantine control over territories in the western Mediterranean quickly waned. By the time the Muslims had emerged from Arabia and swept across North Africa in the first years of the 8th century, the Balearic Islands were an independent Christian enclave. With the exception of several bloody raids by the Muslims and Normans, the islands managed to remain a haven of relative peace and independence. Change, however, was at hand.

A Mediterranean Emporium, by David Abulafia, is a marvellous read and about the only good history of Mallorca in English.

534	707	869
The Byzantine general Belisarius takes control of the Balearic Islands in the name of Emperor Justinian, who until his death in 565 attempted to re-establish the Roman Empire across the Mediterranean.	Muslim Arabs in North Africa raid Mallorca for the first time. Four years later they would begin the conquest of the Spanish mainland.	Norman raiders sack most of Mallorca's population centres. This occurs just 21 years after an Arab raid from Muslim Spain had been carried out, which Mallorca's leaders had agreed to in return for being left in peace.

THE ISLAMIC CENTURIES

An Arab noble from Al-Andalus (Muslim Spain), Isam al-Jaulani, was forced by bad weather to take shelter in the port of Palma in 902. During his stay he became convinced that the town could and should be taken, along with Mallorca and the rest of the Balearic Islands, and incorporated into the Caliphate of Córdoba. On his return to Cordoba the Caliph Abdallah entrusted him with the task and Al-Jaulani returned with a landing party in 902 or 903.

The port town fell easily but Al-Jaulani, who was made Wāli (Governor) of what the Arabs dubbed the Eastern Islands of Al-Andalus, remained engaged in guerrilla-style warfare against pockets of Christian resistance on the islands for eight years of his 10-year rule. By the time he died in 913, the islands had been pacified and he had begun work to expand and improve the archipelago's only city, now called Medina Mayurka (City of Mallorca).

The Muslims divided the island into 12 districts and in the ensuing century Mallorca thrived. They brought advanced irrigation methods and the *alqueries*, the farms they established, flourished. Medina Mayurka became one of Europe's most cosmopolitan cities. By the end of the 12th century, the city had a population of 35,000, putting it on a par with Barcelona and London. The *al-qasr*, or castle-palace (Palau de l'Almudaina), was built over a Roman fort and the grand mosque was built where the Catedral now stands. With the raising of walls around the new Rabad al-Jadid quarter (roughly Es Puig de Sant Pere), the city reached the extents it would maintain until the late 19th century. It was a typical medieval Muslim city, a medina like Marrakech or Fez. Few of those narrow streets that made up its labyrinth, now called *estrets* (narrows), remain.

Medina Mayurka enjoyed close relations with the rest of the Muslim world in the western Mediterranean. Anecdotal evidence of this comes in the person of Ibn al-Labbana, an 11th-century poet born in Dénia, on the Valencian coast, who wound up in Mallorca. Here he mingled with philosophers, mathematicians and other thinkers at the governor's court. By 1075 the Emirs (princes) of the Eastern Islands were independent of mainland jurisdiction.

Al-Jaulani's successors dedicated considerable energy to piracy, which by the opening of the 12th century was the islands' principal source of revenue. As the Spaniards would say, this was *pan para hoy y hambre para mañana* (bread today and hunger tomorrow), for such activities were bound to arouse the wrath of Christian merchant powers. In 1114, 500 vessels carrying a reported 65,000 Pisan and Catalan troops landed on Mallorca and launched a bloody campaign. In April the following year they entered Medina Mayurka. Exhausted after 10 months' fighting, they left Mallorca laden with booty, prisoners and freed Christian slaves when news came that a Muslim relief fleet was on the way from North Africa.

Catalan readers could do worse than read Joan Mas Quetglas' *Història de la Ciutat de Palma*, which is a balanced introduction to the history of the city (and the island).

La Dominación Islamita en las Islas Baleares, written by Álvaro Campaner y Fuertes, remains the single most measured study of three centuries of Arab rule in the Balearic Islands and (for Spanish readers) is a worthwhile acquisition.

903	1075	1114–1115
A Muslim army takes control of Mallorca in the name of the Caliph of Córdoba in Spain. Local Christian warriors would resist another eight years in redoubts across the island (particularly the Alaró castle).	Mallorca becomes an independent *taifa* (small kingdom) in the wake of the civil conflicts that shattered the Caliphate of Córdoba into a series of *taifas* across Spain.	A Catalan–Pisan crusading force lands in Mallorca to put an end to the piracy that is damaging their Mediterranean trade. They take Medina Mayurka (Palma) in 1115 and free 30,000 Christian slaves before leaving the island.

In 1116 a new era dawned in Mallorca, as the Almoravids (a Berber tribe from Morocco) from mainland Spain took control. The Balearics reached new heights in prosperity, particularly under the Wāli Ishaq, who ruled from 1152 to 1185. But trouble was not far off. The Moroccan warrior Almohad tribe landed in Spain and swept all before them. A tussle for the islands was inevitable and in 1203 the Almohads achieved full control.

No doubt all this internecine strife between Muslim factions had not gone unnoticed in Christian Spain, where the Reconquista (the reconquest of Muslim-held territory by the Christian kingdoms) had taken on new impetus after the rout of Almohad armies in the Battle of Las Navas de Tolosa in 1212. By 1250 the Christians would take Valencia, Extremadura, Córdoba and Seville, and the last Muslims would be expelled from Portugal. In such a context it is hardly surprising that a plan should be hatched to take the Balearic Islands too, especially as Mallorca continued to be a major source of piracy that seriously hindered Christian sea trade.

For an introduction to Jewish history in Mallorca, check out www.memoriajueva.org and www.memoriadelcarrer.com.

JAUME I EL CONQUERIDOR

On 5 September 1229, 155 vessels bearing 1500 knights on horseback and 15,000 infantry weighed anchor in the Catalan ports of Barcelona, Tarragona and Salou and set sail for Mallorca. Jaume I (1208–76), the energetic 21-year-old king of Aragón and Catalonia, vowed to take the Balearic Islands and end Muslim piracy there. Jaume I (later dubbed The Conqueror) landed at Santa Ponça and, after two swift skirmishes, marched on Medina Mayurka, to which he laid siege. Finally, on 31 December, Christian troops breached the defences and poured into the city, pillaging mercilessly. In the following months, Jaume I pursued enemy troops across the island but resistance was feeble. The rest of the Balearics fell later: Ibiza in 1235 and Menorca in 1287, in a nasty campaign under Alfons III.

With the conquest of Mallorca complete, Jaume I proceeded to divide it up among his lieutenants and allies. The Arab *alqueries* (farmsteads), *rafals* (hamlets) and villages were handed over to their new *senyors* (masters). Many changed name but a good number retained their Arab nomenclature. Places beginning with Bini (Sons of) are Arab hangovers. Many took on the names of their new lord, preceded by the possessive particle *son* or *sa* (loosely translated as 'that which is of…'). Jaume I codified this division of the spoils in his *Llibre del Repartiment*.

Among Jaume's early priorities was a rapid programme of church-building, Christianisation of the local populace and the sending of settlers from Catalonia (mostly from around the city of Girona). For the first century after the conquest, Ciutat (the city) held the bulk of the island's population. The Part Forana ('Part Outside' Ciutat) was divided into 14 districts but all power in Mallorca was concentrated in Ciutat. Beneath the king, day-to-day government was carried out by six *jurats*, or 'magistrates'. In 1382 (some sources say in 1447) a new system of island government was introduced, called Sac

1148	1203	September 1229
Mallorca signs a trade agreement with the Italian cities of Genoa and Pisa, opening up Mallorcan markets to the Italians and reducing the threat of further Christian assaults on the island.	The Almohads in peninsular Spain defeat the Almoravid regime in Medina Mayurka and take control of the island.	Under Jaume I, king of the Crown of Aragón, Catalan troops land at Santa Ponça in Mallorca, defeat the Muslims and camp before the walls of Medina Mayurka.

THE JEWS IN MALLORCA

The first Jews appear to have arrived in Mallorca in AD 70, the same year the Romans largely destroyed Jerusalem and its temple. Under Muslim rule, a small Jewish minority thrived in Medina Mayurka (the name the Moors gave to Mallorca). The Christian conquest in 1229 would eventually bring great and mostly unpleasant change.

In Mallorca, as elsewhere in Spain, the Jewish community enjoyed nominal protection from the king and noble classes. Although barred from most professions and public office, they were esteemed for their learning and business sense. Jewish doctors, astronomers, bankers and traders, generally fluent in Catalan and/or Spanish, Latin, Hebrew and Arabic, often played key roles. It was a Jew from Zaragoza who carried on Jaume I's ultimately fruitless truce talks with the Muslim rulers of Mallorca during the 1229 siege of the capital.

By the end of the century, there were perhaps 2000 to 3000 Jews in Ciutat (Palma). They were evicted from the area around the Palau de l'Almudaina and moved to the Call (Catalan equivalent of a ghetto) in the eastern part of Sa Calatrava, in the streets around Carrer de Monti-Sion. They were locked in at night and obliged to wear a red and yellow circular patch during the day. In 1315 their synagogue was converted into the Església de Monti-Sion (p77) and they would not have another until 1373. In 1391, rioting farmers and workers crashed through the Call in Palma (and the smaller one in Inca) and killed some 300 Jews, whom they considered unduly rich usurers. Not a few had blamed them for the several bouts of plague that had ravaged the island, accusing them of poisoning well water. Any excuse would do to vent anger. Royal protection seemed to do the Jews little good and the assassins got off.

In spite of all this the community held on. It was at this time, one of general prosperity for the trading city, that Jewish cartographers, led by the Cresques family, achieved the height of fame for

i Sort (Bag and Luck). Simply put, the names of six candidates to be named *jurats* for the following 12 months were pulled out of four bags. This system would remain more or less intact until 1715.

The Christian Catalan settlers basically imposed their religion, tongue and customs on the island and the bulk of the Muslim population was reduced to slavery. Those that did not flee or accept this destiny had only one real choice: to renounce Islam. The Jewish population would also have a roller coaster time of it (above).

Plunge into the life and times of the Middle Ages in Mallorca at www .mallorcamedieval.com.

In the Part Forana the farmsteads came to be known as *possessions* and were the focal point of the agricultural economy upon which the island would largely come to depend. The *possessions* were run by *amos* faithful to their (frequently absentee) noble overlords and were often well-off farmers themselves. They employed *missatges* (permanent farm labour) and *jornalers* (day wage labourers), both of whom generally lived on the edge of misery. Small farm holders frequently failed to make ends meet, ceded their holdings to the more important *possessions* and became *jornalers*.

On Jaume I's death in 1276, his territories were divided between his two sons. This was, perhaps, an unwise decision. The eldest, Pere II, became

December 1229	**1343**	**1391**
Jaume I enters the city, which his troops proceed to sack. They leave it in such a state that a bout of plague the following Easter kills a good number of the inhabitants and invading soldiers.	Pere III of the Crown of Aragón invades Mallorca and takes the crown from Jaume III. Jaume III would try to take it back six years later but would die in the Battle of Llucmajor.	Hundreds of Jews die in a pogrom as farmer-workers and labourers sack the Call (Jewish quarter) of Palma. Months later all those involved would be released without sentence for fear of causing greater unrest.

their extraordinary maps, which were used by adventurers from all over Europe. Abraham Cresques (c 1325–87) and his son Jafuda (c 1350–10) created one of the best-known such maps in 1375 (now in the national library in Paris, after Pere IV of Aragón made a gift of it to Charles V in 1380).

In 1435 the bulk of the island's Jews were forced to convert to Christianity and their synagogues were converted into churches. At the beginning of the 16th century they were forced to move from the Call Major to the Call Menor, centred on Carrer de Colom. Along parallel Carrer de l'Argenteria (Silversmiths' St) you can still see the family names of converted Jewish families who for centuries have worked in the gold and silver trade here. They were now Christians but were under suspicion of secretly practising Jewish rites. The arrival of the Inquisition in Mallorca in 1488 heightened the search for such 'crypto-Jews'. The Inquisition celebrated the last auto-da-fé (trial by fire) of such so-called *judaizantes* in 1691, burning three citizens at the stake (coincidentally, the property of such 'heretics' was confiscated). The Inquisition in Mallorca was dismantled in 1820. Throughout this period it remained virtually impossible for *conversos* (the converted) and their descendants to exercise any of the professions from which their forbears had been barred as Jews.

Known as *xuetes* (from *xua*, a derogatory term referring to pork meat that the converted Jews supposedly continued not to eat), they were as shunned by the rest of the Christian populace as they had been before. 'Mixed marriages' between 'old Christians' and converts were exceptional (and even today are frowned upon by some). Officially some 15 family lines (although in reality there were many more) of *xuetes* were targeted, their Christian family names immediately recognisable. They soldiered on as best they could but only in the 19th century did they finally breathe easier. A veritable flurry of 19th-century writers and poets came from *xueta* families. Today the descendants of these families (who even in the mid-20th century were shunned by many other Mallorquins) are estimated to number between 15,000 and 20,000.

master of Catalonia, Aragón and Valencia, while Jaume II became king of an independent Mallorca and master of Roussillon and Montpellier (the latter two in France). Pere, however, considered himself the rightful heir to the united territories. In 1285 Pere's son Alfons II took Mallorca (before becoming king in 1291). In 1295 Jaume the Just, Alfons' brother and successor, handed the island back to his uncle, who ruled until his death in 1311.

Jaume II was succeeded by his younger son Sanç (r 1311–24) and Jaume III, who was ousted by Pere III in 1343 and forced into exile in Perpignan. He tried to recover the island six years later but was defeated and killed at the Battle of Llucmajor. The independent kingdom of Mallorca was now tied into the Crown of Aragón, although it retained a high degree of autonomy.

The fortunes of Mallorca, and in particular Palma, closely followed those of Barcelona, the Catalan headquarters of the Crown of Aragón and merchant trading hub. In the middle of the 15th century, both cities (despite setbacks such as outbreaks of the plague) were among the most prosperous in the Mediterranean. Palma had some 35 consulates and trade representatives

To learn more about the island's grand country mansions, or *possessions*, for centuries the foundation of the island's rural economy, see www .possessionsdemallorca .com.

1488	1521	1706
The Inquisition, which had operated from the mainland, is formally established in Mallorca. In the following decades hundreds would die, burned at the stake as heretics.	Armed workers and farm labourers rise up in what is the beginning of the Germania revolt against the nobles. In October 1522, Carlos V sends troops to Alcúdia to quell the revolt.	The Austrian pretender to the Spanish throne in the War of the Spanish Succession (1702–15) takes control of Mallorca. Nine years later the tables are turned and Mallorca is defeated by Felipe V.

THE EVANGELISING SHAKESPEARE OF CATALAN

Born in Ciutat (ie Palma) de Mallorca, the mystic, theologian and all-round Renaissance man before his time, Ramon Llull (1232–1316), started off on a worldly trajectory. After entering Jaume I's court as a page, Ramon was elevated to major-domo of Jaume II, the future king of Mallorca. Ramon lived it up, writing love ditties and enjoying (apparently) a wild sex life.

Then, in 1267, he saw five visions of Christ crucified and everything changed. His next years were consumed with profound theological, moral and linguistic training (in Arabic and Hebrew). He founded a monastery (with Jaume II's backing) at Miramar (p117) for the teaching of theology and Eastern languages to future evangelists. His burning desire was the conversion of Jews and Muslims and he began to travel throughout Europe, the Near East and North Africa to preach. At the same time he wrote countless tracts in Catalan and Arabic and is considered the father of Catalan as a literary language. In 1295 he joined the Franciscans and in 1307 risked the ire of Muslims by preaching outside North African mosques. Some say he was lynched in Tunisia by an angry mob while others affirm he died while en route to his native Mallorca in 1316. He is buried in the Basílica de Sant Francesc in Palma (p76). His beatification was confirmed by Pope John Paul II and the long, uncertain process of canonisation began in 2007.

sprinkled around the Med. The city's trade community had a merchant fleet of 400 vessels and the medieval Bourse, Sa Llotja, was an animated focal point of business.

Not all was rosy. The plague hit repeatedly (1348, 1375, 1384, 1388, 1396, 1400, 1439, 1475, 1483, 1503), decimating the population. In the Part Forana farm labourers lived on the edge of starvation and crops failed to such an extent in 1374 that people were dropping dead in the streets. Frequent localised revolts, such as that of 1391 (the same year that furious workers sacked the Call in Ciutat, see the boxed text, p28), were stamped out mercilessly by the army. A much greater shock to the ruling classes was the 1521 Germania revolt, an urban working-class uprising provoked largely by crushing taxes extracted from the lower classes. They forced the viceroy (by now Mallorca was part of a united Spain under Emperor Carlos V) to flee. In October 1522 Carlos V sent in the army, which only re-established control the following March.

By then Mallorca's commercial star had declined and the coast was constant prey to the attacks of North African pirates. The building of *talayots* around the island (many still stand) is eloquent testimony to the problem. Some of Mallorca's most colourful traditional festivals, such as Moros i Cristians in Pollença (p137) and Es Firó in Sóller (p121) date to these times. As Spain's fortunes also declined from the 17th century, Mallorca slid into provincial obscurity. Backing the Habsburgs in the War of the Spanish Succession (1703–15) didn't endear Mallorca to the finally victorious Bourbon monarch, Felipe V, who in 1716 abolished all the island's privileges and autonomy.

A humble (and by all accounts rather sober) Franciscan missionary from Petra, Fra Juníper Serra (1713–84), oversaw the founding of a mission in the Americas in 1776 that would become the city of San Francisco.

1773	1809	1822
King Carlos III orders that the Jews of Palma be allowed to live in whatever part of the city they wish and that all forms of discrimination and mistreatment of the Jewish population be punished.	Thousands of French troops captured in battle in mainland Spain are sent for internment to the Illa de Cabrera, where they live in appalling conditions. The survivors would not be released until 1814.	More than 5000 people die in a bout of yellow fever in Palma, just two years after an outbreak of bubonic plague had devastated the area around Artà.

MALLORCA IN THE CIVIL WAR

The fortunes of Mallorca through the 18th and 19th centuries followed those of the rest of Spain. The biggest events in the first decades of the 20th century were the destruction of most of Palma's city walls and its rapid urban expansion. National politics could not fail to colour local life and the 1931 nationwide elections brought unprecedented results. The Republicans and Socialists together won an absolute majority in Palma, in line with the results in Madrid. The Confederatión Espanola de Derechas Autónomous (Spanish Confederation of the Autonomous Right) won the national elections in 1933 and all the left-wing mayors in Mallorca were sacked by early 1934. They were back again in a euphoric mood after the dramatic elections of 1936 again gave a landslide victory to the left.

For many generals this was the last straw. Their ringleader, General Francisco Franco, launched an uprising against the central Republican government in July 1936. It began in North Africa, and Franco's allies quickly led similar revolts across Spain. Government loyalists and left-wing militias defeated many of these uprisings (including in the three main cities, Madrid, Barcelona and Valencia).

In Mallorca the insurrection found little resistance. On 19 July rebel soldiers and right-wing Falange militants burst into Cort (the town hall) and arrested the left-wing mayor, Emili Darder (he and other politicians would be executed in February 1937). They quickly occupied strategic points across

The North African (Barbary) pirates who were such a scourge to the Balearic Islands also operated beyond the Mediterranean. In June 1631 a squadron of these pirates landed at Baltimore, in Ireland.

A RIGHT ROYAL DILETTANTE

As the first battles of the Italian campaign raged in 1915, Archduke Ludwig Salvator sat frustrated in Brandeis Castle in Bohemia, writing furiously but impeded by the fighting from returning to his beloved Balearic Islands. He died in October that year of blood poisoning after an operation on his leg.

Ludwig had been born in 1847 in Florence, the fourth son of Grand Duke Leopold II. He was soon travelling, studying and visiting cities all over Europe. From the outset he wrote of what he saw. His first books were published one year after his first visit to the Balearic Islands in 1867. He returned to Mallorca in 1871 and the following year bought Miramar (p117). He decided to make Mallorca his main base – a lifestyle choice that many northern Europeans would seek to imitate over a century later.

Salvator was an insatiable traveller, what the Spaniards would call a *culo inquieto* (anxious arse). In his private steam-driven yacht Nixe (and its successors) and other forms of transport, he visited places as far apart as Cyprus and Tasmania. Hardly a year passed in which he didn't publish a book on his travels and studies, possibly the best known of which are his weighty tomes on *Die Balearen* (The Balearics). His love remained Mallorca (where royals and other VIPs visited him regularly) and, in 1877, local deputies awarded him the title of Adopted Son of the Balearic Islands. Four years later he was made an honorary member of the Royal Geographic Society in London.

1837	1851	1902
A passenger steamer between Barcelona and Palma goes into service, creating a regular link between the mainland and Mallorca. Among its first passengers were George Sand and Frédéric Chopin, in 1838.	A moderate earthquake damages the Catedral in Palma and causes panic but no casualties. The main façade, badly cracked, would later be done in the style we see today.	The greater part of Palma's old city walls (their position is roughly followed by the line of the Avingudes today) are demolished to allow urban expansion.

Palma with barely a shot fired. More resistance came from towns in the Part Forana, but was soon bloodily squashed.

By mid-August battalions of Italian troops and warplanes sent by Franco's ally, the dictator Benito Mussolini, were pouring into Mallorca. The island became the main base for Italian air operations and it was from here that raids were carried out against Barcelona with increasing intensity as the Civil War wore on. Sporadic Republican air raids on Palma that continued well into 1937 were far less effective. In Palma the Rambla was renamed Vía Roma (curiously, few notice that the northern extension of the Rambla is *still* called Vía Roma).

One of the most profound accounts ever written of the Spanish Civil War is Hugh Thomas' *The Spanish Civil War*.

On 9 August 1936 a Catalan–Valencian force (apparently without approval from central command) retook Ibiza from Franco and then landed at Porto Cristo on the 16th. So taken aback were they by the lack of resistance that they failed to press home the advantage of surprise. A Nationalist counter-attack begun on 3 September, backed by Italian planes, pushed the hapless (and ill-equipped) invaders back into the sea. Soon thereafter the Republicans also abandoned Ibiza and Formentera. Of the Balearic Islands, only Menorca remained loyal to the Republic throughout the war.

With Franco's victory in 1939, life in Mallorca followed that of the mainland. Use of Catalan in public announcements, signs, education and so on was banned. Rationing was introduced in 1940 and stayed in place until 1952. Of the nine mayors the city had from 1936 to 1976, four were military men and the others conservative.

BOOM TIMES

In 1950 the first charter flight landed on a small airstrip on Mallorca. No-one could have perceived the implications. By 1955 central Palma had a dozen hotels and others stretched along the waterfront towards Cala Major.

The 1960s and 1970s brought an extraordinary urban revolution as mass tourism took off. The barely controlled high-rise expansion around the bay in both directions, and later behind other beaches around the coast, was the result of a deliberate policy by Franco's central government to encourage tourism in coastal areas. Many of the more awful hotels built in this period have since been closed or recycled as apartment or office blocks.

The islanders now enjoy – by some estimates – the highest standard of living in Spain, but 80% of their economy is based on tourism. This has led to thoughtless construction on the islands and frequent anxiety attacks whenever a season doesn't meet expectations. The term *balearización* has been coined to illustrate this short-termism and wanton destruction of the area's prime resource – its beautiful coastlines.

How to retain tourist income while minimising the environmental impact is a growing concern in Mallorca, but it would seem a good percentage of the population is more preoccupied with making a fast euro from the building business.

February 1903	**April 1912**	**June 1922**
The opening of the Gran Hotel, a superb Modernista building, in Palma signifies the first signs of a new business in Mallorca – tourism.	The train line linking Palma with Sóller opens. Until now poor roads across the mountains had made it easier for the people of Sóller to travel north by sea to France than south by land to Palma.	The first postal service flight takes place between Barcelona and Palma. The service would use flying boats parked in hangars at Es Jonquet in Palma.

Construction remains *the* hot potato subject in Mallorcan politics. Restrictions in the Serra de Tramuntana make it (theoretically) difficult to build in the mountains and limits on hotel construction make it nearly impossible to create more massive high-rise hotels. But urban and coastal sprawl, legal or otherwise, continues to eat up territory. As investigations into the trafficking of rural land that theoretically cannot be built on continue, it has emerged that hundreds of licences to build on such land have been handed out for years.

The Andratx construction scandal speaks volumes about what really goes on. The scale of corruption in this case was such that the right-wing Partido Popular (PP) mayor was arrested in November 2006. And yet the PP was the most voted party in three quarters of the municipalities in the May 2007 election. In the regional elections held at the same time PP leader, Jaume Matas, fell short of an absolute majority by one seat. He found himself on the outer as the remaining six parties joined forces to create a coalition under the Socialists of Francesc Antich. Antich's key ally is the conservative autonomy-oriented Unió Mallorquina (led by the wily Maria Antònia Munar, elected president of the Balearic Islands parliament), formerly aligned with the PP. What made Munar switch sides? 'To put a brake on the destruction of the Balearic Islands', she said.

On 16-18 March 1938, Italian air force bombers based in Mallorca launched 17 raids on Barcelona, killing about 1300 people. Apparently Mussolini ordered the raids, without the knowledge of the Spanish Nationalist high command.

19 July 1936	1983	May 2007
The army and right-wing militias take control of Mallorca for General Franco as he launches his military uprising against the Republican government in Madrid.	The autonomy statute for the Balearic Islands region (together with those of other Spanish regions) is approved eight years after the death of Franco.	Mallorcan Socialist Francesc Antich ends right-wing Partido Popular rule after regional elections by forming a coalition government with promises to put a brake on construction projects.

The Culture

REGIONAL IDENTITY

Mallorquins, like the inhabitants of the other Balearic Islands, have a naturally strong sense of home and identity. Few think of themselves as 'Balears'. The islands form a convenient administrative unit but each has its own *consell* (government). Historically, they have never thought of themselves as a unit.

A degree of Mallorquin identity is expressed through their language, *mallorquí*, a dialect of *català* that has evolved since the conquest in 1229 (p27). Though their tongue (which people continued to use at home) was edged out of the public realm under Franco, it has largely returned with little fuss.

However, since the return of democracy in 1978 a curious situation has emerged. In a backlash to centuries of perceived repression by 'the Spaniards', Catalan nationalists in Barcelona (the capital of the northeast Spanish region of Catalonia) have mounted a vigorous campaign to reclaim, protect and promote Catalan identity through the Catalan language. Some mainland nationalists hold dear the idea of *Els Països Catalans* (The Catalan Lands), which create a supposedly unified Catalan-speaking world encompassing Catalonia, Valencia, parts of Aragón, the Balearic Islands, 'Catalunya Nord' and parts of Sardinia, all conquered at some stage by the Catalan king of the mainland Crown of Aragon, Jaume I (see p27) and his successors. Needless to say, the idea gets far from unequivocal support from these areas. It continues to be a complex and contentious issue.

The insistence by some Catalan nationalists that 'standard Catalan' be the sole vehicle of communication in this largely fictitious entity has many Mallorquins' backs up. Indeed some find this apparently imperious attitude from Barcelona more irksome than any perceived centralism from Madrid. The anecdote goes that when Mallorquins visit people in Barcelona, the latter inquire: ¿Com va això en nostres illes? (How are things in our islands?); *Tot bé en NOSTRES illes, gràcies* (Everything's fine in *our* islands, thank you) comes the indignant reply.

A distorted view of Catalan nationalism has sparked much unfair, unthinking graffiti in other parts of Spain. But Catalans might be more hurt still to see the following spray-painted invective in Mallorca: ¡No sirem mai Catalans! ¡Puta Catalunya! (We will never be Catalans! Fuck Catalonia!).

However, overall Mallorquins are somewhat reserved and comfortably self-assured, safe in the knowledge that they live in one of the most beautiful parts of Europe – all those millions of tourists can't be wrong!

For all you ever wanted to know on Balearic Island statistics, search through www.caib.es /ibae/ibae.htm.

DOS & DON'TS

Mallorquins tend to be more economical with 'please' and 'thank you' than Anglo-Saxons. This is linguistic custom and doesn't imply lack of appreciation – politeness expresses itself in different ways. Many Mallorquins will instinctively mutter a *buenos días* (good day) or *adiós* (goodbye) when entering or leaving a café or shop and would be perplexed by the way many northern Europeans slink in and out. People walking past your table in a restaurant may well wish you *bueno provecho* or *qué aproveches* (bon appetit), something most northern Europeans wouldn't dream of doing.

When two women, or a man and woman, meet, even if it's for the first time, they greet each other with a light kiss on each cheek; peck right then left.

LIFESTYLE

The *mañana mañana* approach to life so cheerfully chortled over in Peter Kerr's books on life in Mallorca (see p18) persists today, up to a point. Long lunches remain a part of the daily ritual, although the post-prandial nap known as the siesta is left to the privileged few. Indeed, according to some studies, Spaniards spend more time at work than most other Europeans do.

Most locals attribute growing stress and a faster rhythm of working life to Spain's convergence with the rest of Europe. Mallorquins have whole-heartedly embraced the consumer society and many seem to think nothing of diving deep into debt to satisfy their needs and wishes (mortgages, car loans and more).

That said, Mallorquins have not lost their live-for-the-present *joie de vivre*. Time at the beach (not all day like the roasting northern Europeans), hearty meals (especially on weekends and in boisterous groups), good wine and nights out until dawn are part and parcel of Mallorcan life. And, for all the stress of modern life, the islanders always seem to have time for a coffee, an *aperitivo* and a chat.

ECONOMY

In the early 20th century, Joan March (1880–1962) became rich by buying up big landholders' property, breaking it up and reselling parcels to small farmers who had set aside a little cash. In doing so he helped forge a broad, conservative, property-owning electorate. To this day, Mallorquins tend to lean right.

Although not rich by northern European standards, in the centuries preceding the Civil War Mallorca was self-sufficient and generated enough produce for export, thus allowing for the accumulation of capital. Long gone are the days when Mallorca depended on agriculture for its wellbeing. Sure, oranges (from Sóller), wine, potatoes, carob beans, almonds, olives (a huge variety!), pork products and grain continue to be produced, but they are now largely consumed locally and contribute only a tiny amount to the economy.

These days Mallorca, like the rest of the Balearic Islands, depends on tourism for its livelihood. The figures are eloquent: some 72% of the islands' GDP comes from services and another 10% from construction – according to one 2007 study the Balearic Islands have covered more territory in cement and asphalt than any other region since 1996, laying 10,000,000 sq metres of asphalt and building 171,900 flats and houses. Given that the latter is largely tied to tourism, about 80% of Mallorca's economy is commonly attributed to tourism. Just 1% of GDP comes from agriculture and 5% from industry (such as shoes, leather and cultured pearls, among other items).

The popularity of Mallorca and the other islands (especially Ibiza) have made the Balearic Islands one of Spain's wealthiest regions, behind Madrid, Catalonia, Navarra and the Basque Country, but ahead of the remaining 12 autonomous regions.

POPULATION

The population of Mallorca has more than doubled since 1960. Almost half of the 790,760 people officially resident on the island live in the capital, Palma de Mallorca. Much of the rest of the population is concentrated along the coast and in a few interior centres such as Manacor and Inca. Most have fled the land as agriculture has increasingly taken a back seat to services industries.

In 1959, Charlie Chaplin stayed at the Hotel Formentor. The story goes that a reporter waited six hours to do a one-minute interview with a not-very-funny Chaplin. In response to the question 'Could I ask you two questions', Chaplin replied, 'Oui, what's the other one?'

The bulk of Mallorca's potato production around Sa Pobla and Muro, in the island's east, is destined for UK dinner tables.

COMING HOME

Antonio Bauzá was born in Petra (where his grandfather was mayor) in 1975, but left the island at 18 to go to university in Pamplona. In 2006 (some 12 years later) he returned home having lived in Madrid, Milan and London. He works in media relations and lives in Palma with his Italian-born wife, Alessandra.

Do Mallorquins always come home? I think Mallorquins move less than other people, and those Mallorquins who do, always think about coming back. They long for the island. I, too, went away with the idea that I would come back. Maybe it's the island mentality.

Did you find the island much changed? Before it was more like a country town where everyone knew each other. Now it is culturally much more open and mixed. But there are two worlds: Palma and the coast, and the interior of the island. When I go back to Petra, I feel things move more slowly.

Have the changes been good or bad? Both. I miss certain things about Palma. It might seem silly but Palma has lost some of its provincial air, when people went about all dressed up for Mass or to go for a walk along (Avinguda) Jaume III. They knew and greeted each other. Now the city has become more impersonal. I often walk along Jaume III now and I don't recognise anyone! The upside? Palma has become much more international. Look at the bars and restaurants! Before finding a foreign restaurant was rare. Indian, Thai restaurants didn't exist. And the bars are much more cosmopolitan.

Has the Mallorquins' quality of life improved? In money terms, no. The average Mallorquin's buying power has fallen. The crowding on the beaches and elsewhere is another disadvantage. OK, everyone wants to milk the tourism cow. Which is fine but, as a Mallorquin, it bothers me. I remember as a kid going to Platja des Trenc or Cala Ratjada and the beaches were empty! Overall, though, quality of life is great. Having lived away for so long I appreciate what may appear trivial: the sunshine, having the sea so close…

Would you move away from the island again? Well, I know my wife would love to return to Italy. I'd miss many of the advantages of living here but if I had to go, I'd go. *Em sabria greu* (I'd be sorry), but I'd have no real problem.

MULTICULTURALISM

Of the total population of Mallorca, 129,400 (about 17%) are foreign-born. The official resident German population numbers 22,000, well ahead of the Brits at 12,300 and Moroccans at 12,500. Some 41,000 Latin Americans, primarily from Argentina, Colombia and Ecuador, also live here. In addition to this, about 185,000 residents originally come from mainland Spain. In other words, little more than half the island's population was born in Mallorca.

The Campos-born Benedictine missionary, Romualdo Sala (1821-95), who worked in Australia's western desert from 1852, founded the New Norcia mission in Western Australia, which can still be visited today.

While Mallorquins seem to have little overt problem with immigration, they can sometimes be heard to grumble that many mainland Spaniards do little to pick up Catalan (or its Mallorcan dialect). And not a few non-Spanish-speaking foreigners seem to have trouble even with Spanish. There are flip sides: German residents in particular are active in all the Mallorcan political parties, and around 40 German candidates stood in the island's municipal elections in 2007, though none were elected.

The bulk of the African and Latin American populations concentrate in peripheral areas of Palma, although smaller communities thrive in most towns, providing cheap labour. Much of this migration is recent and, while it is too early to speak of integration, friction between the various communities is low.

Those curious to find out more about authors writing in Catalan, in Mallorca and elsewhere in the Catalan-speaking world, should check out www.escriptors.cat.

RELIGION

About 80% of the population attests to being Catholic. The Catholic Church has long played a preponderant role in Mallorcan and Spanish society, but the demise of Franco in 1975 brought something of a backlash and today not much more than 20% of the population regularly attend Mass. Small Protestant and Muslim minorities are made up almost exclusively of foreign-born residents.

ARTS
Literature
In one sense Mallorcan literature began with the island's medieval conqueror, Jaume I (1208–76), who recorded his daring deeds in *El Llibre dels Fets* (The Book of Deeds). He wrote in Catalan, a language that the Palma-born poet and visionary evangeliser Ramon Llull (1232–1316) would elevate to a powerful literary tool. A controversial figure, who many feel should be declared a saint, Llull has long been canonised as the father of the literary Catalan tongue.

Few Mallorquins grapple with Llull's medieval texts but most know at least one poem by Miquel Costa i Llobera (1854–1922), a theologian and poet who, along with other like-minded writers, sought to promote literature written in *mallorquí*. His *El Pi de Fomentor* (The Formentor Pinetree, 1907), which eulogises Mallorcan landscapes through a pine on the Formentor peninsula, is *the* Mallorcan poem.

It is difficult to know whether to classify the writings of Archduke Ludwig Salvator (Lluís Salvador to the locals) as those of a local or foreign traveller. Many Mallorquins consider him one of their own and his tomes on the Balearic Islands, *Die Balearen,* are a source of pride to islanders. Regional president, Francesc Antich, said *Die Balearen* 'is one of the fundamental works of our culture'. For more on the Archduke, see p31.

One of the island's greatest poets was the reclusive Miquel Bauçà (1940–2005). His *Una Bella Història* (1962–85) is a major anthology.

Llorenç Villalonga (1897–1980), born into an elite Palma family and trained in medicine, was one of Mallorca's top 20th-century novelists. Many of his works, including his most successful novel, *Bearn* (1952), portray the decay of the island's landed nobility.

Baltasar Porcel (b 1937, Andratx) is the doyen of contemporary Mallorcan literature. *L'Emperador o l'Ull del Vent* (The Emperor or the Eye of the Wind, 2001) is a dramatic tale about the imprisonment of thousands of Napoleon's soldiers on Illa Cabrera.

Carme Riera (b 1948, Palma) has churned out an impressive series of novels, short stories, scripts and more. Her latest novel, *L'Estiu de l'Anglès* (The English Summer, 2006), tells of a frustrated Barcelona estate agent's decision to spend a month learning English in a middle-of-nowhere UK town.

Guillem Frontera (b 1945, Ariany) has produced some engaging crime novels, particularly the 1980 *La Ruta dels Cangurs* (The Kangaroo Route), in which the murder of the detective's ex-girlfriend muddies his Mallorca holiday plans.

Tomeu Matamalas (b 1952, Manacor) is a musician, painter and writer who has produced several novels. *Bel Canto* encloses two stories: one recounts the love of pianist Andreu for Alicia, while the other tells the story of the priest Mossèn Antoni Mascaró and, through him, the music scene in Mallorca in the late 19th century.

An asteroid discovered by Mallorcan astronomers in 1997 was named 9900 Ramon Llull after the island's great medieval philosopher, writer and evangelist.

German readers can find anything and everything they ever wanted to know about Archduke Ludwig Salvator at www .ludwig-salvator.com.

One of the most beautiful descriptions written of the island was the Catalan painter Santiago Rusiñol's *Mallorca, L'Illa de la Calma* (Mallorca, the Island of Calm, 1922), in which he takes a critical look at the rough rural life of many Mallorquins.

DON'T GRUMBLE, GIVE A WHISTLE

Some historians claim the funny white, green and red clay figurine-whistles known as *siurells* were introduced to Mallorca by the Phoenicians and may have represented ancient deities. Classic figures include bulls, horse-riders and dog-headed men. You'll occasionally see them in museums but they are mostly found nowadays in shops as mass-produced souvenirs.

The German writer Albert Vigoleis Thelen (1903–89) spent the five years from 1931 to 1936 in Palma. His time on the island inspired his greatest, largely autobiographical, novel, *Die Insel des Zweiten Gesichts* (The Island of the Second Vision, 1953).

Music

Mallorca, like any other part of Spain, has a rich heritage in folk songs and ballads sung in *mallorquí*. At many traditional *festes* in Mallorcan towns you'll hear the sounds of the *xeremiers*, a duo of ambling musicians, one of whom plays the *xeremia* (similar to the bagpipes) and the other a *flabiol* (a high-pitched pipe). Younger bands sometimes give these Mallorcan songs a bit of a rough-edged rock sound.

Los Valldemossa, who sang Mallorcan folk songs with a jazz feel in Palma's clubs, had some success overseas – they wound up playing the London circuit and, in 1969, won the Eurovision Song Contest. They stopped playing in 2001 but their CDs still abound.

The island's best-known singer-songwriter is Palma's Maria del Mar Bonet i Verdaguer (b 1947). She moved to Barcelona at the age of 20 to join the Nova Cançó Catalana movement, which promoted singers and bands working in Catalan. Bonet became an international success and is known for her interpretations of Mediterranean folk music, French *chanson* (Jacques Brel and company) and experiments with jazz and Brazilian music.

An altogether different performer is Concha Buika. Of Guinean origins, she was born in Palma in 1972 and rose through the Palma club circuit with her very personal brand of music, ranging from hip-hop to flamenco to soul. Her second CD, *Mi Niña Lola*, came out in 2007.

Argentine-born starlet Chenoa got her break when she stunned all in the TV talent show *Operación Triunfo*. Since 2002 she has churned out four albums and has become one of the most popular voices in Spanish-Latin pop.

For those who thought Ibiza was the exclusive Mediterranean home of club sounds, Daniel Vulic (DJ and German radio director in Mallorca) brought out *Cool Vibes Vol 1*, a compilation of strictly Mallorcan chillout and club music in 2007.

> Fans of the latest Mallorcan singing sensation, Chenoa, can find out all they need to know about her at www .chenoafanclub.com.

Architecture

FROM TALAYOTS TO MOSQUES

Remains of the *talayots* (enigmatic structures) of the Balearic peoples in Mallorca abound. See the History chapter for more information on these people (p23).

The Romans may have been mighty builders but comparatively little evidence of their prowess remains. Their principal city was Pol·lentia, whose scant remains you can still admire (p142).

Likewise, few reminders of the three centuries of Muslim rule have survived. After the Christian conquest in 1229, mosques and other buildings were gradually replaced. Traces of Palma's city walls, public baths and a handful of other details are all that remain.

> The Pisans who, with the Catalans, invaded and sacked Mallorca in 1114-15, took two porphyry pillars from Palma's Great Mosque and made a gift of them to Florence. They now flank the bronze doors of the Baptistery in Florence.

ROMANESQUE

The return to Christian rule in 1229 came too late for the implementation of a Romanesque style (characterised by the use of semicircles in doorways, windows and apses) predominant in northern Catalonia. Enthusiasts will see one sample in the Palau de l'Almudaina (p73) – better still, if you can get inside, is the chapel of the Temple.

SAVE OUR CENTRE!

Sitting behind a desk covered in paperwork, stationery, a computer and telephones on the ground floor of 14th-century Ca'n Weyler, Javier Terrasa exudes a mix of enthusiasm and world-weariness. He is one of a coterie of committed citizens who runs **Associació per a la Revitalització dels Centres Històrics** (ARCA; Association for the Revitalisation of Historical Centres; www.arcapatrimoni.net). Upstairs are two extraordinary Gothic ogive arches, a splash of Palma's rich medieval heritage.

What is ARCA? An apolitical organisation of citizens (financed largely by membership subscriptions) who love their artistic heritage. ARCA was set up in 1987 when Palma's old historic centre was largely ignored and abandoned. This area (just west of Passeig d'es Born) was not a pleasant place, with petty crime, drugs... Some of the old city's main streets and squares were OK but much of the rest was rundown. Until a short time ago, this barrio (Puig de Sant Pere) was in bad shape.

And now? Things have changed, money has been put into restoration and people are living here again. Indeed to such an extent that the old city is becoming an area where only the wealthy can afford to live! Of course, not all the work done has respected the heritage of buildings as much as we'd have liked.

Is such work in any way supervised? There is commission for the historic centre, and any work requires a permit. Of course where people don't even apply for the permit...

ARCA came into being to promote the revitalisation of the old centre and heritage protection. Was anyone else interested? In the late 1980s we had a Socialist town hall (under Mayor Ramon Aguiló), which had the idea of completely rebuilding the 18th-century barrio of Sa Gerreria from scratch. That was one of our biggest campaigns (with other groups).

Was it a success? We managed to save a few buildings. Another big campaign was to save Sa Riera (Palma's river), which the same mayor wanted to cover up and turn into a pedestrian zone. That battle we won.

In some countries, the realisation that ancient monuments attract the tourist dollar has helped direct finance to such monuments' maintenance. Has tourism in Mallorca had a similar impact? Countries like Greece live largely from their history. Let's face it, the bulk of tourists who come to Mallorca for a week aren't going to spend time in Palma – one day maybe.

Mallorca is covered in ancient monuments, especially talayots, but most seem abandoned. Many are heritage listed but those that have been set up to be visited can be counted on one hand. The fact that many are left sitting on farmland is probably their best form of protection. Heritage buildings are in no danger as long as nothing is at stake financially. As soon as economic interests become involved, trouble starts. The construction boom has damaged a lot.

Are attitudes changing? In the last elections (2007) we had 50,000 people demonstrating against the continued destruction on the island – a record.

GOTHIC

The Catalan slant on the Gothic style, with its broad, low-slung, vaulting church entrances and sober adornment, inevitably predominated in Catalan-conquered Mallorca. The single greatest Gothic monuments are Palma's Catedral (p68) and Sa Llotja (p82).

Guillem Sagrera (c1380–1456), a Catalan architect and sculptor who had previously worked in Perpignan (today in France), moved to Mallorca in 1420 to take over the direction of work on the Catedral. He is considered the greatest architect and sculptor of the period in Mallorca. He designed one of the Catedral's chapels and the Gothic chapter house, and, more importantly, he raised Sa Llotja.

As in other parts of Spain, Muslim influences were evident in some aspects of building through the Gothic period. In Mallorca this mudéjar style is not immediately evident in external façades, but a handful of beautiful *artesonados* (coffered wood ceilings) remain. Those in Palma's Palau de l'Almudaina (p73) are outstanding. The beautiful *artesonado* in the manor house at the

Jardins d'Alfàbia (p129) appears to be a Muslim relic, one of the few remaining architectural-artistic testaments to Muslim times.

RENAISSANCE & BAROQUE

Renaissance building had a rational impulse founded on the architecture of classical antiquity, but it seems to have largely passed Mallorca by. Some exceptions confirm the rule, such as the (later remodelled) main entrance to Palma's cathedral, the Consolat del Mar building and the mostly Renaissance-era sea walls. A handful of Palma's noble houses betray Renaissance influences (especially along Carrer del Sol, where for a moment you might think yourself transported to Medici Florence) as does the basilica (p132) in the Monestir de Lluc. Although decorated in baroque fashion, it is basically late Renaissance, and was designed by sculptor and architect Jaume Blanquer (c1578–1636).

The more curvaceous and, many would say, less attractive successor to the Renaissance was a moderate, island-wide baroque that rarely reached the florid extremes that one encounters elsewhere in Europe. It is most often manifest in the large churches that dominate inland towns and the *patis* (courtyards) that grace old Palma's mansions (see p80). In the case of the churches, existing Gothic structures received a serious reworking, evident in such elements as barrel vaulting, circular windows, bloated and curvaceous pillars and columns. Church exteriors are in the main sober (with the occasional gaudy façade). An exception can be found in the *retablos* (*retaules* in Catalan), the grand sculptural altarpieces behind the altar in most churches. Often gilt and swirling with ornament, this was where baroque sculptors could let their imaginations loose.

MODERNISME

Towards the end of the 19th century, the Catalan version of Art Nouveau architecture was all the rage in Barcelona. Symbolised by Antoni Gaudí, who worked on the renovation of Palma's Catedral (p68) and was the man behind Barcelona's unfinished La Sagrada Família, the eclectic style soon had its adepts, both local and Catalan, in Mallorca. They sought inspiration in nature and the past (especially Gothic and mudéjar influences), and developed a new freedom and individual creativity.

Another great Catalan Modernista architect was Lluís Domènech i Montaner (1850–1923), who left his mark on the magnificent former Grand Hotel (p79).

The undulating façade of **Can Casasayas** (Map pp70-1; Plaça del Mercat 13 & 14), built for the wealthy Casasayas family known for their historic Frasquet sweets shop (p88), is a typical feature of Modernisme. One half of the building was residential and the other today houses offices. In the original design they were to be joined by a bridge.

Gaspar Bennàssar (1869–1933) was one of the most influential architects in modern Palma, his native city. He played with various styles during his long career, including Modernisme. An outstanding example of this is the **Almacenes El Águila** (Map pp70-1; Plaça del Marqués de Palmer 1), built in 1908. Each of the three floors is different and the generous use of wrought iron in the main façade is a herald of the style. Next door the use of *trencadís* (ceramic shards) in the **Can Forteza Rey** (Map pp70-1; Carrer de les Monges 2) façade is classic Gaudíesque. **Can Corbella** (Map pp70-1; Plaça de la Cort 6), on the other hand, oozes a neo-mudéjar look.

The seat of the Balearic Islands Parliament is located in the Círculo Mallorquín, a high society club on Carrer del Conquistador that local Modernista architect Miquel Madorell i Rius (1869–1936) renovated in 1913.

TO THE 21ST CENTURY

Little worthy of praise has been built in or outside Palma since Modernisme fell out of favour. Modern construction on a grand scale has added countless soulless hotel and apartment blocks to both the city and swathes of the coast.

Major projects in Palma include the regeneration of the Sa Gerreria district with new, mid-rise apartments. Plans for a new waterfront Palau de Congressos (convention centre) behind Platja de Can Pere Antoni have been stalled by the regional coalition government.

Painting & Sculpture

FROM THE STONE AGE TO MUSLIM MALLORCA

Little evidence has come down to us of the artistic ambitions of the Talayotic people who preceded the Roman conquest of the island. Decoration of ceramics was minimal and the single greatest indication of creative activity are bronze figurines found in various sites dating to about the 4th century BC. A fine collection is on show in Palma's Museu de Mallorca (p75).

Of the Roman period, fragments of mosaics, ceramics and some sculpture have survived, the bulk on show in Alcúdia's Museu Monogràfic de Pol·lentia (p143) and Palma's Museu de Mallorca. In the latter, you can also see fragments of Byzantine mosaics and traces of Muslim artwork, mostly calligraphy in wood and stone, along with pretty ceramics.

THE CHRISTIAN REVIVAL

Subsumed after the 1229 conquest into the Catalan world of the Crown of Aragón, Mallorca lay at a strategic point on sea routes in a Catalan lake. This fostered the movement of artists and not a few were attracted from the mainland, particularly Valencia, to Mallorca.

The revival earliest works, transmitted by Catalan artists, were influenced by the Gothic art of the Sienese school in Italy. Later International Gothic began to filter through, notably under the influence of the Valencian artist Francesc Comes, who was at work in Mallorca from 1390 to 1415.

Important artists around the mid-15th century were Rafel Mòger (c 1424–70) and Frenchman Pere Niçard, who worked in Mallorca from 1468 to 1470. They created one of the era's most important works, *Sant Jordi*, now housed in Palma's Museu Diocesà (p74). The outstanding sculptor of this time was Guillem Sagrera (see p39), who did much of the detail work on Sa Llotja.

Pere Terrencs (active c 1479–1528) returned from a study stint in Valencia with the technique of oil painting – the death knell for egg-based pigments. His was a transitional style between late Gothic and the Renaissance. In a similar category was Córdoba-born Mateu López (d 1581), who trained in the prestigious Valencia workshops of father and son Vicent Macip and Joan de Joanes (aka Joan Vicent Macip, 1523–79), both signal artists. In 1544 López landed in Mallorca where he and his son became senior painters.

Gaspar Oms (c 1540–1614) was Mallorca's most outstanding late-Renaissance painter. The Oms clan, from Valencia, dominated the Mallorcan art scene throughout the 17th and 18th centuries.

Miquel Bestard (1592–1633) created major baroque canvases for churches, such as the Convento de Santa Clara (p77) and the Església de Monte-Sion, in Palma. Guillem Mesquida Munar (1675–1747) concentrated on religious motifs and scenes from classical mythology.

MODERN MALLORCA

The 19th century brought a wave of landscape artists to Mallorca. Many came from mainland Spain, particularly Catalonia, but the island produced

In 1956 film star and party animal Errol Flynn (1909-59) sailed his schooner, *Zaca*, to Palma with his third wife, Patricia Wymore. Here they lived, partied and tried to forget problems of debt and court summonses in the USA, usually by drowning them in booze. Eventually they left and Flynn died shortly after. Italian art collector Roberto Memmo bought and refitted Flynn's boat in the 1990s.

Anaïs Nin set an erotic short story, *Mallorca*, in Deià. It appeared in the volume *Delta of Venus* and deals with a local girl who gets into an erotic tangle with a pair of foreigners and pays a high price. Nin stayed in Deià for a year in 1941.

its own painters too. More than half a dozen notables were born and raised in Palma. Joan O'Neille Rosiñol (1828–1907) is considered the founder of the island's landscape movement. He and his younger contemporaries Ricard Anckermann Riera (1842–1907) and Antoni Ribas Oliver (1845–1911), both from Palma, were among the first to cast their artistic eyes over the island and infuse it with romantic lyricism. The latter two concentrated particularly on coastal scenes.

From 1890 a flood of Modernìsta artists from Catalonia 'discovered' Mallorca and brought new influences to the island. Some of them, such as Santiago Rusiñol (1861–1931), had spent time in Paris, which was then the hotbed of the art world. Locals enthusiastically joined in the Modernìsta movement. Palma-born Antoni Gelabert Massot (1877–1932) became a key figure, depicting his home city in paintings such as *Murada i Catedral a Entrada de Fosc* (1902–4). Other artists caught up in this wave were Joan Fuster Bonnín (1870–1943) and Llorenç Cerdà i Bispal (1862–1955), born in Pollença.

Meanwhile Llorenç Rosselló (1867–1902) was shaping up to be the island's most prominent sculptor until his early death. A handful of Rosselló's bronzes as well as a selection of works by many of the painters mentioned here can be seen in Es Baluard (p80).

By the 1910s and 1920s symbolism began to creep into local artists' vocabulary. Two important names in Mallorca painting from this period are Joan Antoni Fuster Valiente (1892–1964) and Ramón Nadal (1913–99), both from Palma.

Pollença-born Dionís Bennàssar (1904–67) can best be considered an interesting provincial artist. His works range from local views of his home town through to still lifes and nudes. You can see a good selection of these at his former home in Pollença (p135).

CONTEMPORARY

Towering above everyone else in modern Mallorca is local hero and art icon, Miquel Barceló (b 1957, Felanitx). His profile has been especially sharp in his island home after the unveiling in 2007 of one of his more controversial masterpieces, a ceramic depiction of the miracle of the loaves and fishes housed in Palma's Catedral. The artist, who lives in Paris and Mali and has a studio in Naples, was a rising star by the age of 25. Although he is best known as a painter, Barceló has worked with ceramics since the late 1990s. However, the commission for the Catedral was on a hitherto unimagined scale for the artist.

Less well known but nonetheless prolific is Palma-born Ferran García Sevilla (b 1949), whose canvases are frequently full of primal colour and strong shapes and images. Since the early 1980s he has exhibited in galleries throughout Europe. Joan Costa (b 1961, Palma) is one of the island's key contemporary sculptors, who also indulges in occasional brushwork.

One cannot leave out 20th-century Catalan icon, Joan Miró (1893–1983). His mother came from Sóller and he lived the last 27 years of his life in Cala Major, just outside Palma. Working there in a huge studio, he maintained a prolific turn-out of canvases, ceramics, statuary, textiles and more, faithful to his particular motifs of women, birds and the cosmos. You can visit his Palma house now turned museum (p102).

Cinema

The first cinema projections by the Lumière brothers were held in Palma in early 1897, a little over a year after their premier in Paris. These moving images caught on and soon after permanent movie theatres were springing up around the island. One of the earliest local film companies, Mallorca Film, made short documentaries and a couple of fictional works.

The first foreign-made film shot in Mallorca was *El Secreto del Anillo* (The Secret of the Ring), made in 1913 under Italian direction with French and Spanish personnel. The Civil War (1936–39) and the early Franco years all but saw an end to film production in Mallorca. Then, from the 1950s and 1960s, the island was rediscovered as a set for foreign films, most now justifiably forgotten.

Mallorca has produced a handful of film directors. Antoni Aloy had some success with the US–Spanish co-production *Presence of Mind* (*El Celo*, 2000), starring Sadie Frost, Harvey Keitel and Lauren Bacall, in which a private tutor comes to an island to take on the education of two orphaned children and finds herself dealing with some unpleasant characters of past and present. Aloy is working on his second feature film, *Panteras,* a black comedy about the escape of five ladies from their senior citizens' home.

Rafel Cortés Oliver released his first feature movie, *Yo* (I), in 2007. It tells of a German who comes to work in Estellencs and feels himself accused of a wrongdoing. His attempts to prove his innocence (which no-one actually doubts) only serve to complicate matters.

In 1949 the US-French-Spanish co-production *Captain Black Jack,* starring George Sanders, was filmed on location in Mallorca and caused quite a stir among the local populace. Film critics were less enthralled by this story of an American smuggler in the Mediterranean.

SPORT
Football

Mallorca's football side, **Reial Club Deportivo Mallorca** (RCD; www.rcdmallorca.es), known simply as Real Mallorca, has been taking to the field since 1916. It has been a middling side in the Spanish national Liga, where it has spent more time in the second division than the first. When in the top division, Real Mallorca has managed to come third twice (the last time in 2000–01) and it won the Copa del Rei (King's Cup) in 2003.

Cycling

Mallorquins are keen cyclists. On weekends you can see tribes of them in full kit zipping around back roads all over the island. In 2007 Palma hosted the World Track Cycling Championship at Palma Arena velodrome.

Among Mallorca's greatest cyclists was six-times track champion, Guillem Timoner i Obrador (b 1926, Felanitx). He triumphed in 'stayer' competitions, in which the cyclist rides behind a motorcycle. Porreres boy Joan Llaneras (b 1969) is an Olympic track champion who took gold in Sydney in 2000 and silver in Athens in 2004.

As an unknown 20-year-old Joan Collins starred in Noel Langley's romp, *Our Girl Friday,* filmed at Peguera in 1953.

Tennis

Rafel (Rafael in Spanish, 'Rafa' for short) Nadal (b 1986, Manacor) needs little introduction to anyone who even skims the sports pages. Three-time champion on the clay courts of Roland-Garros in France and number two seed behind the (mostly) unbeatable Roger Federer, he is Spain's greatest ever tennis phenomenon, overshadowing another fine Mallorcan player, Palma's Carles Moyà (b 1976).

Bullfighting

Although it does not have the following it enjoys in parts of mainland Spain, *la lidia* takes place in Palma, Inca, Muro, Alcúdia and Felanitx. Only during the 1950s, as international tourism began to take off, did interest in the fights begin to grow in Mallorca. Since the 1980s, interest (local and foreign) has ebbed considerably. The season kicks off on Sant Joan (the feast day of St John, 24 June) in Muro and continues until the end of August, with several events held in Palma (see p97).

Want to write fan mail to Rafel Nadal, or just keep up with his prodigious progress? Check out his official site at www.rafaelnadal.com.

Castellers

A recent import from Catalonia (since 1996), this tradition dates back to the 19th century and reached its golden age in the 1880s. The idea is to 'build' human layers of a 'castle' and then undo it without everyone tumbling in a heap. The first level is a wide and solid scrum known as the *pinya*. The most popular teams can get a thousand people chiming in! Above this you build your castle. About the best any team has recorded is a *quatre de nou* or *tres de nou*: a four-by-nine or three-by-nine castle. That means nine storeys of people, three or four in the core levels tapering to two then one person at the top.

For more information on Mallorca's *castellers*, check out www.mallor caweb.net/castellers.

Food & Drink

Traditional Mallorcan cuisine is much better suited to the harsh countryside living of centuries past than to the summery, bare-it-all-in-a-bikini Mallorca many visitors experience today. Rich, thick soups and stews, savoury pork dishes and flavour-packed sausages remain the backbone of the Mallorquins' diet.

Dependent on the land and the surrounding sea, Mallorcan cuisine at its best is a delicious reflection of the island's climate, seasons, terrain and history. In centuries past, a stream of invaders and conquerors crossed the island; while many were the cause of hard times, they also brought new fruits and vegetables, spices and recipes, leaving a culinary legacy that lingers today. Arabian influences include apricots, pine nuts, capers, honey, almonds and spices; the British inspired Menorca's *maó* cheese; and Catalans encouraged pork farming and winemaking.

The beautifully bound hardcover book *The Taste of a Place: Mallorca*, by Vicky Bennison, is a cookbook, history book and culinary guidebook in one.

Mallorcan cuisine has gotten more daring in recent years. Young chefs, as part of a trend seen throughout the Mediterranean, are bringing a revival to Balearic food. The combination of local ingredients, age-old recipes and international flair is the basis of oftentimes surprisingly original dishes by Mallorcan-based Michelin-starred chefs like British Marc Fosh (Read's Hotel), Basque Koldo Royo (Koldo Royo) and German Gerhard Schwaiger (Tristan).

THE MALLORCAN KITCHEN

Traditional Mallorcan cuisine is above all resourceful, making use of the ingredients found on the island, especially pork, fish, and local vegetables and herbs. To learn more about Mallorcan cuisine, consider taking a cooking class (p61), or simply wander around the wonderful fresh markets that set up weekly in towns across the island.

The fabulous coffee-table book *Majorca Culture and Life*, published by Könemann, has many engaging, thoughtful essays on Mallorcan cuisine past and present.

Specialities

No meal in Mallorca begins without a dish of olives and a hunk of *pa amb oli* (bread with oil), made with traditional *pa moreno* (rye bread). It's sometimes topped with chopped tomatoes. Menorca's cheddar-like *maó* is the Balearics' best-known cheese, but Piris, a square, aged cow cheese made in Campos, is similar in style. Although seafood paella is ubiquitous, Mallorca's most traditional rice dish is *arros brut* (dirty rice), a soupy dish made with pork, rabbit and vegetables.

Pork is found in some measure in countless sausages, stews, soups and even some vegetable dishes and desserts. The centuries of hunger Mallorquins endured taught them to appreciate every part of the pig; even today, they use everything but the squeal. Other favourite meat dishes include *frit Mallorquí*, a fried mix of tasty lamb parts; it too was born out of a desperate need for protein. Grilled rabbit or lamb is widely enjoyed as well.

In the Middle Ages, peasants made bread with carob seeds because they couldn't buy wheat and drought conditions made growing it difficult.

TOP FIVE RESTAURANTS

- Celler Ca'n Ripoll (p157)
- Restaurant Clivia (p138)
- Béns d'Avall (p122)
- Refectori (p90)
- Port Petit (p193)

CHEF LLUC PUJOL CAPÓ

After a delicious (and filling) meal at his cosy, family restaurant Ca'n Carlos (p90), in the heart of Palma, chef Lluc Pujol Capó sat down for a chat about his favourite Mallorcan dishes. Pujol Capó is known for his modern takes on traditional island cuisine.

What are the 'can't miss' dishes in Mallorca? That's hard, because there are so many. *Suquet de peix* is a fish stew. It's spectacular. Another dish, which we serve here, is *xai Mallorquí*, lamb made with an orange, honey and vinegar crust. And the *frit Mallorquí*, which people love until they find out what it is: a stir-fry of lamb lungs, heart and liver.

How is Mallorcan cuisine changing? It's becoming more modern, taking traditional regional recipes and putting new spins on them. As in other Mediterranean regions, it's the young chefs who, right out of cooking school, are experimenting with using local ingredients to create international dishes.

Can you give us one of your favourite recipes? One is wrapped grouper with cabbage, pork belly and *sobrassada* purée.

Ingredients

50g of chopped pork belly
grouper spine and head for broth
water, salt and pepper
sherry
onion
tomato
150g of grouper fillet
chopped garlic and parsley

1 cabbage leaf
raisins
pine nuts
slice of *botifarrón* or other blood sausage
1 potato
sobrassada
1 walnut
olive oil

Instructions

Boil the pork belly in a broth flavoured with grouper spine, sherry, onion and tomato at a low temperature for three hours, then grill it with its juices. Meanwhile, rub the grouper with garlic and parsley, and place in the centre of a poached cabbage leaf. Add raisins, pine nuts and *botifarrón*, and wrap, securing with string. Add a little broth and bake for 12 minutes at 150°C. Boil the potato until it's soft, then blend with *sobrassada*, walnut, olive oil and salt. To serve, spoon the pork belly on a plate, topped with the wrapped grouper and accompanied by the purée. Drizzle with a bit of broth.

Dried Mallorcan sausages are iconic. Traditionally made by families as a way to keep meat year-round, *sobrassada* (tangy pork sausage flavoured with paprika), *botifarra* (flavourful pork sausage) and *botiffarón* (a larger version of *botifarra*) are some of the best island sausages.

It's true that much of the fish eaten on Mallorca is flown in from elsewhere, but many species still fill the waters near the island. *Atún* (tuna), *besugo* (sea bream), and *rape* (monkfish) are some of the most common fish caught here. Especially appreciated is *cap roig*, an ugly red fish found around the Illa de Cabrera. Fresh seafood is best served grilled with just a bit of salt and lemon. Another delicious way to eat it is *'a la sal'*, or baked in a salt crust. A *marisquada* is a heaping tray of steamed shellfish – plan to share.

Learn all you ever needed to know about *sobrassada* at www.sobrassada demallorca.org.

Mallorca isn't known for its desserts (fruit and ice cream are the most common), but exceptions include *gató Mallorquí* (a dense almond cake) and *quarts* (cake topped with meringue and sometimes also chocolate). The Mallorcan pastry par excellence is the beloved *ensaïmada*, a soft round bun made with a spiral of sweet dough and topped with powdered sugar. Sometimes, *ensaïmades* are filled with cream or a sugary paste called *pasta de angel*.

DRINKS

Mallorcan *vino* (wine) has earned a reputation for quality in past years and is served at nearly all island restaurants. Spanish *cervezas* (beers) like Estrella Damm, San Miguel and Cruzcampo are served in most bars alongside a few imports. The most common way to order a beer is to ask for a *caña*, or small draught beer.

Spirits include all the major international brands as well as local specialities. *Herbes*, a herbal liquor made with up to two dozen different plants including mint, rosemary, lavender and anise is served in both *seco* (dry) and *dulce* (sweet) versions. Also popular is Palo (literally 'stick'), a herbal liquor that tastes akin to a dark brandy.

Learn all you'll ever need to know about *ensaïmada* at www.ensaimada demallorca.com.

HABITS & CUSTOMS

Stopping to sit down and slowly savour a meal is one of the best things about eating in Mallorca. Lunch, the biggest meal of the day, deserves a break of at least an hour (maybe much longer) even on a busy work day. On Sundays, the midday family meal may last until the late afternoon. Social dinners are equally drawn out, with each step from appetisers to post-dinner drinks being relished to the fullest. If you're extended the honour of being invited to dine in someone's home, bring a small gift of wine or chocolates and prepare yourself for a feast. A Mallorquin host will go all-out to entertain guests.

At www.illesbalearsqual itat.es you'll find a wealth of information about agrotourism routes, wine regions and other speciality island products.

For the most part, table manners in Mallorca mirror those elsewhere in Europe. In restaurants wait staff are notoriously curt; don't take it personally. Whether they are polite or not, a 10% tip is considered generous.

CELEBRATIONS

Mallorquins don't need much of an excuse to throw together a celebratory meal, although the extensive Catholic calendar certainly does give them plenty to celebrate. Each holiday or major saint day has its own special recipes and pastries.

Sign up for a day trip through Mallorca's wine country at www.ma jorcawinetour.com.

The *matanza*, or pig slaughter, was traditionally one of the biggest celebrations of late winter; it still is in a few rural communities. The whole family gets together to kill and prepare the sausages and meats they'll eat in the coming months. While it's a messy business, the day ends with a huge feast.

SOBRASSADA

Mallorca's best-known sausage, the addictively tangy *sobrassada*, is an island icon. 'These days, *sobrassada* is made in factories and sold in shops, but not long ago it was a family affair,' explains Bartomeu Frau i Oliver, owner of Embotits Aguilo in Sóller. The factory, more than one hundred years old, produces 1500kg of La Luna–brand *sobrassada* each week. The *sobrassada*-making process at Embotits Aguilo hasn't changed much since the days when it was made in family kitchens following the *matanza* (pig slaughter). Chopped pork is ground with red pepper and sea salt. The mixture sits overnight and is then poured into natural pork casings and hung in a humid, temperature-controlled room to age for about two months. Depending on the conditions and the producer's approach, it may be darker or lighter, softer or harder. *Llonganissa*, for example, is a young soft sausage sold in long, thin links. 'One isn't better than the other,' Frau i Oliver says. 'They're just different.'

'*Sobrassada* is everywhere in Mallorca – we use it in soups, with bread, in rice dishes and stews, with honey, with figs, with eggs, on pizza...it's a very adaptable condiment, and just about any island dish can be served with it. My personal favourite is sliced thin and grilled over hot coals in winter. Delicious!'

EATING OUT

No Mallorcan town, big or small, is without its fair share of cafés and restaurants. Café culture is very much a part of life here, and any excuse is a good one to meet for coffee, go for drinks after work or get a group of friends together for dinner.

It's often hard to distinguish between a café, a bar and a restaurant. Any may serve food and a single establishment might morph from a low-key morning café to a lunchtime bistro to a lively bar after dark. Also, bars come in several forms. *Cervecerías* are more or less the Spanish equivalent of a pub, while anything actually called 'pub' is likely to serve stout and show lots of football. *Taberna* are generally rustic and may serve tapas or meals as well. In any of the above you might be charged more if you get a table or sit outside.

Restaurants have a similar gamut of styles. Anything with *ca'n* or *ca's* in its name (words that, like the French *chez,* designate someone's home or property) serves traditional fare in a family-style atmosphere, while anything dubbed *celler* evokes the image of a country wine-cellar-turned-restaurant, although some of these traditional eateries were never actual cellars. A *marisquería* will specialise in seafood and shellfish and is likely to be pricey.

> The annual *matanza*, or slaughtering of the pig, was a major event on Mallorca's social calendar and is still carried out amid feasting and partying in rural areas today.

When & What to Eat

Mallorquins eat late, no matter what the meal. As in the rest of Spain, travellers will have to reset their stomach clocks if they want to catch even a glimpse of the locals.

> Although the text is in Spanish, *Restaurantes de Mallorca*, by Lucía Alemany, has a stellar list of the island's best eateries.

Most people start the day with a simple coffee at home, but it's also common to head out to *esmorzar* ('breakfast' in Catalan) mid-morning. This is the ideal time to try the sugary *ensaïmada* and wash it down with a *café con leche* (coffee with milk) or a *zumo de naranja natural* (freshly squeezed orange juice). You could also get a pastry or a small ham or cheese sandwich, known as 'sandwich mixto'. In touristy areas expect to see restaurants advertising 'full English breakfast', where you can find eggs and sausage. Many hotels and guesthouses take a more German approach, serving muesli and yogurt, toast with sliced cheese, and fruit.

> Starting with the assumption that to know Mallorcan cuisine you must first know the land it comes from, Sunflower Guides' *Mallorca Walk & Eat* combines nature walks with restaurant and culinary tips.

Lunch, the most important meal of the day, is served from 1pm to 4pm. The best value is the *menú del día*, a fixed-price lunch menu that offers several options each for *primeros platos* (starters), *segundos platos* (entrées) and *postres* (desserts), bread and a drink for €10 to €20. Even when not ordering a *menú*, Mallorquins generally order two courses and a dessert when they go out for lunch. And it's not a bit frowned upon to drink wine or beer with a meal.

Even Mallorquins' stomachs start growling by 7pm or so. This is a great time to stop for tapas. An import from the mainland, tapas aren't as widespread here as in other Spanish cities, but many bars and cafés will have a small selection of snacky things to choose from. Olives, potato chips or a dish of almonds are the ideal accompaniment to a *caña*.

CAFÉ CULTURE

Café, or coffee, is served at breakfast, lunch and dinner and whenever you need a pick-me-up. *Café con leche* (espresso with milk), served in a big mug, is probably the closest thing to a cappuccino you'll find, and is generally considered a morning drink. Later in the day, Mallorquins order either a *café solo* (espresso served alone), a *cortado* (espresso served with a splash of milk) or a *carajillo* (espresso served with brandy).

MALLORCAN WINE

Mallorca has been making wine since Roman times but only in recent years has it earned a reputation for quality. Just over 30 cellars, with 2500 hectares between them, make up the island's moderate production, most of which is enjoyed in Mallorca's restaurants and hotels. The wineries are huddled in the island's two DOs (Denominaciones de Orígen), Binissalem (p154) and an area in the centre of the island that includes towns like Manacor, Felantix and Llucmajor (p162), where growing conditions are ideal. International varieties like Cabernet Sauvignon are planted alongside native varieties, like Manto Negro, Fogoneu and Callet. Local white varieties include Prensal Blanc and Girò Blanc, which are blended with Catalan grapes like Parellada, Macabeo and Moscatell or with international varieties like Chardonnay.

The best wines are the spicy, balanced reds, which tend to be full-bodied, expressive brews that nearly always include Manto Negro in their blend. White and rosé wines have yet to achieve the quality mark of Mallorcan reds and so far represent only a quarter of production.

The best winery here is Anima Negra, which makes modern, distinctive reds. Also look out for Bodegues Ribes, Bodegues Macià Batle, Finca Son Bordils and the organic winery Jaume de Puntiró.

The dinner hour begins at 9pm, though many places open by 7pm or 8pm to accommodate tourists. Nearly all close their kitchens by midnight. A meal begins with *pa moreno* and perhaps a *pica pica*, when many small appetisers are put out for everyone to share. Next comes the *primer plato*, which may be a salad, pasta, grilled vegetable plate or something more creative. The entrée is either fish (often served *a la plancha*, pan grilled) or some kind of meat – pork, lamb, steak or rabbit. Desserts are most often a simple *helado* (ice cream), flan or fruit.

> To try Mallorcan food at home, check out the long list of recipes at www.spain-recipes.com/balearic-recipes.

VEGETARIANS & VEGANS

While veggie lovers may come to loathe the sight of so much pork and sausage, don't despair – wonderful produce is also served year-round. Mallorca's poor soil and steady sun lead to small, compact fruits and vegetables. The island is especially proud of its fava broad beans, peppers, aubergines, artichokes, cauliflowers and green asparagus, which grows wild across the islands. Figs, apricots and oranges (especially around Sóller) are abundant.

Unfortunately for herbivores, many traditional veggie dishes are prepared with salted pork, bacon, meat broth or lard. For example, the bean stew *fava pelada pagesa* is cooked with bacon, and *ensaïmades* are made with lard. The thick *sopas Mallorquins,* hearty vegetable stews, may or may not include pork fat.

Safe bets for vegetarians include *tortillas,* thick omelettes made with potatoes or veggies, and *tumbet,* the typical sautéed vegetable dish. Many restaurants offer a grilled vegetable plate and fresh salads like *trampó,* a cold dish made with tomato, onion, special pale green Mallorcan peppers and olives. The Spanish *gaspacho* (cold tomato soup) is popular too. A cheese sandwich is a reliable fill-in if you just want a simple snack.

> *Ensaïmada* pastries are made with strong flour, water, sugar, eggs, mother dough and pork lard; vegans beware.

Vegetarian-friendly restaurants in this guide are denoted with the symbol **V** . Organic food is sold at some local fresh markets (see individual town sections for opening times), at health food stores and at farm shops like **Finca Son Barrina** (☎ 971 504540; www.mallorcaorganics.com; Carretera Inca-Llubí Km6; 🕑 9am-8pm Fri & Sat).

EATING WITH KIDS

Mallorca is a kid-friendly place and its restaurants are no exception. You can expect to get lots of smiles if you have cute kids with you but few restaurants go out of their way to accommodate them. Kids' menus, booster seats and

PICKY EATERS

Nature has been kind to Mallorca and the locals take full advantage of it. In early autumn they head to the hills in search of tasty *esclata-sang*, a mushroom of the milk-fungus family that's called *rovellon* in Catalonia. In summer it's time to pick the slender green asparagus that grows in rocky, shrub-filled areas. Any time is a good time to restock on herbs like rosemary and thyme, which are abundant throughout the Mediterranean. You can also pick *fonoll marí* (samphire), a leafy coastal herb that's marinated and used in salads.

highchairs are the exception, not the norm. This is why you'll see most parents either bobbing their babies on their laps or simply keeping them in the stroller. Letting a kid wander around a restaurant – as long as they're not breaking wine bottles or bothering anyone – is usually OK too.

Many restaurants are happy to adjust their standard dishes to children's tastes. Simple grilled meats, French fries, spaghetti and *tortillas* are all common kids' plates. If you've brought baby food with you, just ask for it to be warmed up in the kitchen; most places will have no problem with this.

EAT YOUR WORDS

While many restaurants that cater to tourists will automatically place an international menu in front of you, smaller places may only have menus in Mallorquin Catalan.

Mayonnaise was invented on nearby Menorca, when egg yolks, olive oil, lemon juice and salt were combined for the first time, in the 18th century.

Catalan
I'd like ...
Voldria ...   vool·*dree*·a ...
  a table for two
  una taula per a dues persones   *oo*·na *ta*·oo·la per a *doo*·az per·*so*·nes
  the menu in English
  la carta en Angles   la *kar*·ta an an·*gles*
  a drink
  una beguda   *oo*·na be·*goo*·da
  a glass of water
  un vas d'aigua   oon vas de *a*·ee·gwa
  a glass of wine
  una copa de vi   *oo*·na *ko*·pa de vee
  a glass of beer
  una copa de cervesa   *oo*·na *ko*·pa de sur·*ve*·sa
  the bill
  el compte   al *koomp*·ta
  the non-smoking section
  la zona per a no fumadors   la *zo*·na per a no foo·ma·*dors*

I'm ...
Jo soc ... jo sok ...
  a vegetarian
  vegetarià   ve·je·ta·ree·*a*
  diabetic
  diabètic   dee·a·*be*·teek

I'm allergic (to ...)
  Tinc allergia (a ...)   teenk a·*ler*·jee·a (a ...)
I only eat kosher food.
  Només menjo kosher.   noo·*mess* men·joo *ko*·sher

What is the speciality of the house?

Quina és l'especialitat de la casa?   kee·na es les·pe·sya·lee·tat de la ka·sa?

Does this dish have meat?

Aquet plat té carn?   a·ket plat te karn?

Spanish

I'd like ...

Quisiera ...   kee-*sye*-ra ...

a table for two

una mesa para dos personas   oo-na *me*-sa *pa*-ra dos per-*so*-nas

the menu in English

la carta en Inglés   la *kar*-ta en een-*gles*

a drink

una bebida   oo-na be-*bee*-da

a glass of water

un vaso de agua   oon *va*-zo de *a*-gwa

a glass of wine

una copa de vino   oo-na *ko*-pa de *vee*-no

a glass of beer

una copa de cerveza   oo-na *ko*-pa de sair-*ve*-sa

the bill

la cuenta   la *kwen*-ta

the non-smoking section

la zona de no fumadores   la *zo*-na de no fu ma-*do*-res

I'm ...

Soy ...   soy ...

a vegetarian

vegetariano/a   ve-khe-ta-*rya*-no/a (m/f)

diabetic

diabético/a   dee-a-*be*-tee-ko/a (m/f)

I'm allergic (to ...)

Tengo alérgia (á ...)   ten-go a-ler-*jee*-a (a ...)

I only eat kosher food.

Solo como comida kosher.   so-lo *ko*-mo co-*mee*-da *ko*-sher

What is the speciality of the house?

Cuál es la especialidad de la casa?   kwal es la es-pe-sya-lee-*dad* de la *ka*-sa

Does this dish have meat?

Este plato tiene carne?   es-te *pla*-to ti-e-ne *kar*-ne

Food Glossary

a la plancha	a la *plan*·cha	pan grilled
aceite de oliva	a·*they*·te do·*lee*·va	olive oil
alioli	a·lee·*o*·lee	garlic mayonnaise
atún	a·*toon*	tuna
berenjena	be·ren·*khe*·na	aubergine
botifarra	boo·tee·*fa*·ra	typical blood sausage
botiffarón	boo·tee·fa·*ron*	large blood sausage
calamares	ka·la·*ma*·res	calamari or squid
camaiot	ka·ma·*yot*	a paté-like pork sausage with a thick fatty rind
cap roig	kap·*roach*	'red head', a tasty fish from the Illa de Cabrera
cerdo	*ther*·do	pork
conejo	co·*ne*·kho	rabbit
cordero	kor·*de*·ro	lamb

desayunar	de·sa·yoo·*nar*	breakfast
dorada	do·*ra*·da	gilthead
ensaïmada	an·sai·*ma*·da	typical Mallorcan pastry
esclata-sang	as·kla·ta·*sung*	a prized mushroom in the milk-fungus family
favas	*fa*·bas	broad white beans
frit Mallorquí	*freet* ma·yor·*kee*	sautéed lamb offal
fruta	*froo*·ta	fruit
gambas	*gam*·bas	shrimp
granizados	gra·nee·*tha*·dos	flavoured ice drinks
helado	e·*la*·do	ice cream
jamon serrano	ha·*mon* se·*ra*·no	cured ham
la cena	la *the*·na	dinner
la comida	la co·*mee*·da	lunch
langosta	lan·*go*·sta	crayfish
llonganissa	yon·ga·*nee*·sa	young, thin *sobrassada* sausage
lubina	loo·*bee*·na	sea bass
mejillones	me·khee·*yo*·nes	mussels or acorn barnacles
mero	*me*·ro	grouper
merluza	mer·*loo*·tha	hake
pa amb oli	pa amb *o*·lee	bread with oil
paella	pa·*ye*·ya	rice and seafood dish
pan moreno	pan moo·*re*·no	dense rye bread
pargo	par·*go*	sea bream
pasta de angel	pas·ta de *an*·jel	angel paste, a sweet filling used in *ensaïmada*
pimientos	pee·mee·*yen*·tos	peppers
Piris	*pee*·rees	cheddar-like cheese made in Campos
pulpo	*pool*·po	octopus
quarts	*kwarts*	cake topped with meringue and sometimes chocolate
queso	*ke*·so	cheese
raor	ra·*or*	a rare local fish caught in late summer
rape	*ra*·pe	monkfish
rovellon	ro·ve·*yon*	a local mushroom
sepia	*se*·pya	squid
setas	*se*·tas	mushrooms
sobrassada	so·bra·*sa*·da	tangy sausage
sopas Mallorquinas	so·pas ma·yor·*kee*·nas	thick Mallorcan stew-like soups
suquet de peix	soo·*ket* de *peysh*	fish stew
tortilla de patatas	tor·*tee*·ya de pa·*ta*·tas	potato omelette
tumbet	tum·*bet*	layers of fried vegetables topped with tomato sauce
trampó	tram·*po*	summer salad made with tomatoes and peppers
zumo de naranja	*thoo*·mo de na·*ran*·kha	orange juice

Environment

Mallorca is an incredibly diverse island where limestone cliffs, spectacular caves and sandy coves meet blooming fields of wild flowers, eerie olive groves and damp forests to form one of the Mediterranean's most storied landscapes.

THE LAND

The largest island of the Balearic archipelago, Mallorca extends over 3626 sq km in the western Mediterranean, just 175km off the coast of Spain. Technically the Balearics are an extension of mainland Spain's Sistema Penibético (Beltic mountain range), which dips up to 1.5km below the Mediterranean and peeks up again to form the islands of Mallorca, Menorca, Ibiza and Formentera. The stretch of water between the archipelago and the mainland is called the Balearic Sea.

Mallorca is shaped like a rough trapezoid, with the jagged Serra de Tramuntana forming an imposing barrier on its western flank, and the broken hills of the Serra de Llevant adding scenic variety in the east. A series of plunging cliffs interspersed with calm bays marks the south, while capes like the Cap de Formentor and the long shell-shaped bays at Pollença and Alcúdia dominate the north. In the centre of the island extends the vast fertile plain known as Es Pla.

The island's defining geographic feature is the Serra de Tramuntana, whose forested hillsides and bald peaks stretch for 90km and are home to Mallorca's highest summit, Puig Major (main peak 1445m). On the other side of the island, the Serra de Llevant maxes out at just 509m at the Santuari de Sant Salvador.

Mallorca, particularly along its eastern and southern coasts, is drilled with caves created by erosion, waves or water drainage. There are so many that spelunking enthusiasts are still discovering them. The caves range from tiny well-like dug-outs to vast kilometres-long tunnels replete with lakes, rivers and astounding shapes sculptured by nature's hand. For more information see p61. The best-known caves are the Coves del Drac and Coves d'es Hams, both outside Porto Cristo (p177).

WILDLIFE
Animals

Small birds, lizards, turtles, frogs and bats make up the bulk of the native populations. Mammals include feral cats (a serious threat to bird populations), ferrets, rabbits, hedgehogs and the occasional mountain goat (although most have owners). While there are only a handful of hard-to-find snakes, reptiles aren't absent on Mallorca: lizards are among its most popular creatures, especially on the Illa de Sa Dragonera, where they have the run of the island.

Invertebrates shouldn't be overlooked: interesting spiders, more than 300 moth species and 30 kinds of butterflies fill the island. In the evening cicadas and grasshoppers make their presence known.

The Mediterranean is rich with life as well. Sperm whales, pilot whales and finback whales feed not far offshore. Also swimming here are bottlenose dolphins, white-sided dolphins and other species. Scuba divers often spot barracuda, octopus, moray eels, grouper, cardinal fish, damsel fish, starfish, sea urchins, sponges and corals.

The *Complete Guide: Beaches Mallorca + Cabrera*, by Miguel Ángel Álvarez Alperi, takes an in-depth look at more than 300 island beaches and their surroundings.

Thousands of caves, large and small, tunnel underneath the surface of Mallorca. Many are still waiting to be discovered.

Among the most complete guides available to Mallorca's caves are the *Cuadernos de Espeleogía I and II* (Speology Notebooks I & II), by José Bermejo.

BIRDS

Mallorca's balance of wetlands, craggy cliffs and grassy plains has attracted a thriving, varied bird population that's made the island a bird-watching hot spot (see p59 for more information), especially during the migration periods in spring and autumn. The richest habitat is the Parc Natural de S'Albufera (p148), home to a full two-thirds of the species that live permanently or winter on Mallorca. Other great bird habitats are the Embassament de Cúber (p125), the Vall de Bocquer near Port Pollença (p139), the sea cliffs of Formentor (p141) and the Illa de Sa Dragonera (p110). Commonly sighted birds include black vultures, Eleonora's falcons, Audouin's gulls, purple herons, serins, warblers, bee-eaters, ospreys, scops owls and hoopoes.

With more than 200 species it's all but impossible to predict what you'll see. The birds can be divided into three categories: sedentary (those that live on the island year-round), seasonal (those that migrate south after hatching chicks or to escape the cold winters in northern Europe) and migratory (those that use Mallorca as a brief resting point before continuing their journey).

Wetlands species include small birds like red-knobbed coots and warblers as well as long-legged wading birds like flamingos, black-winged stilts, herons and egrets. You can also spot rare ducks like the white-headed duck or marble duck.

The peaks of the Serra de Tramuntana are circled by huge birds of prey, including vultures, falcons and eagles. The trails around Puig Roig are a good place to spot vultures, whose wingspan can reach 3m.

Along the coast gulls are seen in abundance, especially the common Audouin's gull that nests in seaside cliffs. Others nesting here include shearwaters, storm petrels and the Mediterranean shag.

Inland, look out for songbirds like larks, nightingales and chats.

A series of interesting articles about Mallorca's natural spaces can be found at www.mallorcaweb.com/reports/natural-areas.

More than 200 bird species can be found on Mallorca.

If you plan to go birding, invest in a guide like *Finding Birds in Mallorca*, by Dave Gosney.

MALLORCA'S PARKS

The creation of protected wildlife areas has helped stabilise Mallorca's wildlife and make it accessible to visitors. Now a full 40% of the island falls under some form of official environmental protection status.

park	features	activities	page
Parc Nacional Marítim-Terrestre de l'Arxipèlag de Cabrera	an archipelago of 19 islands and islets; home to 130 bird species and incredibly diverse marine life	hiking in the scrubby hills around the Castel de Cabrera, scuba diving, lolling on wondrously uncrowded beaches	p186
Parc Natural de S'Albufera	a vital wetland sheltering 400 plants and 230 species of birds, many of them on the migration path from Europe to Africa	bird-watching (coots and sedge warblers), cycling along the quiet paths that slice through the marsh	p191
Parc Natural de Mondragó	rolling dunes, juniper groves, vibrant wetlands and unspoilt beaches within easy reach of the big east coast resorts	strolling through forests and near wetlands, picnicking on a gorgeous beach	p148
Parc Natural de la Península de Llevant	flora and fauna	walking, bird-watching	p169
Parc Natural de Sa Dragonera	two small islets and the 4km-long Dragonera island, with its harrowing cliffs, pristine coves and countless caves; endangered gull population	snorkelling, scuba diving	p110

LLUÍS GRADAILLE TORTELLA

As director of Jardí Botanic de Sóller (Sóller's Botanic Garden, p121), Lluís Gradaille Tortella works daily with the Balearics' wonderfully varied flora.

What are Mallorca's most iconic plants? There are many, like *Paeonia cambessedesii*, a beautiful pink peony endemic to Mallorca and locally called *dits de sang* (fingers of blood). You could also see a lot of *Naufraga balearica*, a damp-loving endemic plant with delicate white flowers.

What can you tell us about Mallorca's medicinal plants? Mallorca, like most Mediterranean lands, has a strong tradition of using medicinal plants. More than 100 are still used today and are said to calm nerves, ease headaches or even to help avoid the presence of demons.

What is Mallorca's most pressing environmental problem? There are many, but invasive species – non-native plants that can take root anywhere and don't allow other species to survive – are threatening our endemic flora. They are destroying our natural ecosystems.

What can people do to help? Use autochthonous plants in your garden. These also have the benefit of needing less water and being easier to care for.

ENDANGERED SPECIES

Threatened species of Mediterranean birds, tortoises and toads are growing in number thanks to the conservation and controlled breeding efforts of Mallorca's parks and natural areas. Endangered species here include the spur-thighed tortoise and Hermann's tortoise, the only two tortoises found in Spain, and bird species like the red kite.

The programmes are showing results; the endemic Mallorcan midwife toad's status was recently changed to 'vulnerable' from 'critically endangered'. But there's not such good news about the Balearic shearwater, a water bird that has suffered greatly because of feral cats. It recently moved from 'near threatened' to 'critically endangered'.

Plants

From the delicate pink and white blooms of almond trees and the red berries of evergreens, to the vast fields of springtime wild flowers and exotic blooms of cliff-dwelling plants, Mallorca's landscape is defined by its enticing flora. The Balearic Islands claim more than 100 endemic species and provide a fertile home to countless more.

On the peaks of the Serra de Tramuntana, Mallorca's determined mountain flora survives harsh sun and wind. Thriving species tend to be ground huggers or cliff species like *Scabiosa cretica* (full plants with exotic-looking lilac blooms), which burrow into rock fissures to keep their roots well drained and cool.

A full English-language directory of Balearic plants is online at http://herbarivirtual.uib.es.

On Mallorca's rocky hillsides and flat plains, where oak forests once grew before being burned or destroyed to create farmland, drought-resistant scrubland flora now thrives. Expect to see evergreen shrubs like wild olives and dwarf fan palms, as well as herbs like rosemary, thyme and lavender. Other plants include heather, broom, prickly pear (which can be made into jam) and 60 species of orchids.

Where evergreen oak forests have managed to survive you'll find holly oaks, kermes oaks and holm oaks growing alongside smaller, less noticeable species like violets, heather and butcher's broom. Most interesting to botanists are endangered endemic species like the shiny-leaved box *(Buxux balearica)* and the needled yew *(Taxus baccata)*, a perennial tree that can grow for hundreds of years. A specimen in Esporles is thought to be more than two thousand years old.

At least 100 of Mallorca's plants are endemic, that is, they occur naturally only on the island.

Humidity-seeking ferns (more than 40 species of them) have found marvellous habitats near Mallorca's caves, gorges and streams. Look out for the chaste tree (an appreciated medicinal plant), oleander and tangled patches of blackberries. Endemic plants include the lovely *Paeonia cambessedesii,* a pink peony that lives in the shade of some Serra de Tramuntana gullies, and *Naufraga balearica,* a clover-like plant that lives on shady Tramuntana slopes. In other damp areas, clusters of poplars, elms and ash trees, all introduced species, form small forests.

On the shore, plants have had to adapt to constant sea spray, salt deposits and strong winds. One of Mallorca's most beloved coastal species is samphire *(fonoll marí),* a leafy coastal herb that was given to sailors as a source of scurvy-preventing vitamin C. These days it's marinated and used in salads. Other common species are the spiny cushion-like *Launaea cervicornis,* and *Senecio rodriguezii,* whose purple, daisy-like flowers earned it the nickname of *margalideta de la mar* (little daisy of the sea).

In the wetlands, marshes and dunes of Mallorca, a variety of coastal freshwater flora prosper. Duckweed is one of the most common plants here, though it is often kept company by bulrush, yellow flag iris, sedge and mint. These sand-dwelling species often have white or pale-green leaves and an extensive root system that helps keep them anchored in the shifting sands.

ENVIRONMENTAL ISSUES

Not surprisingly, overdevelopment is the main environmental issue facing Mallorca. The uninhibited construction that began in the 1960s and '70s has influenced everything from birds' nesting habits to plant habitats, rainwater runoff and water shortages. Although the government is more environmentally aware than in decades past, there are still conflicts, such as a proposed shopping and leisure centre that would destroy the Ses Fontanelles wetland near S'Arenal, or the urban corruption scandal involving a town hall–approved housing project that would have destroyed part of a protected forest in Andratx (when the scandal was uncovered in 2006 it led to a wave of arrests).

The high-rise hotels of mega resorts like Magaluf, S'Arenal and Cala d'Or may be the most glaring examples of overdevelopment, but just as damaging is the proliferation of chalets and sprawling village-like resort complexes that are quickly eating up land. Per square metre, these residential tourism homes use more water and more electricity than traditional hotels, and as their numbers grow they are encroaching more and more into the natural habitats of island wildlife. At its core the problem is simple and has no obvious solution: there is simply more demand than supply when it comes to Mallorcan land.

For information on environmental issues and how you can get involved, go to www .gobmallorca.com.

One of the most pressing concerns for environmentalists, and an indirect result of the construction boom, is the prevalence of invasive plant species. Many destructive species were first introduced in local gardens but have found such a good home in Mallorca that they're crowding out endemic species. A good example is *Carpobrotus edulis,* called 'sour fig' in England and locally dubbed *patata frita* (french fry) or *dent de león* (lion's tooth) because of its long, slender leaves. A robust low-lying plant, it chokes native species wherever it goes.

RESPONSIBLE TOURISM – WATER CONSERVATION

We all should do our part to conserve H20, starting with some common-sense strategies, such as limiting shower time, turning off the tap when not using water and requesting that hotel towels not be laundered every day – instead, hang them up to dry and re-use.

Even more noticeable is the water shortage, produced by the combination of low rainfall, outdated water collection and treatment facilities, and a demand that completely overwhelms the resources available.

New highways and motorways are another source of tensions, with many environmental groups fighting the construction of major roadways, which destroy habitats, redirect water routes and increase traffic.

Influential environmental groups include **Amics de la Terra** (Friends of the Earth; www.amicsdelaterra.org in Spanish), **Grup Balear d'Ornitologia i Defensa de la Naturalesa** (Balearic Group of Ornithology & Defence of Nature; www.gobmallorca.com), and the **Fundació Pel Deseanvolupament Sostenible de les Illes Balears** (Foundation for the Sustainable Development of the Balearic Islands; www.targetaverda.com), promoters of the Targeta Verda (p17).

Activities

Mallorca is all about the great outdoors. No doubt it's the mild climate and ever-changing natural beauty that lured you here, so now it's time to get out and enjoy. A favourite walking destination for a generation, Mallorca is now garnering fame as a cycling hot spot. Amateurs and pros alike have discovered that the island's hilly country roads are the perfect places to feel the burn.

On the coast there's sailing, kite surfing, sea kayaking and windsurfing. Marshy areas like the Parc Natural de S'Albufera are wonderful bird-watching areas. Or head inland for more adventurous pursuits like caving or descending canyons. The culturally minded can explore Mallorca's agrotourism routes, where you can see how cheese, wine and other local products are made. Signing up for courses, whether they be day-long cooking classes or more intense language immersions, is the ideal way to get under the island's skin.

Several companies offer day trips or activities, among them the Sóller-based **Tramuntana Tours** (☎ 971 632423; www.tramuntanatours.com; excursions average per person incl transport €25), which offers walking, mountain biking, road cycling and fishing trips all around the island.

If you're looking for short, easy-access walks, check out Sunflower Guides' Landscapes of Mallorca.

WALKING

From the bald limestone peaks in the west to the fertile plains of the interior and the rocky coastal trails of the east, trekkers have their pick of splendid walks on Mallorca. The Consell de Mallorca has gotten serious about marking and maintaining the island's trails, many of which have been used for centuries. Keen hikers can tackle the Ruta de Pedra en Sec (Route of Dry Stone, GR 221, p112), which is a five- to seven-day walk running from Port d'Andratx to Pollença, crossing the Serra de Tramuntana. Signposting is currently under way on the Ruta Artà-Lluc (GR 222), which will eventually link the two towns. As in the rest of Spain all GR (long-distance) trails are signposted in red and white. At a few points along the GR 221 there are *refugis de muntanya* (rustic mountain huts) where trekkers can stay the night.

The website www.exploradors.com pertains to the Balearic Islands Rambling Association and has helpful information about walking guides and routes.

The best hiking maps are the 1:25,000 Tramuntana Central, Tramuntana Norte and Tramuntana Sur maps by Editorial Alpina. If you need more than a good map, call on island guides like **Rich Strutt** (☎ 609 700826; www.mallorcanwalkingtours.puertopollensa.com; day hike per person incl transport €25-33), an English-speaking guide who offers tailored day hikes or longer treks for groups of four or more. Also recommended is **Jaume Tort** (☎ 618 215766; www.mallorca-camins.com; day hike per couple incl transport €100); see opposite. Both guides work all over the island.

Lead your own hikes with the detailed and easy-to-follow Walk! Mallorca North and Mountains by Charles Davis.

See individual chapters in this book for details on area walks.

CYCLING

Nearly half of Mallorca's 1250km of roads have been 'adapted' for cycling, with measures ranging from simple signposts to separate bike lanes (like the excellent lanes along Palma's waterfront). The better roads are just one more draw for cyclists, who descend in droves to sample Mallorca's hilly terrain and peaceful countryside, especially from March to May and late September to November, when the weather is refreshingly cool.

Mountain bikers will find plenty of trails here as well, ranging from flat dirt tracks, to rough'n'tumble single-track climbs. There is no 'best' area for biking; trails cover the island like a web and, depending on your skills and

> **JAUME TORT, MOUNTAINEERING GUIDE & MAP CREATOR**
>
> As a hiking guide, mountain lover, and the creator of a series of Tramuntana trekking maps for the bestselling Spanish company Editorial Alpina, Jaume Tort has walked more of Mallorca than most people.
>
> **The world is filled with walking destinations. Why Mallorca?** In one of the most important tourist destinations of the Mediterranean you can find a rural area as beautiful and unspoilt as the Serra de Tramuntana. Most of the 10 million tourists that visit us each year spend their holiday at the beach, so the mountainous regions and the wild coastal areas are still lonely and virgin.
>
> **Where is your favourite place to hike?** The coastal area of the Santuari de Lluc. Smugglers' trails, deep gorges, cliffs, rugged peaks…and private properties.
>
> **Did you run into problems creating the Alpina trekking maps?** I've never had problems with guard dogs (which are always tied up in Mallorca), but to enter private properties I've had to jump more fences than I can count, and once I got into an argument with the caretakers of a rural estate.
>
> **What advice do you have for those who want to take their tent to Mallorca?** That they leave it at home. In Mallorca there is just one simple campground in Lluc, and open-air camping isn't allowed. The best options are the *refugis de muntanya* (mountain refuges), which have caretakers and are located in pretty areas.

interests, anywhere can be the start of a fabulous ride. Be sure to get a good highway or trekking map before you set out.

Check in local tourist offices for route information and details about bike rental agencies. Prices can vary between €8 for a touring bike and €18 for a mountain bike per day. Kids' bikes and kiddie seats are widely available as well. The **Federació de Ciclisme de les Illes Balears** (Cycling Federation of the Balearic Islands; ☎ 971 757628; www.webfcib.org in Spanish & Catalan) can provide contact information for local cycling clubs. A growing number of hotels cater specifically to cyclists, with garages and energy-packed menus.

The 1:75,000 *Mallorca Cycle Map* by Cycline will help you plan routes across the island.

Two suggested cycling routes are on p100 and p146.

GOLF
There are nearly two dozen golf courses across Mallorca, most of them near Palma or along the coasts. Expect a round of 18 holes to cost €75 and up (nine holes is about two-thirds that price), with cart rental €25 to €40. Prices dip in summer when it's often simply too hot to have fun.

Some 50,000 cyclists come to ride on Mallorca's roads each year.

Tourist offices distribute the *Mallorca Golf* brochure, with details and contact information for all island courses. Or contact the **Federació Balear de Golf** (Balearic Golf Federation; ☎ 971 722753; www.fbgolf.com) for general golfing info.

BIRD-WATCHING
As a natural resting point between Europe and Africa, and as one of the few Mediterranean islands with considerable wetlands, Mallorca is a wonderful birding destination. Grab your wildlife guide and head to the Parc Natural de S'Albufera (p148), a marshy bird-watchers' paradise where some 230 species, including moustached warblers and shoveler ducks, vie for your attention. The park provides free binoculars to holders of a Targeta Verda (p17).

Other good spots include the Vall de Bocquer near Port de Pollença (p139) and natural parks like the Parc Natural de Mondragó (p191) and the Reserva Natural de S'Albufereta in northern Mallorca. The best time for birding is spring and autumn, the peak migration times. The web forum www.birdforum.net has an extensive listing of Balearic birding sites. See p54 for more information.

GETTING OUTSIDE...WITH KIDS

After the beach, where can you take the kids? The theme parks and zoos that dot Mallorca are obvious choices. The Puig de Galatxó Parc de Natura in western Mallorca, a park with adventurous activities like rock climbing and zip lining, is a fun option for kids eight and older.

Get out on the water with a cruise on a glass-bottomed boat (p177) or take a day trip to the Illa de Cabrera (p186). Snorkelling around coves like Font de Sa Cala (p171) is a great way to have fun while learning about marine life. Or see sharks and Mediterranean sea creatures up close at the Palma Aquarium (p101).

On dry land rent bikes and make the most of the island's bike paths, like the flat stretch running along Palma's waterfront (p100). Horseback riding is a thrill for older kids, and even toddlers will enjoy the pony rides available at many of the stables. To hike with kids, choose a short- to medium-length trail with lots of diversions; a coastal path is ideal. See p169 and p182 for a couple of specific ideas.

Just off the highways of the Serra de Tramuntana are two dozen or so public recreational areas, parks and rural estates that now have barbecue pits and play areas for kids.

HORSEBACK RIDING

With its extensive network of rugged trails making their way over the hilly countryside and alongside the Mediterranean, Mallorca is a magnet for equestrians. Many towns and resorts also have stables where you can sign up for a class (€10 to €20) or join a group for an excursion (about €25 per hour) or day trip (around €100). Some stables also offer pony rides for small children. Cala Ratjada (p170), Colònia de Sant Jordi (p185) and Pollença (p134) are all popular riding areas. Get more information from tourist offices or the **Federació Hípica de les Illes Baleares** (Equestrian Federation of the Balearic Islands; ☎ 971 154225; www.hipicabaleares.com in Spanish; Carrer del Metge Camps, Es Mercadal, Menorca).

The website www.mal lorcanautic.com has loads of information on sailing Mallorca's coast.

WATER SPORTS

With 550km of coastline, Mallorca makes it easy to enjoy the Mediterranean. In practically every resort you'll find opportunities to get out on the water.

Sailing & Cruising

Among the 35 marinas that ring Mallorca's coast, many offer yacht charters, sailboat rentals and sailing courses. There are large sailing schools in Palma (p85), Port de Pollença (p139) and other resorts; expect a nine-hour course to cost €100 and up.

Spain's king, prince and infantas are avid sailors. Each summer they participate in Mallorca's Copa del Rey (King's Cup).

If you charter or bring your own yacht, your options for sailing are unlimited. Popular routes include sailing around Palma to the Illa de Cabrera and back, sailing along the rugged Tramuntana coast (p119), or making the loop right around the island. For details on moorings and marinas, try to pick up the free *Harbours & Marinas Guide,* published annually by Tallers de Molí, at tourist offices or marinas. If you anchor your yacht in open water, follow the guidelines published by the **Conselleria de Medi Ambient** (☎ 971 176800; www.caib.es; Avinguda de Gabriel Alomar i Villalonga 33, Palma de Mallorca) to protect the sea floor. Another good source of information is the **Federació Balear de Vela** (Balearic Sailing Federation; ☎ 971 402410; www .federaciobalearvela.org in Spanish; Avinguda de Joan Miró 327, Palma de Mallorca).

The glass-bottomed boats that drift up and down the eastern coast are a fun way to enjoy the water without having the responsibility of a boat. See individual resort sections for details.

Surfing, Windsurfing & Kite Surfing

While the relatively calm wind and waves of Mallorca don't make the island a natural hot spot for fans of surfing, windsurfing or kite surfing (aka kite boarding), there are a few places to ride the waves. Port de Pollença (p139), on the Badia d'Alcúdia, is the epicentre for these sports. Most courses include four or more hours of instruction time and cost €75 and up.

Scuba Diving

The northern and western coasts and the islands of Dragonera and Cabrera are all great places to scuba dive, thanks to their rich marine habitats and clear waters. For scuba shops, gear rental, classes or to sign up for a dive, head to Sóller (p119), Santa Ponça, Port de Pollença (p139) or Alcúdia (p142). If you're just looking for an excuse to dive, nearly any resort will be able to provide you with basic gear, even on the east coast where the underwater sights are generally less spectacular. Expect a dive to cost at least €35; equipment rental is extra.

> There's a great overview of Mallorcan diving at www.divesitedirectory.co .uk/balearics_mallorca.

Sea Kayaking

The craggy coast and generally calm conditions of Mallorca make it well suited to sea kayaking, a sport that is just beginning to gain a loyal following. Guide and rental companies are clustered around Alcúdia and Port de Pollença.

The Port de Pollença–based **Kayak Mallorca** (☎ 696 151340; www.kayakmallorca .com; half-day trip per person incl transport €45; La Gola, Port de Pollença) organises trips for any level all around the island. Get in touch with the **Federación Balear de Piragüismo** (Balearic Federation of Canoeing & Kayaking; ☎ 971 792019; www.fibp.org in Spanish; Carrer Joan Miró 327, Palma de Mallorca) for details on courses for kids and adults, as well as a list of nautical clubs with a kayak presence.

ADVENTURE SPORTS

If you're looking for something even more thrilling, canyoning might be for you. Trudging down gorges and gullies can be dangerous if you're not well prepared (going with a guide is essential), but it can also be exhilarating. The Monument Nacional Torrent de Pareis in western Mallorca is the island's best canyoning destination.

Mallorca's pocked limestone terrain means caving conditions are fantastic. One of the best is the long Cova des Pas de Vallgornera (p184), although there are countless explorable caves here, with more being discovered and catalogued each year. To be safe, employ the help of a local expert like **Jose Antonio Encinas** (☎ 609 372888; www.inforber.com/mallorcaverde, an interesting site in Spanish), who leads caving trips.

> Many of Mallorca's hiking trails were first laid out by tobacco smugglers during the oppressive Franco regime of the mid-20th century.

For courses or guides in caving, canyoning or rock-climbing excursions, you could also contact the British-run **Rocksport Mallorca** (☎ 629 948404; www .rocksportmallorca.com), based in Port de Pollença.

For more information on Mallorca's caves see p53.

COURSES

Signing up for a course is a wonderful way to get more out of your holiday. Language classes are widely available, although many of them are geared toward long-term students. For full details on Spanish courses in Spain, check in with Spain's national language institute, the **Instituto Cervantes** (www.cervantes.es).

To learn more about cooking in Spain, get in touch with Fosh Food (p85) in Palma, where two-hour classes costing €45 and up teach gourmet cooking techniques in English and sometimes German.

Yoga classes are available in several spas and rural hotels. They're also offered by private teachers like those at **Yoga Mallorca** (www.yoga-mallorca.com), who, for €28 per hour, will travel to your hotel for a private class.

Courses in sailing, windsurfing, kayaking and rock climbing are spottily available on the island; see individual sports sections in this chapter for more details.

Plan your agrotourism route with www.illesbalearsqualitat.es, a wonderful source if you're curious about the island's food, wine and rural heritage.

AGROTOURISM

See how cheese is made, visit a ceramics factory or tour a winery. Agrotourism is booming in Mallorca, and the local government has even set up guided tours to dozens of local factories and workshops. The helpful map *Agrorutes del Bon Gust* (Agroroutes of Good Taste), published by the Conselleria d'Agricultura i Pesca (Fish and Agriculture Council), provides the contact details and locations for nearly all visitable factories, giving you enough information to make a self-styled agricultural tour of the island.

If you're interested in wineries make a beeline for Binissalem (p154); for cheese factories, hit Campos (p164); for *sobrassada* production, head to Artà (p167) or Sóller (p119). All factory contact details are online at www.illesbalearsqualitat.es.

Palma &
the Badia de Palma

Set on a magnificent broad bay, Palma de Mallorca is a city of light that can happily compete with any European regional capital. Its old heart oozes centuries of history in its twisting lanes, powerful churches, traditional pastry shops and baroque mansions. For those who think of Mediterranean islands as being all about sand and sea, the cultural charge and sophistication of this city can come as a surprise. The wedding of culture, history and seaside recreation is perhaps best symbolised in the position of its Gothic cathedral, one of Europe's finest, overlooking the sparkling Mediterranean and a short walk to the nearest beach.

The city lies at the midpoint of a sweeping bay, the Badia de Palma. To the west, a series of idyllic, aqua-hued beaches and inlets have managed to retain their beauty despite the tourist development. People of all walks of life crowd into the resorts to swing, chill and, in some cases, wreak nocturnal havoc in the heart of the Magaluf party zone. Other beaches spread east from central Palma, with more Euro-partying happening at Platja de Palma and S'Arenal. Then, suddenly, all the ruckus ends at the quiet, residential eastern tip of the bay, with several hidden inlets to swim in.

HIGHLIGHTS

- Admire the fantasy of Barceló within the magnificent Gothic **Catedral** (p68)
- Shudder at the sharks in the brand-new **Palma Aquarium** (p101)
- Wander into the exquisite Gothic cloister of the **Basílica de Sant Francesc** (p76)
- Take in the contemporary art inside the one-time city walls at **Es Baluard** (p80)
- Get lost in Old Palma's labyrinth and search out the courtyards of **baroque mansions** (p80)
- Get a quick lesson in modern Spanish art at the **Museu d'Art Espanyol Contemporani** (p78)
- Wander around the towers and enjoy the view from **Castell de Bellver** (p83)

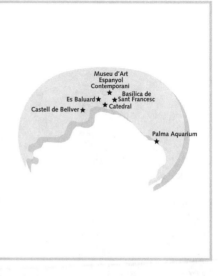

PALMA DE MALLORCA

pop 375,770
Palma de Mallorca is Mallorca's only true
city. The old quarter is an attractive blend of
tree-lined boulevards and cobbled laneways,
Gothic churches and baroque palaces, designer bars and slick boutiques.

HISTORY
Known to the Romans as Palmeria or Palma,
to the Muslims as Medina Mayurka (City of
Mallorca) and to their Christian successors as
Ciutat de Mallorca or Ciudad Capital (City
Capital), to most Mallorquins the city contin-
ues simply to be Ciutat. Officially the name
Palma de Mallorca began to impose itself in
the early 18th century.

By the 12th century the Muslim city was
one of the most flourishing capitals in Europe.
After the Christian conquest in 1229, it again
entered a period of prosperity as a trade centre
in the 14th century. By the 16th century, along
with the rest of the island, it was sinking into a
protracted period of torpor. The great seaward

> ## OUR TOP PICKS
>
> ■ **Hotel** Hotel Palacio Ca Sa Galesa (p86)
> ■ **Restaurant** Refectori (p90)
> ■ **Bar** Hostal Corona (p94)
> ■ **Market** Mercat de l'Olivar (p89)
> ■ **Festival** Corpus Christi (p85)

walls that you see today were largely built in
the 16th and 17th centuries, when the city's
seasonal torrent, the Riera, was diverted from
its natural course along Passeig d'es Born to its
present location west of the city walls.

The old city centre then went into decline.
Even today, parts of the former fishing district
of Es Puig de Sant Pere and the tight web of
lanes in the Sa Gerreria area in the eastern half
of the old city (between Carrer del Sindicat and
Carrer del Temple) retain an air of neglect. Large
slabs of the latter have been torn down since the
mid-1990s to make way for new blocks of flats.
The bulk of the sea walls were demolished at the
beginning of the 20th century to allow rapid
expansion of the city. But the heart of the city

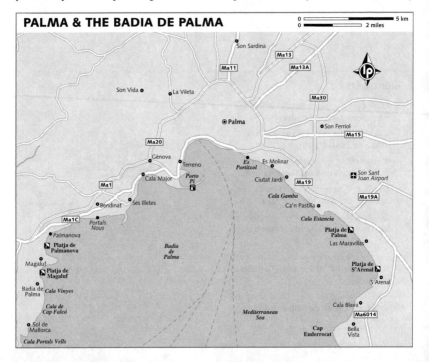

PALMA & THE BADIA DE PALMA

has been spruced up beyond recognition since tourist cash began to flow into the island in the 1960s and a report in 2007 claimed that property around the Dalt Murada was among the most expensive in all Spain.

ORIENTATION

Palma sits halfway along the Badia de Palma. The oldest parts of the city are enclosed within Passeig de Mallorca (west), the Avingudes (the north and east avenues) that roughly mark the line of the old city walls, and the waterfront. The train and bus stations lie within about 400m of each other just off Avinguda de Joan March, northeast of the city centre. The airport bus stops here.

The oldest part of the city, Sa Calatrava (where the Catedral and Palau de l'Almudaina stand) is separated from the waterfront by the Parc de la Mar. The bulk of the sights and most charming hotels are bunched together here. Es Puig de Sant Pere, across Passeig d'es Born, is poorer on specific sights but rewards wandering along its narrow lanes and is full of places to eat and drink.

The area between Plaça Major, Plaça d'Espanya and Passeig de Mallorca is less intriguing but contains some key sights, hotels and restaurants. The Santa Catalina district, west of Passeig de Mallorca, is teeming with restaurants and bars, while Es Portitxol, Es Molinar and Ciutat Jardí, along the coast east of the centre, offer beaches, eateries and cafés. Finally, the Passeig Marítim and Plaça de Gomila areas in western Palma are home to many of the city's clubbing options.

Beyond, spreading especially to the north and east, are rings of suburbs and industrial zones (called *polígonos*) that have spread since the 1960s.

INFORMATION
Bookshops

Dialog (Map pp70-1; ☎ 971 228129; www.dialog-palma.com; Carrer del Carme 14; ☷ 9.30am-2pm & 4.30-8.30pm Mon-Fri, 10am-1.30pm Sat) This is a gold mine of books on Mallorca in German and English.

Fiol Llibres (Map pp70-1; ☎ 971 721428; www.abbooks.com; Carrer dels Oms 45a; ☷ 10am-1.30pm & 5-8pm Mon-Fri, 10am-1.30pm Sat) The shelves groan under the weight of secondhand books and some antique gems.

Trading Place (Map pp70-1; ☎ 871 941350; www.tradingplacemallorca.com; Carrer del Pou 35; ☷ 10am-1.30pm & 5-8pm Mon-Fri, 10am-1.30pm Sat) Exchange and sale of secondhand books.

Cultural Centres

Alliance Française (☎ 971 714101; www.alliancefrancaise.es; Carrer de Sant Feliu 9) Drop by for a shot of Gallic culture (film cycles, exhibitions and the like).

International House (☎ 971 726408; www.ihes.com/pal; Plaça de la Cort 11) This is mainly a centre for English, German and Spanish tuition. Qualified teachers may find work here.

Emergency

Emergency phone numbers valid in Palma and across the island:

Ambulance (☎ 061)
Bomberos (Fire Department; ☎ in Palma 080, rest of the island 085)
General EU emergency number (☎ 112)
Guardia Civil (☎ 062)
Policía Local (☎ 092; Avinguda de Sant Ferran 42)
Policía Nacional (☎ 091; Carrer de Ruiz de Alda 8)

Internet Access

Azul Cybercafé (Map pp70-1; ☎ 971 712927; www.azulgroup.com; Carrer de la Soledat 4; per hr €2.90; ☷ 8.30am-8pm Mon-Fri, noon-6pm Sat)

Internet Resources

www.palmademallorca.es The official site of the City of Palma (Ajuntament), with links to tourist pages, events and various municipal services. Also has interactive map of the city.

www.visit-palma.com Asociación Hotelera de Palma de Mallorca website, with hotel and general information for Palma de Mallorca.

Left Luggage

There is no left luggage service at the airport or port.

Media

For local and national newspapers see p196. For local news in English have a look at either *Euro Weekly News Mallorca* (www.euroweeklynews.com) or the *Daily Bulletin* (www.majorcadailybulletin.es). More substantial are the weekly German-language newspapers, *Mallorca Magazin* (www.mallorcamagazin.net) and *Mallorca Zeitung* (www.mallorcazeitung.es).

For an idea of what's on, try the fortnightly *Youthing* and quarterly *V&mos* (www.vamos-mallorca.com), which you'll find in Palma's tourist offices. *Dígame* (www.digamemallorca.com) is a free monthly with island-wide events, but isn't that detailed. Other free monthlies are *Quecuando* and *TodoPalma*.

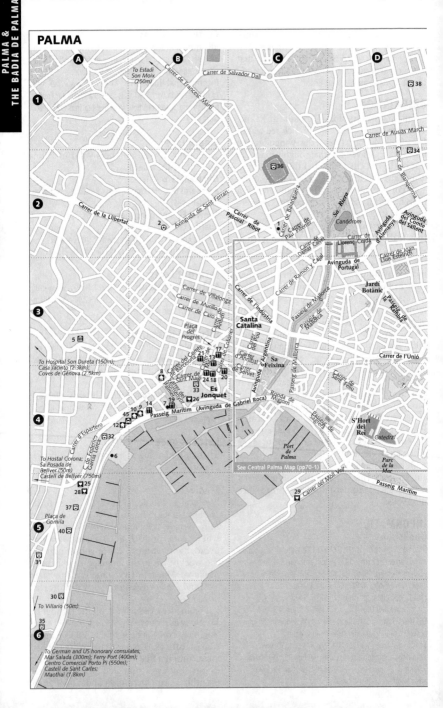

PALMA

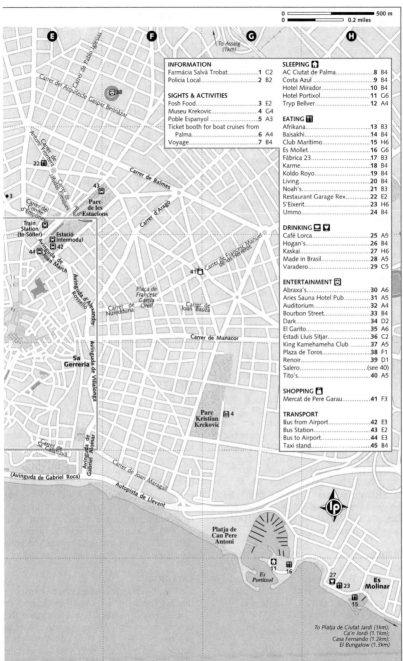

0 _____ 500 m
0 _____ 0.2 miles

To Assaig
(1km)

INFORMATION
Farmàcia Salvà Trobat..............1 C2
Policia Local............................2 B2

SIGHTS & ACTIVITIES
Fosh Food................................3 E2
Museu Krekovic........................4 G4
Poble Espanyol.........................5 A3
Ticket booth for boat cruises from
  Palma...................................6 A4
Voyage....................................7 B4

SLEEPING
AC Ciutat de Palma....................8 B4
Costa Azul...............................9 B4
Hotel Mirador..........................10 B4
Hotel Portixol.........................11 G6
Tryp Bellver............................12 A4

EATING
Afrikana.................................13 B3
Baisakhi................................14 B4
Club Marítimo.........................15 H6
Es Mollet...............................16 G6
Fàbrica 23.............................17 B3
Karme..................................18 B4
Koldo Royo.............................19 B4
Living...................................20 B4
Noah's..................................21 B3
Restaurant Garage Rex............22 E2
S'Eixerit...............................23 H6
Ummo...................................24 B4

DRINKING
Café Lorca.............................25 A5
Hogan's................................26 B4
Kaskai..................................27 H6
Made in Brasil........................28 A5
Varadero...............................29 C5

ENTERTAINMENT
Abraxa's...............................30 A6
Aries Sauna Hotel Pub..............31 A5
Auditorium............................32 A4
Bourbon Street.......................33 B4
Dark....................................34 D2
El Garito...............................35 A6
Estadi Lluís Sitjar....................36 C2
King Kamehameha Club 37 A5
Plaza de Toros........................38 F1
Renoir..................................39 D1
Salero...............................(see 40)
Tito's...................................40 A5

SHOPPING
Mercat de Pere Garau..............41 F3

TRANSPORT
Bus from Airport......................42 E3
Bus Station............................43 E2
Bus to Airport.........................44 E3
Taxi stand..............................45 B4

Carrer del Arquitecte Gaspar Bennàzar

Carrer del Pablo Iglesias

38

Carrer de Antoni Frontera

Carrer de Balmes

22

43

•3

Carrer del comte d'Empúries

Parc
de les
Estacions

Carrer d'Arago

Train
Station
(to Sóller)

Estació
Intermodal

42

44

Avinguda de
Joan March

Carrer de Francesc Manuel
de los Herreros

Avinguda d'Alexandre
Rosselló

Plaça de
Francesc
Garcia
Orell

41

Carrer de
Nuredduna

Carrer de
Joan Bauzá

Sa
Gerreria

Avinguda de Villalonga

Carrer de Manacor

Carrer de
Sa Calatrava

Avinguda de
Gabriel Alomar

Carrer de Joan Maragall

(Avinguda de Gabriel Roca)

Autopista de Llevant

Parc
Kristian
Krekovic

4

Platja de
Can Pere
Antoni

Es
Portixol

11   16

27

23   Es
Molinar

15

To Platja de Ciutat Jardi (1km);
Ca'n Jordi (1.1km);
Casa Fernando (1.2km);
El Bungalow (1.3km)

WI-FI ACCESS

Wi-fi access is far from common in Palma. The occasional restaurant and café is set up for it, as are some of the better hotels (in which you usually pay). Of course, you can just flip your laptop open and hope to get lucky!

You'll find most of them in the tourist offices and distributed in bars.

There is a growing stable of glossy monthlies in English and German. The free *abcmallorca* (www.abc-mallorca.com) has articles on the city and island. *Contemporary Balears* (www.contemporarybalears.com) is published three times a year and has interesting articles and listings. Look out for it in hotels and some restaurants, bars and galleries. The quarterly *Inpalma,* distributed to hotels, has a curious mix of views and reviews.

The annual *Mallorca Geht Aus!* (€8.80; also available in Germany, Austria and Switzerland) has more than 200 glossy pages packed with stories and reviews of anything from *fincas* (farmhouses) to clubs.

Medical Services

Hospital Son Dureta (☎ 971 175000; Carrer de Andrea Doria 55) To get here from the centre, take bus 5 (from Passeig de Mallorca), 29 (from Passeig Marítim) or 46. For an ambulance, call ☎ 061 or the Red Cross on ☎ 971 202222.

In the main newspapers (such as the *Diario de Mallorca*) you will find a list of pharmacies open from 9am to 10pm and others (a handful) from 10pm to 9am. Some handy ones:

Farmácia Castañer-Buades (Map pp70-1; ☎ 971 711534; Plaça de Joan Carles I 3; ⏰ 9am-midnight)

Farmácia Munar Masot (Map pp70-1; ☎ 971 726817; Avinguda d'Alexandre Rosselló 19; ⏰ 9am-midnight)

Farmácia Salvà Trobat (Map pp66-7; ☎ 971 458788; Carrer de la Balanguera 3; ⏰ 24hr)

Money

Bank branches, ATMs and exchange offices abound at Palma's airport (but not the ferry port) and around the centre of town (eg Plaça d'Espanya, Plaça Major, Passeig d'es Born, Carrer de Sant Miquel).

Post

Post office (Map pp70-1; Carrer de la Constitució 6; ⏰ 8.30am-8.30pm Mon-Fri, 9.30am-2pm Sat)

Tourist Information

The island's general tourist office is in Palma (see p203). You can get lots of local city info at ☎ 010, with luck even in English. In addition several city tourist offices are scattered across the city.

Airport tourist office (Map pp70-1; ☎ 971 789556; ⏰ 8.30am-8pm Mon-Sat, 9am-1.30pm Sun)

Main municipal tourist office (Map pp70-1; ☎ 902 102365; www.palmavirtual.es; Casal Solleric, Passeig d'es Born 27; ⏰ 9am-8pm)

Municipal tourist office (Map pp70-1; Parc de les Estacions; ⏰ 9am-8pm)

DANGERS & ANNOYANCES

Palma is fairly safe. The main concern is petty theft – pickpockets and bagsnatchers. Some streets can be dodgy at night, when the occasional junkie, prostitute and pimp comes out to play. This is especially so around the Sa Gerreria district south off Carrer del Sindicat, an area still known as the *barri xinés* (Chinese quarter, which has nothing Chinese about it but is rather a curious appellation for 'red light district'). The streets around Plaça de Sant Antoni and the nearby avenues, such as Avinguda de Villalonga and Avinguda d'Alexandre Rosselló, are worked by prostitutes at night. They pose no threat but their pimps and customers might.

SIGHTS
Old Palma

The heart of the old city (the districts of Sa Portella and Sa Calatrava) has always been centred on its main place of worship (where the Catedral now stands) and the one-time seat of secular power opposite it. The bulk of Palma's sights are jammed into this warren of tight, twisting lanes and sunny squares, where massive churches abound alongside noble houses. The bright Mediterranean light and glittering sea, never far away, lend it a matchless cheer. After selecting some key sights, simply get lost in the maze and poke your nose in wherever takes your fancy.

CATEDRAL

Cast your mind back, when you contemplate this extraordinary sun-kissed monument to Christianity, to earlier days. Here stood the central mosque of Medina Mayurka, capital of Muslim Mallorca for three centuries. When Jaume I and his marauding men forced their way into the city in 1229, the decision had probably already been taken to destroy this symbol of the infidel.

Work on the **Catedral** (La Seu in Catalan; Map pp70-1; ☎ 971 723130; www.catedraldemallorca.org; Carrer del Palau Reial 9; adult/student/under 10yr €4/3/free; ✆ 10am-6.30pm Mon-Fri, 10am-2.30pm Sat Jun-Sep, 10am-5.30pm Mon-Fri, 10am-2.30pm Sat Apr-May & Oct, 10am-2.30pm Mon-Fri, 10am-2.30pm Sat Nov-Mar), one of Europe's largest, did not begin until 1300. Rather, the mosque was used in the interim as a church and dedicated to the Virgin Mary (as was customary in 'reconquered' mosques). Medieval construction times were slow, and as the cathedral was slowly raised, the mosque it replaced was dismantled. Work wasn't completed until 1601.

The awesome structure is predominantly Gothic, apart from the main façade (replaced after an earthquake in 1851) and parts of the interior. It is remarkable for many things, not the least that its sacristans allowed the likes of madcap Modernista Antoni Gaudí and, more recently, contemporary art icon Miquel Barceló to get their hands on it and let their imaginations run riot.

The main façade is startling, quite beautiful and completely mongrel. The original was a Renaissance cherry on the Gothic cake, but an earthquake in 1851 (which caused considerable panic but no loss of life) severely damaged it. Rather than mend the original, it was decided to add some neo-Gothic flavour, which with its interlaced flying buttresses on each flank and soaring pinnacles forms a masterful example of the style. The result, according to the experts, is a hybrid of the Renaissance original (in particular the main doorway) and an inevitably artificial-feeling, 19th-century pseudo-Gothic monumentalism.

Entry to the church is from the north flank, through a series of four rooms that, with the cloister, form what seems like an afterthought tacked on to the side. You get tickets in the first room and then enter a sacristy, which hosts the main part of the small **Museu de la Catedral**, at the centre of which is a huge gold-plated monstrance. Interesting items include a portable altar, thought to have belonged to Jaume I. Its little compartments contain saints' relics. Other reliquaries can be seen, including one purporting to hold three thorns from Christ's crown of thorns. Such relics had enormous value in medieval Christian Europe. Next come two chapterhouses, one Gothic (by Guillem Sagrera) and the second baroque. The latter is dominated by a *relicario de la vera cruz* (reliquary of the true cross).

On passing through one of the side chapels into the cathedral itself, your gaze soars high to the cross vaults, supported by slender, octagonal pillars. The broad nave and aisles are flanked by chapels. The walls support three levels of exquisite stained glass, including five magnificent rose windows. The grandest (the *oculus maior* or 'great eye') is above the main altar and is said to be the biggest in the world. Visit in the morning and see the stunning effect of its coloured light and shapes reflected on the west wall. This spectacle is at its best in February and November.

Gaudí carried out renovations from 1903 to 1914. His most important contribution was opening up many of the long bricked-up windows, adding new stained glass and improving lighting. What most people notice today, however, is the strange baldachin that hovers over the main altar. Topped by a fanciful sculpture of Christ crucified and flanked

---

PALMA IN TWO DAYS

Palma makes a great city break and with a will to cram you can do a lot in a weekend. Start touring with the obvious: **La Catedral** (opposite) and the **Palau de l'Almudaina** (p73). You could spend hours wandering the old town lanes and, to add a little structure, throw in visits to **Can Marqués** (p75), **Casa-Museu Joaquim Torrents Lladó** (p76) and the **Banys Àrabs** (p76). The first two are fine Palma mansions and the latter is what remains of medieval Arab baths. Lunch at **La Taberna del Caracol** (p89). Restart touring with the **Basílica de Sant Francesc** (p76) and **Es Baluard** (p80), where you can stop for a drink on the battlements. For a night out, make for nearby Santa Catalina, with dinner at **Fàbrica 23** (p91), drinks at **Idem Café** (p94) and clubbing along **Passeig Marítim** (p95). The following day is beach day. Make for the strand at **Ciutat Jardí** (p84) and book lunch at the waterside **El Bungalow** (p92). Catch a few more rays and then move around the coast for chilled afternoon drinks at **Puro Beach** near **Cala Estancia** (p101). After sunset head for dinner at **Refectori** (p90).

CENTRAL PALMA

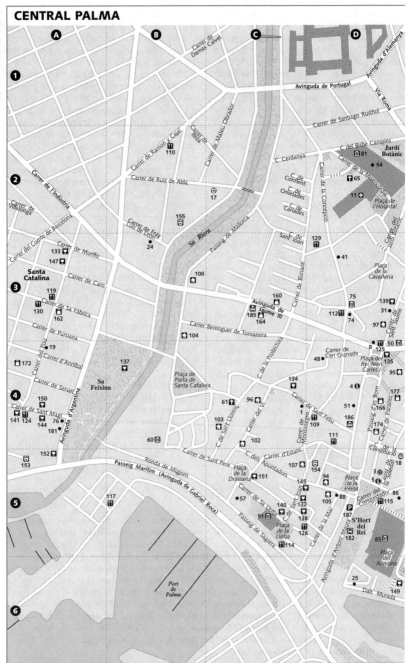

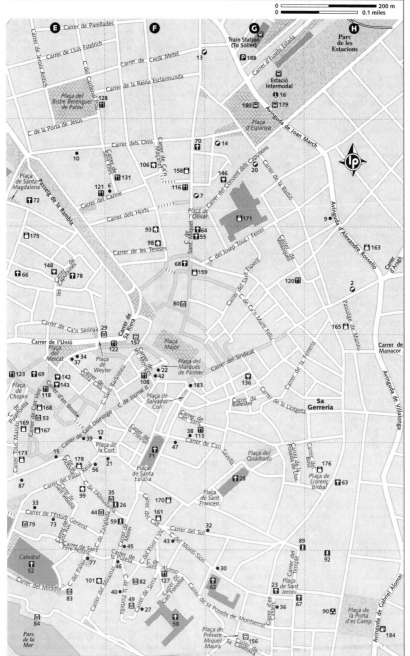

by the Virgin Mary and St John, it looks like the gaping jaw of some oversized prehistoric shark dangling from the ceiling of an old science museum. Some 35 lamps hang from it and what looks like a flying carpet is spread above it. The genius of Barcelona Modernisme seems to have lost the plot here, but then this was supposed to be a temporary version. The definitive one was never made.

Not content with this strangeness, the parish commissioned contemporary Mallorcan artist Miquel Barceló (an agnostic) with the remake of the Capella del Santíssim i Sant Pere, at the rear of the south aisle. Done in 15 tonnes of ceramics, this dreamscape representing the miracle of the loaves and fishes was unveiled in 2007. Slabs of clay seem to have been plastered onto the chapel walls. On the left, fish and other marine creatures burst from the wall. The opposite side has a jungle look, with representations of bread and fruit. In between the fish and palm fronds, and standing above stacks of skulls, appears a luminous body that is supposed to be Christ but is modelled on the short and stocky artist.

Other notable elements of the interior include the giant organ, built in 1798 (free recitals are held at 12.30pm on the first Tuesday of each month), and the two pulpits, the smaller of which was partly redone by Gaudí.

PALAU DE L'ALMUDAINA

Now as in medieval times, the island's maximum secular authority (in the person of the King of Spain) resides at least symbolically opposite the Catedral in the **Palau de l'Almudaina** (Map pp70-1; ☎ 971 214134; www.patrimonionacional.es; Carrer del Palau Reial s/n; adult/student €3.20/2.30, audioguide €2; 🕑 10am-6pm Mon-Fri, 10am-2pm Sat Apr-Sep, 10am-2pm & 4-6pm Mon-Fri, 10am-2pm Sat Oct-Mar; note that ID may be requested). The royal family are rarely in residence, except for the occasional ceremony, as they prefer to spend summer in the Palau Marivent (in Cala Major).

The Romans are said to have built a *castrum* (fort) here, possibly on the site of a prehistoric settlement. The Wālis (governors) of Muslim Mallorca altered and expanded the Roman fort, while Jaume I and his successors modified it to such an extent that little of the Muslim version remains. The forbidding walls are strengthened by squat towers. A higher dungeon-like tower rises from the heart of the residence and is topped by a bronze statue of the Guardian Angel (which must make a fine lightning rod).

The first narrow room you enter has a black-and-white ceiling, symbolising the extremes of night and day, darkness and light. You then enter a series of three grand rooms. Notice the bricked-in Gothic arches cut off in the middle. Originally these three rooms were double their present height and formed one single great hall added to the original Arab fort and known as the Saló del Tinell (from an Italian word, *tinello,* meaning 'place where one eats'). Like a similar medieval hall (on which it was loosely modelled) in Barcelona's Museu de d'Història de la Ciutat, this was used as a giant banqueting and ceremonial hall. After the roof collapsed in 1578, the Spanish king Felipe II had the area split horizontally in half, creating two floors. The rooms are graced by period furniture, tapestries and other curios. The following six bare rooms and terrace belonged to the original Arab citadel.

In the main courtyard, or **Patio de Armas**, troops would line up for an inspection and parade before heading out into the city. The lion fountain in its centre is one of the palace's rare Arab remnants. Up the grand Royal Staircase are the royal apartments, a succession of lavishly appointed rooms (look up to the beautiful coffered timber *artesonado* ceilings), whose centrepiece is the **Saló Gòtic**, the upper half of the former Saló del Tinell, where you can see where those Gothic arches wind up. Next door to the apartments is the royal **Capella de Sant'Anna**, a Gothic chapel whose entrance is a very rare Mallorcan example of late Romanesque in rose and white marble.

After the death of Jaume III in 1349, no king lived here permanently again. The palace housed governors, lieutenants or monarchs passing through. It also housed courts and military governors.

In the shadow of the Almudaina's walls, along Avinguda d'Antoni Maura, is **S'Hort del Rei** (the King's Garden). It is not as green as it perhaps once was, but the shady benches are a nice spot to take a load off. Near here is a grand arch, the **Arc del Wali**, one of the city's few reminders of its Arab past. When the Riera, the city's river, coursed along what is now Passeig d'es Born and the sea lapped the city walls, this was the seaward entrance into the Arab palace and early shipyards. For another rare remnant of Arab days, head up Avinguda d'Antoni Maura from the Arc del

Wali to Plaça de la Reina, then south through a series of three uneven arches into Carrer de la Mar. Together they form the **Porta de l'Almudí**, a Muslim-era gate.

MUSEU DIOCESÀ

Opened in 2007 in its magnificent new home of the Palau Episcopal (bishop's residence), the **Museu Diocesà** (Map pp70–1; ☎ 971 213100; Carrer del Mirador 5; admission €3; ☺ 10am-2pm Tue-Fri) is a fascinating excursion for those interested in Mallorca's Christian artistic history.

The first thing you see is a mind-boggling **retaule** (*retablo* in Spanish, an altarpiece) depicting the Passion of Christ (c 1290–1305) and taken from the Convent de Santa Clara (p77). The characters are in medieval dress (no-one much knew how people looked or dressed in preceding centuries) and the episodes are shown with effusive detail: Palm Sunday, the Last Supper, St Peter's kiss of betrayal. Christ flailed looks utterly unperturbed, while the image of his being nailed to the cross is unsettling. Off to the right, a key work is Francesc Comes' *St Jaume de Compostela* (St James, known to the Spaniards as the Moor-slayer). Pere Niçard's *Sant Jordi* (St George), done around 1468–70, is remarkable for its busy detail. The City of Mallorca (Palma) is shown in the background as St George despatches the dragon. Below this painting is a scene by Niçard and his boss Rafel Mòger depicting the 1229 taking of Palma. The final room in this wing is the Gothic **Oratori de Sant Pau**, a small chapel. The stained glass window was a trial run done by Gaudí in preparation for the windows he did in the Catedral.

Now backtrack and walk through a succession of rooms past works by anonymous and key Mallorquin artists such as Pere Terrencs and Mateu López (father and son). Also here is an 18th-century statue of St Dominic, one of the few remnants of the grand Dominican monastery destroyed in the heart of Palma in the mid-19th century. Upstairs is a thin collection of baroque art, ceramics (mostly from mainland Spain) and some lovely views out over the bay.

Adjoining the Palau Episcopal is the **Jardí del Bisbe** (Map pp70–1; Carrer de Sant Pere Nolasc 6; ☺ 9am-1pm & 3-6pm Mon-Fri, 10am-3pm Sat May-Oct, 9am-3pm Mon-Fri, 10am-3pm Sat Nov-Apr). This modest botanic garden is an oasis of peace. Have a quiet stroll among the palms, pomegranates, water lil-

ies, thyme, artichokes, cumquats, orange and lemon trees and more. Or just sit on a bench and contemplate.

WALLS & PARC DE LA MAR

Most of Palma's defensive walls were destroyed in the late 19th century to allow easier expansion of the city. Only a section of the Renaissance sea wall, the Dalt Murada, remains impressively intact, albeit no longer lapped by the Mediterranean, as a considerable chunk of land has since been won from the sea to create the Passeig Marítim ring road and tree-lined waterfront. Construction of this last section of the city's defensive perimeters began in 1562 and limped along until 1801.

In 1984 the Parc de la Mar (with its artificial lake, fountain and green spaces) was opened. Looking tatty in parts (the white public benches have seen better days), it is still a pleasing part of the view from the stout walls, and a pleasant place for a breezy drink at one of two terrace cafés in summer.

Within a section of the walls at the level of the artificial lake, vaulted chambers once used as barracks have been converted into the **Museu Ses Voltes** (Map pp70–1; ☎ 971 728739; admission free; ☺ 10am-1.45pm & 5-8.30pm Tue-Sat, 10am-1.45pm Sun & holidays), seat of temporary exhibitions.

PALAU MARCH

For a burst of modern art, try this **mansion** (Map pp70–1; ☎ 971 711122; www.fundbmarch.es; Carrer de Palau Reial 18; admission €3.60; ☺ 10am-6.30pm Mon-Fri, 10am-2pm Sat Apr-Oct, 10am-5pm Mon-Fri, 10am-2pm Sat Nov-Mar). Once one of several residences of the phenomenally wealthy March family, this private palace was built in 1939–45 on part of the site occupied by gardens of the demolished Sant Domingo monastery. It boasts an outdoor terrace display of modern sculpture including works by Eduardo Chillida, Henry Moore, Auguste Rodin, Barbara Hepworth, Andrea Alfaro and Pietro Consagra. Centre stage is taken by the enormous *Orgue del Mar* (1973) by Barcelona's Xavier Corberó. It looks like a cross between a sex toy and giant centipede slithering between towers.

Inside is a somewhat disappointing mix. On the ground floor the only permanent item is the extraordinary 18th-century Neapolitan baroque *belén* (nativity scene). Hundreds of incredibly detailed figures, from angels to kings, shepherds to farm animals and market scenes, make up this unique representation of

Christ's birth. Such scenes (although rarely of such quality) are popular in Spain and southern Italy, where they are put on display in the run-up to Christmas. The ground floor is otherwise taken up with temporary exhibitions.

Upstairs, the Barcelona artist Josep Maria Sert (1874–1945) painted the main vault and music room ceiling. The vault is divided into four parts, the first three representing three virtues (audacity, reason and inspiration) and the last the embodiment of those qualities in the form of Sert's client Juan March.

MUSEO DE MUÑECAS

You might want to pop into this odd shop-cum-museum dedicated to old dolls, the **Museo de Muñecas** (Museu de Nines Antigues in Catalan; Map pp70–1; ☎ 971 729850; Carrer del Palau Reial 27; adult/child/under 6yr €3.50/2.50/free; ☼ 10am-6pm Tue-Sun). Climb the steep stairs to the shop, where you buy a ticket and are ushered through the back to two rooms jammed with old dolls from all over the world, made of anything from cardboard to porcelain.

In the first room, countless versions of a popular Spanish doll, Mariquita Pérez, which first appeared in 1938 in San Sebastián, steal the show. Many of the dolls in the second room date to the 19th or early 20th centuries. Cardboard Spanish dolls from the 1940s show how tough times were after the Civil War. There is a Portuguese coach driver, or cheeky 'piano dolls' to perch on your Steinway. Or what about the utterly un-PC gollywogs? And what are the tiny dolls with the huge bare breasts all about?

CAN MARQUÉS

Documents trace this **mansion** (Map pp70–1; ☎ 971 716247; www.casasconhistoria.net; Carrer de Zanglada 2a; adult/student & senior €6/5; ☼ 10am-3pm Mon-Fri, 11am-2pm Sat) to the 14th century, making it one of the oldest as well as one of the most intriguing noble houses in Palma. Gathered around four courtyards and showing elements of Gothic, baroque and even Modernista influences, the house offers a unique insight into how Palma's wealthier citizens lived around the early 20th century. Enter the main *pati* (courtyard) where the family coach once clattered in and climb the Modernista stairway to the main floor of the house, where the public can undertake a circuit through 10 rooms.

The immense **Sala d'Entrada** was a formal reception area and designed to impress the visitor with the owner's evident wealth. Next come three rooms, each used for entertaining guests of differing importance. The last of these, reserved for special guests, connected with the *alcoba*, an opulent looking bedroom that was for show only. Perhaps most interesting are the kitchen (fully equipped and ready for the servants to come and prepare the masters' meals) and dining room (with its washbasin in the corner for cleaning greasy hands).

If you turn left (north) on leaving Can Marqués, you immediately reach Carrer de l'Almudaina and **Can Bordils** (Map pp70–1), a 16th-century mansion with a 17th-century courtyard. It is home to the **Arxiu Municipal** (Carrer de l'Almudaina 9; ☼ 9am-2pm & 4.15-7.45pm Mon-Wed, 9am-2pm Thu-Fri), which sometimes holds temporary exhibitions.

More intriguing for the history buff is the arch across the street to the right (east) of Can Bordils. This **Arco de l'Almudaina** (Map pp70–1) is part of a rare stretch of defensive wall and tower, as you can plainly see from the other side of it. It is said to have been in use from antiquity until about the 13th century. Although largely medieval in appearance, it is almost certain that this was part of the Roman wall.

MUSEU DE MALLORCA

Housed in Ca la Gran Cristiana (aka Palau Aiamans), a rambling ensemble of 17th-century mansions, this **museum** (Map pp70–1; ☎ 971 717540; Carrer de la Portella 5; ☼ 10am-7pm Tue-Sat, 10am-2pm Sun) holds an extensive collection of archaeological artefacts, religious art, antiques and ceramics.

Much of the museum is temporarily off limits due to ongoing renovation but the archaeological collections are all open. Over 15 rooms, the prehistoric and Talayotic periods of the island are explored. Bones, ceramics, utensils, models of caves and burial chambers are accompanied by explanatory panels in Catalan, Spanish and English. The high point is a collection, in a dark room downstairs, of ancient bronze statuettes. Most date to the 4th century BC and depict warriors and other figures. They were unearthed all over the island.

Next up come Roman ceramics, amphorae, remakes of sunken Roman merchant vessels, tombstones, glassware and the like. A few

Byzantine coins and mosaics survive, along with a thin collection of Arab artefacts, mostly ceramics and funerary calligraphy on stone and timber.

On re-entering the main courtyard, cross to the other side of the building for a modest collection of artworks from the 13th to the 19th centuries. A handful of works by important Mallorquin masters, including Francesc Comes, Rafel Mòger and Pere Terrencs, are scattered among the rest. The collections of 20th-century Mallorcan and Modernìsta art are still under wraps.

CASA-MUSEU JOAQUIM TORRENTS LLADÓ

This fine old **house** (Map pp70-1; ☎ 971 729835; Carrer de la Portella 9; adult/student & senior €3/1.80; ۞ 11am-7pm Tue-Fri, 10am-2pm Sat mid-Jun–mid-Sep, 10am-6pm Tue-Fri, 10am-2pm Sat mid-Sep–mid-Jun), with a timber gallery overlooking a courtyard, belonged to the Catalan artist Joaquim Torrents Lladó (1946–93), who moved to Mallorca in the 1960s. The 1st and 2nd levels feature timber floors, 19th-century furniture and a changing display of the painter's work, ranging from portraits to labels for Codorniu champagne. Temporary exhibitions are occasionally staged here too.

BANYS ÀRABS

The **Arab baths** (Map pp70-1; ☎ 971 721549; Carrer de Serra 7; adult/child €1.50/free; ۞ 9am-7.30pm Apr-Nov, 9am-6pm Dec-Mar) are the single most important remaining monument to the Muslim domination of the island. That is not saying an awful lot. All that remains are two small chambers, one with a domed ceiling supported by a dozen columns. Each of the columns is topped by a different capital: the Muslims were great recyclers and the capitals possibly came from demolished Roman buildings. This was the *caldarium*, or hot bath, while the other room was probably the *tepidarium* (warm bath). Normally there would also have been a third, cold bath, the *frigidarium*. As the Roman terms suggest, the Arabs basically took over a Roman idea, here in Mallorca and throughout the Arab world. These ones probably were not public but attached to a private mansion. The baths are set in a pretty garden, where you can sit and relax.

ESGLÉSIA DE SANTA EULÀLIA

One of the first major churches raised after the 1229 conquest, the **Església de Santa Eulàlia** (Map pp70-1; ☎ 971 714625; Plaça de Santa Eulàlia 2; ۞ 9am-10.30pm & 5-8pm) is a soaring Gothic structure with a neogothic façade (a complete remake, which was done in 1894–1924). It is the only such church in Mallorca, aside from the Catedral, that has three naves. The baroque *retablo* is rather worn and you can't get to the chapels in the apse.

BASÍLICA DE SANT FRANCESC

Work on this Franciscan **basílica** (Map pp70-1; ☎ 971 712695; Plaça de Sant Francesc 7; admission €1; ۞ 9.30am-12.30pm & 3.30-6pm Mon-Sat, 9.30am-12.30pm Sun & holidays) began in 1281 in Gothic style and its baroque façade was completed in 1700. It is well worth a visit for the splendid, sunny **Gothic cloister**, a two-tiered, trapezoid affair. The elegant columns in various styles indicate it was some time in the making. The simplest and oldest stretch lies diagonally opposite the entrance, while the most refined and complex columns lie off to the right of the entrance. Inside the lugubrious church, the fusion of styles is clear. The high vaulted roof is classic Gothic, while the glittering, curvaceous high altar is a baroque lollipop, albeit in need of a polish.

In the first chapel (dedicated to Nostra Senyora de la Consolació) on the left in the apse is the church's pride and joy, the tomb of and monument to the 13th-century scholar and evangelist **Ramon Llull** (p37). He is Mallorca's favourite son (apart perhaps from the tennis genius Rafel Nadal, p43). Llull's alabaster tomb is high up on the right. Drop a few coins in the slot for the campaign to have him canonised (he has only made it to beatification). Check out the **Capilla de los Santos Mártires Gorkomienses**, on the right side of the apse. In 1572, 19 Catholics, 11 of them Franciscans, were martyred in Holland. In this much-faded portrayal of the event, you can see them being hanged, disembowelled, having their noses cut off and more.

FROM SANT FRANCESC TO THE CONVENT DE SANTA CLARA

From the Basílica de Sant Francesc, head east along Carrer del Temple. In front of you, where the street bends off to the right, you will make out what was once a medieval Arab gate, the **Porta del Temple**, which was converted into housing in the 19th century.

The Knights Templar who had accompanied Jaume I were granted the right to occupy an Arab fortress known as the Almudaina Gumara at the eastern edge of the city. The extent towers mark what was the inner gate into the fort from the city. The knights were unceremoniously expelled in 1307 and the property taken over by the Knights of St John. In 1811 the monastery and chapel were taken over by the city and for more than 100 years most of it has been occupied by a home for disadvantaged children.

Stroll through the gate (which is due to be restored) and down a quiet lane, flanked by high walls, behind which you can see tree tops. At the end of the lane is the atrium of an early **Gothic chapel** the Templars built. You can, on occasion, wander through the external Romanesque entrance (although everyone will tell you there is *nothing* Romanesque on the island) to inspect the Gothic chapel entrance (also with Romanesque elements, like the columns). Inside is an explanatory display on the history of what is simply known as the **Temple** (Map pp70–1). Getting into the chapel itself is a matter of luck – generally it is closed. If you manage it, you can admire two Romanesque side chapels on either side as you enter. Following on from them is a beguilingly simple, early Gothic single nave.

A short walk north of the Temple would bring you to the **Església de Nostra Senyora del Socors** (Map pp70-1; Plaça de Llorenç Bisbal), with its oddly lofty baroque bell tower.

South along Carrer del Temple you run into another church, the largely baroque **Església de Sant Jeroni** (Map pp70-1; Plaça de Sant Jeroni), part of a convent complex founded in the 15th century. If you manage to get inside (the convent is still home to a handful of cloistered nuns) you will be able to see its Gothic cloister. The church faces the **Antic Col·legi de la Sapiença** (Map pp70–1), a still-functioning seminary across a quiet, narrow square. One block further east and you strike a portion of the Arab city wall (with some heavy blocks from the Roman wall at the base), beyond which is a park named after the city gate that once stood here: **Porta d'es Camp** (Gate of the Countryside). The Muslims knew it as Bab al-Jadid (the New Gate).

Head west along Carrer del Monte-Sion. You could make a quick detour down Carrer d'en Calders and look into the courtyard of **Can Caldés** (Map pp70–1; Carrer del Monte-Sion 3), a noble mansion of Gothic origins (it still retains a few Gothic touches) and a peaceful garden designed in the early 20th-century Modernista style.

Two blocks further west rises the gaudy baroque façade of the **Església del Monti-Sion** (Map pp70-1; Carrer del Monte-Sion; ☉ 5.15-7pm). Converted from a Gothic synagogue (p28) after a serious baroque makeover, inside and out, in the 16th to 17th centuries. As you wander in, a priest sitting in a booth by the entry may flip a switch and light up the curves'n'swirls baroque *retablo* at the back of the church. Gothic giveaways include the ogive arches in front of the chapels, the key vaulting in the ceiling and the long, low Catalan Gothic arch just inside the entrance. Across the road from the church is a baronial mansion from the same period, the **Cal Baró de Pinopar** (Map pp70–1; Carrer del Monte-Sion 17), whose forbidding appearance was clearly designed to keep nosey parkers at bay. Similarly imposing is the 17th-century **Can Lloeta** (Map pp70–1; Carrer del Monte-Sion 6), two blocks west.

Turn south along the church's flank, right on Carrer de Sant Alonso and left again. You are at the entrance to a dusty expanse, at the rear of which rises the **Convent de Santa Clara** (Map pp70-1; Carrer de Can Fonollar 2; ☉ 9am-12.30pm & 4.15-6.45pm). The church is a gloomy, neglected baroque affair. Locals prefer to pop into the adjacent building, because the handful of cloistered nuns maintain a centuries-old tradition of baking sweets for sale. You will see a *torno*, a kind of timber turnstile set in a window. Ring for a nun, order what you want and put money into the turnstile. This swivels around and out come your *bocaditos de almendra* (almond nibbles) or *rollitos de anís* (aniseed rolls), at €3 for 200g.

PLAÇA DE LA CORT & AROUND

Dominating the square that has long been the heart of municipal power in Palma is the **Ajuntament** (Cort; Map pp70-1; Plaça de la Cort 1). The baroque façade hides a longer history: the town hall building grew out of a Gothic hospital raised here shortly after the island's conquest. On the top floor of the main façade sits **En Figuera**, as the town clock is affectionately known. The present mechanism dates to 1863 and was purchased in France, but a clock has tolled the hours here for centuries. You can generally enter the foyer only, in which you will see a Gothic entrance, a fine sweeping staircase and, probably, half a dozen *gegants* (huge figures of kings, queens and other characters that are paraded around town on people's shoulders during fiesta) in storage.

The regional parliament of the Balearic Islands is at home in the 1913 Modernìsta **Círculo Mallorquin** (Carrer del Conquistador) building.

The private **Centre Cultural Contemporani Pelaires** (Map pp70-1; ☎ 971 720375; www.pelaires.com; Carrer de Can Verí 3; ⌚ 10am-1.30pm & 4.30-8pm Mon-Fri, 10am-1.30pm Sat) is as interesting for its architecture as for its content (rotating art exhibitions). The building, Can Verí, is a beautiful 17th-century town house that was for a while also used as a convent. This narrow pedestrian lane is rather chichi, home to galleries, antique shops and fashion boutiques.

Plaça Major & Around

Plaça Major is a typically Spanish central square, lined with arcades, shops and cafés. Lively by day, it falls eerily silent at night. To the east, Carrer del Sindicat spokes out towards the avenues that mark the limits of historic Palma. It crosses a long-run-down district known as Sa Gerreria, now in upheaval as a major programme of apartment building is in full swing. Off Plaça Major, the shopping boulevard, Carrer de Sant Miquel, leads north towards the vast **Plaça d'Espanya**. Watched over by an equestrian statue of Jaume I El Conqueridor (resting on a stone block that was part of the city walls), it hosts banks, fast-food stores, cafés and a mostly motley late-night crowd. The square is the scene of a market in the run-up to Christmas.

Plaça Major and Carrer de Sant Miquel are on high ground that falls away to the west down to shady Passeig de la Rambla. For simplicity's sake, we have included in this section the northern stretch of the old town contained by the avenues to the north, Passeig de Mallorca to the west and Carrer de l'Unió and Avinguda de Jaume III to the south.

MUSEU D'ART ESPANYOL CONTEMPORANI

This 18th-century **mansion** (Map pp70-1; ☎ 971 713515; www.march.es/arte/palma; Carrer de Sant Miquel 11; admission free; ⌚ 10am-6.30pm Mon-Fri, 10.30am-2pm Sat) makes a good introduction to Spanish modern art. On permanent display are some 70 pieces (held by the Fundación Juan March), a veritable who's who of mostly 20th-century artists. The collection starts with the big guns of the first half of the 20th century, such as Pablo Picasso, Joan Miró, Juan Gris (of Cubism fame), the sculptor Julio González and Salvador Dalí.

Various movements in Spanish art follow, such as that inspired in Barcelona by the *Dau al Set* review (1948–53) and led by Antoni Tàpies. Meanwhile, in Valencia, Eusebi Sempere and Andreu Alfaro were leading the way down abstract paths. Sempere's *Las Cuatro Estaciones* (1980), in a series of four panels with interlocking shapes made of fine lines, reflects the four seasons in subtle changes of colour. Other names to watch for are Manuel Millares, Fernando Zóbel and Miquel Barceló, who is represented by a huge ceramic pot with bulging skull shapes (*Grand Pot avec Crânes sur une Face,* 2000) and a canvas, *La Flaque* (The Puddle, 1989).

ESGLÉSIA DE SANT MIQUEL & AROUND

Raised after the conquest of Mallorca, the **Església de Sant Miquel** (Church of St Michael; Map pp70-1; Carrer de Sant Miquel 21; ⌚ 9.30am-1.30pm & 5-7.30pm) is a striking mix. It was one of the first four churches built on the site of the mosque where the island's first Mass was celebrated on 31 December 1229. The façade and entrance, with its long, low arch, is a perfect example of 14th-century Catalan Gothic. The squat, seven-storey belltower is also a Gothic creation. Otherwise, the church, with its barrel-vaulted ceiling, is largely the result of a baroque makeover.

Further up Carrer de Sant Miquel, on the right as you make for Plaça d'Espanya, the **Claustre de Sant Antoniet** (Map pp70-1; Carrer de Sant Miquel 30; ⌚ 10am-1.30pm & 5-8pm Mon-Fri, 10am-1.30pm Sat) is a baroque gem that belongs to the BBVA bank. The two-tiered, oval-shaped enclosure was built in 1768 and is now used for temporary art exhibitions. It was originally attached to the **Església de Sant Antoni de Viana** (Map pp70-1; Carrer de Sant Miquel s/n; ⌚ 11am-1pm) next door. Augustinian fathers occupied this site from shortly after the 1229 conquest, but this church was built in 1757 to 1768. The unusual interior is a series of ellipses.

About 200m north stands the **Església de Santa Caterina de Siena** (Map pp70-1; Carrer de Sant Miquel 48). As testimony to the ebbing of Catholic fervour in Spain, it has been handed over to the Russians for use as an Orthodox church.

CASAL BALAGUER

This somewhat neglected building with the grand if unevenly cobbled courtyard, graced by four thin, leaning palms, is home to a faded but weighty art institution, the **Círculo** de **Bellas Artes** (Map pp70-1; ☎ 971 723112; Carrer de l'Unió 3; ⏱ 11am-1.30pm & 5.30-8.30pm Tue-Fri, 11am-1.30pm Sat during exhibitions only). Art exhibitions are occasionally held here.

CAIXAFORUM

This **exhibition centre** (Map pp70-1; ☎ 971 178500; www .lacaixa.es/ObraSocial; Plaça de Weyler 3; ⏱ 10am-9pm Tue-Sat, 10am-2pm Sun) is run by one of Spain's biggest building societies, the Barcelona-based La Caixa. CaixaForum is housed in the wonderful Modernìsta building (the island's first) that once was home to the Grand Hotel, a city landmark that was built in 1900–03 by the Catalan master architect Lluís Domènech i Montaner and the first building in Palma with electricity and a lift. The hotel was shut down during the Civil War and never recovered. As well as the art exhibitions, lectures, workshops, film cycles, concerts and other activities are frequently put on. Pick up a free programme at reception.

Locals flock to the ground-level **café** (☎ 971 728077; ⏱ 9am-10pm Mon-Sat, 10am-2pm Sun).

FUNDACIÓ SA NOSTRA

The big Balearics building society, Sa Nostra, has a **cultural foundation** (Map pp70-1; ☎ 971 725210; www.sanostra.es; Carrer de la Concepció 12; admission free; ⏱ 10.30am-9pm Mon-Fri, 10.30am-1.30pm) in Can Castelló, where it stages exhibitions. It is worth popping by just to look at the fine 18th-century courtyard. The original house dates to the previous century, and it even has a few Modernìsta touches from renovation work done in 1909. At the time of writing it was closed for further renovation. Just in front of it is **Font del Sepulcre** (Well of the Sepulchre), a Gothic baptismal font left over from a long-disappeared church. Inside it is a 12th-century Muslim-era well. Carrer de la Concepció used to be known as Carrer de la Monederia, as the Kingdom of Mallorca's mint was on this street.

MONESTIR DE LA PURÍSSIMA CONCEPCIÓ DE LES CAPUTXINES

Behind the forbidding walls of this **convent** (Map pp70-1; ☎ 971 720720, 636 430000; Carrer de les Caputxines 14) lives a small community of Clarisan nuns. By tradition they still wash and iron delicate clothing, especially first communion and baptism outfits, for a modest fee. It is possible to visit with the Itineraris Culturals guided visits (see p85). Otherwise, if you happen to see the church doors open (around the 8am or 5pm Mass is the best bet), wander in and see if you can at least make it to the cloister.

CARRER DE SANT JAUME

Despite its baroque façade, the **Església de Sant Jaume** (Map pp70-1; Carrer de St Jaume 10; ⏱ 11.30am-1.30pm & 5.30-8.30pm) is one of Palma's older surviving Gothic churches, a grey soaring eminence, and one of the first four parish churches to be built, from 1327 'under the protection of the Royal House of Mallorca'. It is said that the Bonapart family (later better known as Bonaparte) lived around here until they moved to Corsica in 1406. Napoleon could have been a Mallorquin!

At the northern end of the road rises the baroque **Església de Santa Magdalena** (Map pp70-1; Plaça de Santa Magdalena; ⏱ 9am-12.30pm & 5.30-7.30pm Mon-Sat). Its main claim to fame is as the resting place of Santa Catalina Thomàs of Valldemossa (p115). Her clothed remains are visible through a glass coffin held in a chapel to the left of the altar and are an object of pilgrimage. They say the future saint sat weeping by a great clump of stone one day as none of the convents would accept her because she was too poor. Then someone told her that the convent once attached to the Església de Santa Magdalena would take her in. She was overjoyed. The stone in question is now imbedded in the rear wall of the 14th-century **Església de Sant Nicolau** on Plaça del Mercat.

CENTRE CULTURAL LA MISERICÒRDIA & AROUND

This enormous complex mostly contains offices and a soothing garden facing Passeig de La Rambla. A former chapel, accessed from the other side, is now used as a temporary **exhibition space** (Map pp70-1; ☎ 971 718053; Carrer de la Misericòrdia 2; ⏱ 10am-1pm & 4-6pm Mon-Fri, 10am-1pm Sat). From Plaça de l'Hospital you can also enter the huge courtyard, at the far end of which is the rather eccentric **Museu de l'Esport** (☎ 971 219620; Plaça de l'Hospital 4; ⏱ 9am-2pm Mon-Fri), dedicated to Mallorcan sportsmen and sportswomen. For the low-down on everything from tennis champion Rafel Nadal to local kayaking heroes, this is the place to come. Follow the signs and take the lift to the second floor, where the museum looks like just another office.

Within the **Hospital General** (founded in the 16th century), on the same square, you can behold the Gothic façade of the **Església de Sant Crist de la Sang** (Map pp70-1; Plaça de l'Hospital; ⌚ 7.30am-1pm & 4-8pm Mon-Fri, 7.30am-1pm & 5-8pm Sat, Sun & holidays). The church is the object of pilgrimage and devotion, since the *paso* (a sculpted image used in processions) of 'Holy Christ of the Blood' is considered to be miraculous. If you happen on a Mass, it is moving to see the devotion of the faithful who climb up behind the altar to venerate the image of Christ crucified, with long, flowing *real* hair and embroidered loincloth. Just on your left as you enter the church is a 15th-century Nativity scene, probably imported from Naples.

Es Puig de Sant Pere

Passeig d'es Born is capped by Plaça del Rei Joan Carles I (named after the present king and formerly after Pope Pius XII), a traffic roundabout locally known as Plaça de les Tortugues, because of the obelisk placed on four bronze turtles. This is where rowdy RCD Mallorca football fans come to celebrate their exploits in the field. A block from here on the east side of the avenue, on the corner of Carrer de Jovellanos, the distorted black face of a Moor, complete with white stone turban, is affixed high on the corner of a building. Known as the **Cap del Moro** (Moor's Head), it represents a Muslim slave who is said to have killed his master, a chaplain, in October 1731. The slave was executed and his hand lopped off and reportedly attached to the wall of the house where the crime was committed. Chronicles claim the withered remains of the hand were still in place, behind a grille, in 1840!

Passeig d'es Born is like Barcelona's La Rambla, albeit considerably quieter. Like La Rambla, it follows what was the natural course of the city's modest stream (more a sewage outflow than river). While in Barcelona the stream was eventually built over, here it was diverted beyond the then city walls (along Passeig de Mallorca).

ES BALUARD

A stroll west along Carrer de Sant Pere from Plaça de la Drassana (named after the ship-

---

EXPLORING PALMA'S HISTORIC COURTYARDS

Born of the necessities of a hot Mediterranean and Middle Eastern climate, the typical privileged Roman *domus* (house) was built around one or more cool courtyards. The Muslim Arabs continued the practice and the Christian conquerors of Arab Spain saw no reason not to adopt the system. The *patio andaluz* (Andalucian courtyard) is today something of a call sign for that southern Spanish region.

In Mallorca nobles and wealthy merchants from the time of Jaume I's conquest onward continued the tradition. The Gothic houses of the well-to-do maintained the idea of a cool, plant-filled central courtyard, around which the rest of the house was built. Access from the street was via a narrow entrance, and a stone external staircase led up to the first (or noble) floor of the house. Enormous change came with the baroque style of the 17th and 18th centuries. Entrances were widened to allow the entry of coaches and horses and designs were more voluptuous.

These great houses, around 150 in Palma, belonged to the crème de la crème of society: nobles, landed gentry, judges, businessmen and so on. The Mallorcan *pati* (courtyard) was not merely a pleasant private space. It often had a semi-public role. Prominent families maintained armies of servants, who tended to hang about in the courtyard. Even former employees would drop by. Frequently the *pati* was treated as a public meeting place. Neighbours would pop in for a chat or to take shelter from heat or rain.

Today the doors to quite a few such *patis* are opened by day, although often you cannot walk in far off the street. The tourist office has lists of the more interesting ones. In late spring around 50 are opened for guided visits and concerts in the context of the Corpus Christi celebrations (see p85).

Among the more interesting *patis* to look out for:

- **Can Salas** (Can Jordà; Map pp70-1; Carrer de la Puresa 2), whose entrance could be the oldest in the city
- **Can Catlar del Llorer** (Map pp70-1; Carrer de Can Savellà 15), one of the few that is largely Gothic (the narrow entrance and octagonal columns are giveaways) in a street jammed with mansions
- **Can Oleza** (Map pp70-1; Carrer d'en Morey 9), which boasts a series of broad arches and tubby baroque columns

building yards that once stood here) takes you past tightly packed houses to one of the great surviving corner bastions of the Renaissance-era seaward walls. **Es Baluard** (Museu d'Art Modern i Contemporani; Map pp70-1; ☎ 971 908200; www.esbaluard .org; Porta de Santa Catalina 10; adult/student & senior €6/4.50, temporary exhibitions €4/3; ☼ 10am-10pm Tue-Sun mid-Jun–Sep, 10am-8pm Tue-Sun Oct–mid-Jun), a modern and contemporary art museum, now lives here.

A 21st-century concrete complex has been cleverly built in and among the fortifications, which include the partly restored remains of an 11th-century Muslim-era tower (on your right as you arrive from Carrer de Sant Pere). The effect is a playful game of light, surfaces and perspective. Before you enter, contemplate the views of the port and city.

Inside, the ground floor houses the core of the permanent exhibition, starting with a section on Mallorcan landscapes by local artists and others from abroad. Some of the most idyllic, filled with uplifting, ochre-tinged Mediterranean light, are those by the Catalan Modernìsta artist Santiago Rusiñol, who did a

lot of work in and around the town of Bunyola (midway between Palma and Sóller). A broad swathe of local and mostly Catalan landscape artists are also on show here (see also p41).

Next comes a mixed and revolving international bag of mostly 20th-century artists. Canvases on display can range from the pointillism of Edouard Vuillard to the disturbing works of Oskar Kokoschka, from the calm of René Magritte nudes to the giant collages of Antoni Tàpies. Also on show are some works by Miró, ceramics by Picasso and a cabinet of drawings and sketches by key artists ranging from Henri Matisse to Amedeo Modigliani. Overall the collection is intriguing rather than a must-see on the international gallery circuit.

Before, during or after the visit, take a seat at the Café Bar Marítimo, a great snack location on the ramparts.

CASAL SOLLERIC
This grand 18th-century baroque mansion (Map pp70–1) with the typical Palma courtyard of graceful broad arches and uneven stone

- **Can Vivot** (Map pp70-1; Carrer de Can Savellà 4), with loping arches on round pillars; frequently closed
- **Can Berga** (Map pp70-1; Plaça del Mercat 12), since 1942 the Palacio de Justicia (courts)
- **Can Marqués** (p75)
- **Casa-Museu Joaquim Torrents Lladó** (p76)

Others open to the public because they house museums, public offices and the like:
- **Museu de Mallorca** (p75)
- **Centre Cultural Contemporani Pelaires** (p78)
- **Casal Balaguer** (p78)
- **Fundació Sa Nostra** (p79)
- **Casal Solleric** (above)
- **Estudi Lul·lià de Mallorca** (p84)
- **Can Bordils** (p75)
- **Can Caldés** (p77)

Other favourites:
- **Can Forteza del Sitjar** (Map pp70-1; Carrer de la Concepció 24)
- **Can Alemany** (Map pp70-1; Carrer de l'Estudi General 5)
- **Can Espanya-Serra** (Map pp70-1; Carrer de la Portella 8)
- **Cal Marquès del Palmer** (Map pp70-1; Carrer del Sol 7), with a unique sculpted Renaissance façade
- **Can Zagranada** (Map pp70-1; Carrer de Gran Granada 10)
- **Cal Comte de San Simón** (Map pp70-1; Carrer de Sant Jaume 7), radically different from the traditional mansions of Palma; this one was built in 1854–56 in neoclassical style

paving is at once a **cultural centre** (☎ 971 722092; Passeig d'es Born 27; ☼ 10am-2pm & 5-9pm Tue-Sat, 10am-1.30pm Sun), bookshop and tourist information office. Displays are usually free and found over a couple of floors. The part facing Passeig d'es Born was actually the rear of the original house, built in 1763. Archduke Ludwig Salvador thought its courtyard 'one of the most beautiful in Palma'.

SA LLOTJA
The gorgeous, if weather-beaten, 15th-century sandstone Gothic **Sa Llotja** (Map pp70-1; ☎ 971 711705; Plaça de la Llotja s/n; ☼ 11am-1.45pm & 5-8.45pm Tue-Sat, 11am-1.45pm Sun for exhibitions only), opposite the waterfront, was built as a merchants' stock exchange and is used for temporary exhibitions. Designed by Guillem Sagrera (see p39), it is the apogee of civilian Gothic building on the island and was completed in 1450. Inside, six slender, twisting columns lead to the lofty vaulted ceiling. In each corner of the building rises a fanciful octagonal tower. The flanks are marked with huge arches, fine tracery and monstrous-looking gargoyles leaning out overhead.

CONSOLAT DE MAR
Virtually next door to Sa Llotja, the Consolat de Mar (Map pp70–1) was founded in 1326 as a maritime tribunal. The present building, one of Mallorca's few examples of (albeit impure) Renaissance design, was completed in 1669. It was tacked onto, and faces, a late-Gothic chapel completed around 1600 for the members of Sa Llotja. The Consolat de Mar houses the presidency of the Balearic Islands regional government.

ESGLÉSIA DE SANTA CREU
Work on this much-neglected Gothic **church** (☎ 971 712690; Carrer de Sant Llorenç 1; admission €3; ☼ 11am-12.30pm Mon, Tue, Thu & Fri), just downhill from what was once the Santa Catalina gate, began in 1335. The main entrance (Carrer de Santa Creu 7) is a baroque addition. What makes it interesting is the Cripta de Sant Llorenç (crypt of St Lawrence), an early Gothic place of worship dating possibly to the late 13th century. Some paintings by Rafel Mòger and Francesc Comes are scattered the interior. You can peer into it from windows on the street. In spite of the official timetable, the museum seems to be eternally shut.

Santa Catalina & Around
A curious district of long, grid-pattern streets and traditional low-slung one- and two-storey houses, Santa Catalina was for a long time a somewhat raggedy and even dodgy part of town. In recent years it has known something of a renaissance as a cheerful wining and dining area. There are no real sights but it is interesting to walk around for the atmosphere, especially around lunchtime and on weekend evenings.

Essentially a mariners' district until recent years, it was not officially constituted as the *barri* (district) of Santa Catalina until 1865.

A hospital (since demolished) was built in the 14th century in this then wide-open area and ministered to ill and impoverished mariners. As early as the 17th century, windmills were raised in the area (still known as Es Jonquet) south off Carrer de Sant Magí, the oldest street in the *barri*. Es Jonquet remains a world unto itself, with modest houses (some old and done up, others abandoned and some replaced by soulless modern affairs) and a couple of ruined windmills that pumped potable water into the higher parts of this district until 1900. A series of four windmills (now converted into bars and restaurants) lines Carrer de l'Indùstria. One of them dates from around 1644.

From 1904, the now shuttered-up **Hostal Cuba**, on the corner of Carrer de Sant Magí and Avinguda d'Argentina, was a reference point for sailors, fishermen and other folks who slept here overnight or simply came for a drink. Depending on whom you talk to, its corner tower is reminiscent of a lighthouse or minaret. Across Avinguda d'Argentina, the **Sa Feixina** (or Faixina) park was long a parade and training ground for troops. It is home to a monument inaugurated by General Franco to the casualties of the Nationalist cruiser *Baleares*, sunk by Republican forces on 6 March 1938. Of the crew, 788 died and 469 survived (some saved by neutral UK destroyers patrolling in the vicinity).

Passeig Marítim & Western Palma
Western Palma boasts a handful of sights. The Castell de Bellver is the most worthwhile, if only for the views. Night owls will get to know the Passeig Marítim for its bars and club scene.

POBLE ESPANYOL
This **Spanish Village** (Map pp66-7; ☎ 971 737075; Carrer del Poble Espanyol 39; adult/student & senior €5/3;

MEANDERING PAST MODERNÌSTA GEMS

Palma is sprinkled with eye-catching buildings that resulted from the strange and fecund, if brief, period of architectural imagination known as Modernisme. For more on this flourishing movement at the turn of the 20th century, see p40.

Examples are the former **Grand Hotel** (CaixaForum; p79), the pastry shop, **Forn des Teatre** (p89), the nearby twin buildings of **Can Casasayas**, the undulating **Can Corbella**, **Can Forteza Rey** (Can Rei) and adjacent **Almacenes El Águila** (p40).

The **Palma–Sóller train station** (Map pp70–1) was also built in this style in 1912. Several buildings on nearby Plaça d'Espanya, including **Bar Cristal** (Map pp70-1; Plaça d'Espanya 4) betray Modernìsta influences. The more you wander around with an attentive eye, the more examples, often minor, you will turn up.

9am-7pm Apr-Sep, 9am-6pm Oct-Mar) imitates a similar institution in Barcelona, which in turn is a copy of bits of Spanish towns from all over the country. It's cheesy but intriguing and contains replicas of everything from typical Andalucian streets to Canary Islands houses, from the grand Bisagra gate of Toledo to Granada's Muslim Alhambra. Most of the replicas are smaller than the originals but could inspire one to travel further afield in Spain. You will also find shops, a couple of bars and eateries and even a pair of language schools. Buses 5, 29 and 46 take you close (alight at Avinguda d'Andrea Doria 41).

CASTELL DE BELLVER

Set atop a pleasant park, the **Castell de Bellver** (Bellver Castle; ☎ 971 730657; Carrer de Camilo José Cela s/n; adult/senior & student €2/1; 8am-8.30pm Mon-Sat, 10am-7pm Sun & holidays Apr-Sep, 8am-7.15pm Mon-Sat, 10am-5pm Sun & holidays Oct-Mar) is a 14th-century circular castle (with a unique round tower), the only one of its kind in Spain. Parts of the castle are shut on Sunday. Jaume II ordered the castle built atop a hill known as Puig de Sa Mesquida in 1300 and it was largely complete 10 years later. It was conceived above all as a royal residence but seems to have been a white elephant, as only King Sanç (in 1314) and Aragón's Joan I (in 1395) moved in for any amount of time. In 1717 it became a prison.

The best part of a visit is to mosey around the castle and enjoy the views over the surrounding woods to Palma and out to sea. The ground-floor **Museu d'Història de la Ciutat** (City History Museum) couldn't be less interesting; it's basically just some explanatory panels and a modest collection of pottery. Upstairs you can visit a series of largely empty chambers, including the one-time kitchen. Three rooms are given over to a desultory collection of clas-

sical statuary assembled by Cardenal Antoni Despuig (1745–1813). Climb to the roof and check out the prisoners' graffiti etched into the stonework. Unfortunately, more recent visitors have felt fit to add their own immortal traces.

About the nearest you can get to the castle by bus (3, 46 or 50) is Plaça Gomila, from where you'll have to hoof it about 15 minutes (1km) up a steep hill.

CASTELL DE SANT CARLES

More of a fort, the St Charles 'Castle' is home to the **Museu Històric Militar** (☎ 971 402145; Carretera del Dic de l'Oest s/n; 9am-1pm Mon-Fri, 10am-1pm Sat). The great guns in camouflage paint indicate you have reached the stellar-shaped fortress overlooking Porto Pi. It was built in 1610 and 1612 and later expanded. Its principal task was the protection of the approaches to Palma. Inside, the display contains some of the usual suspects for this kind of museum: plenty of weaponry (swords, pistols, rifles from many eras and countries), uniforms, flags, battle dioramas and so on. In Room 3 is a special section dedicated to Palma-born General Weyler, known for his harsh (and ultimately futile) campaign to crush rebellion in Cuba (1895–98).

Es Portitxol, Es Molinar & Ciutat Jardí

Virtually in front of Avinguda de Gabriel Alomar, at the edge of Palma's historic centre, starts a pleasant, artificial beach, **Platja de Can Pere Antoni**. Within walking distance of the city centre, it is not bad for a morning dip. Below the waterfront apartments is a series of restaurants and cafés.

A 1km walk from the city centre end of the beach brings you to **Es Portitxol**. The 'little port' has a quiet abundance of pleasure craft and is closed off inland by the motorway (at a discreet distance). You can walk, cycle or rollerblade here along the Passeig Marítim from central Palma. The main attraction is a snazzy hotel-restaurant, Hotel Portixol (p88).

Not far inland from Es Portitxol spreads the dishevelled **Parc Kristian Krekovic**. The **Museu Krekovic** (Map pp66–7; ☎ 971 219606; Carrer de Ciutat de Querétaro 3; adult/child €1.80/0.45; ☻ 9.30am-1pm & 3-6pm Mon-Fri, 10.30am-1pm Sat, closed Aug) looks on to the park and is dedicated to the work of eccentric Bosnian artist Kristian Krekovic (1901–85), who spent the last 25 years of his life in Mallorca after a long period studying the Incas and Peruvian tribes. The result is three rooms of monumental canvases in a thunder-and-lightning crash of colour. They mostly depict ancient warriors, chiefs, virgins, musicians and masked figures. Bus 12 runs close by.

From Es Portitxol, continue walking around the next point and enter **Es Molinar**. This simple, waterfront 'suburban' district of low fishing folks' houses has become a dining haunt, with a handful of places at the Es Portitxol end. Walk along the waterfront cycle path, among snippets of protected beach. The area is marked off to the east by a stream, the Torrent Gros. Over the bridge is **Ciutat Jardí**, a low-key residential area with a broad, sandy beach. The area was created as 'garden city' from 1917, along the lines of British concepts for green residential areas. It was dominated by the luxury **Hotel Ciutat Jardí**, built in 1921 to 1922 in imitation of part of a maharaja's palace in Tripura (India). The beach is great for kids as the water is calm and there are loads of swings and other distractions just off the beachside promenade. Some good restaurants make the idea of a quiet day here tempting. A walk beyond the beaches takes you to the next bay, **Cala Gamba**, a marina with a scruffy beach.

ACTIVITIES

The easiest 'activity' is going to the beach. For city beaches, see p92). **Platja de Palma** and **S'Arenal** (p101) together form an almost 5km-long white strand. The little coves and beaches west of the city, starting with Cala Major, are pretty (their backdrop isn't always so). If all that sand seems too much trouble, pop by **Aquamar Spa Center** (☎ 971 456612; www.aquamarcenter.com; Carrer de Fray Luis de León 5; admission €12-58; ☻ 10am-9pm Mon-Sat, 10am-2pm Sun except Jul-Aug) for

a circuit of spa baths, massage and more. Depending on the services you want to use you may need to book ahead.

Various boat cruises are available. Some are detailed in the *Excursions En Barca* brochure, available at tourist offices. **Cruceros Iberia** (☎ 971 717190; ☻ Tue, Thu & Fri mid-May–mid-Oct) organises day trips to Sant Elm (p110), leaving at 9.30am and returning at 3pm (the trip takes two hours each way), for €52.50 per person including lunch and hotel transfers.

Attraction (☎ 971 227702; www.attractioncatamarans.com) does catamaran trips to Ca'n Pastilla by day (€50 a head) and Magaluf by night (€55 a head). The latter is basically a party excursion.

Marenostrum (☎ 971 456182; www.marenostrum-catamarans.com) puts on a daily catamaran tour (from May to October) to either Portals Vells (p9) or Cala Vella (depending on wind direction), just east of the Badia de Palma. The trip (€53 per person) includes food on board and snorkelling gear.

For a quick one-hour whiz around the bay (for info call ☎ 659 636775), there are departures from the same spot three to five times a day, Monday to Saturday (March to October) for €9 per person.

Boats leave from in front of the Auditòrium (Map pp66–7) and tickets for most tours are available at a booth near the embarkation point.

COURSES

Palma is a great town to live in for a while, and what better way to get involved than by taking up a class? Many of the town hall's district cultural centres offer evening courses at low cost for long-termers. For a list go to the English-language page of the **Universitat de les Illes Balears** website (☎ 971 173380; www.uib.es/en; Carretera de Valldemossa Km7.5) and click on 'Spanish Courses' and then on 'Other Spanish Courses'. The university itself offers various semester courses of Spanish for foreigners, as well as intensive summer courses (€400 for 60 hours' tuition). Other options:

Dialog (Map pp70-1; ☎ 971 719994; www.dialog-palma.com; Carrer del Carme 14), the predominantly German language bookshop, offers two-week intensive Spanish courses (€350).

The **Estudi Lul·lià de Mallorca** (Map pp70-1; ☎ 971 711988; www.estudigeneral.com: Carrer de Sant Roc 4) offers intensive summer courses in Spanish language and culture (€400).

GALLERY ALLEY

Contemporary art enthusiasts will get a buzz out of the plethora of galleries that populate the narrow streets just west of the Passeig d'es Born. Top art houses include:

- **Sala Pelaires** (☎ 971 723696; www.pelaires.com; Carrer de Pelaires 5) An arm of the Centre Cultural Contemporani Pelaires (p78) and Palma's first contemporary gallery, this is a wonderful place to see works by top Spanish artists.
- **Galeria La Caja Blanca** (Map pp70-1; ☎ 971 722364; www.lacajablanca.com; Carrer de Can Verí 9) Edgy Mallorcan and international artists are showcased in this stark, minimalist space.
- **Joan Guaita Art** (Map pp70-1; ☎ 971 715989; Carrer de Can Verí 10) This sleek gallery is well known for its emphasis on contemporary Latin American artists.

Die Akademie (Map pp70-1; ☎ 971 718290; www.dieakademie.com: Carrer de Morei 8) runs a variety of Spanish language courses and is housed in a late-Gothic mansion.

Marc Fosh, who runs the Michelin-star Reads in Santa Maria del Camí (p153), also heads up the gourmet laboratory **Fosh Food** (Map pp66-7; ☎ 971 290108; www.foshfood.com; Carrer de Blanquerna 6). Cooking classes by various chefs, local and international, are held most days and cost €45 to €60. Book ahead. It doubles as a gourmet delicatessen and is curiously surrounded by a sushi bar, self-proclaimed Thai fusion restaurant and Indian eatery!

Want to learn to be a yacht or catamaran skipper in the Med? **Voyage** (Map pp66-7; ☎ 971 222907; www.voyageseaschool.com; Avinguda de Gabriel Roca 4) runs courses in conjunction with the UK Royal Yachting Association.

PALMA FOR CHILDREN

With the city's beaches and related water activities (including boat tours) an easy option, Palma should be stress-free for kids and their adult guardians. Children will love to explore the Bellver and Sant Carles castles (p83 and p83); you can combine art with fun on the ramparts at Es Baluard (p80); and young girls and boys might find the Museo de Muñecas (p75) intriguing. See also the aqua parks and other theme parks on p104.

Sets of swings, climbing things and other diversions for young children are scattered about town. There is an immense assortment in Parc de les Estacions (Map pp70–1), near the bus station, and another good set in Sa Feixina park near Es Baluard (Map pp66–7). You'll stumble across more swings in the shadow of Palau de l'Almudaina (Map pp70–1) and further along near the walls just east of Parc de la Mar (Map pp70–1).

For information on babysitting services, see p196.

TOURS

Itineraris Culturals (Map pp70-1; ☎ 971 720720, 646 430000; www.itineraris.org; Carrer de Sant Domingo 11) offers a series of themed walks around Palma. The walks range from tours of the courtyards of fine mansions to specialised tours for the hearing-impaired. In general the tours take two hours and cost €10 a head. Themes include Monumental Palma, the Jewish Quarter (Call), The City and the Sea, Modernisme in Palma, Stories and Legends of Palma (night tour), Tradition and Modernity: Traditional Trade in Palma, and a special tour of the still-functioning Convent de les Monges Caputxines (October to May only, see also p79).

The hop-on-hop-off **Palma City Sightseeing** (Map pp70-1; ☎ 902 101081; www.mallorcatour.com) circuit bus (Bus 50, 16 stops, €13) has the option of commentary in various languages. Tickets are valid for 24 hours. The bus departs from Avinguda d'Antoni Maura. The service runs every 20 minutes, starts at 10am and stops anytime between 6pm and 10pm depending on the time of year.

FESTIVALS & EVENTS

In addition to regular sailing events (p97), the city seems caught up in a near endless parade of cultural events (get information from tourist offices), ranging from local traditions to international performance.

Festa de Sant Sebastià (19–20 January) On the eve of the feast day of Palma's patron saint, concerts (from funk to folk) are staged in the city squares, along with flaming pyres and the *aiguafoc*, a fireworks display over the bay. It's a big (if chilly) night.

Sa Rueta & Sa Rua (February) Palma's version of Carnaval (celebrated in the last days before Lent starts) involves

PALMA &
THE BADIA DE PALMA

a procession for kids (Sa Rueta) followed later by a bigger one (Sa Rua) with floats and the like.

Semana Santa (March–April) Processions dot the Easter Week calendar, but the most impressive are those on Holy Thursday evening. In the Processó del Sant Crist de la Sang (Christ of the Blood), robed and hooded members of *confraries* (lay brotherhoods) parade with a *paso* (heavy sculpted image of Christ, borne by a team of men). It starts at 7pm in the Església del Crist de la Sang (Map pp70–1), where the *paso* is kept, and returns hours later.

Festival Mundial de Danses Folklòriques (www .worldfolkdance.com; April) A five-day folk extravaganza, with dance groups from around the world performing in central Palma's streets and squares.

MUST (www.dissenymallorca.com; April) A three-day fashion fest with parades and workshops in various locations in central Palma.

Saló Nàutic (www.firesicongressos.com; May) Usually held around the first week of May, this is a major boat fair held at the Moll Vell docks.

Corpus Christi (May–June) The feast of the Body of Christ (the Eucharist) falls on the Thursday of the ninth week after Easter, although the main procession from the cathedral takes place on the following Sunday at 7pm. On that day, carpets of flowers are laid out in front of the Catedral and in Plaça de la Cort. Concert cycles (many held in the city's *patis*, which can also be visited at this time) add a celebratory note for about a month around the feast day.

Nit de Sant Joan (June 23) The night before the feast of St John (24 June) is celebrated with fiery feasting. As night falls, the *correfoc* (fire running) begins in the Parc de la Mar. People dressed up as demons, and armed with pyrotechnical gear that would probably be illegal in hell, leap and dance in an infernal procession. Locals then head for the beaches, where wandering musical groups and pyres add flaming cheer to a partying crowd until dawn.

Estiu de Cultura (www.palmademallorca.es; July–August) Musical events are held in the Castell del Bellver, ranging from classical to flamenco, jazz and Cuban. See the website for dates, prices and where to buy tickets.

Festes de Sant Magí (August 19) A local event in Santa Catalina with music, street theatre and fireworks.

Nits a la Fresca (www.palmademallorca.es; July–August) Catch the open-air cinema, folk music and theatre at a stage set up in Parc de la Mar.

Art Cologne (www.artcologne-palma.com; September) In 2007 this German contemporary art fair launched a four-day annual autumn edition in Palma's airport (terminal A).

Jam Art Mallorca (www.jamartmallorca.com; September) A parallel art event to Art Cologne, concentrating on upcoming international talent.

Nit de l'Art (September) A more established art event; galleries and institutions all over town throw open their doors to expose the latest trends in art.

SLEEPING

Where you stay depends on what you want to get out of your visit. The intimate boutique hotels of the city centre (especially those near the Passeig d'es Born or around the Plaça Major) place you in the thick of the capital's shopping, restaurant and nightlife districts. For views, head to the Passeig Marítim or Passeig de Mallorca. West of the centre cluster several business hotels; these aren't particularly convenient for sightseers but are practical places to stay if having wi-fi and a work centre are important considerations.

Old Palma

The often hard-to-find hotels dotted throughout Palma's historic centre offer a romantic old-world ambience.

Hostal Brondo (Map pp70-1; ☎ 971 719043; www .hostalbrondo.net; Carrer de Ca'n Brondo 1; s/d/tr without bathroom €35/50/60, d with bathroom €65) Brondo's high-ceilinged rooms (try to nab No 3, which has a glassed-in gallery) are furnished in styles varying from Mallorcan to vaguely Moroccan. The friendly owners are as good as a tourist office when it comes to giving advice about the city. Downsides include slightly cramped quarters and street noise.

Hotel Dalt Murada (Map pp70-1; ☎ 971 425300; www.daltmurada.org; Carrer d'Almudaina 6; r €140-200; ⊗) This aristocratic manor-house-turned-hotel dates from 1500 and is filled with art and antique furniture that evoke days gone by. Museum-worthy paintings, chandeliers and canopied beds decorate the rooms, whose ceilings are held up by timber beams. Modern concessions include womb-like Jacuzzis and an elevator.

ourpick Hotel Palacio Ca Sa Galesa (Map pp70-1; ☎ 971 715400; www.palaciocasagalesa.com; Carrer de Miramar 8; s €240, d €300-435; P ⊗ ☐ ☒) Staying in this luxurious 12-room hotel is like being a guest in a private, 16th-century Mallorcan mansion. The antique furniture, soaring ceilings and silk wall coverings are truly indulgent, while welcoming living spaces like a stocked reading room, breezy patio and cheery yellow kitchen (where you can help yourself to tea and cake) keep things from getting too stuffy.

Plaça Major & Around

The hotels in this buzzing central quarter stand elbow-to-elbow with upscale shops, terrace cafés and fine restaurants.

MIDRANGE

Hotel Born (Map pp70-1; ☎ 971 712942; www.hotelborn.com; Carrer de Sant Jaume; s €50-65, d €73-105) Stepping into this 16th-century Can Maroto manor house is like stepping back in time. From the palatial reception area, take the spiral staircase to a red-carpeted hallway where carved wooden doors creak open to reveal simply furnished rooms, whose high ceilings dwarf antique, slightly care-worn furniture. For old-world ambience and a central location, look no further.

Hotel Ca Sa Padrina (Map pp70-1; ☎ 971 425300; www.hotelcasapadrina.com; Carrer de les Tereses 2; s €80, d €100-120; ⚄) Ca Sa Padrina has no reception office, so all communication is via closed-circuit cameras and a telephone with a direct line to the staff of the Hotel Dalt Murada (see opposite). A small sign in the lobby reads, 'If the telephone sounds is [sic] because we see you on the camera and we have to talk with you'. Strange. But once you get over the spooky Big Brother feel, this quaint guesthouse is quite nice. Thankfully there are no cameras in the bedrooms, where antique bathtubs, carved wooden beds and views of the old town set a yesteryear tone.

our pick Misión de San Miguel (Map pp70-1; ☎ 971 214848; www.hotelmisiondesanmiguel.com; Carrer de Can Maçanet 1; r €110-130; P ⚄) A shockingly good deal, this 32-room boutique hotel is a real find. We can't help but think that once the word gets out the prices will go up, but for now Misión is a steal. The hotel is on a hard-to-find side street off Carrer dels Oms, so the stark and spacious rooms are quiet, with free wi-fi, perfectly firm mattresses and rain showers. The restaurant, Trébol, serves a fabulous made-to-order breakfast – the omelette is divine – and to top it off you can enjoy perks like free parking and a romantic patio area.

Hotel Jaime III (Map pp70-1; ☎ 971 725943; www.hmhotels.net; Passeig de Mallorca 14; r €165; ⚄) This urbane hotel overlooking the palm-lined Passeig de Mallorca tries a wee bit too hard to be cool, with kitschy art in the lobby and slightly snooty service. But if you're looking for a fashionable, central place at a reasonable price, this is an excellent option. Rooms boast striking wine-red linens, wenge furniture, flat-screen TVs and free wi-fi. Breakfast is not included in the room price.

TOP END

Convent de la Missió (Map pp70-1; ☎ 971 227347; www.conventdelamissio.com; Carrer del Convent de la Missió 7; r incl breakfast €225-390; P ⚄) A functioning convent from the 1600s until 2003, this intimate boutique hotel has just 14 rooms and a Zen-like calm created by all-white rooms with wispy curtains and airy spaces. Though there's no pool, couples will enjoy the romantic Arab-style hot tub and sauna located in the stone-walled underground cellar. You can also relax on the rooftop terrace or in the artfully designed reading room. Dine in the stylishly minimalist restaurant, Refectori (p90).

Es Puig de Sant Pere

If you stay in this busy, tourist-friendly district, you'll never be more than a few minutes' walk from restaurants, tapas bars and nightclubs.

BUDGET

Hostal Pons (Map pp70-1; ☎ 971 722658; Carrer del Vi 8; s/d/tr without bathroom €25/40/60) If you had a Mallorquin grandmother, her house might look like this. The 22 rooms are quaint, if dusty, with creaky 1950s-style twin beds and, for the lucky, views of an interior patio. The kindly owner has been running this place for 50-plus years and still takes reservations on an old black rotary phone. No elevator.

Hostal Apuntadores (Map pp70-1; ☎ 971 713491; www.palma-hostales.com; Carrer dels Apuntadors 8; s/d €52/64 without bathroom €33/48; ⚄) Right on the main drag (bring earplugs), this unfussy spot makes up for its smallish rooms and lumpy beds with balconies, lots of sunlight and a rooftop terrace that overlooks the cathedral and serves drinks. Wi-fi in reception.

MIDRANGE

Hotel Palau Sa Font (Map pp70-1; ☎ 971 712277; www.palausafont.com; Carrer dels Apuntadors 38; s €90-105, d €145-200; ⚄ 🖵 🖵) Tucked away on a quiet side street, this former 16th-century palace offers 19 sparsely decorated rooms. Wrought iron beds and a few splashes of colour in the form of a pale green headboard or a simple red chair give the rooms a feeling of almost monastic calm. Internet connection for laptops.

Hotel Saratoga (Map pp70-1; ☎ 971 727240; www.hotelsaratoga.es; Passeig de Mallorca 6; s/d €115/180; ⚄ 🖵) Although not as quaint or intimate as other hotels in the area, this swanky four-star can't be beat for convenience. A great location, sea views, full breakfast buffet, large pool and a fab rooftop terrace with views make it a popular place. Rooms are standard business-style hotel fodder, with parquet floors and simple white linens. There's free wi-fi throughout the hotel and live jazz in the 7th-storey Blue Jazz Club (p95).

Hotel San Lorenzo (Map pp70-1; ☎ 971 728200; www .hotelsanlorenzo.com; Carrer de Sant Llorenç; s €115-165, d €135-185; ✗ ♨) Just nine rooms are interspersed around the staircases and patios of this old Mallorcan manor house. At the centre is a wonderfully fragrant terrace garden with a pool and marvellous cathedral views; it's practically begging you to watch the sunset with a drink in hand.

TOP END

Hotel Tres (Map pp70-1; ☎ 971 717333; www.hoteltres .com; Carrer dels Apuntadors 3; s/d €180/270; ✗ 🖳 ♨) With complimentary slippers and robes in each room, king-sized beds and in-room DVD players, there's no doubt about the Hotel Tres' upscale boutique credentials. The décor mixes urbane and eco-chic, with slate-walled showers, cowhide benches and bamboo plants in the bathrooms. If you want a terrace, request Room 101, 201 or 206. Wi-fi in all rooms.

Puro Oasis Urbano (Map pp70-1; ☎ 971 425450; www .purohotel.com; Carrer del Mont Negre 12; s €165-185, d €235-285; ✗ 🖳 ♨) Achingly chic with a décor that crosses Ibiza-style minimalism with Moroccan flair, this 14th-century palace-turned-26-room boutique hotel has positioned itself as the place to see and be seen. By day, lounge on the canopied day beds of the patio or take a dip in the plunge pool; by night join a fashionable crowd for cocktails in the bar. As a guest here, you can also access the Puro Beach (p101) club.

Passeig Marítim & West Palma

Hotels in this area are a 15- to 30-minute walk from the centre (hiring a bike is not a bad idea), but they may be considerably cheaper than city-centre hotels.

AC Ciutat de Palma (Map pp66-7; ☎ 971 222300; www .ac-hotels.com; Plaça del Pont 3; r €85-162; P ✗) The popular business-style hotel chain, AC, has another winner with this reliable four-star hotel a block from the waterfront. Rooms are outfitted with plasma TVs, wi-fi, and a sleek wenge-and-white décor. The look is business chic.

Tryp Bellver (Map pp66-7; ☎ 971 222240; www.sol melia.com; Avinguda de Gabriel Roca 11; r €95-130; P ✗ 🖳 ♨) The waterfront location and generous balconies make the Bellver more than just another four-star chain hotel. The decoration of the 381 rooms is nothing special, but with these sigh-inducing views, you won't be paying much attention to the inside anyway.

Hotel Mirador (Map pp66-7; ☎ 971 732046; www.hot elmirador.es; Avinguda de Gabriel Roca 10; s/d €100/125; P ✗ ♨) Overlooking the port and maritime promenade, the Mirador bills itself as a 'classic' hotel. No Nordic minimalism here; rooms are decorated with overstuffed chairs, sensible lamps and yellow bedspreads.

Costa Azul (Map pp66-7; ☎ 971 731940; www.hotelcos taazul.es; Avinguda de Gabriel Roca 7; r €180; ✗ ♨) Right on the waterfront, the Costa Azul is popular with groups, many of them 50-plus, who book it for its breezy, beach-themed rooms with views and competitive rates.

Es Portitxol, Es Molinar & Ciutat Jardí

Although it's a longish walk, bike ride or bus ride from the centre, this is a great place to enjoy Palma's beaches and sunshine.

Hotel Portixol (Map pp66-7; ☎ 971 271800; www .portixol.com; Carrer de la Sirena 27; s €125, d €210-370; ✗ ♨) Two kilometres south of Palma's centre is the jewel of this fishing-village-turned-resort: the hip Hotel Portixol. With a soothing fusion of cool Mediterranean and Scandinavian styles, this harbour-front hotel has been making guests happy for more than 50 years. Most rooms have terraces with sea views, and all are airy, with DVD players and an orderly, minimalist décor.

EATING

A mess of eateries and bars cater to Palma's visitors in the maze of streets between Plaça de la Reina and the port. Or take a look around the *barri* of Santa Catalina, west of Passeig de Mallorca, especially around the east end of Carrer de Sa Fàbrica. Also pleasant are the waterside eateries in Es Portitxol and Es Molinar.

Old Palma

BUDGET

Forn Sant Crist (Map pp70-1; ☎ 971 712649; Carrer de Paraires 2) A historic pastry shop where you can pick up all sorts of traditional goodies.

Confitería Frasquet (Map pp70-1; ☎ 971 721354; Carrer d'Orfila 4; ☯ 9.30am-2pm & 4.45-8pm Mon-Fri, 9.30am-2pm Sat) Another excellent place to pick up sweet munchies.

MIDRANGE

La Taberna del Caracol (Map pp70-1; ☎ 971 714908; Carrer de Sant Alonso 2; meals €25; Mon-Sat) Descend three steps into this high-ceilinged Gothic basement. Through a broad vault at the back you can see what's cooking. Dark wooden tables are scattered about. Soothing background music, some fine wine and a delicate assortment of tapas (€11.75 for two) make a great start. You might follow with a tender grilled *dorada* (bream, €15).

Cappuccino (Map pp70-1; ☎ 971 717272; Carrer del Conquistador 13; meals €30; 9am-1am Sun-Thu, 9am-2am Fri & Sat) The location is a winner, a terrace at the 'prow' end of Palau March. You could do a light lunch or dinner, ranging from pumpkin soup starters to pasta mains. Or just settle for a slightly overpriced cappuccino.

Plaça Major & Around
BUDGET

Forn des Teatre (Map pp70-1; ☎ 971 715254; Plaça de Weyler 9; 8am-8pm Mon-Sat) This pastry shop has feather-weight *ensaïmada* (a light, spiral pastry emblematic of the island) and is a historic landmark.

Ca'n Joan de S'Aigo (Map pp70-1; ☎ 971 710759; Carrer de Can Sanç 10; hot chocolate €1.40; 8am-9pm Wed-Mon) For a hot chocolate and fine *ensaïmades* (which come with apricots, cream or whipped cream) you have to stop by what might be described as an antique-filled milk bar dating from 1700. The house speciality, however, is *quarts*, a feather-soft sponge cake item with almond-flavoured ice cream (served in a glass with a spoon) that children love to eat. The place fills with families and children from around 6pm.

Sa Pastanaga (Map pp70-1; ☎ 971 724194; Carrer de Sant Elies 6b; meals €12.20; lunch Mon-Fri; V) Lo-cals queue here for the nicely priced vegetarian set lunches in this one-time shop. Yellow walls and exposed beams lend a huggy feel to the place. Starters (juice or salad) could be followed by *crema de carbassò i pèsols* (pumpkin and peas with cream) and a main course of *burritos de verdura amb salsa de formatge* (vegetable burritos in a cheese sauce).

Bar España (Map pp70-1; ☎ 971 724234; Carrer de Ca'n Escurrac 12; meals €15-20; 6pm-midnight Mon, 10am-midnight Tue-Sat) Pick your own *pintxos* (Basque Country tapas) at the bar (where you can't smoke) and sample with house wine. Or take them to a table (smoker-friendly). Bullfight posters adorn the walls and it fills to bursting at lunch and on weekend evenings.

S'Esponja Café (Map pp70-1; ☎ 971 723701; Carrer del Metge Matas 2; dinner daily, closed Mon in Aug) A jug of *sangría* and *pa amb oli* (with unusual variants on the theme, such as the *capresse*, a mozzarella and tomato combo), perhaps followed by a little cake, is not a bad way to start the night at this funky eatery.

MIDRANGE

Restaurant Celler Sa Premsa (Map pp70-1; ☎ 971 723529; Plaça del Bisbe Berenguer de Palou 8; meals €20-25; Mon-Sat Sep-Jun, Mon-Fri Jul & Aug) A visit to this local institution is almost obligatory. It's a cavernous tavern filled with huge old wine barrels and has walls plastered with faded bullfighting posters. The food is hearty and the atmosphere jolly.

El Botxo (Map pp70-1; ☎ 971 717830; Carrer de Velázquez 14; meals €20-25; Mon-Sat) This is an amusing barn of a place and not bad for a few *raciones* (smallish dishes about halfway between a main dish and tapas). Most of the tables are equipped with their own beer taps. Set up an account and pour your own as you

DIY MEALS

Palma's produce markets are a great way to get under the skin of the city as you bustle about the fresh produce stands. You can stock up on all you need to put together your own meals, from cheeses and cold meats to fruit and veg (and plenty more if you have access to a stove). The most engrossing is the central **Mercat de l'Olivar** (Map pp70-1; Plaça de l'Olivar), especially good for fish and meat. At lunchtime Monday to Saturday, head here for several lively tapas bars serving fresh food to market workers and shoppers.

Equally busy and with few tourists are the **Mercat de Santa Catalina** (Map pp70-1; Plaça de la Navegació) and **Mercat de Pere Garau** (Map pp66-7; Plaça de Pere Garau). On Saturday mornings the latter is good for gourmet products. Locals who love fresh produce will tell you it is the best market for fruit and vegetables, as this is where farmers from around the island converge with the fruits of their labours.

go. You can see what each table is consuming and spending on a big monitor.

El Gallego (Map pp70-1; ☎ 971 710313; Carrer del Carme 16; menú €9.40, meals €20-30; ⊙ lunch Mon-Thu, lunch & dinner Fri & Sat summer, lunch Sun-Wed, lunch & dinner Thu-Sat winter) A hearty, noisily good-natured Spanish eatery opens up before you as you enter (the waiters seem like they are on speed). Stop for a quick glass of wine at the bar on your right. Seafood lovers might be tempted by the *cigalas a la plancha* (grilled crayfish, €24.90).

Cappuccino (Map pp70-1; ☎ 971 719764; Carrer de Sant Miquel 53; ⊙ 9am-10pm) We don't often recommend chains, and certainly not more than once. But this spot is hard to walk past. The Cappuccino crowd have converted a startling 18th-century mansion into a stylish café-restaurant.

Restaurant Garage Rex (Map pp66-7; ☎ 871 948947; Carrer de Pablo Iglesias 12; menú del día €12, meals €30-35; ⊙ Mon-Sat; ✗) Back in the 1960s this was the first Mallorcan garage where you could have your car washed. Now you can wash your liver with Cava (sparkling wine) at the bar in this minimalist lounge restaurant. The cooking has creative touches but nothing too loopy. Think *rollitos de lenguado rellenos de gambas con salsa de almendras* (slices of sole rolled up and stuffed with prawns in an almond sauce) followed by a triple-choc brownie. On Friday and Saturday nights the place stays open to 2.30am for a little post-prandial cocktail lounging.

Ca'n Carlos (Map pp70-1; ☎ 971 713869; Carrer de l'Aigua 5; meals €35-40; ⊙ lunch & dinner Mon-Sat) Step into this basement restaurant for finely prepared fish, meat and rice dishes (the latter abundant and creamily delicious at €12 a head). You might opt for a fat calamari stuffed with monkfish and mushrooms (€20). Ochre-washed walls lend warmth to this split-level charmer.

La Bodeguilla (Map pp70-1; ☎ 971 718274; Carrer de Sant Jaume 1-3; meals €35-45; ⊙ 1-11.30pm Mon-Sat; ✗) This gourmet eatery does lightly creative interpretations of dishes from across Spain, such as *cochinillo* (suckling pig), from Segovia and *lechazo* (young lamb, baked Córdoba-style in rosemary). It also offers a tasting menu of tapas for €21 a head.

TOP END

ourpick Refectori (Map pp70-1; ☎ 971 227347; Carrer de la Missió 7a; meals €70-80; ⊙ lunch & dinner Mon-Fri, dinner Sat; ✗) Lovingly prepared Mediterranean grub

with a special touch is the order of the day in the refectory of the Convent de la Missió. Alleluia! The restaurant has a modern air, with angular high-backed chairs and rigorously white, black and timber décor. You can opt for tasting menus or go *a la carta*. The *filetes de lenguado y mozzarella con crema de guisantes y mejillones a la menta* (sole filets and mozzarella with a cream of peas and mint clams) is to be savoured with due reverence. There is a set lunch for €40.

Es Puig de Sant Pere
BUDGET

Bon Lloc (Map pp70-1; ☎ 971 718617; Carrer de Sant Feliu 7; menú €12.50; ⊙ lunch Mon-Sat; Ⓥ) With its mighty timber ceiling, fans and discreet lighting, this is a soothing setting for a good, healthy four-course *menú del día* that might include a *crema fría de zanahoria* (cold carrot cream soup) and *pastel de patata* (potato pie).

MIDRANGE

ourpick La Bóveda (Map pp70-1; ☎ 971 714863; Carrer de la Boteria 3; meals €25; ⊙ daily) You have to love this place, one of the few to transmit an essential Spanish boisterousness in this heavily touristed district. Sure, the bulk of the punters are from anywhere but Palma, but the elements are genuine enough: Andalucian wall tiles, high ceilings, fans, and people crammed in to munch on generous tapas and larger *raciones*. All the classics are here, such as *pimientos de Padrón* (green peppers, some of which are hot). The *revuelto al ajo y langostinos* is one of several great scrambled egg dishes (really!), this one with garlic and prawns.

Bruselas (Map pp70-1; ☎ 971 710954; Carrer de s'Estanc 4; meals €30-40; ⊙ lunch & dinner Mon-Fri, dinner Sun) Once a Belgian-owned piano bar (hence the name), this is a carnivore's pleasure dome. Argentine meat dishes are the central theme in the stone-vaulted locale: anything from spare ribs to rib eye steak is on the menu. Wash down with a throaty Mallorcan red, such as Son Bordils Negre.

TOP END

Aramís Bellini (Map pp70-1; ☎ 971 725232; Carrer de Sant Feliu 7; meals €50-60; ⊙ lunch & dinner Mon-Fri, dinner Sat Sep-Jul; ✗) Tucked away off the street, this is a carefully orchestrated gourmet hideaway, with dark-timber floors and art on the walls. It does a variety of tempting international dishes such as *pechuga de pato con purée de limón y albaricoques* (duck breast with a lemon and apricot puree; €19). The midday *menú del día* is good value at €14.

Santa Catalina & Around
BUDGET

Sa Llimona (Map pp70-1; ☎ 971 736096; Carrer de Sa Fàbrica 27a; meals €12-18; ⊙ Mon-Sat) A trifle too bright and smacking of 'snack bar', this is nonetheless a good spot for an inexpensive *pa amb oli*. You can order it in various combinations, with several cold meats and cheeses, and always accompanied by salad and olives.

Afrikana (Map pp66-7; ☎ 971 287007; Carrer de Dameto 17; meals €20; ⊙ Mon-Sat; V) Get your fingers messy in this pan-African delight, with dishes extending from Ethiopia to Benin. There's a good vegetarian selection, like the Angolan beans, coconut cream and curry mix. For a whiff of the sea, try *gombo* (from Benin): prawn and shrimps mixed with okra and other vegetables.

Noah's (Map pp66-7; ☎ 971 220122; Plaça del Progrès 15; meals €20; ⊙ Mon-Sat; X V) Afghan food is the speciality here, with spicy lamb (€13.20) a key dish, along with some vegetarian options. Not very Afghan options, like the salads and pasta (all around €9), broaden the options. There is a *menú del día* for €10.50.

Karme (☎ 653 829091; Carrer de Sant Magí 60; meals €20; ⊙ daily) Sit at high stools for a drink and a nibble of tapas in this laid-back bar-eatery. Classics like *alitas de pollo* (chicken wings) or *revuelto* (scrambled eggs) sit alongside rather un-Spanish items such as *arroz al curry* (rice curry).

MIDRANGE

Diecisiete Grados (Map pp70-1; ☎ 871 943368; Carrer de Sa Fàbrica 12; meals €20-25; ⊙ daily) A pleasingly modern restaurant with a few pavement tables and lots of original tapas and small dishes. Chomp into a *brocheta de magret de pato y naranja* (skewer of duck and orange) or push the boat out with a *chuletón* (huge chop), which comes in at €34 a kg. They have some good wines, unfortunately at exorbitant prices.

La Baranda (Map pp70-1; ☎ 971 454525; Carrer de Sant Magí 29; meals €30; ⊙ 8pm-1am) An easy-going Italian, with exposed stone and warm-yellow hued walls and simple timber furniture and art scattered about, this is a good choice for wood-oven pizzas, pastas and homemade cake for dessert.

Ummo (Map pp66-7; ☎ 871 953873; Carrer de Sant Magí 66; meals €30-40; ⊙ closed 1st half Aug) Choose between Basque dishes or *pintxos* at this relaxed little restaurant. The chef, from San Sebastián, has worked in such prestige establishments as Koldo Royo (p92). Fresh vegetables and *bacalao* (dried cod) feature in his ever-changing menu. Quite unusually for Spanish eateries, you can bring your own wine.

Brunello (Map pp70-1; ☎ 971 221424; Carrer de Ramon y Cajal 15; meals €40; ⊙ Mon-Sat) It doesn't look like much, sitting beneath undistinguished apartments, but this is a fine choice for Italian grub, from creamy risottos (€11 to €14) to a classic Tuscan beef *tagliata* with rocket. Or how about sirloin beef in a truffle sauce?

Living (Map pp66-7; ☎ 971 455628; Carrer de Cotoner 47; meals €45; ⊙ Mon-Sat; X) From the outside it seems modest enough, but inside you'll find a little gourmet secret. How about the feather-light *risotto de mariscos con tempura de verduras y consomé de lemongrass* (seafood risotto with vegetable tempura and lemongrass consomé) to start? Various fish and meat dishes follow and they have a tasting menu for €45.

TOP END

Fàbrica 23 (Map pp66-7; ☎ 971 453125; Carrer de Cotoner 42; meals €45-55; ⊙ Tue-Sat; X) For good market-based Med cooking, this gourmand fave (long since moved from Carrer de Sa Fàbrica) is hard to beat. The menu changes regularly and generally there is only a handful of dishes each day, covering meat, fish and vegetarian tastes. There is a *menú del día* for €19 and it is usually a good idea to book ahead.

Passeig Marítim & West Palma
MIDRANGE

Baisakhi (Map pp66-7; ☎ 971 736806; Avinguda de Gabriel Roca 8; meals €30; ⊙ dinner Tue-Sun) Several Indian joints decorate this stretch of the waterfront, but this is one of the better ones. Settle in for a candlelit spread among the Indian antiques. As a rule there is a single tasting menu that is changed regularly, which staff talk you through.

Casa Jacinto (☎ 971 401858; Camí de la Tramvía 37; meals €30-35; ⊙ Wed-Mon) A classic since the 1980s, this huge and no-nonsense eatery far from the centre of town attracts Mallorquins from far and wide for copious servings of mainland Spanish and local food, especially grilled meats.

ourpick **Casa Eduardo** (Map pp70-1; ☎ 971 721182; Travessia Pesquera (Mollet); meals €35-45; ☺ lunch & dinner Tue-Sat, lunch Sun) What better place to get stuck into fish than behind the fresh fish market? This place has been serving meals since the 1940s and has come up with such things as lobster paella (€25 a head)! A mixed seafood platter comes in for €30 and catch of the day is priced by the kilo. Waiters in black vests move about swiftly on the roof terrace below ceiling fans and neon lights. The restaurant sometimes closes up in winter.

Villario (☎ 871 946454; Dársena de Can Barbará s/n, Passeig Marítim; meals €40-45; ☺ dinner Tue-Sun) Here is a minimalist designer dining den of inventive, international dishes; you might find Italian cheeses mixed with chicken in a buckwheat crepe, or sautéed rabbit and prawns. Make a night of it; facing the little harbour are three late-night bars.

TOP END

Caballito de Mar (Map pp70-1; ☎ 971 721074; Passeig de Sagrera 5; meals €40-50; ☺ daily Jun-Sep, Tue-Sun Oct-May; ✗) One of Palma's seafood beacons, the 'Little Seahorse' presents its critters in a contemporary key. The *gazpacho de bogavante* (a humble cold tomato soup turned into a lobster delight) is unique. After such a start you could opt for fresh fish of the day or red shrimp from Sóller. Grab a seat on the sunny terrace.

Koldo Royo (Map pp66-7; ☎ 971 732435; Avinguda de Gabriel Roca 3; meals €80-110; ☺ lunch & dinner Mon-Fri, dinner Sat; ✗) Considered one of Mallorca's great eating experiences, this Basque gastrodome offers a limited menu in its downstairs bistro, *menú del día* (€30, children €14), and the full linen treatment upstairs, where you dine at dark timber tables laid with silver service. With luck you'll get a port view. Why not start with *gambas con puré de ajo, melocotón y aceite de gambas* (shrimps with a purée of garlic, peach and shrimp oil)?

Es Portitxol, Es Molinar & Ciutat Jardí

Several eateries suggest themselves around the little port, more stretch along the west end of the waterfront road (Carrer del Vicari Joaquín Fuster) in Es Molinar and some fine seafood places grace Ciutat Jardí. Remember that where fish is sold by weight (as is usually the case in the places below) it will almost always be more expensive than you anticipate.

El Bungalow (☎ 971 262738; Carrer d'Esculls 2, Ciutat Jardí; meals €20-30; ☺ lunch & dinner Tue-Sat, lunch Sun Apr-Oct, lunch Tue-Sun Nov-Mar, closed mid-Dec–mid-Jan; ✗) Sit on the broad terrace close to the water's edge at the southern end of the main beach and order the day's catch. You can see clear across the bay to central Palma. El Bungalow is renowned above all for its paella (€14 per person).

Club Marítimo (Map pp66-7; ☎ 971 273479; Carrer del Vicari Joaquín Fuster 2, Es Molinar; meals €30-40; ☺ daily) For fresh fish of the day in a simple, portside atmosphere, this place is a faithful stop. Or you can indulge in tapas in the roadside courtyard. They are also known for their rice dishes. Service is uneven but the portions are generous.

S'Eixerit (Map pp66-7; ☎ 971 273781; Carrer del Vicari Joaquín Fuster 73, Es Molinar; meals €35; ☺ daily) Best on a warm evening for a feast of fish or paella in the leafy garden out the back, this place is a great favourite with locals, who fill the night air with animated banter.

Ca'n Jordi (☎ 971 491909; Carrer de l'Illa de Xipre 12, Ciutat Jardí; meals €50; ☺ daily; ✗) One of the stalwart seafood restaurants in Palma (a classic that needs no introduction to Palmenses), which attracts local businessfolk and seafood lovers. On your way in to this over-lit but otherwise tastefully presented eatery you will see fresh fish (sold by weight) awaiting your choice.

Casa Fernando (☎ 971 265417; Carrer de Trafalgar 27, Ciutat Jardí; meals €50; ☺ Tue-Sun, closed mid-Dec–mid-Jan; ✗) No sea views here, but countless photos of local and more distant celebs grin at you from the walls of this ordinary-looking restaurant. Basic linen graces the timber tables in this fishy, ill-lit den, providing a style counterpoint to Ca'n Jordi but virtually the same recipe – well-prepared catch of the day, sold by weight.

Es Mollet (Map pp66-7; ☎ 971 247109; Carrer de la Sirena 1, Es Portitxol; meals €60-70; ☺ Mon-Sat) With its covered veranda just over the road from a little bay (Cala Portitxolet), this is a classic seafood joint, where your main course, the freshest catch of the day, is sold by weight (€45 to €60 per kg). There's a price to pay, but these people select their produce from local fishers and grill it to utter perfection.

DRINKING

Palma offers a wide variety of bars in various parts of town, but the city will never be voted Spain's party capital. For the truly raucous summer tourist scene, head for Platja de

Palma or Magaluf (p104). Most locals hit the bars on Friday and Saturday nights, although the more restless get out on a Thursday too.

Old Palma

Bar Bosch (Map pp70-1; ☎ 971 721131; Plaça de Joan Carles I; ⏱ 7.30am-2am Mon-Sat) The outdoor tables of this knockabout bar are a favourite meeting and stopping point for locals and visitors alike. Known for its *llagostas* (little hot bread rolls with ham or similar), it is an easy-to-find place for the first beer or two of an evening before kicking off elsewhere in the old town.

Guirigall (Map pp70-1; Carrer d'En Brossa 14; ⏱ 7pm-1.30am Mon-Sat) Hidden deep in the heart of the old medieval labyrinth, this postage-stamp-sized bar has a conspiratorial feel (you may get looked over from the upstairs bar as you swing the door open). Get a beer and head downstairs for a spot at a bench.

Gibson (Map pp70-1; ☎ 971 716404; Plaça del Mercat 18; ⏱ 8am-3am) This chirpy cocktail bar with outside seating on the square is still busy with (mostly local) punters on a weekday night when everything else around has pulled the shutters down.

Ses Voltes (Map pp70-1; Parc de la Mar; ⏱ 10am-1am) Lurking in the shadows of Palma's former sea wall, this is a pleasant terrace for summer tippling. Early some evenings they have a little live music. You can also get snacks and light meals. Sunday is Hangover Day (Domingo de Resaca), with laid-back sounds and, presumably, some hair of the dog.

Plaça Major & Around

L'Orient (Map pp70-1; ☎ 971 723202; Carrer del Convent dels Caputxins 5a; ⏱ 7pm-1am Sun-Thu, 7pm-2.30am Fri & Sat) This boisterous place with heavy timber benches is where locals come to travel a beery globe. On offer are countless beers from Belgium, Germany, the UK and more. Try a Cobra from India or even Cuban ambers.

Bar Flexas (Map pp70-1; Carrer de la Llotgeta 12; ⏱ 1-5pm & 8pm-midnight Mon-Fri, 9pm-1am Sat) A lively locals' bar with a whiff of grunge, this is a great spot for a noisy chat far from the tourist haunts. The image of the Virgin Mary near one door is a contrast with the provocative erotic image at the back. Long mirrors reflect the drinking activity, ceiling fans blow the hot summer air around and punters drift across the tiled floor to grab a spot at the timber tables.

Pincell (Map pp70-1; Carrer de les Caputxines 13; ⏱ 8pm-midnight Tue-Thu & Sun, 8pm-3am Fri & Sat) No sign re-veals the existence of this deep vaulted cellar where locals gather for a *pomada* (Menorcan gin and lemon soft drink) at long timber tables. Young rebels with causes, such as independence from the Spanish state, often gather for animated discussion.

Ca'n Àngel (Map pp70-1; Carrer de Sant Jaume 27; ⏱ 7pm-1am Sun-Thu, 7pm-3am Fri & Sat) Skip down the stairs into this smoky locals' haunt. Play pool out the back or settle at a timber booth for a premixed *pomada* (€10) and conspiratorial chat.

Es Puig de Sant Pere

Abaco (Map pp70-1; Carrer de Sant Joan 1; cocktails €15; ⏱ 8pm-1am Tue-Thu, 8pm-3am Fri & Sat) Behind a set of ancient timber doors is the bar of your wildest dreams. Inside, a Mallorcan *pati* and candlelit courtyard are crammed with elaborate floral arrangements, cascading towers of fresh fruit and bizarre artworks.

Atlantico Café (Map pp70-1; ☎ 971 722882; Carrer de Sant Feliu 12; ⏱ 10pm-4am Mon-Sat) Of the bars along this street, this is probably the most enticing. Think 'Hotel California' for the music, US car numberplates on the walls (along with generous swathes of graffiti) and cocktails (€6).

Bodeguita del Medio (Map pp70-1; ☎ 971 717832; Carrer de Vallseca 18; ⏱ 9pm-3am) For a taste of Cuba, head in here for a *mojito* (rum, lemon, mint and ice, one of Hemingway's faves) or three. The walls are covered in punters' scribblings and the music usually has a Caribbean swing.

Café La Lonja (Map pp70-1; ☎ 971 722799; Carrer de Sa Llotja de Mar 2; ⏱ 10am-1am Mon-Thu, 10am-3am Fri, 7pm-3am Sat) With its curved marble bar, tiled chessboard floor and smattering of tables and benches, this place is as appealing for breakfast as it is for a very generous *pomada*. Many choose to sit outside in the shadow of Sa Llotja.

The Escape Bar (Map pp70-1; ☎ 971 724968; Plaça de la Drassana 13; ⏱ 10am-2am) A largely international crowd (with a seafaring tilt) fills up the two rooms of this small bar in the early stages of the evening. Grab one of a couple of tables out the front for an afternoon refreshment or come along in the morning for a full English breakfast (€9.20). They also whip up some imaginative dishes at lunchtime.

Santa Catalina & Around

Once run down and dodgy, the Santa Catalina area has become a favourite spot for hitting a modest but intriguing selection of bars. Carrer de Sant Magí and Carrer del Pou each offer a selection. It can be fairly subdued on any day except Friday or Saturday.

Soho (Map pp70-1; Avinguda d'Argentina 5; 6.30pm-2.30am Sun-Thu, 6.30pm-3am Fri & Sat) This self-proclaimed 'urban vintage bar' has a green-lit beer fridge, red walls (with some '60s décor), low white ceilings, and Bob Geldof and other '80s and '90s hit-makers. The laid-back crowd mostly seems oblivious to the traffic pounding past the footpath tables. It is one of several similar bars at this end of the avenue.

Café Lisboa (Map pp70-1; Carrer de Sant Magí 33; 11pm-1am Sun-Wed, 11pm-4am Thu-Sat) The curved timber bar gives this place a homy appeal. When they throw in some Latin and bossa nova sounds, it gets even better. It fills up quickly on evenings that live music is staged.

Idem Café (Map pp70-1; 971 280854; Carrer de Sant Magí 15a; 8pm-3am) A deep, dark-red baroque feel attracts cocktail-drinking night owls. Past the front bar and deeper inside are two separate spaces. Some of the wall art is risqué and the place has something of the air of an old-style but gay-run bordello.

T-Acuerdas? (Map pp70-1; Carrer de Sant Magí 22; 9.30pm-3am Sun-Thu, 10.30pm-4am Fri & Sat) For a noisy slice of Spain, this music bar is the place. Spanish hits (the bar's name means 'do you remember?') dominate the soundtrack at this small but fun bar that local punters cram into on the weekends.

Aretha (Map pp70-1; 971 734485; Carrer del Pou 8; 7pm-2am Mon-Thu, 7pm-3am Fri & Sat) Soulful sounds mix with general pop at this pleasing little bar where drinks can be enjoyed with crepes. The main bar area (exposed stone at one end and red walls all around) leads into another, sunset-yellow cosy enclosure out back. Happy hour is at 9pm.

Miel (Map pp70-1; 646 465354; Carrer del Pou 12; 7pm-2am Mon-Thu, 7pm-3am Fri & Sat) The music and crowd are mixed and relaxed in this funky bar with low lighting and lounges.

Passeig Marítim & West Palma

A stroll along Passeig Marítim between Carrer de Monsenyor Palmer and the ferry port on a Friday and Saturday night will reveal a parade of enough bars, karaoke dens and clubs to keep you busy until dawn. There's more mischief up in the heights behind the boulevard too. Many places that are a cross between bars and clubs stay open until 4am on this strip, and sometimes later.

Varadero (Map pp66-7; 971 726428; Carrer del Moll Vell s/n; 9am-2am Sun-Thu, 9am-4am Fri & Sat) This bar's splendid fore position makes it feel as though you have weighed anchor. The squawking of seagulls mixes with lounge sounds as you sip your favourite tipple and gaze east across the bay or back to the splendid cathedral from the sprawling terrace.

Hogan's (Map pp66-7; 971 289664; www.pubhogans .com; Carrer de Monsenyor Palmer 2; noon-3am) It's 'Irish', it's noisy and it's full of foreign visitors and expats. But it also gets a good crew of locals. Speaking of crews, people in search of work on the boats could do worse than make this their first port of call. Bands usually play from 11pm on Wednesday and Saturday nights.

our pick **Hostal Corona** (971 731935; www.hostal -corona.com; Carrer de José Villalonga 22; 6pm-1am Tue-Sun) With its palm trees and cornucopia of plants, the generous garden of this little Modernìsta hotel (the house is known as Can Quetglas and was once a private villa) is the perfect setting for a drink under the stars. If you get a chill, head inside for an indoor tipple. You can sleep here too, and eat a modest meal in the 1st-floor restaurant.

Sa Posada de Bellver (971 730739; www.saposada .esmejor.com; Carrer de Bellver 7; 1pm-2am) Way uphill from Plaça Gomila, step through the greenery into what could be somebody's home. Doubling as a simple restaurant, it comes into its own when a little music is laid on (from 10pm Friday and Saturday). It's a relaxed place for a few drinks in a Mallorcan atmosphere. It can close up earlier on weeknights if business is slow.

Made in Brasil (Map pp66-7; 670 372390; Avinguda de Gabriel Roca 27; 8pm-4am Mon-Sat) The name is a little misleading, as anything South American goes, from salsa to lambada. A good place to give your body a shakedown while sipping on Caribbean tipples like *mojitos* and *caipirinhas*.

Es Portitxol, Es Molinar & Ciutat Jardí

A handful of simple bar-cafés dot the waterfront of Es Molinar and Ciutat Jardí, but neither area is a nightlife zone. The bar restaurant of the Hotel Portixol (p88) is a nice spot for a relaxing cocktail, inside or out.

Kaskai (Map pp66-7; 971 241284; www.kaskai.com; Carrer del Vicari Joaquín Fuster 71, Es Molinar; 1pm-2am) This place sells itself as something of a mixed modern cuisine experience, with Asian and local dishes, but it works better as a chilled-out bar. The dominant black and blood-red décor and candlelit tables invite you to dally over a few drinks, which might well be accompanied by a DJ session from Thursday to Saturday.

ENTERTAINMENT

From live concerts to opera, from a good movie to a summer bullfight, from sailing regattas to a football match, there's plenty to do in Palma. You can book tickets to many events by phone or online through **Servicaixa** (☎ 902 332211; www.servicaixa.com). You can also get tickets to many events at El Corte Inglés department store (Map pp70–1).

Live Music

Most of Palma's live acts perform on the stages of intimate bars around Sa Llotja, although in recent years neighbours' complaints have shortened the opening hours or even shut down some venues. Jazz in all its many varieties is popular but, depending on the night, you may also find rock'n'roll, soul and flamenco. Concerts begin between 10pm and midnight and wrap up no later than 2am. Check www.vamos-mallorca.com (in English) for concert details.

Assaig (☎ 971 905292; www.assaig.com; Carrer del Gremi Porgadors 16, Polígono de Son Castelló) More than just a concert hall, this cultural centre in northern Palma is a place for up-and-coming artists to practise and promote their music. Free concerts are held on the café stage, while more-formal shows are put on at the larger concert hall.

Blue Jazz Club (☎ 971 727240; Passeig de Mallorca 6; ✆ Thu 11pm-1am) Located on the 7th floor of the Hotel Saratoga, this sophisticated club offers after-dinner jazz from 11pm till 1am on Thursday nights.

Bluesville (Map pp66-7; Carrer de Ma d'es Moro 3) As dark and smoky as a blues bar should be, this intimate spot a stone's throw from the busy Carrer Apuntadors hosts free blues concerts at midnight, attracting a young hippy crowd.

Bourbon Street (Carrer de Sant Magí 79) Stop by for jazz, blues, soul and rock'n'roll: Thursday and Sunday concerts begin at 8pm; on Friday and Saturday they begin at 11pm.

Jazz Voyeur Club (☎ 971 905292 www.jazzvoyeur .com; Carrer dels Apuntadors 5) A tiny club no bigger than most people's living rooms, Voyeur hosts live jazz bands nightly, starting at 10pm. Red candles burn on the tables and a few plush chairs are scattered about, though you should get here early if you want one.

Clubs

The epicentre of Palma's clubbing scene hovers around the Passeig Marítim (Avinguda de Gabriel Roca) and the Club de Mar, where you'll find the city's largest and most popular *discotecas*. No matter what time of year, there's plenty going on, especially Thursday through Saturday nights, when locals and tourists from across the island come to groove.

Although most clubs open around midnight or earlier, don't expect to find much action until at least 2am. Things will continue going strong until 5am, when glassy-eyed clubbers

---

GAY & LESBIAN PALMA

The bulk of gay life on the island happens in and around Palma. For useful sources of information and websites, see p198. Left your sex toys at home? Head for **Erotic Toy Stories** (Map pp70-1; ☎ 971 727865; Passatge Maneu 10). The biggest concentration of gay bars is on Avinguda de Joan Miró, south of Plaça de Gomila. To get your night going, you could start with the following:

- **Café Lorca** (Map pp66-7; ☎ 971 451930; www.cafelorca.com; Carrer de Federico García Lorca 21; ✆ 10am-3am) A key stop on the Palma gay circuit, this immaculately presented bar is great for brunch, coffee and cake, dance music and the late-night chill-out hour. It also stages regular events.

- **Dark** (Map pp66-7; ☎ 971 725007; www.darkpalma.com; Carrer de Ticià 22; ✆ 4.30pm-2.30am daily, 5.30pm-10.30am Sat, Sun & holidays) For all your dark room encounters, this is the place. Look for the small illuminated sign and the deep blue glow.

- **Aries Sauna Hotel Pub** (☎ 971 737899; www.ariesmallorca.com; Carrer de Porras 3; ✆ 4pm-midnight, bar 10pm-6am) Housed in the gay-friendly hotel about 100m south of Plaça de Gomila, this sauna makes no bones about its purpose.

- **Black Cat** (Avinguda de Joan Miró 75; ✆ midnight-5am) One of the most popular gay clubs in Palma, Black Cat has a dark room downstairs and often stages drag shows.

stumble outside. Some may head home, while others head to the 'afters', early-morning clubs (some around Plaça de Gomila) that keep the music going past the breakfast hour.

Admission prices range from €10 to €18, though if you're not dressed to impress you may be turned away no matter how much cash you're willing to spend.

Abraxa's (Map pp66-7; ☎ 971 455908; www.abraxasmal lorca.com; Passeig Marítim 42; ☽ 10pm-6am Thu-Sat Sep-Jun, nightly Jul-Aug) Formerly known as Pacha (of the famous Ibiza line), this is Palma's most established club. Hordes of dancers of every nationality descend on Abraxa's two dance floors, spilling onto the terrace and grooving to the house music spun by Europe's top DJs.

Art Deco (Map pp70-1; www.artdecodisco.com; Plaça del Vapor 20; ☽ 10pm-late) A longtime favourite, this elegant club spins everything from oldies to contemporary pop from its perch above the Passeig Marítim. Salsa classes offered Thursdays at 10.30pm.

ourpick El Garito (☎ 971 736912; www.garitocafe .com; Dàrsena de Can Barberà; ☽ 7pm-4.30am) A trendy club with a bohemian air, Garito is a must for music lovers. The DJs and live performers could be doing anything from fusion jazz to house, disco classics or electro beats. This is also a great place to hang out for a drink on the terrace earlier in the evening.

King Kamehameha (☎ 971 939200; www.king -kamehameha.com; Passeig Marítim 29; ☽ midnight-late) Pulsating with up-to-the-minute electronic tracks and a young, international crowd, this intimate club on the water is one of Palma's newer venues but has quickly endeared itself to night owls. It also has a relaxed terrace bar out the front for a drink without the clubbing.

Mar Salada (☎ 971 702709; www.marsalada.net; Moll de Pelaires s/n; ☽ 10pm-late) Famed as the favourite club of Spain's Prince Felipe – at least before he became a father of two – this laid-back venue in the Club de Mar draws a sophisticated crowd. The standard entry is around €12 but, to keep the pedigree, erm, royal, some punters might be charged more.

Tito's (☎ 971 730017; www.titosmallorca.com; Passeig Marítim 33; ☽ 11.30pm-6am Jun-Sep, 11.30pm-6am Thu-Sun Oct-May) A classic Palma nightspot (founded in 1923), this megaclub boasts two dance floors, five bars, stage shows and elevators down to the Badia de Palma. In summer, theme nights like 'Latex' and 'Italian Style' spice things up.

Salero (Passeig Marítim 33; ☽ 11pm-6am) Just beside Tito's, Salero is Palma's salsa club par excellence. Great Latin music, a varied though friendly crowd, and occasional salsa classes add to its appeal.

Cinema

Palma has seven cinema complexes, each with several screens. If you want to see movies in their original language, your best chance is at **Renoir** (Map pp66-7; ☎ 971 205408; www.cinesrenoir .com; S'Escorxador, Carrer d'Emperadriu Eugènia 6; tickets €6), which has four screens and generally runs sessions from about 4.30pm to 10.30pm.

Theatre

Auditòrium (Map pp66-7; ☎ 971 734735; www.auditori umpalma.es; Passeig Marítim 18; ☽ box office 10am-2pm & 4-9pm) This spacious, modern theatre is Palma's main stage for major concert performances (as well as congresses), ranging from opera to light rock. The Sala Mozart hosts part of the city's opera programme (with the Teatre Principal).

Teatre Principal (Map pp70-1; ☎ 971 713346; www .teatreprincipal.com; Carrer de Riera 2; ☽ box office 10.30am-1.30pm & 5.30-8.30pm Mon-Fri, 10.30am-1.30pm Sat) Built in 1854 and restored in 2007, this is the city's prestige theatre for drama, opera and more. The renovation works re-created the theatre's heyday majesty of 1860 and combined it with the latest technology.

Teatre Municipal (Map pp70-1; ☎ 971 710986, 971 739148; Passeig de Mallorca 9; ☽ box office 1 hr before show) Here you might see anything from contemporary dance to drama.

Teatre Municipal Xesc Forteza (Map pp70-1; ☎ 971 710986; Plaça de Prèvere Miquel Maura 1; admission €5-15; ☽ box office 1 hr before show) Concerts, ballet and theatre take turns here.

Sport
CYCLING
The non-competitive **Volta Cicloturista a Mallorca** (www.vueltamallorca.com) cycling event starts at the Castell Bellver in late April. It is open to all who wish to race around the island by bike over three days.

FOOTBALL
Palma's top division **RCD Mallorca** (www.rcdmal lorca.es) is one of the better sides battling it out in the Primera Liga. They have never finished as champions but usually wind up with a respectable spot about halfway down the ladder.

The side has played at the **Estadi Son Moix** (Camí dels Reis s/n, Polígon Industrial, Can Valero), about 3km north of central Palma, since 1999. The old Estadi Lluís Sitjar, closer to the centre of town, is due to be demolished and replaced with a new stadium. You can get tickets at the stadium or call ☎ 971 739941.

SAILING

Sailing is a big deal in Palma and numerous regattas are held in the course of the year. The **Copa del Rey** (King's Cup), held over eight days in July and August, is a high point. The king, Juan Carlos I, and his son Felipe frequently race on competing boats. **PalmaVela** (www.palmavela.com), held in April, has hundreds of yachts of all classes from around the world. **Trofeo SAR Princesa Sofía** (www.trofeo princesasofia.org), also held in April, is one of six regattas composing the World Cup Series and attracts Olympic crews from all over the world. The **Superyacht Cup** (www.thesuperyachtcup .com), held over three days in October, is one of the major races for super yachts of anything from 25m to 90m. The **Ciutat de Palma-Regata Nova IX** is a huge event for smaller boats held over four days in December.

The **Real Club Náutico** (www.realclubnauticopalma .com), the most prestigious of Palma's yacht clubs, organises more than 20 events (some in collaboration with other clubs) during the year.

BULLFIGHTING

Bullfights take place about half a dozen times from mid-July to the end of August at the **Plaza de Toros** (Map pp66-7; ☎ 971 751639; Carrer del Arquitecte Gaspar Bennàzar 32). The fact that the season is so short is an indication that the activity is not that widely followed in Mallorca. If you are interested you can obtain tickets at the ring. The programme usually begins around 6pm.

SHOPPING

Start your credit card swiping in the chic boutiques around Passeig d'es Born. The Passeig itself is equal parts high street and highbrow, with chain stores like Massimo Dutti and Zara alongside elitist boutiques. In the maze of pedestrian streets west of the Passeig, you'll find some of Palma's most tempting (and expensive) stores.

More great shops, including the department store El Corté Inglés, are just north of the Passeig along the arcaded Avingunda de Jaume III. Continue strolling to the grid of pedestrian-friendly streets just above Jaume III, where traditional shops and designer boutiques rub shoulders.

For family-run shops, local artisan goods and high-street brands, make your way to Carrer dels Oms, north of the Plaça Major. From here, turn down Carrer Sant Miquel, a busy pedestrian street that's like one long outdoor mall, and cross the Plaça Major to reach Via Sindicato, another popular shopping area.

The area's largest mall is the **Centro Comercial Porto Pi** (Avinguda de Gabriel Roca 54), a complex with dozens of stores, restaurants and a bowling alley at the far western end of the Passeig Marítim, some 2km from the centre.

Popular souvenirs include traditional ceramic pottery, handmade baskets, blown glass, island-made textiles, Majorica pearls, delicatessen items like *sobrassada* sausage, and local wines and liquors. Great contemporary finds are shoes by a local firm, or a work by a local artist.

FOOD & DRINK

Colmado Manresa (☎ 971 731631; Carrer de Sa Fàbrica 19) This old-timey grocer in Santa Catalina is where the locals head for typical island products like *sobrassada, ensaïmades,* brown bread, olive oil and marmalade.

Les Illes d'Or (☎ 971 723411; Carrer del Convent de Sant Francesc 10) You'll find a decent selection of local wines, olive oils and pastries at this upscale souvenir shop.

FASHION & FURNISHINGS

Camper (☎ 971 714635; Avinguda de Jaume III 16) The best known of Mallorca's famed shoe brands, funky, eco-chic Campers are now trendy worldwide.

CRAFTY PALMA

If you're looking for Mallorcan-made glassworks, ceramics, baskets or other artisan goods, stroll around the **Passeig de la Artesania** (Crafts Walk; Plaça de l'Artesania & Carrer del Bosc), a well-marked route that includes more than a dozen shops and workshops. The museum-like **Sa Gerreria** (Map pp70-1; ☎ 971 213650; Carrer del Bosc 14) gives background information on the city's historic guilds and artisan traditions.

El Corte Ingles (☎ 971 770177; Avinguda de Jaume III 15) Spain's ubiquitous department store, this is a one-stop shop for everything from clothing to curtains. There's another branch on Avinguda de Alexandre Rosselló 12.

Farrutx (☎ 971 715308; Passeig d'es Born 16) This local brand's exquisite leather shoes for women are guaranteed to make you drool.

Janer (☎ 971 727674; Carrer de Can Verí 1) Minimalism is out at this opulent furniture shop, where you'll find major ticket items and handsome home accent pieces.

Món (☎ 971 724020; Plaça del Rosari 2) You can find great deals at this outlet, where flirty, feminine fashions from labels like Essentiel and Hoss hang on the racks. They're the still-desirable leftovers from the mother store, Addaia (Carrer Sant Miquel 57).

ARTISAN & LOCAL SPECIALITIES

Bordados Valldemossa (☎ 971 716306; Carrer de Sant Miquel 26) Embroidered linens, many made on the island, fill this old-timey shop.

Cerería Picornell (☎ 971 715727; Carrer del Call 7) Find modern and old-fashioned wax candles of every size and shape at this shop in Old Palma, open since 1785.

Quesada (☎ 971 715111; Passeig d'es Born 12) The typical Mallorcan two-toned patterned textiles called *roba de llengües* (striped cloths) have been sold here since 1890.

Rosario P (☎ 971 723586; Carrer de Sant Jaume 20) Artisan boutiques like this dot central Palma. Here you'll find delicate hand-painted tops, dresses and shawls, all made with light-as-breath silk.

Vidrierias Gordiola (☎ 971 711541; Carrer de la Victoria 8; ⊙ closed Sat afternoon) At this old-fashioned glass shop, run by one of Mallorca's most

---

MARKET WATCH

Flea markets, speciality markets and artisan markets abound in Palma. For handicrafts, head to the artisan markets on **Plaça Major** (⊙ 10am-2pm Mon & Sat Mar-Jul & Sep-Dec, daily Aug-Sep) or **Plaça des Meravelles** (⊙ 8pm-midnight May-Oct). A sprawling **flea market** (⊙ 10am-2pm) takes over the Avingudes west of the city centre (Avinguda de Gabriel Alomar and Avinguda de Villalonga) each Saturday. The **Christmas market** (⊙ 10am-8pm) takes over the Plaça Major from 16 December to 5 January.

---

well-known glass-makers, you'll find everything from traditional goblets and vases to surprisingly modern works of art. Gordiola has another branch in the Passeig de la Artesania (p97) and a factory on the outskirts of Palma.

GETTING THERE & AWAY
Air

Palma's Son Sant Joan airport lies 8km east of the city and receives an impressive level of traffic. For details on how to reach Mallorca by air, turn to p206.

Boat

Palma is also the island's main port. For details on ferry services from neighbouring islands and the Spanish mainland, see p209.

Bus

All island buses depart from (or near) the **bus station** (Map pp70–1; Carrer d'Eusebi Estada). For more details see p211. Services head in all directions, and places like Valldemossa, Sóller, Pollença and Alcúdia are easily reached by regular services. Other coastal and inland centres are served by less-frequent bus lines. A handful of areas are more easily reached by train (p211).

Car & Motorcycle

The big-league car-hire agencies have representatives at the airport and along Passeig Marítim, along with several cheaper companies. Several other companies are scattered about the city centre. You can pick up a list of car-hire places in Palma and around the island from tourist offices. One of the best deals is **Hasso** (☎ 902 203012; www.hasso-rentacar.com), which offers a Ford Ka for €35 for a day or €20 a day for six days or more (including insurance and unlimited mileage). **Pepecar** (☎ 807 414243; www .pepecar.com) has several rental outlets on the island, starting with the airport (look for the Centauro counter). It rents cars like Ford Kas or larger vehicles for up to seven passengers, which can cost less than €30 a day. You can rent scooters from **Europa Moto Rent** (Map pp70–1; ☎ 971 287129; www.europamotorent.com; Avinguda d'Argentina 9). A Piaggio Zip (50cc) costs €35 a day, while a 500cc Gilera Nexus costs €70.

Train

Two train lines run from Plaça d'Espanya. The **Palma–Sóller railway** (opposite) is a popular panoramic run. The other line (☎ 971 177777) is more prosaic, running northeast to Inca (€1.80) and then splitting into a branch to Sa Pobla (€2.65; 58 minutes) and another to Manacor (€3.70; 66 minutes). The Sa Pobla train makes more stops and takes 40 minutes to reach Inca, while the Manacor train takes 25 minutes. They start running at 5.50am and finish at 10pm on weekdays. Those for Sa Pobla generally leave Palma at 10 minutes before the hour and those for Manacor leave at 20 minutes after the hour. Departure times on weekends (when both lines are all-stops trains) vary but the frequency remains about the same.

GETTING AROUND
To/From the Airport

Bus 1 runs every 15 minutes from the airport to Plaça d'Espanya (on the train station side) in central Palma (€1.85, 15 minutes) and on to the entrance of the ferry terminal. It makes several stops along the way, entering the heart of the city along Avinguda de Gabriel Alomar i Villalonga, skirting around the city centre and then running back to the coast along Passeig de Mallorca and Avinguda d'Argentina. It heads along Avinguda de Gabriel Roca (aka Passeig Marítim) to reach the Estació Marítima (ferry port) before turning around. Buy tickets from the driver.

Taxis are generally abundant (when not striking) and the ride from the airport to central Palma will cost around €15 to €18.

To/From the Ferry Port

Bus 1 (the airport bus) runs every 15 minutes from the ferry port (Estació Marítima) across town (via Plaça d'Espanya) and on to the airport. A taxi from/to the centre will cost around €7 to €10.

Bus

There are 25 local bus services around Palma and its bay suburbs run by **EMT** (☎ 971 214444; www.emtpalma.es). Single-trip tickets cost €1.10, or you can buy a 10-trip card for €8.

Car & Motorcycle

Parking in the centre of town can be complicated. Some streets in the historic centre are for pedestrians only and the remaining streets are a mix. It is possible to park for free in some, but most are either no-parking zones or metered parking. The ring roads (the *avingudes*, or *avenidas*) around the centre and some adjoining areas are also given over to metered parking. These areas are marked in blue and generally you can park for up to two hours (€2.40), although time limits and prices can vary. The meters generally operate from 9am to 2pm and 4.30pm to 8pm Monday to Friday, and 9am to 2pm on Saturday.

THE SLOW CHUG NORTH TO SÓLLER

Since 1912 a narrow-gauge **train** (☎ 971 752051, 902 364711; www.trendesoller.com; one way/return €9/14, child 3-6yr half price, under 3yr free) has trundled along the winding 27.3km route north to Sóller. The fragile-looking timber-panelled train, which replaced a stagecoach service, departs from Plaça de l'Estació seven times a day and takes about 1¼ hours. The route passes through ever-changing countryside that becomes dramatic in the north as it crosses the Serra de Alfàbia, a stretch comprising 13 tunnels and a series of bridges and viaducts.

The trip begins through the streets of Palma but within 20 minutes you are in the countryside. At this stage the view is better to the left towards the Serra de Tramuntana. The terrain starts to rise gently and to the left the eye sweeps over olive gardens, the occasional sandy-coloured house and the mountains in the background. Half an hour out of Palma you call in at Bunyola. You could board here to do just half the trip (one way/return €4.50/9) to Sóller.

Shortly after Bunyola, as the mountains close in (at one point you can see Palma and the sea behind you), you reach the first of a series of tunnels. The so-called panoramic train (the 12.15pm service) stops at a marvellous lookout point, the Mirador Pujol de'n Banya, shortly after the Túnel Major (or main tunnel, which is almost 3km long and took three years to carve out of the rock in 1907–10). The view stretches out over the entire Sóller valley. From there, the train rattles across a viaduct before entering another tunnel that makes a slow 180 degree turn on its descent into Sóller, whose station building was carved out of an early 17th-century noble mansion. Return tickets are valid for two weeks.

In many of the streets beyond the ring roads, parking is free. If you are driving a hire or foreign-plated car, you may want to leave it in a car park, of which several are dotted about the city and have been marked on the Central Palma map (pp70–1).

Metro

A metro line operates from Plaça d'Espanya to the city's university (which could be handy if you wind up doing Spanish courses there). A single trip costs €0.65; return costs €1.20.

Taxi

For a taxi call ☎ 971 728081, 971 755440, 971 401414, 971 743737 or 971 200900. For special taxis for the disabled, call ☎ 971 703529. Taxis are metered but for trips beyond the city fix the price in advance. A green light indicates a taxi is free to hail or you can head for one of the taxi stands in the centre of town, such as those on Passeig d'es Born. Several are indicated on the Central Palma and Palma maps (pp70–1 and pp66–7). Flagfall is €1.80; thereafter you pay €0.67 per kilometre (€0.96 from 9pm to 7am and on weekends and holidays). There's a €0.55 supplement for every piece of luggage. Other extras include €2.50 for the airport and €1.70 for the port.

Bike

Bicycle is a good way to get around the historic centre and there's a bike track along the shoreline from Porto Pi to S'Arenal. **Palma on Bike** (Map pp70–1; ☎ 971 718062; www.palmaonbike .com; Plaça de Salvador Coll 8) has everything from city bikes to get around Palma to trekking and mountain bikes. Rates start at €12 for a day to €49 for a week and include insurance and a helmet.

CYCLE TOUR: PALMA TO CAPOCORB VELL

Covering a huge swathe of the sparkling Badia de Palma, this circular ride follows an easy-going seafront cycle path, then heads slightly inland towards Cap Blanc on the island's south coast. **Capocorb Vell** (p183), the remains of a prehistoric village, makes an interesting place to stretch your legs, and a convenient lunch stop. The return journey winds through peaceful country lanes, before a deserved downhill reverses the route back to S'Arenal and the city. Most people will want to cover the 67km in a full day, but

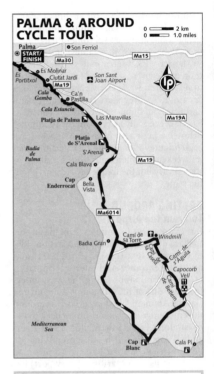

PALMA & AROUND CYCLE TOUR

0 —— 2 km
0 —— 1.0 miles

RIDE FACTS

Start/finish Palma/S'Arenal
Distance 67km/40km
Difficulty easy to moderate
Bike road or touring bike

the route could easily be shortened by catching a bus to S'Arenal and starting the ride from there. You'll find plenty of rental outlets along S'Arenal's beachfront but if you're after a road bike try **Ciclos Quintana** (☎ 971 442925; ciclosquintana@yahoo.es; Carrer de San Cristóbal 32; per hr €18), just up from the main drag.

Pick up the waterfront bike path anywhere in central Palma and head southeast. Hugging the coast for most of the way, the path is a breezy sweep to Ca'n Pastilla, from where you follow the seafront road to the end of the long sandy strip of **Platja de Palma** and its extension of S'Arenal (see opposite). From here, follow the wooden signs for Cap Blanc. Although along a major road, the 23km ride cuts through pleasant enough countryside, and motorists are used to lycra-clad two-wheelers plying the route. The road rises to 150m but none of the ascents is too gruelling.

You're unable to get to the lighthouse at the cape (and you won't see it en route either), so it's best to scoot on round the bend, rather than taking the signed road to the right. When you come to a junction (with signs right to Cala Pi), take a left for Capocorb Vell, whose entrance is just on the left.

A rustic **bar** at the ruins serves drinks, ice creams and a basic selection of *pa amb oli* with cheese, ham, tuna and anchovies (all €5).

Exit the bar to the right and take the Camí de Betlem, a quiet country lane (also signed Carreró de Betlem and marked as a cycle route). Follow this to the junction, and continue on to the Camí Estabits de s'Àguila, which rolls along surrounded by farmland. Turning a sharp right, it becomes the Camí de s'Àguila. After 200m, a left turn will bring you onto the Camí de sa Caseta, beautifully shaded by overhanging trees and lined by dry-stone walls. The end of the lane is marked by a **windmill** and, to the left, a church. Turn left here, where a wooden sign points you along the tranquil Camí de sa Torre to S'Arenal. Take a right when you hit the Ma6014 and follow the wooden signs to Platja de Palma.

From here, you can easily retrace your tracks all the way back to the capital.

THE BAY OF PALMA

The broad Badia de Palma stretches east and west away from the city centre. Some of the island's densest holiday development is to be found on both sides, but the beaches, especially to the west, are quite striking in spite of the dense cement backdrop.

EAST OF PALMA

Beyond the quiet beach of Ciutat Jardí and the Cala Gamba marina, you arrive in the mass beach-holiday area focused on Platja de Palma and S'Arenal. A couple of nearby escape hatches allow respite from the madding crowds.

Ca'n Pastilla to S'Arenal

In the shadow of the airport, heavily built-up **Ca'n Pastilla** is where Palma's eastern package holiday coast begins. The **Platja de Ca'n Pastilla** marks the western and windier end of

the 4.5km stretch of beach known as **Platja de Palma**. You can hire windsurfing gear and take windsurfing and kite surfing lessons at **Bellini** (☎ 971 262126; www.bellinifunboats.com; Carrer del Vaixell s/n; windsurf hire/lesson per hr €20/€35), around Balneario 15 (western end of the beach) beneath Hotel El Cid. Just west of Ca'n Pastilla is the pleasant **Cala Estancia**, a placid inlet whose beach is perfect for families with tots to keep under surveillance. The waterfront, with a pedestrian walkway, is backed by low-rise developments with hotels, eateries, cafés and bars.

Just a two-minute walk further west from Cala Estancia along the waterfront is the über-laid-back, sunset chill lounge, **Puro Beach** (☎ 971 744744; www.purobeach.com; ✪ 11am-2am), an all-white bar with a tapering outdoor promontory area that is perfect for sundowners, DJ sessions and fusion food. Blend in with the monochrome décor and wear white to emphasise your designer tan. If you ever felt like having a business card that just said 'The Dude', this is where you'd most likely flash it. Turn up for 11am yoga sessions, breakfast until noon, or waft in for dinner and cocktails at night.

Platja de Palma and its eastern extension, **Platja de S'Arenal**, are backed by a phalanx of 1970s mass-built hotels and holiday apartments, bars and pubs, tacky souvenir shops and fast-food joints. The beach is beloved especially of young German package partiers. Since 2005 Platja de Palma has been the stage for the annual **Palma de Mallorca Surf Action** (www.palmademallorcasurfaction.com) event, which attracts demos, stands and leading figures in windsurfing, kite surfing, wakeboarding, light sailing, skating and more.

The **Palma Aquarium** (☎ 971 264275; www.palmaaquarium.com; Carrer de Manuela de los Herreros i Sorà 21; adult/child under 18 yr/child under 3 yr €18.50/15/free; ✪ 10am-6pm) is one very good reason for visiting Platja de Palma. Five million litres of salt water fill the 55 tanks, home to sea critters from the Mediterranean (rays, sea horses, coral and more) and far-away oceans. The central tank, through which you walk along a transparent tunnel, is patrolled by 20 sleek sharks. In total some 8000 specimens are found here.

In S'Arenal, the only 'sight', apart from the not always edifying sights on the beach, is **La Porciúncula** (☎ 971 260002; Carrer de Fra Joan Llabrés 1; admission €1.50; ✪ 9.30am-1pm & 3.30-6pm Mon-Sat), a 1968 Franciscan church with a huge

6 sq metre stained glass window a few blocks inland from the beach. You can also visit the humble original church and a modest Mallorcan ethnological and coin collection.

Aqualand (☎ 971 440000; www.aqualand.es; adult/child €21/13; ☺ 10am-6pm Jul-Aug, 10am-5pm mid-May–Jun & Sep) is a typical watery amusement park, with rides, aqua gym, and kids' amusements. It's on the Ma6014 road just outside S'Arenal by the Cala Blava roundabout.

S'Arenal hosts produce and **flea markets** on Tuesdays and Thursdays.

EATING, DRINKING & NIGHTLIFE

There are several hundred hotels and apartment blocks jammed into the 5km stretch from Ca'n Pastilla to S'Arenal but there is little to recommend staying here. You can easily reach the beaches from Palma and if you're after the raucous nightlife, that too is a bus ride away (and a €15 to €20 taxi ride back).

There is no shortage of places to eat in Platja de Palma and S'Arenal, anything from German sausages to paella, although quality rarely surpasses mediocre. But who cares? What most people come for is the partying, not fine food. A predominantly German crowd pours in for endless drinking and deafening music, a phenomenon known as Ballermann (after the name of a famous beachside drink and dance local – Balneari 6). Ballermann to a German is synonymous with a good, and loud, time. There are even Ballermann CDs.

The core of the nightlife takes place in enormous beer gardens on or near Carrer del Pare Bartomeu Salvà, known to German revellers as Schinkenstrasse (Ham St) and about three-quarters of the way along the beach east towards S'Arenal (orientation points are Balneario 5 and 6 on the beach). Among the biggest attractions are **Bierkönig** and **Bamboleo**, while the nearby **MegaPark** (housed in a fake Gothic abbey) on Carrer de Llaüt is a temple to all-night partying. Popular clubs include **Paradies** and **Riu Palace** (www.riupalace.com), in the Riu Centre building on Carrer de Llaüt. The clubs tend to open from 8pm to 4am. The beer gardens are open by the early afternoon and close by 2am to 3am. They are sometimes closed for breaching noise-level limits (65 decibels is the legal outside noise limit).

GETTING THERE & AWAY

Bus 23 runs from Plaça d'Espanya to Ca'n Pastilla and parallel to Platja de Palma through S'Arenal and on past La Porciúncula to Aqualand (one hour). Buses run every half-hour or so and once every two hours they go on to Cala Blava (€1.15; one hour 50 minutes). Bus 15 runs from Plaça de la Reina and passes through Plaça d'Espanya on its way to S'Arenal every eight minutes. For the aquarium, get off at Balneari 14.

WEST OF PALMA

The Badia de Palma stretches to the southwest of central Palma in a series of little bays and beaches that are the nucleus of a series of heavily built-up resort areas. The beaches themselves are mostly very pretty and clean; the tourism at its English-breakfast-and-binge-drinking worst in Magaluf. Beyond, the coast quietens considerably until rounding Cap de Cala Figuera to reach the bucket-and-spade areas of Santa Ponça and Peguera (p107).

Cala Major

Cala Major, once a jet set beach scene about 4km southwest of the city centre, is a pretty beach and the first you encounter on your way west of the city. Sandwiched in between the multistorey hotels and apartments right on the beach is a motley crew of bars, snack joints and dance joints. The main road from Palma is lined with souvenir shops, kebab stands and the like.

Inland from the waterfront is a major art stop, the **Fundació Pilar i Joan Miró** (☎ 971 701420; http://miro.palmademallorca.es; Carrer de Joan de Saridakis 29; adult/student & senior/under 17 yr €5/2.80/free; ☺ 10am-7pm Tue-Sat, 10am-3pm Sun & holidays mid-May–mid-Sep, 10am-6pm Tue-Sat, 10am-3pm Sun & holidays mid-Sep–mid-May). Top Spanish architect Rafael Moneo designed the main building in 1992, next to the studio in which Miró had thrived for decades. No doubt influenced by his Mallorquin wife, Pilar Juncosa, and the fact that his mother was from Sóller, Miró moved to Palma in 1956 and remained there until his death in 1983. His friend, the architect Josep Lluís Sert, designed the studio space for him above Cala Major.

The foundation has 2500 works by the artist (including 100 paintings) along with memorabilia. A selection of his works hangs in the Sala Estrella, an angular, jagged part of Moneo's creation that is the architect's take on the artist's work. The rest of the building's exhibition space is used for temporary shows. Miró sculptures are scattered about

GETTING AWAY FROM IT ALL

Nothing could be further removed from the beer gardens of Platja de Palma than residential Cala Blava, 2.5km southwest of S'Arenal. There are several rocky locations for a dip, and one sandy beach, Cala Blava (Carrer D'Ondategui). After the fork in the Ma6014 road (to Cala Blava and Cala Pi), take the first right – it's a few hundred metres down to the beach (bus stop Carrer D'Ondategui 36). Look for the Pas a Sa Platja sign and stairs opposite Carrer de Mèxic.

The continuation south of Cala Blava is Bella Vista. Part of the coast is off limits as a protected area, but you could slip down to the Calò des Cap d'Alt for a swim in crystal-clear waters. It is a narrow rocky inlet that a handful of locals visit for some quiet sea and sunbathing. Hungry? Stop at **Restaurante Panorámica Playa** (☎ 971 740211; Passeig de les Dames 29, Bella Vista; meals €25-30; ☼ daily) and tuck into some fish on the terrace, which has magnificent views of the Badia de Palma. Walk down the steps for a dip in the 'pool' – a platform from which to launch yourself into the sea.

On the west side of the Badia de Palma, you could head south of Magaluf to a couple of pretty inlets. Cala Vinyes has placid water, and the sand stretches inland among residential buildings. The next cove, Cala de Cap Falcó, is an emerald lick of an inlet surrounded by tree-covered rocky coast. Don't wait too long, as the developers are getting closer and closer. These two gems are both within 2km to 3km of southern Magaluf. Follow signs south for Sol de Mallorca and then the signs for each of these locations. Bus 107 from Palma reaches Cala Vinyes via Magaluf.

outside. Walk past and behind Sert's studio to **Son Boter**, an 18th-century farmhouse Miró bought to increase his privacy. Inside, giant scribblings on the whitewashed walls served as plans for some of his bronze sculptures.

Maothai (☎ 971 703043; Passeig de Joan Miró 244; meals €35-40; ☼ lunch & dinner Mon-Fri, dinner Sat & Sun), just across the road from Palau Marivent (the summer palace), is King Juan Carlos I's local Thai. A friendly if noisily located spot in cheery yellow paint and burnt-brown floor tiles, it offers reasonably authentic dishes.

Take Bus 3 or 46 from the Palma city centre (Plaça d'Espanya) for Cala Major.

Coves de Gènova

About 1km roughly north of the Fundació in the satellite settlement of Gènova, you can poke about the stalactites and stalagmites of the **Coves de Gènova** (☎ 971 402387; Carrer d'es Barranc 45; adult/child under 10 yr €8/3.50; ☼ 10am-1.30pm & 4-7pm Tue-Sun Apr-Oct, 10am-1pm & 4-6pm Tue-Sun Nov-Mar). Discovered in 1906, the caves are not as interesting as the Coves del Drac in the east of the island (p177), but are a pleasant enough distraction. You reach a maximum depth of 36m and will be shown all sorts of fanciful, backlit shapes. The temperature is always around 20°C in the caves, and water has been dripping away for many millennia to create these natural 'sculptures'.

Palma folk love to come up here for hearty eating in one of several crowded restaurants.

One of the best known is **Ca'n Pedro** (☎ 971 402479; Carrer del Rector Vives 4; meals €30; ☼ Tue-Sun), famous for its snails. It has another place at Carrer del Rector Vives 14 (closed on Wednesday).

From Palma or Cala Major, take Bus 46 to Coves de Gènova. Alight at Camí dels Reis 19, from where it's about a 300m walk.

If you have wheels, follow the signs to **Na Burguesa** off the main road from the centre of Gènova (a short way north of the Coves turn-off). About 1.5km of winding, poor road takes you past the walled-in pleasure domes of the rich to reach a rather ugly monument to the Virgin Mary, from where you have sweeping views over the city (this is about the only way to look *down* on the Castell Bellver) and bay.

Ses Illetes & Portals Nous

The islands (*illetes*) in question lie just off pine-backed beaches. This is altogether a much classier holiday–residential zone. The coast is high and drops quite abruptly to the turquoise coves, principally Platja de Ses Illetes and, a little less crowded, Platja de Sa Comtesa. Parking is a major hassle.

The hippest spot of the moment is **Virtual Club** (☎ 971 703235; www.virtualclub.es; Passeig d'Illetes 60; ☼ 10am-midnight), a waterside pleasure dome with thatched huts and shades, wicker chairs and wicked DJ sounds. There's also a kind of cavernous bar that fills with strange strobe lighting at night. Glam it up for cocktails and food.

Virtually a part of Ses Illetes is **Bendinat**, named after the private castle of the same name (a neo-Gothic reworking of the 13th-century original that can only be seen from the Ma1 motorway). The area is jammed with high-class hotels and villas that are not for the financially faint-hearted. Next up is **Portals Nous**, with its super marina for the super yachts of the super rich at restaurant-lined **Puerto Portals**. The beach that stretches north of the marina is longer and broader than those mentioned above. At its northern end, sip cocktails and munch on snacks at **Chiringuito Roxy Beach** (9am-10pm daily Jun-Sep).

Local Palma Bus 3 reaches Ses Illetes from central Palma (you can pick it up on Passeig de la Rambla or Avinguda de Jaume III).

Buses 103, 104, 106 and 111 from Palma's bus station call in at Portals Nous (€1.35; 30 to 50 minutes).

Palmanova & Magaluf

About 2km southwest from Portals Nous's plastic surgery beauty and €500 notes is a whole other world. Palmanova and Magaluf have merged to form what is the epitome of the sea, sand, sangria and shagging (not necessarily in that order) holiday that has lent all of Mallorca an undeserved notoriety.

Palmanova's **tourist office** (☎ 971 682365; Passeig de la Mar; 9am-6pm) is on the waterfront, while the Magaluf **tourist office** (☎ 971 131126; Carrer de Pere Vacquer Ramis 1; 9am-6pm) is a block back from the sea. Check the local hoteliers' website (www.palmanova-magaluf.com).

The four main beaches between Palmanova and Magaluf are beautiful and immaculately maintained. The broad sweeps of fine white sand, in parts shaded by strategically planted pines and palms, are undeniably tempting and the development behind them could be considerably worse.

Three theme parks operate in the area. **Marineland** (☎ 971 675125; www.marineland.es; Costa d'En Blanes; adult/child €20.50/14.50; 9.30am-6pm mid-Mar–Nov) has dolphin shows, an aquarium, reptiles and so on. It is at the Puerto Portals

roundabout between Portals Nous and Palmanova. At the south end of Magaluf you strike **Western Water Park** (☎ 971 131203; www.westernpark.com; Carretera de Cala Figuera; adult/child €21/13; 10am-6pm Jul-Aug, 10am-5pm Jun & Sep), with wave pools, sea lions, falcon shows and Wild West–themed eateries and shops. Across the road is **Aqualand** (☎ 971 130811; www.aqualand.es; Carretera de Cala Figuera; adult/child €21/13; 10am-6pm Jul-Aug, 10am-5pm mid-May–Jun & Sep), similar to its counterpart in S'Arenal (p102).

Divers should see what's available at **Big Blue Diving** (☎ 971 681686; www.mallorcaonline.com/sport/bigblue; Carrer de Martí Ros García 6) in Magaluf.

On Saturday morning in Magaluf, a fairly standard crafts and knick-knacks market sets up around Carrer Blanc (a good four blocks from the beach) for the area's few early risers.

While restless young Germans party at the Platja de Palma beer gardens, their British equivalents are letting themselves loose on the nightspots of Magaluf. This is big stag- and hen-night territory, and few holds are barred. The drinking antics of the Brits in Magaluf have long been legendary (for all the wrong reasons) but it's undeniably a curious night out. The bulk of the action is concentrated around the north end of Carrer de Punta Ballena. Pubs and bars are piled on top of one another (much like some of their punters late in the evening) and clubs to look for at this end of the street include **Bananas**, **Boomerang** and the cult classic **BCM**.

Feel like trying your luck? Have a spin of the wheel at the **Gran Casino Mallorca** (☎ 971 130000; www.casinodemallorca.com; Sol de Mallorca; 6pm-5am). The slot machines are open from 3pm. Follow the signs for Sol de Mallorca for 2km from south Magaluf.

The most direct bus from Palma is the 105 (€2.60; 45 minutes), which runs 11 times a day. Bus 107 (seven times a day) takes five minutes longer as it stops at Marineland en route. The 106 (one hour) is the most frequent service.

The 110B (three times a day Monday to Saturday) connects Santa Ponça (p107) with Palmanova and Magaluf (€1.35; 30 minutes).

Western Mallorca

Some of the most spectacular coastline in the Mediterranean forms an impervious rock barrier to powerful north winds that, in winter especially, can batter Mallorca. Tourism took off with the bucket-and-spade masses on the southern beaches in the 1960s, but the island's first tourists made a beeline for the Serra de Tramuntana long before.

Deià became an artists colony in the early 20th century and a bevy of Catalan painters led by Barcelona Modernìsta Santiago Rusiñol would applaud the sunsets there as if in a theatre. Deià and nearby inland Valldemossa, site of a grand monastery, are undeniably pretty (and much visited) towns.

They are only the beginning. A grand depression that opens to the northwest's only port, Port de Sóller, is an enchanting world. The air of shady Sóller and picture-postcard villages like Fornalutx and Biniaraix is heavy with the intoxicating perfume of the oranges and lemons that were long the area's economic mainstay.

Each of the burnt-orange villages along the coast has its own outlet to the sea, where turquoise waters lap tiny pebbly strands. Among the most enticing are those of Deià and Lluc Alcari. In the southwest, Sant Elm offers a 'proper' sandy beach. Yachting folk promenade between buzzy Port d'Andratx and Port de Sóller.

It is hard to pull away from the magic of the glittering sea, but inland excursions bring other rewards in villages like Orient and Esporles, the mystic calm of the Monestir de Lluc and the medieval castle ruins above Alaró.

HIGHLIGHTS

- Dive the transparent depths off the **Illa del Toro** (p107) near Santa Ponça
- Wander the steep and scented lanes of **Deià** (p117), one of Mallorca's prettiest towns
- Walk through citrus, almond and olive groves to the villages of **Biniaraix** and **Fornalutx** (p128)
- Discover the tranquil beauty and Modernìsta flair of the island's orange capital, **Sóller** (p119)
- Feel your heart leap as you take the dramatic hairpin drive to **Sa Calobra** (p131)
- Climb to the impregnable fortress ruins of **Castell d'Alaró** (p130)
- Marvel at the monastic peace of **Monestir de Lluc** (p132)

Sa Calobra ★
Monestir de Lluc ★
★★ Biniaraix & Fornalutx
Deià ★   ★★ Sóller
Castell d'Alaró ★
★
Illa del Toro

THE SOUTHWEST

Heavily if not always tastelessly developed in parts, the southwest corner of the island holds a couple of delightful coastal surprises. It remains to be seen whether these last redoubts of natural beauty will resist human greed. Judging by the building scandals and phalanxes of cranes in and around Andratx, it might be an idea to get in quick before the cement-mixers do.

TO CAP DE CALA FIGUERA

The residences of the rich in the soulless suburban-style development of Sol de Mallorca, 2km south of Magaluf, look across the Punta de S'Estaca to three dreamlike inlets collectively known as **Portals Vells**. Their view over the turquoise-emerald waters is enviable. Will the developers' grip stretch to the other side?

To reach Portals Vells, take the road from south Magaluf (the number 8 roundabout by Aqualand) in the direction of El Toro and, after 800m, the narrow road south through

OUR TOP PICKS

- **Hotel** Muleta de Ca S'Hereu (p126)
- **Restaurant** Bens d'Avall (p122)
- **Town** Valldemossa (p114)
- **Beach** Cala de Deià (p118)
- **Festival** Es Firó (p121)

the golf course rather than swinging right (west) for El Toro. About 2km through pine woods brings you to a junction. To the left is signposted 'Playa Mago', which is two narrow inlets. The one on the right has a restaurant and is generally frequented by nudists, while the longer inlet with the narrow, shady beach to the right is prettier.

Nicer than either is **Cala Portals Vells**, another 1.8km south from the junction. Turquoise waters lap the beach, whose sands stretch back quite a distance beneath rows of straw umbrellas. To the south a walking trail leads to caves in the rock walls, one of them containing the rudiments of a chapel.

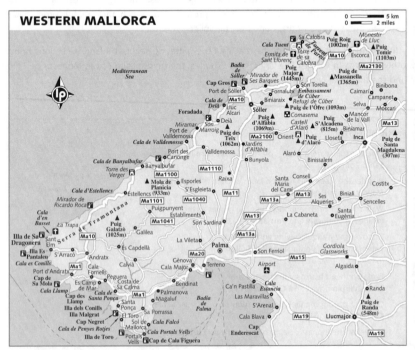

Right on the beach, **Es Repòs** (☎ 971 180492; meals €30-35; Ⓨ lunch Apr-Jun, Sep & Oct, lunch & dinner Mon-Sat, lunch Sun Jul & Aug) serves relaxed, sea-salty punters a simple array of seafood, salads and refreshments.

A few hundred metres back up from the beach, the road south to the **Cap de Cala Figuera** lighthouse is blocked off as private property.

SANTA PONÇA, PEGUERA & AROUND

South of Magaluf, the road west leads to the holiday residential district of El Toro and then on to adjoining Santa Ponça (and its indistinguishable extensions of Ses Rotes Velles and Costa de Sa Calma). The whole area has largely been created out of nothing to meet the demands of mass tourism.

The Santa Ponça **tourist office** (☎ 971 691712; Carrer des Puig de Galatzó 1; Ⓨ 9am-6pm Mon-Fri, 9am-3pm Sat) is on the main beach. Check also www .santa-ponsa.com.

Entering El Toro from Magaluf, you could follow the signs to the marina of Port Adriano, opposite which stretches **Cala de Penyes Rotjes** (Red Cliffs Beach). It is pleasant enough but without shade, and the red cliffs are partly made up of ochre apartment blocks. South of this, a long point faces an islet that divers should note: **Illa del Toro**. At around 30m down the island's steep walls there are lashings of sea life, including plenty of moray eels.

Keep to the coast road approaching Santa Ponça and you will arrive at a lookout point, **Cap Negret**, from which you can see the marine reserve of **Illa Magrat** and the tiny **Illa dels Conills**. From here the road passes villas, the shady **Caló d'en Pellicer** beach and **Jungle Park** (☎ 630 948295; www.jungleparc.es; Avinguda de Jaume I 40a; admission €14; Ⓨ 10am-8pm daily mid-Jun—mid-Sep, 10am-6pm Fri-Sun May—mid-Jun & mid-Sep—Oct), which offers a little adrenaline rush as you walk along rope bridges, swing through the branches and engage in other Tarzanesque activities.

The main **Santa Ponça beach** is broad and sandy and backed by a mix of high- and low-rise development. The beach is fine, the rest a little tedious. Divers should seek out **Zoea** (☎ 971 691444; www.zoeamallorca.com; Club Naútico Santa Ponça, Via La Cornisa), a professional outfit that does boat dives in the area, including Illa del Toro. In September try to be here for the **Festes del Rei Jaume I** on the 9th, when the 1229 landing by the Catalan king in Muslim Mallorca is staged on the beach.

A couple of kilometres west along the Ma1 road is nondescript **Peguera**. The pine-backed beach itself is pretty but some of the apartment blocks wouldn't be amiss in a Soviet suburb. Barely 1km southwest, **Cala Fornells** is more enticing, with its pair of bijou aquamarine strands framed by high, wooded promontories and not overly obtrusive hotels. Relax in the **Hotel Petit Cala Fornells** (☎ 971 685405; petitcf@baleares.com; d per person €90-96; Ⓨ May–mid-Oct; Ⓟ Ⓧ Ⓡ Ⓛ), which sits between the two beaches and offers 24 spacious rooms, sauna, putting green and gym.

Another 2km west, **Es Camp de Mar** is a colourless residential holiday zone (where Claudia Schiffer has a pad) with an acceptable beach. Follow the Ma1020 road out of here for fine views over the coast before turning into high wooded country and then dropping down the other side to Port d'Andratx (p108).

The 102 bus from Palma to Santa Ponça continues to Peguera (€2.60, 55 minutes from Palma). Quite a few of these buses continue to Andratx and Port d'Andratx.

CALVIÀ & ES CAPDELLÀ

Calvià is one of the richest municipalities in Spain thanks to the money pouring in from the mass coastal tourism in Palmanova, Magaluf, Santa Ponça and company, but the sleepy, bucolic capital of the same name doesn't flaunt its wealth.

The **Església de Sant Joan Baptista** was originally raised in the late 13th century and is curious because its 19th-century remake includes a gaudy neo-Romanesque entrance. A handful of restaurants and bars help out with sustenance.

About 1km southwest of the town centre, a modest country house awaits guests in search of tranquillity within a short drive of the coast.

Son Malero (☎ 971 670301; www.sonmalero.com; Camí de Son Malero; d €100-120; ☽ late Dec-early Nov; P ⚘), set in a valley of almonds and carobs, dates to at least 1430. Its six rustic rooms can accommodate 12 people. Three have terraces. You might get to try wines from the *finca's* own cellars.

Four kilometres west of Calvià, **Es Capdellà** is a hamlet set in flourishing country, with almond and citrus groves. It's a minor crossroads you will probably encounter if exploring the southwest.

Three to seven buses run from Peguera via Santa Ponça and Palmanova to Calvià and Es Capdellà. From Santa Ponça they take about 30 minutes to Es Capdellà (although some take longer) and cost €1.35. The three to five daily buses from Palma to Es Capdellà take anything up to 1½ hours (€2.60).

ANDRATX

pop 4995 / elev 132m

Andratx is the largest town in the southwest. Typically for Mallorca, it lies well inland as a defensive measure against pirate attack, while its harbour, Port d'Andratx (right), lies 4km southwest. The tight concentration of houses around a grid of narrow streets offers few specific sights, but is a world away from the coastal mayhem. The wealth and corruption generated by the orgy of building on the coast to the south has left no visible signs here in the municipal capital.

Andratx is pasted like crunchy peanut butter onto the flank of foothills of the Serra de Tramuntana. Its most important buildings stand tall on two rises. The 16th-century **Castell de Son Mas** is an elegant defensive palace with a tower and Renaissance touches in its exterior decoration. Lying on the roundabout for the roads to Estellencs and Es Capdellà, it houses the *ajuntament* (town hall). From it you can see the hulk of the **Església de Santa Maria d'Andratx** (Camí de la Rectoria 62), built in the 18th century on the site of the original 1248 church.

The enormous **Centre Cultural Andratx** (☎ 971 137770; www.ccandratx.com; ☽ 10.30am-7pm Tue-Fri, 10.30am-4pm Sun & holidays May-Oct, 11am-4pm Tue-Fri & Sun Nov-Apr) is 1.2km northeast of Castell de Son Mas along the road to Es Capdellà. It is a modern, private space for art exhibitions housed in an ochre building, a cross between what could be the spaceship *Jupiter* from *Lost in Space* and a supposedly Mallorcan-style

possessió. Temporary exhibitions are staged on two floors gathered around an immense courtyard, along with film programmes, concerts and more. The land around the centre produces oranges, lemons, almonds, figs and olives.

The best thing about Andratx is people-watching. Turn up around 8pm in summer and, in addition to the pleasing afternoon light, you'll see folks in the bars and in the streets, chatting, playing and checking out their motorbikes. Carrer de Sa Constitució, Plaça d'Espanya and Via Roma are best for this, along with Plaça des Pou (whose one-time well is marked by a towering stone cross).

Wednesday morning is market day and another lively moment for a visit.

For simple island fare in a time-warp atmosphere, **Font i Caliu** (☎ 971 137070; Carrer de Juan Carlos I 2; meals €20; ☽ Sun-Fri) is a good choice. Nothing seems to have changed here over the years – there's no fusion fuss and chilling out here. There is a courtyard out the back or you could take an inside table with ageing white linen beneath exposed beams for some *trampó* (a cold vegetable dish), followed by *arros brut* (dirty rice), a typical rice dish jammed with *sobrassada*, rabbit and other optional meats.

For accommodation, head the few kilometres to Port d'Andratx. The Palma to Port d'Andratx bus (102) calls in to Andratx (€3.80, one hour 10 minutes).

PORT D'ANDRATX

pop 1060

Port d'Andratx was once a kind of laid-back Portofino. It is a fine, long natural bay that attracts yachties from far and wide. While it is still a pleasant place for an evening waterfront meal, the blight of construction is rapidly eroding its charm.

The **tourist office** (☎ 971 671300; Avinguda de Mateu Bosch s/n; ☽ 9am-4pm May-Sep, 9am-3pm Mon-Fri, 9am-2pm Sat Oct-Apr) is next to the bus stop. Check email at **Ciber Café** (☎ 971 671010; Carrer de Sa Fàbrica 10; per hr €3; ☽ 1-3pm & 7pm-2am Fri-Wed).

Sights & Activities

The port is short on sights. You could easily slip past the tiny **Església de la Verge del Carme** (Carrer d'Isaac Peral) without noticing it. About 2km south of the port centre is the eccentric **Museo Liedtke** (www.liedtke-museum.com; Carrer de l'Olivera),

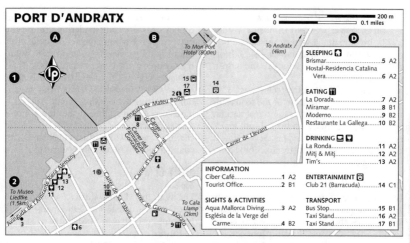

built in 1987–93 into the cliffs near Cap de Sa Mola by German artist Dieter Walter Lietdke. Home to his art and temporary exhibitions, it is also a selling point for Lietdke's theories on life, art, the universe and anything else you care to contemplate. Finding it open could be a matter of chance, but the coastal views warrant the detour.

Aqua Mallorca Diving (☎ 971 674376; Avinguda de l'Amirante Riera Alemany 23) is the main local dive shop. One dive with all gear costs €53.

Those with wheels should make a detour for **Cala Llamp**, for at least three reasons: to jump into the sparkling, bottle-green waters in this sandless bay; to marvel at the extent of construction (a bit of investment in the pot-holed roads wouldn't go astray) all around this stretch of rugged coast; and to relax over a drink at the **Gran Folies Beach Club** (☎ 971 671094; www .granfolies.net; 10am-2am). This bar-restaurant is placed right above the rocky cove and offers use of a pool to cavort in between cocktails. It also does breakfast and full meals and runs free yoga classes (the latter on Friday mornings). Take the Ma1020 from the centre of Port d'Andratx and follow the signs over the ridge.

Sleeping

Hostal-Residencia Catalina Vera (☎ 971 671918; Carrer de Isaac Peral 63; s/d €42/68; **P**) A couple of hundred metres back from the harbour, this is a lovely guesthouse retreat with rooms set around a tranquil garden courtyard. The best doubles have balconies.

Brismar (☎ 971 671600; Avinguda de l'Almirante Riera Alemany 6; s/d from €67/95; Mar-Nov) The only wa-terfront hotel, this is a straightforward place with a bar and reasonably spacious if unexciting rooms. If the budget will stretch, ask for rooms with sea views (€90 for a single, €116 for a double).

Mon Port Hotel (☎ 971 238623; www.hotelmon port.com; Finca La Noria, Camí de Cala d'Egos; s €103-145, d €148-222; **P**) Away from the hub of the action, on the west side of the bay, this is a pamper palace. Pools, gym, massages, facials, sauna…you name it. Everything for your 'wellness' is on offer.

Eating

The waterfront is lined with restaurants, all with dining areas right on the water. A few worthwhile options lie hidden a block or two inland.

Restaurante La Gallega (☎ 971 671338; Carrer de Isaac Peral 52; meals €30; Tue-Sun, Dec-Oct) Try north-ern Spanish seafood faves, such as a quarter-kilo of *percebes* (a strange-looking mollusc) for €37, at this popular, no-nonsense back-street eatery.

La Dorada (☎ 971 671648; Avinguda de Mateu Bosch 31b; meals €30-40; Feb-Oct) You are assured of a stylish presentation (those nice square plates) and well-prepared dishes. The *filete de dorada en salsa de trufa* (gilthead bream fillet in truf-fle sauce) is delicate and the *parrillada de pescado* (mixed fish grill) abundant. On cooler nights, retreat inside and grab an upstairs table by a window.

Miramar (☎ 971 671617; Avinguda de Mateu Bosch 18; breakfast €9, meals €35; ◷ daily) In business since 1927, this remains a waterfront classic that serves decent seafood and meat dishes. It offers an abundant set lunch for €19 and is open for breakfast too.

Moderno (☎ 971 673035; Carrer de García Morato 24b; meals €35; ◷ 7pm-1am) Back on the hill road leading to Cala Llamp (just past the petrol station) is this charming mansion turned into an elegant Italian restaurant and bar. Several lowlit dining areas lead to a rear terrace. Some folks just hang about the bar by the entrance.

Drinking

In summer the waterfront is a minor party zone. **Mitj & Mitj** (☎ 971 672608; Avinguda de l'Almirante Riera Alemany 9) attracts a mixed crowd to its waterside terrace, as does the more lounge-style **La Ronda** (Avinguda de l'Almirante Riera Alemany 9) next door. **Tim's** (Avinguda de l'Almirante Riera Alemany 6) is for the under-25s and pulses to the barely controlled hormones of a mostly foreign clientele. These locales generally open from 7pm to 4am (March to November) but this depends largely on how busy they get.

Everyone then heads for **Club 21** (Barracuda; Avinguda de Mateu Bosch s/n; www.mallorca-nightlife.com; ◷ midnight-6am), to dance the night away.

Getting There & Away

Most of the 102 buses from Palma continue from Andratx to the port (€1.35, 10 minutes). Bus 100 runs seven or eight times a day between Andratx and Sant Elm, calling in at Port d'Andratx en route. Taxis (☎ 971 235544, 971 136398) will whisk you to Palma (€30) or the airport (€43).

S'ARRACÓ

Two kilometres west of Andratx and 4km north of Port d'Andratx, this smiling hamlet, bundled fish-bone-style along the main road, dates to about the 18th century. The rich territory around it attests to its rural traditions, although hard times in the 19th century forced many farmers to migrate to France. Today it is simply a pleasantly relaxed place to stop and is blessed with several good restaurants. Those with more than a passing interest could stay in the rustic UK-run **Hotel L'Escaleta** (☎ 971 671011; www.hotelescaleta.com; Carrer del Porvenir 10; s/d €60/95; ❒ ☐). The three-storey house has been sympathetically restored and rooms are each a little different, although some elements are

common, including terracotta floor tiles and timber beds. If even wandering around the village seems like too much effort, relax over a book in the garden. You should crawl out to try a couple of the better restaurants, such as **Es Puput** (☎ 971 674703; Carrer del Atajo 1; meals €40-45; ◷ dinner Tue-Sat Aug-Jun), a German-run gastro-dome offering hybrid Med–Asian dishes. It's hard to avoid salivating at the thought of a tender *solomillo de cordero con coucous al cilantro y yogur al lima* (thick cut of lamb with cilantro couscous and lime yoghurt).

SANT ELM
pop 80

For 5km, the Ma1030 ducks and weaves up hill and down dale to suddenly emerge in this tranquil beach haven at Mallorca's extreme southwest edge.

The **tourist office** (☎ 971 239205; Avinguda de Jaume 1 28b; ◷ 9am-4pm May-Sep, 9am-3pm Mon-Fri, 9am-3pm Sat Oct-Apr) is a short walk from the beach.

Sights & Activities

The main town **beach** is a pleasant sandy strand (no shade) that faces the gently lapping Med to the south. Within swimming distance for the moderately fit is **Illa Es Pantaleu**, a rocky islet that marks one of the boundaries of a marine reserve. That reserve is dominated by the much bigger, 4km-long **Illa de Sa Dragonera**, which looms like an aircraft carrier to the west. Constituted as a natural park, it can be reached by **ferry** (☎ 639 617545; tickets €10; 15 min, 3-4 times daily Feb-Nov) from a little harbour north of the beach in central Sant Elm. The ferry lands at a protected natural harbour on the east side of the island, from where you can follow trails to the capes at either end or ascend the **Na Pòpia peak** (Puig des Far Vell, 349m). The ferry operators also do **glass-bottomed boat tours** around the island. If you want to dive off the island, try **Scuba Activa** (☎ 971 239102; www.scuba -activa.com; Plaça del Monsenyor Sebastià Grau 7; 1 dive incl equipment €57).

To the south of Sant Elm's main beach (follow Carrer de Cala es Conills), **Cala es Conills** is a sandless but pretty inlet.

A couple of nice walks would see you heading north from Plaça del Monsenyor Sebastià Grau, at the northeast end of town. One follows the GR221 long-distance route (p112) for about an hour to **La Trapa**, a ruined former monastery that is being transformed into a hikers' refuge. A few hundred metres from the building is a wonderful lookout point. You can start on the same trail but branch off west about halfway (total walk of about 45 minutes) to reach **Cala d'En Basset**, a lovely bay with transparent water but not much of a beach to speak of.

Sleeping & Eating

Hostal Dragonera (☎ 971 239086; www.hostaldragonera .net; Avinguda del Rei Jaume I 5; s/d with balcony €51/65; ⊗ Feb-Nov) The best of the two hotel options, this is cheap and cheerful and on the main drag. Go for broke and take a room with balcony for sea views (the extra outlay is less than €10). Rooms are smallish and Spartan but clean and light. The place has its own restaurant and sea views are also on the menu for breakfast, lunch and tea.

Indeed, there is no shortage of restaurants with water views. A cluster of them are perched off Plaça de Na Caragola, halfway into the town (past the tourist office). Of these, **El Pescador** (☎ 971 239198; Avinguda de Jaume I; meals €30; ⊗ daily) is reliable. Paella (€16) is a good midday option and meat mains are available, but the best bet is the fish of the day (sold by weight).

Getting There & Away

Seven or eight buses run from Andratx to Sant Elm (€1.35, 40 minutes) via Port d'Andratx and S'Arracó. You can also take the boat between Sant Elm and Port d'Andratx (€7, 20 minutes, once daily February to November).

SERRA DE TRAMUNTANA

Dominated by the rugged Serra de Tramuntana range, Mallorca's northwest coast and its hinterland form a spectacular opposite to the mass coastal tourism you leave behind around Palma. The vertiginous coastline is unforgiving, rocky (mostly limestone) and mostly inaccessible; the villages are largely built of local stone (as opposed to concrete), and the high, rugged interior is much loved by walkers for its beautiful landscapes of pine forests, olive groves and spring wild flowers.

The highest peaks are concentrated in the central mountain range. The highest, Puig Major (1445m) is off limits and home to a military communications base. It is followed

by Puig de Massanella (1365m). The area is virtually bereft of surface watercourses, but rich in subterranean flows that feed the farming terraces of the coast villages.

The main road (the Ma10) starts at Andratx and runs roughly parallel to the coast to Pollença. It's a stunning scenic drive and popular cycling route, especially during spring, when the muted mountain backdrop of browns, greys and greens is splashed with the bright colours of yellow wattles, blood-red poppies and other spring blooms. Plenty of *miradores* (lookout points) recommend themselves as stops to punctuate the trip, as do diversions down to tiny bays for a dip.

ANDRATX TO VALLDEMOSSA

The Ma10 road climbs away from Andratx into the wooded hills that mark the beginning of the majestic Serra de Tramuntana range. After about 6km you get your first sea glimpses from on high. Three kilometres short of Estellencs, pull in at the parking area opposite a restaurant to climb up to the **Mirador de Ricardo Roca**, a stunning lookout point.

Estellencs

pop 350 / elev 151m

Estellencs is a coquettish village of stone buildings scattered around the rolling hills below the **Puig Galatzó** (1025m). A 1.5km road winds down through terraces of palm trees, citrus orchards, olives, almonds, cacti, pines and various primary-coloured flowers to the local 'beach', **Cala d'Estellencs**, a rocky cove with crystal-clear water. Park your steed, go for a swim and enjoy a simple lunch at **Sa Punteta**, a summertime eatery on the rocks overlooking the sea. To ascend Puig Galatzó, a walking trail starts near the Km97 milestone on the Ma10 road, about 2½km west of Estellencs. It's not easy going, so you'll need good maps and plenty of water and food. Reckon on a five- to six-hour round trip. An alternative but easily confused trail leads back down into Estellencs.

An arts and crafts fair is usually held in Estellencs on the third weekend of April.

SLEEPING & EATING

Petit Hotel Sa Plana (☎ 971 618666; www.saplana .com; Carrer d'Eusebi Pascual; d €98; 🅿 🏠 🛋) At the western entrance to the town, this higgledy-piggledy, stone place dominates a rise that catches the evening sun. The five rooms are all quite different and tastefully decorated with period furnishings.

Hotel Maristel (☎ 971 618550; www.hotelmaristel .com; Carrer d'Eusebi Pascual 10; s/d €100/125; 🌐 🔊) More functional, Maristel is on the main drag at the western end of the village. The best rooms have balconies and sea views. Whatever room you get, indulge in the spa facilities.

Finca S'Olivar (☎ 971 618591, 629 266035; www.pan gea.org/fincaolivar; d/tr from €109/195; 🅿 🌐 🖥 🔊) A more curious option, about 1km east of town, this series of renovated stone houses scattered over a sprawling valley property (with olive terraces) is perfect for those in search of total tranquillity. Most of the property is a wi-fi area if you have to bring work along. Or forget the work and do laps in the pool, which seems to hang at the edge of nothing.

Montimar (☎ 971 618576; Plaça de la Constitució 7; meals €25-30; 🕒 Tue-Sun; 🆅) In town, this place opposite the church remains the best of the handful of eateries. The high terrace above the main road affords great views that may distract you from your *arros brut* or vegetarian dishes.

Banyalbufar
pop 460 / elev 112m

Eight kilometres northeast of Estellencs, Banyalbufar is similarly positioned high above the coast. If anything it is an even tighter and steeper huddle and its quiet lanes beckon strollers. All around are carved-out centuries-old, stone-walled farming terraces, known as *ses marjades*. They are kept moist by mountain well water that gurgles down open channels and is stored in cisterns. A steep 1km walk downhill brings you to a shingle cove, **Cala de Banyalbufar**, for a swim. One kilometre out of town on the road to Estellencs is one of the island's symbols, the **Torre des Verger** (aka Torre de Ses Ànimes). This 1579 *talayot* (watchtower) is one of the most crazily situated on

---

THE RUTA DE PEDRA EN SEC

A breathtaking walkers' week in Mallorca would see you traverse the entire mountainous northwest, from Cap de Formentor to Sant Elm. Old mule trails constitute the bulk of the (still incomplete) 150km GR221 walking route, aka the Ruta de Pedra en Sec (Dry Stone Route). The 'dry stone' refers to an age-old building method here and throughout the island. In the mountains you'll see paved ways, farming terraces, houses, walls and more built of stone without the aid of mortar.

The GR221 begins in Pollença (Map p134) near Can Diable and the Torrent d'en Marc stream, but you could start with a day's march from Cap de Formentor. A reasonably fit walker can accomplish the stretch from Pollença to Port d'Andratx in as little as four days, but with an extra few days you can include stops in some of the beautiful villages en route.

The first stretch is an easy walk of about four to five hours gradually curving southwest to the Monestir de Lluc (where you can stay overnight). You will ascend about 600m in the course of the day, before dropping back down a little to the monastery. The following day sees another fair climb to over 1000m, taking you past the Puig de Massanella (1365m), southwest to the Embassament de Cúber dam, past Puig de l'Ofre (1093m), which many like to bag, and down the Biniaraix ravine to Sóller to sleep. You might want to spend a couple of days here to explore the surrounding area.

To Deià you are looking at two to three hours' walking (from Sóller you could follow several trails, not just the GR221) and another two hours for Valldemossa. Those in a hurry could make it as far as Estellencs but, again, you might want to spread the walking over a couple of days. The last day would see you hiking from Estellencs to Sant Elm via La Trapa.

The walking requires a reasonable level of fitness but no special skills or equipment, other than good boots, sun protection, water bottle and so on. Good map-reading and compass skills are essential, as paths are not always well marked (one of the delays in completing the GR221 trail has been that 92% of the Serra de Tramuntana is private property and many rights of way are disputed). With various alternative routes, it is easy to become disoriented.

There are six refuges along the way (to book a sleeping berth, call ahead on ☎ 971 137700). There are also plenty of overnight options in the villages. For more information on the route, check out the Consell de Mallorca's web page, Pedra en Sec i Senderisme a Mallorca (www .conselldemallorca.net/mediambient/pedra).

the island. One step further and it would plunge into the seething Mediterranean far below. Climb to the top and fight off vertigo as you check the horizon for yachts (pirates stopped their business some while ago).

SLEEPING

Hotel Baronia (☎ 971 618146; www.hbaronia.com; Carrer de Baronia 16; s/d €52/65; ✷ ☷) A maze of a building with an olde-worlde feel, Baronia is built in the ruins of a Muslim-era fort (part of the central tower remains). It has modern rooms, some with excellent sea views, and a great cliffside swimming pool. For a little more (€88 for a double) you get half-board and a guaranteed room with a view.

Ca Madò Paula (☎ 971 148717; www.camadopaula .com; Carrer de la Constitució 11; d €105; ✷) At the seaward rim of the village core, this charming stone house is home to four guest rooms, decorated simply with a few antique touches and views out to sea.

Hotel Sa Coma (☎ 971 618034; www.hotelsacoma.com; Camí des Molí 3; s/d €76/118; ℙ ✷ ☐ ☷) Partway down the road to the village cove, this place boasts unbeatable sea views from the balconies of its rooms. The accommodation itself is basic enough but reasonably sized and spotless (however, running water is a trickle).

EATING

Pegasón y el Pajarito Enmascarado (☎ 971 148713; Carrer del Pont 2; meals €20-25; ✷ lunch & dinner Mon-Wed, Fri & Sat, dinner Sun) Hidden from the main road, this cosy cavernous spot offers simple pizzas, pasta and mains like *magret de pato agridulce y espárragos* (sweet-and-sour duck slices with asparagus) at little candlelit tables, some of them sitting uneasily outside.

Son Tomás (☎ 971 618149; Carrer de Baronia 17; meals €30-35; ✷ lunch & dinner Wed-Sun, lunch Mon) A classic, this place almost seems to lean over the main road at the southwest end of town. Crackling suckling pig (*lechona* in Spanish, *porcella* in Catalan) or a chunky *suquet* (a seafood and potato hotpot) await the ravenous.

ourpick **Ca Madò Paula** (☎ 971 148717; www.ca madopaula.com; Carrer de la Constitució 11; meals €40-45) The small dining room is what you might expect at your Mallorquin granny's place. The rear garden is perfect for romantic summer nights. And the menu of international Med grub with a strong Italian leaning is mouthwatering. The pasta options are fine as mains, but you might opt for the *solomillo de avestruz*

a la mostaza de Cassis (sirloin of ostrich in a Cassis mustard).

Port des Canonge

From Banyalbufar, the Ma10 road curls away from the coast. After 6km, a side road squiggles 5km down to this coastal settlement. Clear waters lap the short waterfront, which is backed by fishing boat shelters and pine tree roots hold together the fragile red earthen cliffs. You can walk along a trail through woods towards Banyalbufar, or follow the coast for about five minutes to reach another, hardly frequented, shingle beach. Back in the village, two restaurants cater for hungry lunchers.

Esporles & Inland Circuit

A few hundred metres beyond the Port des Canonge turn-off, the Ma1100 breaks off southward towards Esporles. After 1km you reach a road junction and **La Granja** (☎ 971 610032; www.lagranja.net; Carretera d'Esporles-Puigpunyent; adult/child €10/5; ✷ 10am-7pm Apr-Sep, 10am-6pm Oct-Mar), a magnificent *possessió* that has been turned into something of a kitsch Mallorcaland exhibit, with folks in traditional dress doing traditional things. The grand mansion is, however, well worth the visit, as are its extensive gardens. Some elements of the property date to the 10th century. You could spend hours exploring the period-furnished rooms, olive and wine presses, grand dining room, stables, workshops and some medieval instruments of torture in the cellars. In the gardens a stout old yew tree is estimated by some to be 2000 years old!

From La Granja, those with wheels could make a circuit inland. Follow the Ma1101 south, which plunges through thick woods and slithers down a series of hairpin bends to reach **Puigpunyent**. This typical inland town offers few sights but there are a couple of enticements to stop here. One is the luxury, rose-hued hilltop **Gran Hotel Son Net** (☎ 971 147000; www.steinhotels.com/sonnet; Carrer del Castell de Son Net; d €412-680; ℙ ✷ ☐ ☷), where pampering is the order of the day. This award-winning 17th-century mansion is home to a considerable modern art collection, a renowned restaurant in a grand stone-walled hall, and plush, spacious rooms and suites. A minimum four-night stay is required from May to October.

Rather more down to earth is the **Rose** (☎ 971 614360; Carrer de la Ciutat 3; meals €35; ✷ lunch

WESTERN MALLORCA

GETTING AWAY FROM IT ALL

Those who like detours are in for a treat in Esporles. As you enter the town from the south, a sign along a lane to the left beckons you 4.5km into the mountains to the spectacularly located **La Posada del Marqués** (☎ 971 611230; www.posada-marques.com; Es Verger; s/d €160/203; P ⚅ 🖳 🔊). From the dining terrace and pool, the view sweeps between mountains and across valleys to the distant plains. The 16th-century stone manor offers accommodation in a variety of rooms and suites, decorated with rustic antique good taste and equipped with plasma TVs and DVD players. The restaurant does fine Mediterranean meals (€40 to €45), including pasta that even recalcitrant Italians will have to admit is good.

& dinner Thu-Mon, dinner Wed). Sitting on the junction of the roads leading to Gran Hotel Son Net, Palma, Galilea and central Puigpunyent, this is a breezy roadside restaurant with an appetising mix of meat and fish mains, usually dressed up with a little imagination. Locals love it.

From Puigpunyent, make a quick dash for **Galilea**, a high mountain hamlet about four serpentine kilometres south. Climb to the town church square for views across the valleys and a drink in the bar next door, or head even higher up this straggling place for a greater sense of altitude. **Scott's Galilea** (☎ 971 870100; www.scottsgalilea.com; Sa Costa d'En Mandons 3; s/d €141/187; P ⚅ 🖳 🔊) has a series of luxury studio apartments here.

Back in Puigpunyent, follow the Ma1041 east and make for **Establiments**, a string of villages through which the narrow Ma1040 runs north from Palma to Esporles. Apart from a couple of restaurants with typical Mallorcan fare, such as **Es Porxo** (☎ 971 768643; Carretera d'Esporles; meals €35; ☺ Tue-Sat), there is little to hold you. George Sand and Frédéric Chopin spent time here before moving to Valldemossa in 1838.

Esporles, about 10km northwest, brings you back into the Tramuntana foothills. This shady, ochre village, set beside a generally dry stream, is an open invitation to aimless meandering. A weekly market sets up in Esporles on Saturdays. The plane tree–lined Ma1040 serves as the main road, on which reside a pompous church and five bar-eateries. Of these, **Es Brollador** (☎ 971 610539; Passeig del Rei 10; meals €30; ☺ Sun-Fri), with its tiled floors, high ceilings and rear courtyard, makes a pleasant stop for anything from a morning coffee to lunch or dinner. Esporles can be animated at night, as many folks from Palma have opted to live here and commute to the capital.

Getting There & Away

The Palma–Estellencs bus (€3.30, one hour 20 minutes, four to 11 times a day) passes through Esporles and Banyalbufar.

VALLDEMOSSA
pop 1710 / elev 425m

From the Esporles turn-off, the Ma10 climbs high on its inland thrust to Valldemossa. Known as the 'town of the four valleys' because, well, it is surrounded by four valleys, Valldemossa is a blend of tree-lined, cobbled lanes, stout stone houses and impressive villas. Yes, the place swarms with tourist bus contingents and, yes, the bulk of the restaurants and bars serve average fare at inflated prices. But there is a reason for all this. It may owe most of its fame to the fact that the ailing composer Frédéric Chopin and his domineering writer-lover George Sand spent their 'winter of discontent' here in 1838–39. But Valldemossa is quite simply one of the most beautiful towns on the island.

Information

The **tourist office** (☎ 971 612019; Avinguda de Palma s/n; ☺ 9am-1.30pm & 3-5pm Mon-Fri, 10am-1pm Sat) is on the main road running through town, about two minutes' walk from the main bus stop. Banks abound; one with an ATM is **Banca March** (Carrer de Chopin 13). If you have a problem (not with the ATM), contact the **Policía Local** (Carrer del Rei Sanxo 1).

Sights

Sand, Chopin and the kids stayed in the **Cartoixa de Valldemossa** (Cartuja; ☎ 971 612106; www .valldemossa.com; adult/student & child €7.50/3; ☺ 9.30am-6.30pm Mon-Sat, 10am-1pm Sun Jun-Sep, 9.30am-4.30pm Mon-Sat, 10am-1pm Sun Oct-May), a grand monastery that was turned into rental accommodation (mostly to summer holiday-makers from Palma) after its monks were expelled in 1835.

Their stay wasn't an entirely happy experience and Sand later wrote *Un Hiver à Mallorque* (Winter in Mallorca), which, if nothing else, made her perennially unpopular with Mallorquins (although you will find copies of her rant at souvenir stands). Chopin's poor health, constant rain and damp and the not always warm welcome from the villagers, who found these foreigners rather too eccentric, turned a planned idyllic escape from the pressure-cooker of social life in Paris into a nightmare. Years later Austrian Archduke Luis (Ludwig) Salvador, another eccentric, also moved into the area, living in the S'Estaca property (now owned by US actor Michael Douglas) and then buying other properties.

The monastery is a beautiful building surrounded by gorgeous gardens and enjoying fine views. Jaume II had a palace built on the site in 1310. After it was abandoned, the Carthusian order took over and converted it into a monastery, which, in 1399, was greatly expanded. A series of cells shows how the monks (bound by an oath of silence they could break only for half an hour per week in the library) lived. Following the rules of the order, just 13 monks lived in this cavernous place. Various items related to Sand's and Chopin's time here, including his pianos, are also displayed. Entry includes piano recitals (eight times daily in summer) and Jaume II's 14th-century **Palau del Rei Sanxo** (King Sancho's Palace), a muddle of medieval rooms jammed with furniture and hundreds of years of mementos, gathered around a modest cloister.

For an exquisite view taking in the terraces, orchards, gardens, cypresses, palms, the occasional ochre house through the mountains and the distant plains leading to Palma, walk down Carrer del Lledoners to **Miranda dels Lledoners**. You may notice that most houses bear a colourful tile depicting a nun and the words '*Santa Catalina Thomàs, pregau per nosaltres*' ('St Catherine Thomas, pray for us'). Yes, Valldemossa has its very own saint.

The **Casa Natal de Santa Catalina Thomàs** (Carrer de la Rectoria), her birthplace, is tucked off to the side of the parish church, the **Església de Sant Bartomeu** (Plaça de Santa Catalina Thomàs) at the east end of the town. It houses a simple chapel and a facsimile of Pope Pius VI's declaration beatifying the saint in 1792. Born in 1531, she is said to have had visions of (and was tempted by) the devil from a precocious age. Apparently this was a good thing and she wound up in the Església de Santa Magdalena in Palma (p79), where she died in 1574. Sor Tomasseta, as she is affectionately known, has been venerated by locals as a saint since she was canonised in 1930. Other curious sights around town include a characteristic **cross** (Carrer del Rei Sanxo), once used as a waymarker, and the nearby *lavadero,* where the local women used to do their laundry.

From the sublime we head for the ridiculous. **Costa Nord** (☎ 971 612425; www.costanord .com; Avinguda de Palma 6; adult/senior/child €7.75/6 /4.75; ☼ 9am-5pm Oct-Apr, 10am-6pm May-Sep) was dreamed up by part-time Mallorca resident and Hollywood celebrity Michael Douglas.

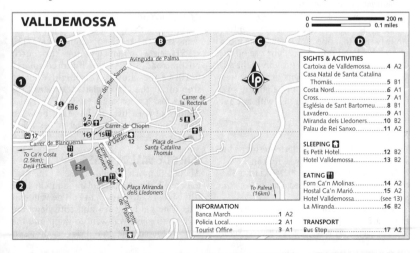

VALLDEMOSSA

SIGHTS & ACTIVITIES	
Cartoixa de Valldemossa.................4	A2
Casa Natal de Santa Catalina	
Thomàs.......................5	B1
Costa Nord.............................6	A1
Cross.............................7	A1
Església de Sant Bartomeu......8	B1
Lavadero.............................9	A1
Miranda dels Lledoners.........10	B2
Palau de Rei Sanxo.............11	A2

SLEEPING 🛏	
Es Petit Hotel.........................12	B2
Hotel Valldemossa...............13	B2

EATING 🍴	
Forn Ca'n Molinas...............14	A2
Hostal Ca'n Marió...............15	A2
Hotel Valldemossa...........(see 13)	
La Miranda.........................16	B2

TRANSPORT	
Bus Stop.............................17	A2

INFORMATION	
Banca March.............................1	A2
Policia Local.............................2	A1
Tourist Office.............................3	A1

His (what should we call it?) show, including a 'documentary' and a mock-up of the master's quarters of the good ship *Nixe*, is rather silly. The vessel belonged to Archduke Luis Salvador (Ludwig to his family), son of the 19th-century Habsburg ruler of Tuscany, Leopoldo II. Luis spent much of his life bobbing around on the Mediterranean in *Nixe* and writing treatises on an astounding range of subjects, including Mallorca, which he came to live on and love. Indeed, he liked it so much that he proceeded to buy as much of it as he could (see opposite).

Festivals & Events

Sunday is market day in Valldemossa. On 28 July, the town celebrates the **Festa de la Beata**, for Santa Catalina Thomàs, in which a six-year-old is chosen to represent the saintly child. In August the **Festival Chopin** (www.festival chopin.com; admission €15-25) sees a series of international classical performers putting on music of Chopin and other greats in the Cartoixa de Valldemossa (p114).

Sleeping

Es Petit Hotel (☎ 971 612479; www.espetithotel-valldem ossa.com; Carrer d'Uetam 1; s/d from €108/120; 🍴 🖳) Set in the heart of Valldemossa, this enticing stone town house is a great midrange option. The buffet breakfast bursts with variety and you get the feeling that everything is done with an eye to detail and comfort. For a little extra, upgrade to a superior room with balcony (single €144, double €160).

Hotel Valldemossa (☎ 971 612626; www.valldemos sahotel.com; Camí Antic de Palma s/n; s/d/ste €235/353/460; 🅿 🍴 🖳 🐾) Composed of two 19th-century stone houses that once belonged to the monastery, this hotel rests on a slight rise off the old Palma road about 300m south of the village, surrounded by olive and orange groves. Of the 12 immaculate rooms, eight are spacious suites. Each is decorated with antique furniture and artwork.

Eating

A sprinkling of cheerful eateries festoons the streets. Few are of culinary significance.

Forn Ca'n Molinas (☎ 971 612247; Carrer de Blan querna 15) For the local speciality of *coca de patata* and other pastries.

La Miranda (☎ 971 612296; Plaça Miranda dels Lledon ers 3; meals €20-25; 🕑 noon-5pm & 7pm-midnight May-Jun, 6pm-midnight Tue-Sun Jul-Oct, noon-5pm Nov-Apr) Settle

in for anything from salad with goats' cheese to a selection of cold meats and cheeses, along with less Spanish options such as risotto. On warm days, you might get lucky and snare a table outside with views down the valley. It's ideal for tapas.

Hostal Ca'n Mário (☎ 971 612122; Carrer de Uetam 8; meals €30; 🕑 daily) If you can grab a window table half the job is done, as you'll have views almost clear to Palma! Enjoy the simple local fare, with a brief selection of fish and meat dishes. It's a shame they don't rent rooms here any more.

Ca'n Costa (☎ 971 612363; meals €30; 🕑 Wed-Mon) About 2.5km out of Valldemossa on the road to Deià, this makes a great roadside rustic stop for *porcelleta al forn* (suckling pig). Take a seat inside the stone house or beneath the straggling pergola. The Valldemossa–Deià buses stop outside.

Hotel Valldemossa (☎ 971 612626; www.valldemo ssahotel.com; Camí Antic de Palma s/n; meals €80-120; 🆅) The hotel's restaurant is considered one of the island's best. It offers a tasting menu (€78) and a vegetarian menu (€59).

Getting There & Away

BUS

The 210 bus from Palma to Valldemossa (€1.50, 30 minutes) runs four to nine times a day. Three to four of these continue to Port Sóller (€2.10, one hour) via Deià. From May to October, various special services run on Saturdays only from resorts on the southeast coast to Valldemossa. Ask at tourist offices.

CAR & MOTORCYCLE

From Palma the quickest way to get to Valldemossa is the 16km run along the Ma1110 via **S'Esgleieta** (so named for the little church on the roadside). A few hundred metres north of the church, you might want to stop off at the **Lafiore glassworks** (www.lafiore .com; 🕑 9am-8pm Mon-Fri, 9am-6pm Sat). Otherwise, Valldemossa is just off the Ma10 between Banyalbufar and Deià (the latter lies 10km to the northeast).

PORT DE VALLDEMOSSA

About 1.5km from Valldemossa on the road to Banyalbufar (the Ma1113) drops 6km to Port de Valldemossa. The giddying sea and cliff views are enough to make you want to jump into the surf on the shingle and algae 'beach' when

MIRAMAR & SON MARROIG

Five kilometres north of Valldemossa is **Miramar** (☎ 971 616073; www.sonmarroig.com; admission €3; ◷ 9.30am-7pm Tue-Sun May-Oct, 10.30am-6pm Tue-Sun Nov-Mar), one of Habsburg Archduke Luis Salvador's former residences. The archduke built this home on the site of a 13th-century monastery, of which only a small part of the cloister remains. The evangelist and patron saint of Catalan literature, Ramon Llull, founded the monastery, where he wrote many of his works and trained brethren in Arabic and the Good Word for the task of proselytising among the infidel Muslims. Walk out the back and enjoy the clifftop views. Nearby, the curious could set off on walking trails either side of the highway to discover the Capella del Beat Ramon (Beatified Ramon's Chapel) and the Cova del Beat Ramon (his cave).

Two kilometres further is one of the archduke's other main residences, **Son Marroig** (☎ 971 639158; www.sonmarroig.com; admission €3; ◷ 9.30am-7.30pm Mon-Sat & holidays Apr-Sep, 9.30am-2pm & 3-5.30pm Mon-Sat & holidays Oct-Mar). It is a delightful, rambling mansion jammed with furniture and period items, including many of the archduke's books. The views are the stuff of dreams. Wander down to the **Foradada**, the strange hole-in-the-rock formation by the water. It's about a 3km walk, and a soothing swim in the lee of this odd formation is the reward.

Private events, banquets and the like are often organised in one or the other of these properties. Son Marroig also hosts the summer **Festival Internacional de Deià** (☎ 971 639178; www .soundpost.org; admission €20), a series of light classical concerts that take place on Thursday nights (starting at 8.30pm or 9pm) from June to September.

you arrive. Behind it cluster a dozen or so houses, one of which is home to the justifiably popular **Restaurant Es Port** (☎ 971 616194; meals €30-35; ◷ Feb-Nov). Try for a table upstairs on the terrace. Seafood is the mainstay, and you might like a hearty *cazuela de rape con mariscos y patatas* (monkfish casserole with seafood and potato in a delicious peanut broth). The *calamares al ajillo con patatas* (cuttlefish cooked in garlic with potato cubes and lightly spiced) is perfectly prepared.

DEIÀ & AROUND

Deià has long attracted foreigners of all sorts. Those who want to live here now pretty much have to be wealthy. A 16th-century house in the old town with four small bedrooms and sea glimpses? That will be €2 million please.

Deià

pop 650 / elev 222m

Deià is perhaps the most famous village on Mallorca. Its setting is idyllic, with a cluster of stone buildings pasted on to a conical hill and dripping into the surrounding valleys. The steep hillsides are terraced with vegetable gardens, citrus orchards, almond and olive trees and even the occasional vineyard. The mountain backdrop is the **Puig des Teix** (1062m). Deià was once a second home to an international colony of writers, actors and musicians, the best known of whom (to Anglo-Saxons at

any rate) was the English poet Robert Graves. Check out **Deià Mallorca** (www.deia.info) and **Enjoy Deià** (www.deia-mallorca.com).

SIGHTS & ACTIVITIES

The Ma10 passes though the town centre, where it becomes the main street and is lined with bars, restaurants and shops. Several pricey artists' workshops and galleries flog locally produced work.

The steep cobbled lanes, with their well-kept stone houses, overflowing bougainvillea and extraordinary views over the sea, farm terraces and mountains, make it easy to understand why artists and other bohemians have loved this place since Catalan artists 'discovered' it in the early 20th century. At the top of Es Puig, the hill at the heart of Deià, is the modest parish church, the **Església de Sant Joan Baptista** (whose **Museu Parroquial**, with a collection of local religious paraphernalia, you might find open on Saturdays).

Opposite is the town **cemetery**. Here lies 'Robert Graves, Poeta, 24-4-1895 – 7-12-1985 E.P.D' (*en paz descanse*, meaning 'may he rest in peace'). His second wife, Beryl Pritchard, who died in 2003, was buried at the other end of the graveyard. Famous for such works as *I, Claudius*, the novelised version of the Roman emperor's life, Graves also wrote reams of verse and a book on his adopted homeland, *Mallorca Observed* (1965).

Graves moved to Deià in 1929 and three years later had a house built here. The **Casa Robert Graves** (☎ 971 636185; www.fundaciorobert graves.com; Ca N'Alluny; admission €5; ☒ 10am-5pm), a five-minute walk out along the road to Sóller, is now a museum. Graves left hurriedly in 1936 at the outbreak of civil war, entrusting the house to the care of a local. The Spanish authorities allowed him to return 10 years later and he found everything as he had left it. 'If I had felt so inclined, I could have sat down and…started work straight away', he later commented. Graves' three-storey stone house, Ca N'Alluny (House in the Distance), is now a testament to his life and work, replete with mementos.

The important-sounding **Museu Arqueològic i Centre d'Investigació de Deià** (Deya Archaeology Museum & Research Centre; ☎ 971 639001; Es Clot; ☒ 5-7pm Sun, Tue & Thu), housed in an ancient mill, was opened in 1962 by US archaeologist William Waldren (1924–2003). It contains a modest but intriguing collection of ceramics and other finds that include skeletal remains of the *myotragus balearicus*, a long-extinct antelope-type animal that was indigenous to Mallorca.

A 3km drive away (head out of town for Sóller), or a slightly shorter walk, from the town is **Cala de Deià**, one of the most bewitching of the Serra de Tramuntana's coastal inlets. A proper bay backed by a handful of houses, the shingle beach gives onto crystal-clear water that just begs to be swum in. Competition for a parking spot (€5 for the day) can be intense. The beach is backed by a simple bar-eatery, **Can Lluc** (meals €15-20; ☒ lunch May-Oct), while on a rocky platform above the water, you can sit down for fresh fish at **Ca's Patró March** (meals €30; ☒ 12.30-8pm Thu-Tue May, Jun, Sep & Oct, 12.30-10pm Thu-Tue Jul & Aug). Three daily buses run from Deià (15-minute trip) from May to October.

Some fine walks crisscross the area, such as the gentle **Deià Coastal Path** to the pleasant hamlet of Lluc Alcari (opposite).

SLEEPING

Fonda Villa Verde (☎ 971 639037; Carrer de Ramon Llull 19; s/d from €46/62) This charming *pensión* in the heart of the hilly village offers homey rooms and splendid views from the sunny terrace. A handful of doubles with their own terrace and superlative views cost €80.

Hostal Miramar (☎ 971 639084; www.pensionmiramar .com; Carrer de Can Oliver s/n; d €84) Hidden in what could almost be described as the jungle above

the main road, and with views across to Deià's hillside church and beyond to the sun-kissed sea, this 19th-century stone house with gardens is a shady retreat. Various artists have chosen to stay in the nine rooms down the years.

S'Hotel des Puig (☎ 971 639409; www.hoteldespuig .com; Carrer des Puig 4; s/d €85/127; ☒ late Jan-late Nov; ☒ ☐ ☒ ☒) The only other hotel in the centre, this is a gem. Rooms ooze a muted modern taste within the ancient stone walls of the house. And out the back are secrets impossible to divine from the street, like the cool pool and terrace.

Hotel Es Molí (☎ 971 639000; www.esmoli.com; Carretera de Valldemossa; s/d €145/238; ☒ ☒) Looking across to the village from a commanding position on the Ma10, this hotel is on the site of a one-time mill, whose water source now feeds the pool and keeps the gardens fresh. The 85 rooms are on the uniform side, but if you can snag one with a balcony and views, you can ignore the dated furniture. The hotel runs the Ca'n Quet (☎ 971 639196) restaurant about 200m up the road on Carretera Valldemossa-Deià. Meals cost €40 to €45; it's open for lunch and dinner Tuesday to Sunday.

La Residencia (☎ 971 639011; www.hotellaresidencia .com; Son Canals s/n; s/d from €316/519; ☒ ☒ ☐ ☒) 'The Res' to its habitués, this is the place to rub shoulders with the rich and famous. A short stroll from the village centre, this former 16th-century manor house is a luxurious resort hotel set in 12 hectares of manicured lawns and gardens. A minimum stay of five nights is required from mid-May to the end of October. You can continue to splash out in the hotel's renowned restaurant, El Olivo (meals €90 to €120).

EATING

The diverse collection of eateries along the main street includes a couple of affordable pizzerias and several expensive restaurants that claim to specialise in local cuisine.

Patricia's Bar (☎ 971 637199; Carrer de Felip Bauza s/n; meals €12-18; ☒ 11am-6pm Thu-Tue) Pull up a pew on the rear terrace and gaze over the village and the big blue. Shake the reverie for a minute to order a baguette, quiche or stuffed potato – probably the cheapest light meal in town and a change from the local fare.

El Barrigón de Xelini (☎ 971 639139; Avinguda del Arxiduc Lluís Salvador 19; meals €20; ☒ 12.30pm-12.30am Tue-Sun) You never quite know what to expect here, but tapas is at the core of things. They have a penchant for mains of lamb too. In the evenings you may find that a bit of live jazz or blues helps digestion further.

Sa Dorada (☎ 971 639509; Avinguda del Arxiduc Lluís Salvador 24; meals €30; ☽ dinner Jun-Sep, lunch & dinner Oct-May) Something of an old-style classic Mallorcan eatery, where the main star is grilled fish of the day. Other Spanish favourites include *entrecot Roquefort*.

Sebastian (☎ 971 639417; meals €45-50; ☽ dinner Thu-Tue, Mar-late Nov) Deià could not miss out on some gourmet, refined fusion options. In restrained fashion, Sebastian meets the requirements, with subtle dishes like *suprema de rodaballo con risotto de espárragos blancos y salsa de trufa* (turbot supreme with white asparagus risotto and truffle sauce).

Es Racó d'es Teix (☎ 971 639501; Carrer de San Vinya Vella 6; meals €70-90; ☽ Wed-Mon, Mar–mid-Nov) Something of a legend on the island, Joseph Sauerschell cooks his way to the hearts of the Michelin folks, so he must be doing something right. He tends to concentrate on elaborate but hearty meat dishes – anything from deer in Armagnac sauce to a delicious suckling pig.

GETTING THERE & AWAY

Deià is 15 minutes up the winding road from Valldemossa on the 210 bus route between Palma (€2.35, 45 to 60 minutes) and Port de Sóller (€1.25, 30 to 40 minutes).

Lluc Alcari

Three kilometres northeast of Deià, this is a magical hamlet encrusted into the rocky mountain-side.

ourpick Hotel Costa d'Or (☎ 971 639025; www.hopo sa.es; s/d without sea views up to €103/162, d with sea views

up to €235; P ✗ ⬛ ⬛ ; ☽ Mar-Oct) The town is largely occupied by this stylish hotel. The spacious rooms have a designer whiff about them (tones of grey in the tiles and immense bathrooms contrast with the white paint and timber shutters), but the position's the thing. Olive terraces and clusters of palms serve as partial camouflage, but seated by the terrace pool, the only thing separating you from the sunset is the bracing sea air. A 15-minute walk down through a pine forest takes you down to a pebbly beach (appreciated by nudists) with crystal-clear water. Robert Graves wrote many of his love poems here.

SÓLLER
pop 9160 / elev 40m

As though cupped in celestial hands, the ochre town of Sóller lies in a valley surrounded by the grey-green hills of the Serra de Tramuntana. Here the mountainous terrain of the northwest coast gives way to a sloping plain. The Arabs saw the potential of the valley, known as the Vall d'Or (Golden Valley), and accounts of orange and lemon groves, watered from sources in the hills, date to the 13th century.

To the north lie open skies and a rattling old tram ride downhill to Port de Sóller and the glittering Mediterranean. Only a few kilometres east lie pretty villages (like Biniaraix and Fornalutx) scattered about this citrus-growing region. This is great territory for soothing country walks or, for the hardier, a good starting point for more challenging mountain trails.

It might seem hard to believe now, but this was once the jumping-off point for

---

THE SEA VIEW

Driving, walking, cycling…whichever way you choose to explore the dramatic coast of the Serra de Tramuntana you are in for some spectacular views. But there's a different approach. Take a sailing route from Port d'Andratx in the southwest, around past Sant Elm and Illa Sa Dragonera and northeast to Port de Sóller, a good, quiet port to overnight in. Places to stop during the day for a dip (they are no good for dropping anchor overnight) are Port des Canonge, Cala de Deià and Lluc Alcari. The inlets of Estellencs and Valldemossa are too shallow for most yachts. The next stage, tracking to Cap de Formentor and rounding it to find shelter in the Badia de Pollença (Map p134), takes longer under equal conditions. Good daytime stops are Cala Tuent, Sa Calobra, Cala Sant Vicenç and Cala Figuera. The total trip is around 60 nautical miles.

One of the main factors to consider is weather. Wind is more of a rule than an exception, which means you can get your sails out. However, depending on conditions, it can also be uncomfortable. In winter it is often dangerous to sail along this coastline. It is possible to charter yachts in Port d'Andratx at **Rieke Group** (www.yachting-andratx.com).

WESTERN MALLORCA

Mallorquin migrants in search of a better life elsewhere. They headed from the port mostly to France and the Americas, especially Puerto Rico.

Not everyone was doing it tough though. Local landowners grew rich in the 19th century on the back of the citrus trade with France. Until the Palma railway was completed in 1912, overland travel had been difficult. With road communications so poor, locals moved about by sea.

Sóller's train station is the terminus for the Palma–Sóller railway (p99), one of Mallorca's most popular and scenic excursions.

The main square, Plaça de la Constitució, is 100m downhill from the train station. It's surrounded by bars and restaurants, and is home to the *ajuntament* (town hall). The tram down to Port de Sóller rumbles through the square.

Simply wandering Sóller's peaceful, often cobbled, streets is a pleasure. In any direction, within a few minutes you exchange tight, winding lanes for country roads boarded by stone walls, behind which flourish orange and lemon groves.

Information

Internet Sin Café (☎ 971 631699; Carrer de Sa Lluna 30; per hr €2.60; ☼ 10am-3pm & 5-11pm Mon-Sat, 5-11pm Sun) This is the local internet stop.

Llibreria Calabruix (☎ 971 632641; Carrer de Sa Lluna 7) A good bookshop for local material plus hiking guides.

Tourist office (☎ 971 638068; Plaça d'Espanya; ☼ 9.45am-1.30pm & 2.45-5pm Mon-Fri, 9.15am-1pm Sat) This is in a one-time postal wagon from the Sóller railway.

The main Sóller website is www.sollernet.com. Also worth looking at is www.viu-soller.com.

Sights

You can start your sightseeing without even leaving the train station. The town has set up a couple of intriguing art exhibitions, the **Sala Picasso** and **Sala Miró** (Plaça d'Espanya 6; admission free; ☼ 10am-6.30pm) with, respectively, a ceramics collection and a couple of series of prints.

One of the architect Antoni Gaudí's disciples, Joan Rubió, got some big commissions in Sóller. The town didn't want to miss the wave of modernity and so Rubió set to work in 1904

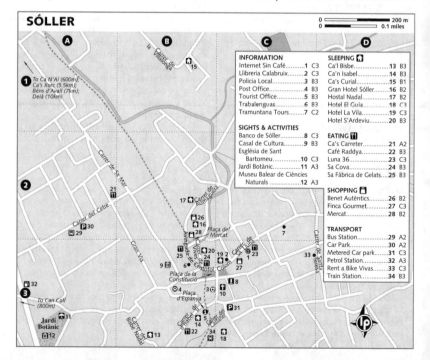

SÓLLER

on the renovation of the 16th-century **Església de Sant Bartomeu** (Plaça de la Constitució). The largely baroque church (built 1688–1723) preserved elements of its earlier Gothic interior, but Rubió gave it an unusual Modernìsta façade. Finding the church open seems to be a matter of divine will.

Across the lane from the church, Rubió set to work on another temple, this time to Mammon. Now the Santander Central Hispano, the one-time **Banco de Sóller** (Placa de la Constitucio s/n) is a still more daring effort, with two massive, circular galleries sticking out into the square. The windows are draped in lacy wrought-iron grills typical of the Modernìstas.

The **Casal de Cultura** (☎ 971 631465; Carrer de Sa Mar 13; admission €2; ☼ 11am-1pm & 4-7pm Mon-Fri, 11am-1pm Sat) museum is housed in an 18th-century house, Ca'n Mo, and contains a curious collection of old-time furniture, farm implements, a few works of art and all sorts of household objects from down the ages.

A wander down to the central **Mercat** (Market; Plaça del Mercat; ☎ 8am-1pm Mon-Sat) is interesting just to see locals going about their shopping business. Saturday is the best day.

A pleasant stroll (about 600m) west from the town centre brings you to the main road to Deià and the entrance to the peaceful **Jardí Botànic** (☎ 971 634014; www.jardibotanicdesoller.org; adult/child under 11yr €5/free; ☼ 10am-6pm Tue-Sat, 10am-2pm Sun), with collections of flowers and other plants native to the Balearic islands, as well as samples from other Mediterranean areas.

At one end of the gardens is the **Museu Balear de Ciències Naturals** (☎ 971 634064; www.museuciencies naturals.org), housed in a once private mansion surrounded by lemon groves.

Most visitors take a ride on one of Sóller's open-sided **trams**, which shuttle 2km down to Port de Sóller on the coast (€3). They depart from the train station every 30 minutes between 7am and 9pm.

Courses
Trabalenguas (☎ 971 635079; www.trabalenguas.net; Avinguda de Cristòfol Colom 3) offers Spanish courses at €165 for a week (20 hours).

Tours
Tramuntana Tours (☎ 971 632423; www.tramuntana tours.com; Carrer de Sa Lluna 72) organises walking and mountain bike tours in the Serra de Tramuntana.

Festivals & Events
Around the second weekend of May, Sóller is invaded by a motley crew of Muslim pirates. This conflict (involving about 1200 towns-folk) between *pagesos* (town and country folk) and Moros (Moors), known as **Es Firó**, is full of good-humoured drama and not a little drinking. It re-enacts an assault on the town that was repulsed on 11 May 1561. The centrepiece of this event is remembered as **Ses Valentes Dones** (Valiant Women). Two sisters, instead of cowering as corsairs barged into their house, took a heavy bar and proceeded to kill several of the pirates, thus contributing to the town's final victory.

Sleeping
You will find a variety of attractive hotels in historic buildings in and around Sóller.

BUDGET
Hostal Nadal (☎ 971 631180; Carrer de Romaguera 27; s/d €23/36) It may be simple, but it's home, and about as cheap as it gets on the island. Rooms are basic but clean and there's a courtyard out the back to flop in after a day's hiking. It has even cheaper rooms without their own shower.

Hotel El Guía (☎ 971 630227; www.sollernet.com /elguia; Carrer del Castañer 2; s/d €51/79) Handily located beside the train station, this is a charming place to meet fellow walkers. Set in an 1880s house with an old well in the courtyard, it offers bright rooms featuring timber trims and modern bathrooms. The restaurant here does decent island cooking too.

MIDRANGE
Hotel La Vila (☎ 971 634641; www.lavilahotel.com; Plaça de la Constitució 14; s/d €72/99; ✖ ☐) Bang on the central square, this hotel offers a choice of four rooms looking over the square towards the mountains or another four with views of the garden in the rear. They are simple and clean, with polished tile floors, flat-screen TVs and elegant bathrooms.

Ca'l Bisbe (☎ 971 631228; www.hotelcalbisbe.com; Carrer del Bisbe Nadal 10; s/d €85/129; ℗ ✖ ☐ ☒) The bishop who once lived here would no doubt appreciate the addition of the pool in this nicely restored bishop's residence. Perhaps he would have snorted at the little gym. Some grand details (such as the stone arches and fireplaces) have remained intact and most of the 25 rooms have their own balcony.

Hotel S'Ardeviu (☎ 971 638326; www.sollernet .com/sardeviu; Carrer de Vives 14; s/d €95/120; ⌣ Feb-Nov; ✹) Hidden down a lane in the centuries-old heart of the town, the seven rooms spread out over this cool stone house vary, some with bare stonework and others whitewashed. Most have exposed timber beams. Wander into the pretty garden, where breakfast is served.

Ca'n Isabel (☎ 971 638097; www.canisabel.com; Carrer de d'Isabel II 13; s/d €123/150; ✹ 💻) With just four rooms, this 19th-century house is a romantically decorated hideaway, with a garden out the back. The best (and dearest) of the fairly simple rooms comes with its own delightful terrace.

ourpick Can Coll (☎ 971 633244; Camí de Can Coll 1; www.cancoll.com; s/d €145/180; P ✹ ♨) Two kilometres west out of the town centre on a high point affording great views, this hotel is set in lemon groves and is something of a chillout zone. The nine spacious rooms are colour-themed by fruit (apple, peach, apricot etc) and decorated with a charming simplicity. Each has its own character. You can munch on the copious breakfast when and where you want.

Ca's Curial (☎ 971 633332; Carrer de La Villalonga 23; d €152-208; P ✹ ♨) Barely out of the centre, this idyllically set hotel offers eight rooms, including three suites. Loll around in the grounds to the scent of the oranges or have a dip in the pool. It's hard to leave this sturdy stone *finca* to go visit anything!

Ca N'Ai (☎ 971 632494; www.canai.com; Camí de Son Sales 50; s/d €150/237; P ✹ ♨) An impossibly romantic Mallorca *possessió* ensconced among generous orange groves (more than 5000 trees, they tell us), this place is a fragment of heaven on earth. You could come here just to dine. Take an outdoor table and enjoy – the Michelin folks did! And watch out for the winter specials.

TOP END

Gran Hotel Sóller (☎ 971 638686; www.granhotel soller.com; Carrer de Romaguera 18; s/d from €192/321; P ✹ 💻 ♨) As the name suggests, this is the big one: a five-star luxury getaway set in a late-19th-century mansion. The rooms are nice without being spectacular. What really makes the place is all the extras, from the gourmet restaurant to the neat ideas they sometimes have, like Chinese massages on the roof.

Eating

Sa Fàbrica de Gelats (Plaça des Mercat) This local ice-cream maker sells lickable treats all over the island. What better place to try one than on home ground? Tangy local oranges go into the orange-flavoured ice cream, a symbol of the town.

Sa Cova (☎ 971 633222; Plaça de la Constitució; meals €25; ⌣ daily) Of the places on the main square, this is the best. Head inside the labyrinthine dining rooms for air-conditioned comfort in a rustic setting or sit on the crowded terrace to enjoy the night air and the almost constant clatter of passing scooters. The paellas and other rice dishes (€11 to €14) are generous.

Ca's Carreter (☎ 971 635133; Carrer del Cetre 9; meals €25-30; ⌣ lunch & dinner Tue-Sat, lunch Sun) Set in a leafy, corner cart workshop (founded in 1914), this is a cool and welcoming spot for modest local cooking, with fresh local fish, a couple of meat options and such specials as *calabacines rellenos de espinacas y pescado* (spinach- and fish-stuffed courgettes).

Luna 36 (☎ 971 634739; Carrer de Sa Lluna 36; meals €25-30; ⌣ Mon-Sat) Mediterranean warmth meets urban chill in this tempting eatery. Ceiling fans slowly push the air around as you sit at your tiny round timber table, chatting over coffee. Or you might prefer the sunny courtyard for a plate of *pulpo al grill con tagliatelle de calamar* (grilled octopus with tagliatelle done with squid).

Café Raddya (☎ 971 630391; Carrer de d'Isabel II 23; meals €30; ⌣ lunch & dinner Tue-Thu & Sat, dinner Fri & Sun; ✗) A leafy courtyard at the rear is the high point of this rambling house converted into a soothing restaurant. German-run, it works with a cool efficiency, bringing such classic Mediterranean dishes to your table as *cordero a la plancha con verduras y patatas* (grilled lamb with vegetables and potatoes).

Ca's Xorc (☎ 971 638280; www.casxorc.com; Carretera Sóller-Deià Km56.1; meals €45-60; ⌣ Apr-Oct; ✗) Excellent island cooking with a restrained creative touch and generally brief if changing menus accompanies the fine views back over the Sóller valley. Fish of the day and goat cheese salad should be rounded off with a creamy *pannacotta*. This classic Mallorcan farmhouse-turned-hotel (12 suites) and restaurant is worth the 5km drive out of Sóller (or about a one-hour walk if you feel so inclined).

ourpick Béns d'Avall (☎ 971 632381; www.bens daval.com; Urbanització Costa Deià, Carretera Sóller-Deià; meals €70-90; ⌣ Wed-Sun; ✗) Benet Vicens is one of the island's foremost chefs. From Sóller, head 5km along the road to Deià. At about Km57, a sign points you 2km down a winding road to the restaurant, with its hopelessly romantic terrace overlooking the sea and surrounded by greenery. Avoid complex decisions and opt for the tasting menu (€78), with 10 scintillating courses, from prawn carpaccio in a champagne marinade to a foie gras and peach combo. The wine list is superlative, the service attentive and the sunset to die for.

Shopping
New shoes, old cheese, fine wine? You can find this and more on Sóller's modest approximation of Oxford St, Carrer de Sa Lluna.

Finca Gourmet (☎ 971 630253; www.fincagourmet .com; Carrer de Sa Lluna 16) This Mallorcan mansion has been converted into a den of sin for the palate, with all sorts of local food and wine products. The building itself invites a browse.

Benet Autèntics (☎ 971 638127; Carrer de Romaguera 20) Not content to feed folks his creative dishes in the restaurant he runs outside town, Benet Vicens also tempts us with delirious sweets and other *amuse-gueules*.

Getting There & Away
BUS
Less romantic but a little faster than the train to and from Palma is the bus. The 211 shoots up the Ma11 road to Sóller (€2.20, 30 minutes) 11 times a week (six to eight runs on weekends), and takes another five minutes to get down to Port Sóller. The 210 takes the long way to/from Palma (€3.30) via Deià and Valldemossa (€1.75, 40 to 50 minutes). Two daily buses run between Ca'n Picafort (on the east coast) and Port de Sóller from May to October (€9.10, 1¾ hours). A local service connects Sóller with Fornalutx (€1.10, 15 minutes) via Biniaraix. It runs four times a day Monday to Friday and twice on Saturdays.

CAR & MOTORCYCLE
Roads converge on Sóller from the south (the Ma11 from Palma via Bunyola and the tunnel), from the southwest (the Ma10 along the Serra de Tramuntana from Valldemossa) and from the northeast (the Ma10 from Pollença). When coming from Palma, you have the option of taking the tunnel (€4.25 toll per car and €1.70 per motorbike) or adding 7km to the trip and taking the switchbacks up to

the pass – with some great views back down towards Palma on the way.

TAXI
Taxis can be found near the train station. The fare to Palma is about €35, or €20 to €22 to Deià. The trip to Fornalutx is €7 to €10.

TRAIN
The Palma–Sóller train journey is a highlight. See p99.

Getting Around
Hire bicycles at **Rent a Bike Vivas** (☎ 971 630234, 654 110851; www.rentabikevivas.com; Carrer de Santa Teresa 20; racing bike per day €13). It has mountain bikes too. Tramuntana Tours (p121) also rents out mountain bikes.

WALKING TO FORNALUTX & THE BINIARAIX VALLEY
An easy wander for just about anyone and well worth the minimal effort is the 6.5km circuit from Sóller to Fornalutx and back via Biniaraix.

Start at Es Pont de Can Rave, a bridge in the northeast of Sóller about 100m east of the football pitch. This places you on the GR221 walking trail. Head north 100m along Carrer de ses Moncades and right along Camí de S'Ermita. This road rises gently; to the right you have lovely views across citrus groves, fig and carob stands to Sóller and the mountains. After 10 minutes, follow the GR221 signs for **Binibassi**, which you will hit within 15 minutes of starting the walk. Do not follow the GR221 signs for Biniaraix. Rather, on entering Binibassi, turn left up the steps and right through the gate marked Coto Privado de Caza. After the gate, wind up to the left (don't follow the Camino Particular). After a five-minute climb, follow the wooden signpost with an arrow pointing right along a dirt trail. Within another five minutes you will reach a Y-junction. Keep heading straight on this now smooth trail past almond terraces and the municipal cemetery. Almost immediately after, **Fornalutx** appears before you. The total walk from Sóller to here is around 30 to 40 minutes.

After lolling around in Fornalutx, walk along the main road past the Restaurant Bellavista. About 200m on, a sign on the left saying Sóller a Peu (Sóller on Foot), leads you down a shortcut that saves the trouble

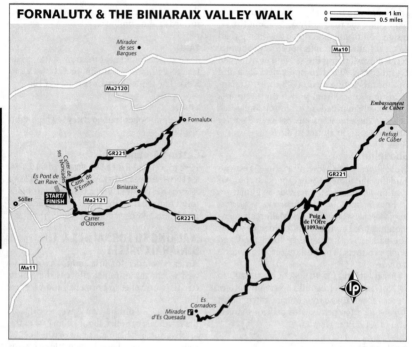

FORNALUTX & THE BINIARAIX VALLEY WALK

WALK FACTS

Start/finish Es Pont de Can Rave, Sóller
Distance/duration (basic Sóller–Fornalutx–
Biniaraix loop): 6.5km; around 1½ hours
Distance/duration (Sóller–Embassament
de Cúber–Sóller loop): around 22km; around
six hours

of following a series of curves in the Ma2121
road (which you are later obliged to follow).
About 10 minutes out of Fornalutx, veer left
at the fork. This road swings west past country
houses and fragrant citrus groves, with Sóller
opening up in the background. Within 20
minutes you enter Plaça de Sa Concepció in
Biniaraix. If you find it open, sit down for a
drink at the **Bar Bodega** (☻ Tue-Sun) on the leafy
square. The walk back to Sóller (1.4km, 15 to
20 minutes) is signposted west off the square.
You'll enter Sóller at Carrer d'Ozones. If you
want to reach the point you departed from,
head right down Carrer de ses Rentadores,
a tight lane that passes a *lavadero* (one-time
outdoor public laundry) and meanders past

houses and gardens to Carrer de ses Fontanelles and on to the bridge.

Hikers with more grit will want to start
early and consider several extensions. One
classic sees you heading southeast from Biniaraix along the GR221 (signposted). Within
a few minutes you cross the usually dry Torrent de Biniaraix and start on a stone donkey trail of steps (1932 of 'em!) that rises
inexorably towards the mountain walls to
the south. The views all around are exquisite
and you are surrounded by terraces (mostly
olives, pines and almonds) as you ascend.
After about 20 minutes you find yourself in
a gorge and 10 minutes later will be walking
alongside a stream bubbling with cool water.
Follow this for 10 minutes or so. An hour
(and some taxing switchbacks on the stone
step trail) out of Biniaraix, you get your first
breathtaking views over the Biniaraix valley, Sóller and the sea. The switchbacks seem
endless, but after another 10 to 15 minutes'
steady climbing, the trail eases off. You will
reach a gate warning of the presence of bulls
(don't be put off!). After a second gate you'll
pass the Ofre farm, scramble a little uphill

and wind up on a track with good tree cover. At the second gate a side trail leads to the **Mirador d'Es Quesada** and **Es Cornadors**, which offer wonderful views (count on two hours there and back). In all, from the first gate to the **Coll de l'Ofre** pass (875m) will take about 20 minutes. The pass is announced by a cross and here you get your last glimpse of the sea to the north. To the northeast you can see the **Embassament de Cúber** dam and **Puig Major** peak, topped by the telltale military radar station. To the south, an ill-defined trail heads for the popular **Puig de l'Ofre** (1093m), about an hour's climb for those who want the extra diversion. About 45 to 60 minutes' gentle walking northeast along the usually dry Torrent de Binimorat and lake takes you to the Ma10 road. If you plan to turn back to Sóller, there is no need to go this far – just reaching the lake is reward enough. All in all, the moderately fit should reckon on about six hours (with a little rest time built in) for the entire walk (not including the Es Cornadors detour or Ofre ascent).

PORT DE SÓLLER

In mid-2007, millions of euros of restoration work in the port left it all looking spanking new. The architecture reflects French and even Puerto Rican influences, as these were the two main destination countries of many Mallorcan emigrants, some of whom returned with cash and imported tastes.

Information

The **tourist office** (☎ 971 633042; Carrer del Canonge Oliver 10; ☷ 9.15am-1pm & 2.45-5pm Mon-Fri) is right in the heart of the town, near the bus terminus. Several banks line Passeig En Través.

Sights & Activities

The bay is shaped something like a jellyfish and makes for pleasant promenading, especially around the northern end, where the heart of the original town is gathered together. The **Museu de la Mar** (☎ 971 630200; Carrer de Santa Caterina d'Alexandria; admission €3; ☷ 10am-2pm & 5-8pm Tue-Sat, 10am-2pm Sun Apr-Oct, 10am-1.30pm & 3-6pm Tue-Sat, 10am-2am Nov-Mar) tells the maritime history of Sóller. It is housed in a 13th-century chapel, the **Oratori de Santa Caterina d'Alexandria**, standing imperiously on a high point overlooking the sea (stand four square to the wind and watch the Med crash against the impervious cliffs). Inside the museum is a display of pho-

tos, documents, models of boats and more. This is followed by an imaginative audiovisual display. Lanes wind down to the port from the museum in a historic (and much renovated) area known as Santa Caterina.

By the fishing port, the tiny 17th-century **Oratori de Sant Ramon de Penyafort** was a chapel and is now used for occasional exhibitions.

The beaches are OK, although hardly the island's best. The pick of the crop is **Platja d'en Repic**. It is backed by a pleasant, pedestrianised and restaurant-lined esplanade.

If you're into water sports, visit the **Escola d'Esports Nàutics Port de Sóller** (☎ 609 354132; www .nauticsoller.com; Platja des Port), where you can hire windsurfing gear (€10 per hr), Lasers (€25 per hr), go water-skiing and more. Dive with **Octopus Dive Centre** (☎ 971 633133; www.octopus-mal lorca.com; Carrer del Canonge Oliver 13; ☷ Easter-Oct), a five-star English-run PADI centre with good equipment. It does boat dives at about 30 sites along the Serra de Tramuntana coast. By Mediterranean standards, there is reasonable fish life, including barracuda, rays and even dolphins.

Tour boats (www.barcosazules.com; adult €11-20, child 6-12yr €5-10, under 6yr free) do trips to Sa Calobra (up to three to four times daily) and Cala Tuent (once a day from Easter to June and in September). Get tickets at a booth on the dock.

Sleeping

More than a dozen hotels offer shelter in Port de Sóller.

Refugi La Muleta (☎ 971 173700; Camí del Far; dm/d €10.40/37.70, bed linen €3.70) Thirty dorm beds await walkers in this simple refuge (a former telegraph station) by the lighthouse, about 2km west of Port de Sóller. You must call ahead (business hours only) to be sure of a spot.

Hostal Brisas (☎ 971 631352; Camí del Far 15; d €55; ☐) Wake up to watch the rising sun flood across the bay into your grandstand room. Not bad for a straightforward *hostal*, with simple, whitewashed rooms, the best with a balcony. From here it's a short wander to Platja d'en Repic.

Hotel Es Port (☎ 971 631650; www.hotelesport.com; Carrer d'Antoni Montis 10; s/d €75/124; ☐ ☒ ☐) A 17th-century fortified mansion is at the core of this large hotel. Part of the pleasure is to wander outside the stone keep and explore the gardens or hang about on the terraces. Or nurse a cocktail by the pool. The bad news: the bulk of the rooms, all with balcony and

WESTERN MALLORCA

PORT DE SÓLLER

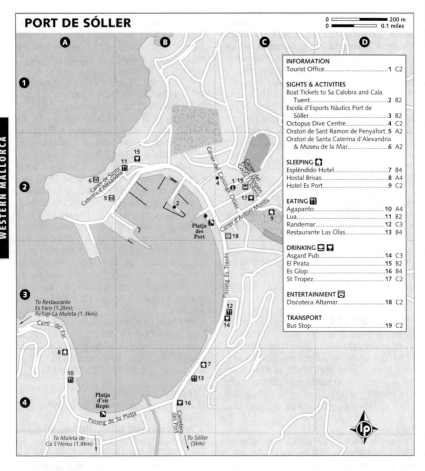

0 — 200 m
0 — 0.1 miles

roomy enough, are in a modern annexe. These doubles (€100) are cheaper.

ourpick Muleta de Ca S'Hereu (☎ 971 186018; www.muletadecashereu.com; Camp de Sa Mar s/n; s/d €96.50/148; P ⚅ ⚃) Your car will hate you for the 1.8km track of switchbacks, but this lordly country mansion, dating to 1672, will enchant you. Eight sprawling rooms and a handful of apartments, some with distant sea glimpses from this mountainside position, are filled with charm and antiques. Wander the olive groves, relax on the terraces or summon the courage to drive down to the beach. You may be woken by donkey braying.

Espléndido Hotel (☎ 971 631850; www.esplendido hotel.com; Passeig Es Través 5; s/d from €105/130; ⚅ ▢) Run by the snappy Hotel Portixol (p88) folks

in Palma, this marvellous 1954 carcass has been transformed into cutting-edge waterfront luxury digs. The hotel's best rooms have terraces that open up straight to the sea. The better rooms can go for up to €270. The hotel also has a spa and gym.

Eating

The Port de Sóller waterfront is lined with eateries, including a handful of pizza and Chinese joints and an Indian.

Randemar (☎ 971 634578; Passeig Es Través 16; meals €30; ⚘ Tue-Sun) You could almost feel like you're turning up to a Great Gatsby–style party in this pseudo-waterfront mansion (which clearly impressed Michelin). The house is divided into several dining areas over a couple of floors, or you could opt for the terrace. There is a fair range of fish and meat dishes, along with pizza, and the apple crumble is a great way to finish up.

Lua (☎ 971 634745; Carrer de Santa Caterina d'Alexandria 1; meals €35; ☼ Tue-Sun ⊠ ⓥ) As narrow as some Amsterdam residences, this cheerful yellow eatery has a big heart. Grab one of the four terrace tables or try for one with a window inside (over a couple of floors) and dig in to a *brocheta de carne y verduras* (two skewers of grilled meat and vegies). For vegetarians, the *parrillada de verduras salteadas en wok* (wok-sauteed vegetables) is perfect. Or ask about the grilled fish of the day.

Restaurante Las Olas (☎ 971 632515; Passeig Es Través s/n; meals €35; ☼ Wed-Mon, Mar-Oct) A long-established classic for fresh fish, this is an old-style, no-nonsense restaurant and is perfect for a midday paella. Another house speciality is *lluvina en fonoll* (sea bass in fennel). Grab a window seat for bay views.

Agapanto (☎ 971 633860; Camí del Far 2; meals €35; ☼ Tue-Sun; ⊠) Take up a spot right at the water's edge or in the high-ceilinged dining room, with its straight-backed timber chairs, chessboard tiled floor and crisp, airy feel. Choice is abundant, from chicken through to seafood, and is by no means strictly local. What about a *brocheta de pescado con salsa de vino y Pernod y arroz basmati* (a fish skewer in a wine and Pernod sauce served with basmati rice)?

Restaurante Es Faro (☎ 971 633752; Carrer del Cap Gros de Moleta; meals €50; ☼ daily) Rule 1: book. The views from most tables (inside or out) from this vantage point take in the entire port and surrounding mountains; reason enough for making the 2km drive or walk up.

Drinking

By day the café-bar-restaurant terraces by the port and along Passeig de Sa Platja are all pleasant for some sit-and-tipple.

For an Irish night out (with Guinness), pop along to the **Asgard Pub** (Passeig Es Través 15; ☼ 4pm-3am), which has been known to stay open after 4am. For something more laidback, with candles and low-voltage club sounds, try **Es Glop** (Carretera des Port 72; ☼ noon-3am). A funky food option (from sushi to ravioli) with drinks

---

LABOUR OF LOVE

Diving instructor Tony White proposed to fellow instructor Jane Falconer under water. 'We were at a wreck and I carved "Will you marry me?" into sand.

'I was trying to get myself out of trouble, because I'd slipped into a hole in the wreck and left Jane behind,' says Tony.

'He's not a good dive buddy – wherever there's a wreck he just scoots off down the nearest hole.'

All's well that ends well and, in March 2007, Tony and Jane opened their dive shop in Port de Sóller.

'We wanted to be in the Mediterranean, not too far from friends and family (in the UK),' says Jane. 'We started looking on the internet and saw this place for sale. We were working in Malta then, and I persuaded my boss to let me come for a week to take a look at it. I just fell in love with it. I had never been to Mallorca before, or even mainland Spain.'

'We love the combination of sea and mountains. We both like walking and I like mountain-biking. Another big attraction is all the caverns and caves along the coast – about half our dive sites have caves. And there is more fish life than in some other parts of the Mediterranean, like Malta or Greece. Perhaps because the area is not over-dived.'

'I think it's also because of fishing,' Tony chimes in. 'Here most of the fishing is done with nets and further out. In Malta, they do a lot more spear-fishing and fishing off the rocks.'

'Interaction with locals is a little slow,' Tony says, 'but we have had a really good reception from the customers who used to visit the shop before.'

'The more Spanish we know the easier life gets,' Jane observes. 'This is only our first year, so we have to see how it goes. But it's a long-term plan. We sold both our houses in the UK to buy this.'

Settling could be a costly business: 'Have you seen the house prices in the estate agents' windows?' Jane cries. 'If we ever get onto the housing ladder here and for some reason have to sell and go back to the UK, we'd have no problem getting back onto the ladder there!'

WESTERN MALLORCA

is **El Pirata** (☎ 971 631497; Carrer de Santa Caterina d'Alexandria 8; ☾ noon-3am).

Rather different is the local kids' all-night hang-out, **St Tropez** (Carrer del Poeta Mossèn Costa i Llobera s/n; ☾ 10.30pm-4am Tue-Sun), good if you like pool, eardrum-rupturing music and adolescent hormones. For more of a mixed dance crowd, have a peak at **Discoteca Altamar** (Passeig Es Través; ☾ 1-6am). It ain't sophisticated, but it's the only club around.

Getting There & Away

Most buses to Sóller have their terminus in Port de Sóller. If driving, you must choose between going to the centre (take the tunnel) or the Platja d'en Repic side (follow the signs). For the tram to Sóller, see p121. There is talk of putting on a direct ferry from Barcelona from 2008. Several car-rental offices line Passeig Es Través.

BINIARAIX & FORNALUTX

From Sóller it's a pleasant 2km drive, pedal or stroll through narrow laneways to Biniaraix. From there, another narrow and scenic route continues north to Fornalutx, through terraced groves crowded with orange and lemon trees. This walk (as you will see on p123) can also be done with several variants.

Biniaraix is a quiet hamlet (that started life as an Arab *alquería* or farmstead) with a shady central square, Plaça de Sa Concepció. **Fornalutx**, probably another *alquería*, is a pretty village of distinctive stone houses with green shutters, colourful flower boxes, well-kept gardens and flourishing citrus groves. Many are owned by expats but it's a far cry from the (comparative) bustle of Sóller. These are the kinds of places people dream about and that lured the ilk of Peter Kerr to live on the island (his trials and tribulations settling in to Mallorca feature in his travel humour tomes *Snowball Oranges*, *Mañana Mañana* and *Viva Mallorca!*).

Wander the lanes around the central Plaça d'Espanya and pop into the **Ajuntament** (Town Hall; Carrer des Vicari Solivellas 1), with its cool courtyard dominated by a palm tree. Outside, water gurgles cheerfully along one of several irrigation channels. You can follow the course of the town stream east past fine houses and thick greenery, or climb the stairs heading north out of the town from the Església de la Nativitat de Nostra Senyora.

A delightfully converted former convent just off the main street, **Fornalutx Petit Hotel** (☎ 971 631997; www.fornalutxpetithotel.com; Carrer de l'Alba 22; s/d €78/142; P ☒ ☒) is a friendly, tranquil place to stay with a half-dozen rooms and a couple of suites. The common areas glow with the warmth of terracotta floors and stonework. Room décor is mostly sober white but soothing. The Sa Capelleta (Little Chapel) suite is aptly named – it is a dreamy cream-coloured Gothic love nest. Have a snooze in the garden hammock, relax in the sauna or just gaze over the orchards from the pool terrace or Jacuzzi.

Ca'n Reus (☎ 971 631174; www.canreushotel.com; Carrer de l'Alba 26; d €120-160; P ☒ ☒) A couple of doors down from the Petit, this place is equally tempting for a romantic escape. The British-owned country mansion was built by a certain Mr Reus, who got rich on the orange trade with France. The eight rooms are all quite different and all have views.

Choose from four restaurants and a handful of cafés in Fornalutx. Two of the former, each with shady roadside terraces and views of the orchards below and mountains to the south, lie about half a kilometre out of the centre on the Ma2121 road leading northeast out of town.

ourpick Ca N'Antuna (☎ 971 633068; Carrer de Arbona Colom 8; meals €35-40; ☾ lunch & dinner Tue-Sat, lunch Sun) is a classic of Mallorca cooking. They do a bubbling cauldron of *caldereta de llagosta* (a thick lobster stew) or a vegetable version of the same thing, but are locally famous for their oven-cooked lamb and other meats. The hand juicer on the sill connecting the kitchen with the terrace is a nice touch – order up lots of local orange juice!

Also good for sweeping views and popular with locals is **Bellavista** (☎ 971 631590; Carrer de Sant Bartomeu 26; meals €30; ☾ lunch & dinner Thu-Sat & Mon-Tue, lunch Sun), which is good for simple grilled fish and a handful of hearty meat dishes.

Café Sa Plaça (☎ 971 631921; Plaça d'Espanya 3; ☾ Wed-Mon) is a great spot for coffee, ice cream or snacks on the main square. A trio of other options stretches just off the square along Carre de Sa Plaça.

See Sóller (p123) for details of the occasional bus service to Fornalutx.

ROAD FROM SÓLLER TO ALARÓ

A nice driving route suggests itself south of Sóller. Climb the valley into the hills (don't take the tunnel) and enjoy the views to Palma as you follow the switchbacks on the other side.

First stop is the roundabout at the bottom of the hill, where you could visit the enchanting **Jardins d'Alfàbia** (☎ 971 613123; Carretera de Sóller Km17; admission €4.50; ☺ 9.30am-6.30pm Mon-Sat Apr-Oct, 9.30am-5.30pm Mon-Fri, 9.30am-1pm Sat Nov-Mar). The endearingly crumbly *possessió* with the baroque façade (which looks like it was stripped from a Florentine basilica) is surrounded by gardens, citrus groves, palm trees and a handful of farmyard animals. There is a shady bar amid this mini-Eden.

The murmur of water gurgling along narrow irrigation canals gives a hint of the place's past, for it began as the residence of an Arab Wāli. The water comes from a generous underground source not far from the house in the Serra d'Alfàbia mountain range (maximum altitude 1069m) that stretches east. Of the original Arab house, virtually nothing remains but the extraordinary polychromatic, pyramidal *artesonado* (coffered ceiling), fashioned of pine and ilex, immediately inside the building's entrance. It is bordered by inscriptions in Arabic and is thought to have been made around 1170, although dispute persists as to whether it was made before or after the Christian conquest. From here you enter an inner courtyard. To the right is the *tafona* (large oil press that was typically a part of any self-respecting *possessió*) and a mix of Gothic, Renaissance and baroque styles. The rambling house is laden with period furniture and an extensive library.

Bunyola

About 2.5km south of the Jardins d'Alfàbia and just east of the highway to Palma lies this drowsy transport junction, known for olive oil and its Palo (herbal liquor) distillery. There's not an awful lot to hold you here, except for a slice of Mallorcan village life in the central square, Sa Plaça, with its single bar. Next to the square is the **Església de Sant Mateu** (☎ 629 310849; Carrer de l'Església 2), built in 1230 but largely redone in 1756.

S'Alqueria Blanca (☎ 971 148400; www.alqueria -blanca.com; s/d €120/160; ☺ Jan-Nov; P ✖ ☎) is a majestic country residence in sprawling grounds about 2km west of Bunyola, with six rooms (three doubles and three suites). The oldest buildings formed the Arab *alquería* and now house these rooms. A whimsical Modernista building was added in 1906 (now the breakfast room). If travelling north from Palma along the Ma11, the turn-off west is

at Km13.6 and it's about 700m further down the trail.

Three bar-restaurants surround the church on Carrer de l'Església, but perhaps you'd prefer to look into **Restaurant Es Carreró** (☎ 971 615440; Carrer Major 17; meals €45; ☺ daily), a few metres east of the square. Take a seat on the romantic roof terrace and tuck into a *filete de dorada en mantequilla de alcaparras y anchoas con espinacas y puré de patatas* (bream fillet in a caper and anchovy butter with spinach and mashed potato).

Three kilometres south of town on the road to Palma, a turn-off west leads to one of Mallorca's grandest *possessions*, **Raixa**. It was restored in 2007 and will house an environmental centre and natural park organisations. Eventually it will also open to the public, but this depends on how long it takes to restore the extensive gardens.

Orient

A treat comes in the 9km road (the Ma2100) northeast from Bunyola to the hamlet of Orient. Nice enough by car, it is a fave with bike riders (in reasonable shape!). The first 5km is a promenade along a verdant valley that slowly rises to a bit of a plain before tumbling over the other side of a forested ridge. The next 2km of serried switchbacks flatten out on the run into Orient. All the way, the Serra d'Alfàbia is in sight to the north.

Orient is a huddle of ochre houses clustered nervously on a slight rise south off the Ma2100. A few houses seem to slide off as if in afterthought on the north side of the road.

ourpick **Finca Son Palou** (☎ 971 148282; www .sonpalou.com; Plaça de l'Església s/n; s/d €129/150; P ✖ ☎ ☎) Climb up Carrer de Sant Jordi to the church of the same name and this quiet village mansion with restaurant. On its 150-hectare land around the town, you can watch the harvesting of apples and cherries, and go for walks and mountain bike jaunts. Rooms have a rustic simplicity, with bucolic terracotta floor tiles, timber furnishings and, in some cases, exposed beams. The better rooms have a terrace.

Barely a breath away is **Mandala** (☎ 971 615285; Carrer Nou 1; meals €45-55; ☺ lunch Tue-Thu & Sun, lunch & dinner Fri & Sat Oct-Apr, dinner Mon-Sat May-Sep), a boutique French fusion restaurant that is highly regarded and requires booking. By the road, **Dalt Muntanya** (☎ 971 615373; www .daltmuntanya.net; s/d €60/100; P ✖ ☎) is another rural retreat, with 18 rooms, restaurant, bar and pool surrounded by greenery. Just 1.5km east of the hamlet stands **L'Hermitage** (☎ 971 180303; www.hermitage-hotel.com; s/d €120/189; ☷ Feb-Nov; P ☒ ☒), a 17th-century country manor that in 1950 was converted into a small monastery. It now offers 24 rooms, shady gardens and a good if somewhat fiscally demanding restaurant. All of this, however, is a little precious for islanders, who flood instead to **Ca'n Jaume** (☎ 971 615153; meals €20-30; ☷ Wed-Mon), a roadside diner that offers as house speciality succulent suckling pig for €16 a head. Follow this with chocolate profiteroles. It's a knockabout place on the left as you enter town coming from Bunyola, with a dozen tables outside and the radio and TV both blaring in rowdy unison inside.

Ancient history buffs might like to follow a narrow road about 2.5km northeast of Orient to the *possessió* of **Comasema**, an imposing, fortified farmhouse complex. About another 500m inside this property is a circular *talayot*. You need to ask permission to walk in to see it and this may not be forthcoming.

Alaró

As the Ma2100 rises away from Orient, surrounded by cypresses and gardens, you could be forgiven for thinking you're in Tuscany. The road meanders about 4km northeast before taking a leisurely turn around the outriders of the mighty bluff that is **Puig d'Alaró** (821m). This rocky peak is matched to the east by **Puig de S'Alcadena** (815m). To the south you can make out the flat interior of Es Pla (The Plain). About halfway between Orient and Alaró, you could call it a day at the remote rural hotel, **S'Olivaret** (☎ 971 510889; www.solivaret.com; s/d €132/184; P ☒ ☒). You can't get too much further out of the way and this is a country idyll. Rooms are generally spacious and some have four-poster beds. It has tennis courts, art on the walls and an indoor pool too.

Eight kilometres from Orient, you arrive in **Alaró**. Head for Plaça de la Vila, flanked by the Casa de la Vila (town hall), parish church and a couple of cafés, and the busier junction of Carrer Petit and Carrer de Jaume Rosselló, with a couple of lively cafés. Alaró makes a pleasant if uneventful spot to stay overnight. **Hostal Ecològic Ca'n Tiu** (☎ 971 510547; www.hostalcantiu.com; Carrer Petit 11; s/d/tr €30/50/60; ☒ ☒ ☐) is a pleasant spot that tries to minimise its

environmental impact (this will include use of solar energy in the future). Guests who arrive by bicycle get 5% off and it has plenty of info on local routes. The 10 rooms are pleasant and fresh, with 100% cotton bed linen. A classier establishment is the central **Hotel Can Xim** (☎ 971 518680; www.canxim.com; Plaça de la Vila 8; s/d €80/100; ☒ ☐ ☒). The eight double rooms are spacious and light, and the hotel restaurant, **Traffic** (meals €35) has a certain local renown for its beef dishes. Those wanting a no-nonsense rural-style getaway could do worse than the **Agroturisme Son Penyaflor** (☎ 971 510071; www.sonpenyaflor.com; per person €49; P ☒), about 1.5km out of town on the road to Castell d'Alaró. Surrounded by oak stands and almond trees, this place offers a series of seven smallish and simple singles and doubles, 12 beds in all. You can rent the entire 12 beds for €36 per person, and the price drops further if you take the place for periods of two days, a week or a month. There are cooking facilities.

A weekly market is staged in Alaró on Saturdays.

From the entrance to the Agroturisme Son Penyaflor, you can see, perched at an improbable, Monty Pythonesque angle, the **Castell d'Alaró**, high up and imperious on the mount of the same name. This excursion is worth the sweat but if the two-hour walk doesn't appeal, you can cover most of the climb by car. The first 3km of switchbacks are asphalted. The next 1.2km is a dirt trail but OK. It leads you to the **Restaurant Es Verger** (☎ 971 182126; Camí des Castell; meals €20-25; ☷ 9am-10pm), a simple place for hearty dishes (they do especially good suckling pig) and good views.

The road continues in poor but driveable state (not after rain) another 1.2km to a parking area at the base of a path that leads (in 15 minutes) to the ruins of what was an impregnable castle. Christian warriors could only be starved out of this redoubt by Muslim conquerors around the year 911, eight years after the latter had invaded the island. Several stone arched doors and parts of the walls of what was clearly a major fortress remain today. You can see Palma, the sea, the Badia d'Alcúdia, the plains and Puig Major. Another minute's walk further uphill brings you to the **Ermita de la Mare de Déu del Refugi**, a 17th-century, fly-infested chapel that locals still visit to give thanks for miraculous events. The **Refugi S'Hostatgeria** (☎ 971 182112), is being renovated and should be ready from 2008 for people who wish to sleep overnight. They have been working on it for several years and much of the building material was lifted by helicopter. How on earth did medieval Mallorquins build the great stone fortress? The snack bar offers three rooms with four beds each (bring your sleeping bag) at €12 a head. You can get sandwiches and drinks in the bar, open from 9am to 11pm.

Getting There & Away

Buses and trains running between Palma and Sóller stop at Bunyola (the bus stop is at Sa Plaça, and the train station a short walk west of the centre). From there local bus 221 runs twice a day east to Orient (€1.10, 30 minutes). This is a microbus service and you need to book a seat in advance (☎ 971 615219).

The Palma–Inca train calls at the Consell-Alaró train station (20 to 30 minutes), where it connects with local bus 320 for Alaró (15 minutes).

CALA DE SA CALOBRA & CALA TUENT

The Ma10 road from Sóller to the Monestir de Lluc is a beautiful drive. The first stop is the **Mirador de Ses Barques**, with restaurant (recommended by locals, closed Monday) and spectacular views, about 6km out of Sóller. The road unravels eastward to cross the Serra de son Torrella range, and at 16km out of Sóller a side road leads north up to the island's highest point, Puig Major. You can't take it, however, as this is Air Force territory and topped by a communications base.

The Ma10 slithers past two artificial patches of liquid blue, the Cúber and Gorg Blau dams. Shortly after the latter, a 12km road branches north off Ma10 and down to the small port of **Sa Calobra**. It was completed in 1935 with the sole aim of allowing tourists to reach the beach by land. You know what they say: it is

better to travel than to arrive. Nothing could be truer of this spectacular scenic drive. The serpentine road has been carved through the weird mountainous rock formations, skirting narrow ridges before twisting down to the coast in an eternal series of hair-raising hairpin bends.

If you come in summer you won't be alone. Divisions of buses and fleets of pleasure boats disgorge battalion after battalion of tireless tourists. It makes D-Day look like play-lunch. Sa Calobra must be wonderful on a quiet, bright midwinter morning. From the northern end of the road a short trail leads around the coast to a river gorge, the **Torrent de Pareis**, and a small cove with fabulous (but usually crowded) swimming spots.

Skip the crowd scenes and, 2km before arriving, follow a turn-off west for **Cala Tuent**, a tranquil emerald-green inlet in the shadow of Puig Major. The broad pebble beach is backed by a couple of houses and a great green bowl of vegetation that climbs up the mountain flanks. About 200m back from the beach, a turn-off leads 1.5km to **Es Vergeret** (☎ 971 517105; Camí de Sa Figuera Vial 21; meals €25-30; Feb-Oct), where the shady terrace looks from on high to the bay below and hearty servings of paella, *tumbet* (vegetable stew) and other dishes can be had. They are especially known for their grilled fish.

One bus a day (bus 355, Monday to Saturday, May to October) comes from Ca'n Picafort (9am) via Alcúdia, Cala Sant Vicenç, Pollença and the Monestir de Lluc. It returns at 3pm. The whole trip takes three hours 50 minutes to Sa Calobra (with a one-hour stop at the Monestir de Lluc) and 2½ hours on the return leg. From Ca'n Picafort you pay €7.60 (€15 return). Boats make excursions to Sa Calobra and Cala Tuent from Port de Sóller (see p125).

WESTERN MALLORCA

SLIPPERY DROPS

For those with a taste for jumping into ravines and streams, canyoning could be the sport for you. The best places for this are concentrated in the central Serra de Tramuntana between Valldemossa and Sa Calobra. By far the most challenging (rated 5–6, for experts only) is the Gorg Blau–Sa Fosca canyon, descending north and then northeast from the dam of the same name. This 2.5km route (there and back) is tough. The drops and scrambling are accompanied constantly by freezing water and there is a 400m stretch in total darkness. Instead of turning back, you could continue north 3.3km along Torrent de Pareis, a much easier route surrounded by majestic rock walls. Either way, a local guide is essential. One group of guides to contact is **Mallorca Canyoning** (☎ 691 230291; www.mallorcacanyoning.com).

WESTERN MALLORCA

MONESTIR DE LLUC & AROUND

Back in the 13th century, a local shepherd claimed to have seen an image of the Virgin Mary in the sky. Later, a similar image appeared on a rock. Another story says that a statuette of the Virgin was found here and taken to the nearest hamlet, Escorca. The next day it was back where it had been found. Three times it was taken to Escorca and three times it returned. 'It's a miracle', everyone cried and a chapel was built near the site to commemorate it, possibly around 1268. The religious sanctuary came later. Since then thousands of pilgrims have come every year to pay homage to the 14th-century (and thus not the original) **statue of the Virgin of Lluc**, known as La Moreneta because of the statuette's dark complexion.

The present monastery, the **Monestir de Lluc** (☎ 971 871525; www.lluc.net; admission free; ☽ 8.30am-8pm), a huge austere complex, dates mostly from the 17th to 18th centuries. The word *monestir* (monastery) is a little misleading as the order of Sacred Heart Missionaries that run it are not, strictly speaking, monks.

Off the central courtyard is the entrance to the rather gloomy, late-Renaissance **Basílica de la Mare de Déu** (built in 1622–91 and bearing mostly baroque decoration), which contains a fine *retablo* done by Jaume Blanquer in 1629, and the statuette of the Virgin Mary. There is also a **museum** (admission €3.30; ☽ 10am-1.30pm & 2.30-5pm) with archaeological bits and bobs, religious objects, ceramics and a modest art collection in eight rooms on a 1st-floor wing just before you reach the basilica.

Outside, the modest **Jardí Botànic** (botanic garden) is worth a stroll, as is the climb up to the **Pujol dels Misteris**, a hill topped by a crucifix whose base is enveloped in barbed wire. Forget the cross and enjoy the lovely valley views behind it.

You might get lucky and hear the Els Escolanets (also known as Els Blauets, the Little Blues, because of the soutane they wear), the monastery's boarding school boys' choir. This institution dates to the early 16th century.

A couple of popular walking routes leave from the monastery. One is a four-hour circuit of **Puig de Massanella** (1365m), in the course of which the landowners will charge you €4. The other is the seven-hour **Puig Roig** (1002m) circuit, a long walk with plenty of ups and downs (but you don't ascend the peak). You can only do this on Sundays, when the landowners open the barriers. Ask for information at **Ca s'Amitger** (☎ 971 517070; ☽ 9am-4pm), a wilderness information office opposite the entrance to the monastery grounds.

Sleeping & Eating

Hospedería del Santuari de Lluc (☎ 971 871525; s/d from €13.50/23.50) The monastery's accommodation section has 97 rooms (of all sizes and some with kitchen access), and is popular with school groups, walkers and pilgrims. The downstairs rooms are dark and best avoided. It is also possible to pitch a tent about 600m from the monastery near the Ma10 road. Get permits from **Ca s'Amitger**.

Several restaurants and cafeterias cater to your tummy's demands. The **Son Amer refuge**, about 1km south of the monastery up the hill along the Ma10, was still not open at the time of writing.

Getting There & Away

Up to two buses a day (May to October) run from Ca'n Picafort to the Monestir de Lluc (€5.25, 1¾ hours) on their way to Sóller and Port Sóller. From Palma, two all-stops buses (bus 330) to Inca continue to Lluc via Caimari on weekends only (or take the train to Inca and change to bus 332). By road, the Ma10 from Sóller or Pollença is a scenic pleasure. A less common approach (if coming from Palma or the south) is via Inca and north up the Ma2130 road via Caimari. The 7km from Caimari are a treat, taking you high through woods and two ravines to reach the Ma10, where you turn right for Pollença (you reach the monastery turn-off after 2km).

Northern Mallorca

Northern Mallorca is a near ideal mix. The mountain chain of the Serra de Tramuntana meets a restrained mass tourism in a gentle 'clash of civilisations' that allows you to pick and mix in the most pleasant fashion.

Two magnificent bays, Badia de Pollença and Badia d'Alcúdia, are formed by a trident of imposing capes (Cap de Formentor, Cap des Pinar and Cap Ferrutx). Their high cliff walls stand defiantly against the might of the Mediterranean Sea and offer an extraordinary palette of fine views, as well as plenty of opportunities to stretch your legs hiking and cycling. Between the capes, the long flat coastline offers resort beaches, wilder stretches backed only by dunes and Aleppo pines, a wetlands nature reserve a-twitter with hundreds of bird species, and aquatic activities from diving and sea kayaking to windsurfing and sailing.

Two of the island's most captivating medieval towns, Pollença and Alcúdia, are nestled here, the latter alongside what remains of Rome's senior Mallorcan settlement, Pol·lentia. Sites more ancient still dot the area, especially around Ca'n Picafort. A couple of hilltop hermitages provide a different perspective on the island's history, and more stunning views of the island.

Accommodation covers the widest possible range, from one of the island's few youth hostels in a superb position on the Cap des Pinar peninsula to the luxury Great Gatsby-esque Hotel Formentor. Fish and chips abound, but culinary diamonds twinkle all over, from traditional hearty island fare to contemporary international seafood spreads.

NORTHERN MALLORCA

HIGHLIGHTS

- Absorb the splendour of the island and the Mediterranean from the lighthouse at **Cap de Formentor** (p142)
- Go back several millennia at the **Necròpolis de Son Real** (p149)
- Savour the peace and bird-watching in the **Parc Natural de S'Albufera** (p148)
- Slip into the translucent depths of **Cala Figuera** (p142)
- Relax at the little inlet beaches of **Cala Sant Vicenç** (p138)
- Take a vow and climb the pilgrims' stairway to Calvari in pretty **Pollença** (p134)
- Make the half-hour descent on foot to reach the remote and paradise-like **Platja des Coll Baix** (p148)
- Inspect the remains of what was Rome's main city in Mallorca, **Pol·lentia** (p142)

Cala Figuera
★★Cap de Formentor
Cala Sant Vicenç ★
★Pollença
★Platja des Coll Baix
Pol·lentia★
Parc Natural ★ de S'Albufera
★ Necròpolis de Son Real

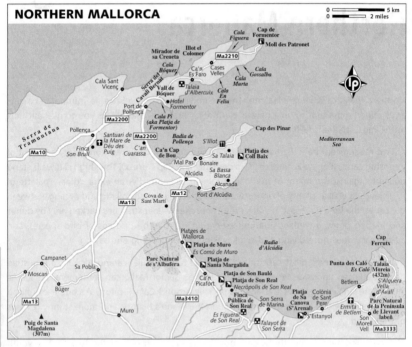

NORTHERN MALLORCA

0 — 5 km
0 — 2 miles

POLLENÇA & AROUND

This tiny corner of the north has a little of everything. The coquettish town of Pollença makes an enticing base for fanning out to the coastal family resorts of Port de Pollença, with its long beach and bustle, and Cala Sant Vicenç, which is like a pearl farm of aqua-tinged inlets. Further east, the Formentor peninsula stretches in mountainous splendour, ending in the dramatic Cap de Formentor – an 18km strip of breathtaking views.

POLLENÇA

pop 11,330 / elev 41m

Everyone from Winston Churchill to Agatha Christie has at some point hung about at Pollença. A little like its coastal cousin, Deià (p117), Pollença used to be a magnet for artists and is now home to a more or less permanent foreign populace.

Known as Al-Bulansa to the Muslims before 1229, the pretty town you see today was largely formed in the 18th century. Just how it inherited the name from Rome's Pol·lentia

(near present-day Alcúdia) is not entirely clear.

Information

The **tourist office** (☎ 971 535077; www.pollensa.com; Carrer de Sant Domingo 17; ☼ 8am-8pm Mon-Fri, 10am-1pm Sun) has information on the town and surrounding area. Check out www.thepollensaguide.com or the printed listings and ads guide *El Puente* (available in the tourist office).

Sights & Activities

They don't call it **Calvari** (Calvary) for nothing. Some pilgrims do it on their knees, but plain walking up the 365 stone steps from

---

OUR TOP PICKS

- **Hotel** Ermita de la Victòria (p148)
- **Restaurant** La Terraza (p146)
- **Town** Pollença (left)
- **Market/food shop** Enseñat (p138)
- **Festival** Moros i Cristians (p137)

> **REGIONAL SPECIALITIES**
>
> Traditionally, the marshlands of S'Albufera have produced two mainstays: rice and eels. The former is used in many dishes, while the latter most often pops up in the *espinagada*, an eel-and-spinach pie. On a sweeter note, Pollença is also known for its honey.

the town centre to an 18th-century hilltop chapel (330m), the **Oratori del Calvari**, is penance enough. Your reward may not be in heaven, but there is a little bar next to the chapel from which to savour the views back across the town.

A church was first raised on the site of the **Església de la Mare de Déu dels Àngels** (Plaça Major) shortly after the conquest in 1229. The present edifice dates, like most major Mallorcan churches, to the 18th century.

The **Museu de Pollença** (☎ 971 531166; www.ajpol lenca.net in Spanish & Catalan; Carrer de Guillem Cifre de Colonya s/n; admission €1.50; ☺ 10.30am-1.30pm & 5.30-8.30pm Tue-Sat, 10.30am-1.30pm Sun Jul-Sep, 10.30am-1.30pm Tue-Sat Oct-Jun) is worth visiting for the chance to get a look at the 17th-century baroque cloister of what was the Convent de Sant Domingo, in which it is housed, and a bright Buddhist Kalachakra mandala donated by the Dalai Lama to the town in 1990.

The convent church, the **Església de Santa Maria de Déu de Roser**, is a baroque job with barrel vault, gaudy retable and medallions in the ceiling. It is used for the Festival de Pollença (right).

A short way up the Calvari steps lurks the **Museu Martí Vicenç** (☎ 971 532867; www.martivicens .org; Carrer del Calvari 10; ☺ 10.30am-6pm Mon-Fri, 10.30-3pm Sat, 11am-1pm Sun). The weaver and artist Martí Vicenç Alemany (born 1926) bought this property, once part of a giant Franciscan monastery which also included the nearby former Església de Monti-Sion, in the 1950s. His works, mostly canvases and textiles, are strewn around several rooms downstairs.

Casa-Museu Dionís Bennàssar (☎ 971 530997; www .museudionisbennassar.com in Spanish & Catalan; Carrer de Roca 14; admission €2; ☺ 10.30am-1.30pm Tue-Sun) was the home of local artist Dionís Bennàssar and is now (with a modern extension) home to a permanent collection of his works. Downstairs are some of his earlier efforts, including etchings, aquarelles and oils, depicting mostly local scenes. Works on the other floors range

from a series on fish that is strangely reminiscent of Miquel Barceló's efforts in Palma's cathedral (p68) to a series of nudes and portraits of dancing girls.

At the north end of town, the **Pont Romà**, a bridge over the Torrent de Sant Jordi, was probably built sometime after the Christian conquest in 1229. It is common for medieval bridges to have become known as Roman bridges in Spain.

South of Pollença, off the Ma2200, what must be one of the most tortuous roads on the island weaves 1.5km in such tight bends towards the hilltop former monastery of **Santuari de la Mare de Déu des Puig** (333m) that you are better off hoofing it. This rambling residence was built in the 14th and 15th centuries and is worth the climb, if only for the magnificent views over Pollença and Alcúdia bays, and the weird, jagged formations of the Formentor peninsula. The Gothic chapel and refectory are highlights of the complex.

Festivals & Events

The town's big event is the **Festes de la Patrona**, which climaxes on 2 August with the staged battle between Moors and Christians (p137).

The **Davallament** (bringing down), an Easter procession held on Good Friday in which the body of Christ is symbolically paraded down the steps of Calvari, is one of the most moving of the island's Easter celebrations.

During the **Festival de Pollença** (www.festivalpol lenca.org) in July and August, various genres of music can be heard in concerts in the Sant Domingo cloister.

Another big event is **La Fira**, a huge general market held on the second Sunday of November in the Convent de Sant Domingo and other locations around town.

Sleeping

Cheap lodgings are not a reality in the town, which has six hotels.

Santuari de la Mare de Déu des Puig (☎ 971 184132; d €20) The budget conscious who love a view and don't mind the inconvenience of being a 45-minute uphill hike from the town could opt for these former hermits' cells. The lodgings are basic and booking ahead is mandatory.

Hotel Desbrull (☎ 971 535055; www.desbrull.com; Carrer del Marqués Desbrull 7; s/d €86/91; 🖭) The best deal in town, with six pleasantly fresh if

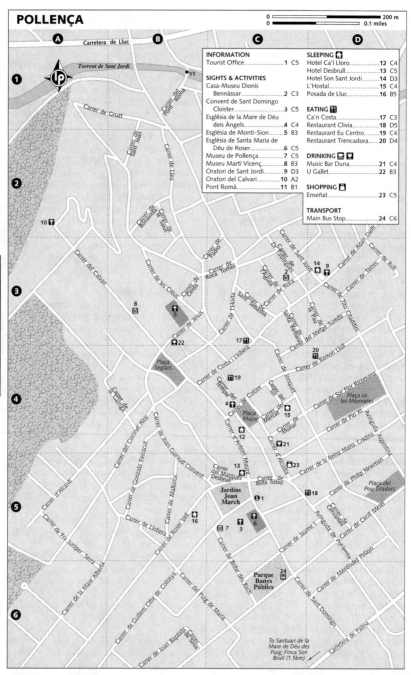

POLLENÇA

0 — 200 m
0 — 0.1 miles

INFORMATION
Tourist Office......................1 C5

SIGHTS & ACTIVITIES
Casa-Museu Dionís
  Bennàssar.......................2 C3
Convent de Sant Domingo
  Cloister..........................3 C5
Església de la Mare de Déu
  dels Àngels.....................4 C4
Església de Monti-Sion.......5 B3
Església de Santa Maria de
  Déu de Roser.................6 C5
Museu de Pollença.............7 C5
Museu Martí Vicenç...........8 B3
Oratori de Sant Jordi...........9 D3
Oratori del Calvari............10 A2
Pont Romà.......................11 B1

SLEEPING
Hotel Ca'l Lloro................12 C4
Hotel Desbrull..................13 C5
Hotel Son Sant Jordi........14 D3
L'Hostal...........................15 C4
Posada de Lluc................16 B5

EATING
Ca'n Costa.......................17 C3
Restaurant Clivia..............18 D5
Restaurant Eu Centro........19 C4
Restaurant Trencadora.....20 D4

DRINKING
Music Bar Duna................21 C4
U Gallet..........................22 B3

SHOPPING
Enseñat...........................23 C5

TRANSPORT
Main Bus Stop.................24 C6

NORTHERN MALLORCA

To Santuari de la
Mare de Déu des
Puig; Finca Son
Brull (1.5km)

coquettishly small doubles in a modernised stone house. White dominates the décor in rooms and bathrooms and, if you like the contemporary art on the walls, you can buy it.

Hotel Ca'l Lloro (☎ 971 535493; http://cal-lloro.com; Carrer d'Antoni Maura 38; s/d €86/107;) A modern spot in the heart of town, this hotel offers straightforward rooms with parquet floors, whitewash and timber furniture (only the strictly necessary items, no clutter here!). Sit on the rooftop terrace for the views.

L'Hostal (☎ 971 535282; www.hostalpollensa.com; Carrer del Mercat 18; s/d €89/111;) Equally simple rooms with white tiled floors, a splash of primal colour in the décor and more modern art on the walls. Downstairs a communal lounge is where you dig into breakfast.

Posada de Lluc (☎ 971 535220; www.posadadelluc.com; Carrer del Roser Vell 11; s €90, d €129-158;) A 15th-century, two-storey town house in central Pollença, it was handed over to the brethren of the Monestir de Lluc (p132) as a resting place for pilgrims. It is now a fetching inn with a variety of rooms. The most straightforward are the doubles on the 1st floor facing the street. Those overlooking the pool and with their own terrace have more of a wow factor.

Hotel Son Sant Jordi (☎ 971 530389; www.hotel sonsantjordi.com; Carrer de Sant Jordi 29; s/d €139/169;) Occupying a fine old house and sharing a bit of square with the 16th-

century Oratori de Sant Jordi chapel, this hotel has rooms with high ceilings, terracotta floors (with varying styles), canopied beds and plenty of light. Out back, a trim garden frames a curvaceous pool. Prices halve from November to January.

Finca Son Brull (☎ 971 535353; www.sonbrull.com; Carretera Palma-Pollença Km49.8; d €264-369, ste up to €800;) This is an exquisite retreat set in a grand 18th-century *possessió* (rural estate) about 1.5km south of Pollença. The standard doubles are a tasteful mix of the old and clean-lined modernity (with Bang & Olufsen TV, DVD player and several telephones!). It also boasts a spa, one of the island's top restaurants and a bar set by the old olive press.

Eating

Plaça Major is surrounded by good-natured eateries and café-bars where you can receive sustenance morning, noon and night. But take a look around the rest of town.

Restaurant Eu Centro (☎ 971 535082; Carrer del Temple 3; meals €25, menú del día €8; Thu-Tue) Tapas and all the old Mallorcan faves, from *tumbet* to *frit Mallorquí* (sautéed lamb offal). Meat lovers might want to have a go at the *lechona* (suckling pig), which, while not the island's best, is not a bad shot. Inside is over-lit, so you might try for one of three tables in the street.

Restaurant Trencadora (☎ 971 531859; Carrer de Ramon Llull 7; meals €30; 11am-1am Tue-Sat, 11am-6pm Sun) With its enormous garden, this is perhaps the hippest place to head for a meal. Lounge about afterwards for a drink or two. Friday nights the speciality is BBQ meats and tapas, while on Sunday, brunch carries on until 4pm. Food-wise, the general category is creative Med.

Ca'n Costa (☎ 971 531276; Carrer de Costa i Llobera 11; meal €40-45; dinner only Mon-Sat) The rambling old building in which the poet Miquel Costa

NORTHERN MALLORCA

i Llobera (p37) was born, and which later housed the town's first cinema, is now the setting for romantic dinners of such oddities as *filete de avestruz* (char-grilled ostrich) and *calamares salteados con chorizo* (calamari sautéed with spicy sausage). They have kids' portions too.

ourpick Restaurant Clivia (☎ 971 533635; Avinguda Pollentia; meals €45-50; ☺ lunch & dinner Tue & Thu-Sun, dinner Mon & Wed) Set in what was once a private house, this spot offers fine food (especially the fish) prepared and presented with panache. The service is attentive and the ambience tranquil. Try the house speciality, *llobarro de palangre al vi blanc* (wild sea bass steamed in white wine).

Drinking

U Gallet (☎ 971 534879; Carrer de Jesus 40; ☺ 10.30am-2.30pm & 7.30pm-3.30am Tue-Sun, 7.30pm-3.30am Mon) This is where the locals come for a drink, far from the madding (and largely foreign) crown down on the central square. The narrow bar ends in a basic lounge area. If this or a barstool doesn't appeal, the timber tables in the street could be the go.

Music Bar Duna (Carrer d'Alcúdia 1; ☺ 10pm-4am) For those needing more of an urban bar feel, this is the place to come, but not before midnight. Punters crowd around the dimly lit horseshoe bar upstairs and try to talk over the thundering DJ sets. Opening times are enigmatic, to say the least.

Shopping

Enseñat (☎ 971 533618; www.ensenyat.com; Carrer d'Alcúdia 5; ☺ 8.30am-1.30pm & 4.30-8.30pm Mon-Sat, 8.30am-1.30pm Sun) It's the place to pick up gourmet groceries, wines, cheeses and meats. They've been in business since the 1940s.

On Sundays, a produce market is held in Pollença.

Getting There & Away

BUS

From Palma, Bus 340 heads non-stop for Pollença (€4.50, 45 minutes, up to 14 times a day). It heads on to Cala Sant Vicenç and Port de Pollença.

CAR & MOTORCYCLE

From Palma, zip along the full length of the Ma13 motorway and follow the turn-off north as this becomes a normal dual-carriageway road. A much more picturesque

approach would see you turn north from Inca up the Ma2130 road and then east along the Ma10.

CALA SANT VICENÇ
pop 270

A tranquil and leafy residential area works itself up into something of a lazy roller of hotels and restaurants on the waterfront, but there is little sense of frenzy. The four jewel-like *cales* (coves) that constitute the *raison d'être* of this low-key resort are worth making for, except perhaps on crowded summer weekends when locals tumble in to compete for the limited towel space.

The **tourist office** (☎ 971 533264; Plaça de Cala Sant Vicenç; ☺ 9am-2pm Mon-Fri, 10am-1pm Sat May-Oct) is about 50m inland from Cala Clara.

The first of the beaches, **Cala Barques**, is sandy until you hit the water, when you have to pick your way over rocks to reach submersion depth. Pretty (well, they're all pretty) **Cala Clara** is similar. **Cala Molins** is the biggest of the four, with a deep sandy strand and easy-going access into the shimmering waters of this tranquil inlet. **Cala Carbó**, around the headland, is the smallest and least visited. It wouldn't take more than 20 minutes to walk the entire distance between the four.

Those with no interest in watching afternoon football matches in a pub could walk about 15 minutes along Carrer Temporal from behind Cala Clara and then down Carrer de Dionìs Bennàssar. You will hit a rise with park benches and the **Coves de L'Alzineret**, seven funerary caves dug in pre-Talayotic times (c 1600 BC) and simply left here for anyone who wants to poke around.

Sleeping & Eating

ourpick Hostal los Pinos (☎ 971 531210; www.hostal-lospinos.com; s/d from €36/60; ☺ May-Oct; P ♠) This hotel is set on a leafy hillside off the road between Cala Molins and Cala Carbó. The best of the simple rooms have partial sea views and are technically suites, with separate sleeping and lounge areas and balconies to hang up your beach towel.

Hotel Niu (☎ 971 530100; www.reisdemallorca.com; Cala Barques; s/d €75/144; ☺ May-Oct; ✳ ▢) You can't get much closer to the water than in this 1928 hotel that was one of the first to open here. Rooms are straightforward but with a touch of old-world charm (in the dark timber fittings and furniture for instance). Some have balconies with superb sea views.

Bistro Balaixa (☎ 971 530659; meals €25; ☾ Sun-Fri) Set back about 100m from Cala Molins on an unnamed street, this is a simple place with internal dining and a terrace below. Pop in for tapas, pasta dishes and a generally odd mix of local, Spanish (*riñones al Jerez*, kidneys cooked in sherry) and Mediterranean options (Italian *bruschette*).

our pick Cal Patró (☎ 971 533899; Cala Barques; meals €30-40; ☾ Wed-Mon Easter-Oct) Locals in search of fish don't hesitate and head straight for the 'Captain's House' for fresh catch of the day (like the delicious *gallo San Pedro*, a rich Mediterranean fish). Or you can keep the price down with fish-farm options. Round off with *gató amb gelat*, a Mallorcan treat of almond tart served with almond-flavoured ice cream.

Café Art 66 (☎ 971 534080; Carrer Temporal s/n; ☾ 4pm-2am daily May-Oct, 4pm-2am Fri & Sat Feb-Apr & Nov) This is the place to chill out later in the day. DJ sessions usually accompany the cocktails and you can opt to lounge about inside or out. The décor is overwhelmingly in keeping with the sea theme, with endless shades of blue.

Getting There & Away
Cala Sant Vicenç is 6.5km northeast of Pollença. Take the road towards Port de Pollença and turn north (left, signposted) after 2km. The 340 Palma–Port de Pollença bus runs to Cala Sant Vicenç (€1.10, 15 minutes, up to six times a day) from Pollença and from Port de Pollença.

PORT DE POLLENÇA
pop 5930

On the north shore of the Badia de Pollença, this resort is popular with British families soothed by fish and chips and pints of ale. Sailboards and yachts can be hired on the beaches. South of town the bay's shoreline becomes quite rocky and the beaches are less attractive.

Information
The **tourist office** (☎ 971 865467; Passeig Saralegui; ☾ 8am-8pm Mon-Fri, 10am-5pm Sat, 10am-1pm Sun May-Sep, 8am-3pm Mon-Fri, 10am-1pm Sat Oct-Apr) is on the waterfront in front of the marina. The English-language website, www.puertopollensa.com, has listings and sundry titbits of information.

For medical assistance, the **Clinica Inle** (☎ 971 864466; Passeig de Londres 26) has a 24-hour ambulance service.

Sights & Activities
The beaches immediately south of the main port area are broad, sandy and gentle. Tufts of beach are sprinkled all the way along the shady promenade stretching around the north end of town. As you head south along the bay towards Alcúdia, the sand (what little there is) becomes a grey gravel mix and is frequently awash with dried and fresh poseidon grass (p144). The tail end of this less than winsome stretch, **Ca'n Cap de Bou** (Map p134) and **Sa Marina** (just before entering Alcúdia proper) are popular with wind and kite surfers but otherwise are no great shakes.

They say some of the island's best diving is in the Badia de Pollença. There is plenty of wall and cave action, some reasonable marine life (rays, octopuses, barracuda and more) along the southern flank of the Formentor peninsula, and more popular spots along the southern end of the bay leading to Cap des Pinar.

Scuba Mallorca (☎ 971 868087; www.scubamallorca.com; Carrer d'El Cano 23; 2 boat dives €70, equipment extra €15) is a PADI five-star outfit and one of a couple of dive centres in town.

Sail & Surf Pollença (☎ 971 865346; www.sailsurf.eu; Passeig de Saralegui 134) hires out sailing (from €20 an hour for a Laser) and windsurfing equipment (from €15 an hour for beginners) and organises courses in both activities at various levels. Just opposite them, on the beach, **Kayak Mallorca** (☎ 971 534870; www.kayakmallorca.com) organises sea kayak trips around the bay and off Cap de Formentor (depending on skill levels and numbers). Or you can just hire a kayak for a bit of solo paddling (€10 for an hour, €30 for a day).

Various **boat tours** (☎ 971 864014, 971 864014) are available from June to September around the bay and to Cap de Formentor (€18.50) and Cala Sant Vicenç (€23). Shuttle boats also ferry people to Platja de Formentor (€8.30, 25 minutes). Snoop around the harbour to see what the options are.

Rent March (☎ 971 864784; Carrer de Joan XXIII 89) hires out all sorts of bikes, from simple no-gears jobs (€5 per day) to Onix Obrea 27-gear cycles (€20 per day). They also rent out scooters.

A weekly market is staged in town on Wednesdays.

NORTHERN MALLORCA

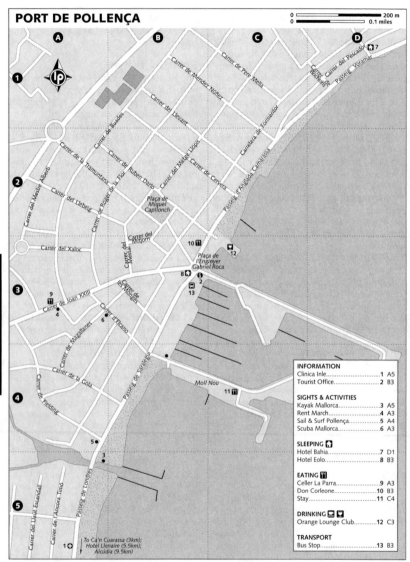

PORT DE POLLENÇA

INFORMATION
Clinica Inle.............................1 A5
Tourist Office........................2 B3

SIGHTS & ACTIVITIES
Kayak Mallorca.....................3 A5
Rent March............................4 A3
Sail & Surf Pollença...............5 A4
Scuba Mallorca.....................6 A3

SLEEPING
Hotel Bahia...........................7 D1
Hotel Eolo.............................8 B3

EATING
Celler La Parra.......................9 A3
Don Corleone.......................10 B3
Stay.....................................11 C4

DRINKING
Orange Lounge Club............12 C3

TRANSPORT
Bus Stop..............................13 B3

To Ca'n Cuarassa (3km);
Hotel Llenaire (5.5km);
Alcúdia (9.5km)

Sleeping

Hotel Eolo (☎ 971 866550; www.hoteleolo.com; Plaça de l'Enginyer Gabriel Roca 2; s/d €38/70; ☺ Mar-Oct) Smack in the heart of the action, just back from the marina, are these straightforward digs, built over several floors and with few frills. Rooms have tiled floors, serviceable bathrooms and are kept neat and tidy. The best part is the view, so try for a room with a balcony. There is a busy pizzeria downstairs.

Hotel Bahia (☎ 971 866562; www.hoposa.com; Passeig Voramar s/n; s/d €66/76, d with sea views €106-134; ☺ Apr-Oct; ▨) A 19th-century villa converted into a hotel, the Bahia occupies a waterfront spot along a shady pedestrian esplanade. If you can shell out the extra for sea views, do so! Rooms are crisp with parquet floors, but those with views (and a couple with balconies) are a treat.

Hotel Llenaire (☎ 971 535251; www.hotelllenaire.com; Camí de Llenaire Km3.8; s/d €218/290; P ♨ 🖳 ☻) The most alluring of Port de Pollença's hotels, this largely 19th-century town house dominates a rise (at a perfect height to look across the bay) about 4km inland from the southern limits of town (signposted). The spirit of the grand stone manor has been maintained and the bedrooms are a combination of old and new, with antique furniture, contemporary art and Persian throw rugs on the exquisite tiled floors.

Eating

Don Corleone (☎ 971 867981; Passeig d'Anglada Camarassa 13; meals €7-10; ♡ Mon-Sat) Sometimes you just feel like a pizza. Problem is, it's easy to be disappointed. This place doesn't look promising, but the pizzas are good enough for Palma folk to make the occasional pilgrimage here.

Celler La Parra (☎ 971 865041; Carrer de Joan XXIII 84; meals €20-30; ♡ daily) In business since the 1960s, this is about as traditionally Mallorcan as it gets around here. True, the 18th-century wine vats have clearly been dragged in from somewhere else, but it serves up genuine island fare. Fresh fish depends on market prices, or you could go for *lechona* at €15 and finish with a classic Spanish dessert, *pijama* (tinned peach slices, a clump of flan, two balls of ice cream covered in whipped cream with chocolate topping).

ourpick Ca'n Cuarassa (☎ 971 864266; meals €40; ♡ 9am-11pm; P) This rambling collection of houses sits opposite the water 3km south of central Port de Pollença and offers a large garden dining space and kids' play area. They do a long menu of island and Spanish food. A good starter might be the *esparragos verdes frescos a la parrilla con salsa de almendras* (fresh green asparagus in almond sauce), followed by *lenguado con salsa de alcaparras* (sole in a caper sauce). They have a kids' menu too.

Stay (☎ 971 864013; Moll Nou s/n; meals €45; ♡ daily) The Gassó family, the same folks who operate Ca'n Cuarassa, completely remodelled this seaside haven of mixed Med cooking in 2006. This is seaside chic, with an extensive outdoor dining area out on the pier. Yachties and their ilk hang here, savouring things like *crema ligera de gambas al Riesling* (shrimp cream

with Riesling) and *cigalas a la parrilla* (grilled Dublin Bay prawns). They have a kids' menu and you can have breakfast here too.

Drinking

Port Pollença doesn't exactly go off. You have to feel for those somewhat lost-looking adolescents wandering about late at night, dreaming of Ibiza clubs and wishing they hadn't been dragged here by their insensitive parents.

Orange Lounge Club (Passeig d'Anglada Camarassa s/n; ♡ 7pm-midnight) This is one place worth seeking out. It sets up by the Hotel Daina's waterfront swimming pool for chilling, cocktail-sipping and light DJ sounds. No-one seems to garner the courage to have a dip though!

Getting There & Away

BUS

The 340 bus from Palma to Pollença continues to Port de Pollença (15 minutes direct or 30 minutes via Cala Sant Vicenç). Bus 352 makes the run between Port de Pollença and Ca'n Picafort (€2.20, one hour), stopping at Alcúdia and Port d'Alcúdia along the way.

CAR & MOTORCYCLE

Port de Pollença lies 7km northeast of Pollença. From here the road to Cap de Formentor unfolds eastward, while the main Ma2200 road heads south around the bay to Alcúdia. There are one motorbike-rental and seven car-rental outlets in Port de Pollença.

CAP DE FORMENTOR

Doubtless one of the most spectacular stretches of Mallorca's coast (and there is sturdy competition), the 18km stretch from Port de Pollença (via the Ma2210) can really only be done with your own motor, bicycle or two legs.

The road quickly climbs away from Port de Pollença, opening up splendid views of the bay. More breathtaking is the **Mirador de Sa Creueta** (232m), 3km northeast of Port de Pollença. From this lookout cliffs plunge into the depths on the peninsula's north coast. To the east, just off the coast, floats the **Illot del Colomer**, a rocky islet. From the same spot you can climb a couple of kilometres up a side road to the **Talaia d'Albercuix** watchtower (380m). It was built to warn of pirates and you can see why; the views extend far out to sea.

NORTHERN MALLORCA

WALKERS' OPTIONS

The peninsula offers several challenges for those with itchy feet, including various trails leading down to largely pebbly beaches and inlets. The walk from Port de Pollença to **Cala Bóquer** is signposted off a roundabout on the main road to Cap de Formentor. This valley walk, with the rocky Serra del Cavall Bernat walling off the western flank, is an easy 3km hike. About 11km from Port de Pollença, separate trails lead off left and right from the road (there is some rough parking here) to **Cala Figuera** on the north flank and **Cala Murta** on the south. The former walk is down a bare gully to a narrow shingle beach, where the water's colours are mesmerising. The latter walk is through mostly wooded land to a stony beach. Each takes about 40 minutes down. Near Cala Murta but tougher to reach by land is **Cala Gossalba**. In all cases pack food and drink.

A couple of other small inlets to check out along the coast between Port de Pollença and Cala Murta are **Cala des Caló** and **Cala En Feliu**. Walkers can also hike to or from the cape along the **Camí Vell del Cap**, a poorly defined track that crisscrosses and at times follows the main road. At Port de Pollença you could then link with the GR221 trail that runs the length of the Serra de Tramuntana.

The Pollença and Port de Pollença tourist offices can give you booklets with approximate trail maps, which for these walks should be sufficient.

From here, the Ma2210 sinks down through the woods some 4km to **Platja de Formentor** (aka Platja del Pi). Parking costs €4 for the day.

The **Hotel Formentor** (Map p134; ☎ 971 899101; www.hotelformentor.net; s/d €300/479; ☺ Apr-Oct; Ⓟ Ⓧ Ⓡ) is a jewel of pre-WWII days and a Mallorca classic. The whole area (including the beach and offshore island) was bought by an Argentine businessman in the 1920s and remains private property. From 1929 the ritzy hotel digs have played host to the likes of Grace Kelly, Winston Churchill, Mikhail Gorbachev, John Wayne and the Dalai Lama. Rooms are pleasing without being the latest in grand luxury. The singles are a little small, but the seaside doubles and suites are a taste of paradise, if only for their privileged position.

From here the road slithers another 11km out to the cape and its **lighthouse**, where you'll find a snack joint, views to Cap Ferrutx to the south and a short walking track (the Camí del Moll del Patronet) south to another viewpoint.

The 353 bus runs from Ca'n Picafort to Cap de Formentor (€2.90, one hour 20 minutes, twice daily May to October) and passes through Port d'Alcúdia, Alcúdia and Port de Pollença. Two extra services run between Port de Pollença and Cap de Formentor. The only other option during May to October is the 360 bus from Palma (€5.80; 1½ hours, Monday to Saturday), which departs at 10.15am and stops at Inca and Alcúdia on the way. The return leg leaves at 3.30pm.

BADIA D'ALCÚDIA

The long beaches of this huge bay dominate Mallorca's northeast coast, its broad sweeps of sand stretching from Port d'Alcúdia to Ca'n Picafort.

ALCÚDIA

pop 15,900 / 20m

Wedged between the Badia de Pollença and Badia d'Alcúdia, Alcúdia sits next door to what was once Mallorca's prime Roman settlement. Remnants of the Roman theatre can be seen and the old town (whose name is about all that remains from the Muslim period) is still partly protected by medieval walls.

Information

The **tourist office** (☎ 971 897100; Carrer Major 17; ☺ 9.30am-3pm & 5-7pm Mon, Wed & Fri, 9.30am-3pm Tue, Thu & Sun, 10am-1pm Sat) is in the heart of the old town. The town hall's website (www.alcudia .net) has interactive street maps. For more listings tips and other information check out www.thealcudiaguide.com and www.alcudia pollensa.blogspot.com.

Sights & Activities

The ruins of the Roman town of **Pol·lentia** (☎ 971 897102; www.pollentia.net; adult/student & senior incl museum €2/1.25; ☺ 9.30am-8.20pm Tue-Sun May-Sep, 10am-4pm Tue-Fri, 10am-2pm Sat & Sun Oct-Apr) lie just outside Alcúdia's walls (the entrance is on Avinguda dels Prínceps d'Espanya). Founded around 70 BC, it was Rome's principal city in Mallorca and is the most important archaeological site on the island. It reached its apogee in the 1st and 2nd centuries AD. A visit takes you through three distinct areas. In the northwest corner is the Portella residential area. Signs indicate the layout of three houses in particular – the first and most interesting is the **Casa dels Dos Tresors** (House of the Two Treasures), which stood from the 1st to the 5th centuries AD and was a typical Roman house centred on an atrium. A short stroll away are the remnants of the **Forum**, which boasted three temples and rows of *tabernae* (shops). Finally, you walk another few hundred metres to reach the somewhat crumbly 1st-century AD **Teatre Romà** (Roman Theatre), nowadays used for performances in August.

Back in town, the same ticket gets you entry to the one-room **Museu Monogràfic de Pol·lentia** (☎ 971 547004; www.pollentia.net; Carrer de Sant Jaume 30; ⏳ 11am-2pm & 4-7pm Tue-Sun May-Sep, 10am-4pm Tue-Fri, 10am-2pm Sat & Sun Oct-Apr), with fragments of statues, coins, jewellery, household figurines of divinities and other odds and ends dug up at the site.

Just across the road in the eponymous church is the **Museu de Sant Jaume** (☎ 971 548665; Plaça de Jaume Ques s/n; adult/child €1/free; ⏳ 10am-1pm Mon-Sat), which could hold your attention if you're into priestly vestments and other religious paraphernalia from the past.

Perhaps more interesting is simply walking around town. Although largely rebuilt, the city walls are impressive. Those on the north side are largely the medieval originals. Near the Porta Roja (Red Gate) are remnants of an **18th-century bridge** and, just beyond, the Plaça de Toros (bullring) has been built into a Renaissance-era fortified bastion. Wandering inside the town is well worthwhile. Almost too squeaky clean, it is dotted with handsome mansions. Among them are **Ca'n Domènech** (Carrer dels Albellons 7), **Ca'n Canta** (Carrer Major 18), **Ca'n Torró** (Carrer d'En Serra 15) and **Ca'n Fondo** (Carrer d'En Serra 13).

Want to take a hike? Some 4.5km east of Alcúdia in a relatively isolated house, Sa Bassa Blanca, is the **Fundació Yannick i Ben Jakober** (☎ 971 549880; www.fundacionjakober.org; Camí de Coll Baix s/n; admission free Tue, by guided, prebooked tour only Wed-Sat, adult/child under 10yr €9/free; ⏳ 9.30am-12.30pm

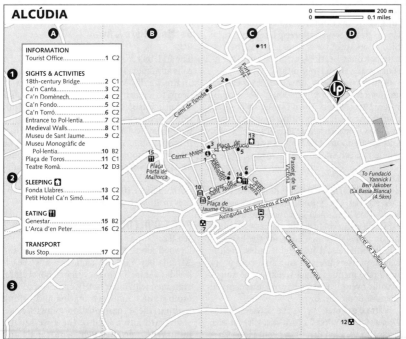

ALCÚDIA

0 ————— 200 m
0 ————— 0.1 miles

INFORMATION
Tourist Office............................1 C2

SIGHTS & ACTIVITIES
18th-century Bridge..................2 C1
Ca'n Canta................................3 C2
Ca'n Domènech........................4 C2
Ca'n Fondo...............................5 C2
Ca'n Torró................................6 C2
Entrance to Pol·lentia..............7 C2
Medieval Walls.........................8 C1
Museu de Sant Jaume..............9 C2
Museu Monogràfic de
  Pol·lentia..............................10 B2
Plaça de Toros........................11 C1
Teatre Romà...........................12 D3

SLEEPING
Fonda Llabres..........................13 C2
Petit Hotel Ca'n Simó..............14 C2

EATING
Genestar.................................15 B2
L'Arca d'en Peter.....................16 C2

TRANSPORT
Bus Stop.................................17 C2

To Fundació
Yannick i
Ben Jakober
(Sa Bassa Blanca)
(4.5km)

& 2.30-5.30pm Tue, guided tours 11am & 4pm Wed-Sat). This is a strange beast, a cultural institution that works on the restoration of artworks and concentrates on children's portraits from the 16th to 19th centuries. Many of these are on permanent display, along with other works of modern and contemporary art. Sculptures by Ben Jakober and Yannick Vu, the British artist couple who live here some of the time, litter the garden. In May you can also visit a rose garden. Follow the signs to Fundació and Bonaire. At the Bodega del Sol restaurant, turn right and keep on down the road, which turns into a potholed track. The foundation is on the right.

Festivals & Events
Tuesday and Sunday are market days in Alcúdia, held on and around Passeig de la Victòria. The big annual market event is the **Fira d'Alcúdia**, held on the first weekend of October and bringing a produce market together with traditional dances, music and parades.

Sleeping
Fonda Llabres (☎ 971 545000; www.fondallabres.com; Plaça de sa Constitució; s/d €30/36; 🛇) Here's a cheerful cheapy overlooking the central square. Good, clean rooms with crisp linen and white tiled floors spread over three storeys. The best have balconies overlooking the square. Downstairs is a lively bar-restaurant.

Petit Hotel Ca'n Simó (☎ 971 549260; www.cansimo .com; Carrer de Sant Jaume 1; s/d €78/106; 🛇 🛋) A renovated 19th-century town house, with seven double rooms. It is wondrous how they managed to squeeze in a little indoor pool, Jacuzzi and fitness room. Out back is a sunny patio, where you can sit down for a meal.

Eating
Genestar (☎ 971 549157; Plaça Porta de Mallorca 1; set meals plus drinks €24; 🕑 lunch & dinner Mon-Sat Sep-Dec, Feb-Jul, dinner Mon-Sat Aug) This modern, designer establishment is an oddly soulless spot just beyond the city walls. Look for the bamboo trunks outside. At just eight tables, enthusiastic punters are served a five-course set meal (the menu changes weekly) that ranges broadly over Mediterranean and international themes. Book ahead.

L'Arca d'en Peter (☎ 971 539178; Carrer d'En Serra 22; meals €25-30; 🕑 May-Oct, lunch & dinner Tue-Sat, lunch Sun Nov-Jan, Mar & Apr) Part of the Petit Hotel Ca'n

---

POSEIDON'S GRASS

Beach lovers are occasionally a little put off by the appearance at the water's edge (or strewn over the beach) of great rafts of what many mistake for algae. This is sea grass, (poseidon grass or *poseidonia*), vital for the hindering of erosion on the seabed. The oxygen it gives off helps clean the water, attracts abundant sealife (some of which lives in among the grass's leaves) and slows global warming by absorbing carbon dioxide. Thick layers of this stuff on some beaches actually help keep them intact. It doesn't make it any more pleasant (especially as it sometimes gives off an unpleasant odour) but perhaps there is some comfort in knowing that its presence is good for the maritime environment.

Simó, this old-town charmer with internal courtyard and exposed stone walls offers mixed Med cookery: anything from *raviolis de foie con salsa de trufas* (foie gras ravioli with truffle sauce) to *carré con polenta al aroma de menta* (lamb and polenta with a hint of mint).

Getting There & Away
BUS
The 351 bus from Palma to Platja de Muro calls at Alcúdia (€4.40, one hour, from five to 16 times a day May to October). The service drops to a maximum of five from November to April. Bus 352 connects Ca'n Picafort with Port de Pollença as often as every 15 minutes from May to October. From Ca'n Picafort it costs €1.40 (45 minutes) to Alcúdia. The frequency drops to 11 a day from November to April. Local service 356 connects Alcúdia with Port d'Alcúdia and the beach of Platja d'Alcúdia (€1.10, 15 minutes, every 15 minutes from May to October).

PORT D'ALCÚDIA
pop 1820
Draped along the northeast corner of the Alcúdia bay, Port d'Alcúdia is a busy beach holiday centre. From the original port centre, crammed with older hotels, eateries and bars around the main town marina and fishing harbour, the accommodation sprawl spreads southward into a kind of (dare we say it?) mini-Venice arrangement with canals and

internal lakes. On the seaward side, pleasant beaches are the name of the game.

Information

Main Tourist Office (☎ 971 547257; www.alcudia.net; Passeig Marítim; ☼ 9.30am-8.30pm Easter-Oct) Located in a booth behind the marina.

Tourist Office (☎ 971 892615; Carretera d'Artà 68) Another branch is located further southwest. It can have unreliable opening hours.

Sights & Activities

About 1.6km southwest of the tourist office on Carretera d'Artà, the **Cova de Sant Martí** is an otherworldly grotto. As early as 1268 a religious sanctuary was installed in this 15m-deep hollow. After a miracle brought rain in 1507, chapels to St Martin and St George were erected inside. Today the oldest part of the human-constructed elements are the slippery, mossy steps leading down into this cool cavern.

About 600m inland from the beach is something more appealing for the kids. **Hidropark** (☎ 971 891672; www.hidropark.com; Avinguda del Tucá s/n; adult/child 3-11yr/under 3yr €17/8/free; ☼ 10.30am-6pm May-Oct) is a typical water park with slides, wave pool and infants' splash pool area.

Numerous excursions run from the port from May to October. **Transportes Marítimos Brisa** (☎ 971 545811; www.tmbrisa.com) offers three daily trips (€16, two hours) on a glass-bottom catamaran to Platja des Coll Baix (p148). A long version of the trip goes to Platja de Formentor (€21, four hours) and runs twice a day. Children go for half price. Other companies abound along the waterfront, offering jaunts around the bay in anything from speed boats to luxury yachts.

Divers should approach **5 Oceanos** (☎ 971 549957; www.5oceanos.com; Avinguda del Mal Pas 1, Bonaire), located in one of the northern suburbs facing the Badia de Pollença. It offers try-out dives (€75 for novices), cave dives and dives around Cap de Formentor.

Parapente Alfabia (☎ 971 891366 or 687 626536; www.parapentealfabia.com) offers the chance to go paragliding. An accompanied flight of about 20 minutes for beginners costs €80. Ask for Oscar.

At **Wind & Friends** (☎ 627 086950; www.windfriends.com; Carrer de Neptú; ☼ Apr-Oct), next to the Hotel

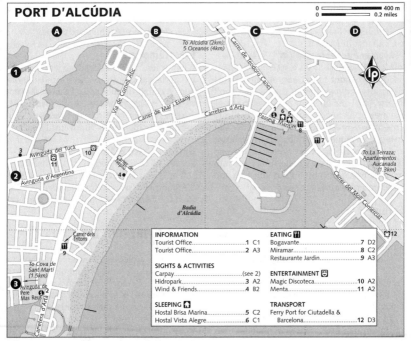

PORT D'ALCÚDIA

Sunwing on the waterfront, you can get organised for sailing, windsurfing and kite surfing. A four-day course in windsurfing will cost €195.

Festivals & Events

The **Festival de Sant Pere** celebrates the port's patron saint, Peter, on 29 June. The week running up to this day is a time of concerts, kids' shows and activities. On the big day a statue of the Sant Pere is paraded on land and sea.

Sleeping

Port d'Alcúdia teems with hotels and apartments. The tourist offices can provide lists and you can also search on www.alcudia hotels.com.

Hostal Vista Alegre (☎ 971 547347; www.hvista -alegre.com; Passeig Marítim 22; s/d €20/35; 🅿) Friendly managers run this tidy hotel just by the marina in the heart of the town. The singles are pokey and have no air-con, while the doubles have either sea views (and breeze) or air-con. The doubles have their own bathroom.

Hostal Brisa Marina (☎ 971 549450; www.hbris amarina.com; Passeig Marítim 22; s/d €35/50, d with sea views €65-75; 🅿) Next door, a similar deal is offered. Although the rooms have a more modern, welcoming feel and crisp décor, there really isn't all that much in it.

Apartamentos Aucanada (☎ 971 545402; www .stilhotels.com; Carrer de S'Illot s/n; apt €90-104; 🅿 May-Oct; 🅿 🖥) About 1.5km east of central Port d'Alcúdia and just short of the exclusive golf course, you wind up in the privileged residential area of Alcanada (Aucanada). This leafy area offers a hotel and these simple one- and two-bed apartments with bright white décor and tiled floors. They come with a kitchen and balcony; the best have wonderful views south over the bay. The complex has a market and children's play area.

Eating

There is no shortage of cheap and cheerful eateries, including Chinese, Indian, fast food and more all over town.

Miramar (☎ 971 545293; Passeig Marítim 2; meals €25-35; 🕑 Feb-Dec) Take up a spot on the ample terrace of this waterfront classic (since 1871) for one of a broad selection of paellas or *fideuà* (roughly a vermicelli noodle version of paella, €11 to €13). Standard fish dishes (sole, bream etc for around €16) are well prepared.

Bogavante (☎ 971 547364; Carrer de Teodoro Canet 2; meals €40-45; 🕑 Tue-Sun mid-Nov–Dec) This place has more stylish pretensions and occasionally has contemporary art on the walls. Timber floors, halogen lighting and a huge tank full of sea critters awaiting their fate are the interior's hallmarks. Opt for classics such as sole meunière or dig deeper into your pocket for fresh catch of the day (sold by weight).

ourpick La Terraza (☎ 971 545611; www.culinari aalcanada.com; Placeta de Pompeu Fabra 7, Alcanada; meals €45-50; 🕑 Easter-Oct) The setting's the thing. Ignore that the building looks like a pink, seashell-covered watchtower and proceed to the seaside terrace for a pre-dinner drink. You can have a set meal for €40 here or proceed to the restaurant proper. They have an extensive menu, especially of creatures from the deep. The *caldereta de pescado y marisco* (€26) is a hearty fish and shellfish hotpot.

Restaurante Jardín (☎ 971 892391; www.restaurante jardin.com; Carrer dels Tritons s/n; meals €45-55; 🕑 Tue-Sun Jun-Sep, Fri-Sun & holidays Oct-Dec, mid-Mar–May) is a garden of culinary delights. The cooking brings *nouvelle* twists to essential Med products, with such offerings as *delicias de Ibérico con gambas* (variety of Spanish cured ham slices with prawns) followed by various fishy options or a succulent *solomillo de buey a la mostaza dulce* (beef sirloin in sweet mustard).

Entertainment

A family resort, Port d'Alcúdia is jammed with UK-style pubs and the like around the old port. A couple of clubs, **Magic Discoteca** (Avinguda del Tucá 1; 🕑 10.30pm-6am May-Oct) and **Menta** (www .mentadisco.net; Avinguda del Tucá 5; 🕑 7.30pm-6am), keep the gyrating night owls happy until dawn.

Getting There & Away

See Alcúdia (p144) for bus information.

You'll find eight car-rental outlets in Port d'Alcúdia. Boats leave for Ciutadella on the island of Menorca (see p209) from the ferry port.

CYCLE TOUR: PORT D'ALCÚDIA & AROUND

This ride is a pleasant dawdle through tranquil wetlands, followed by an old town turn and a real rollercoaster ride around the bay. It's best spread over a full day with frequent stops to take in the surroundings.

Setting out from Port d'Alcúdia's Passeig Marítim, head south towards C'an Picafort,

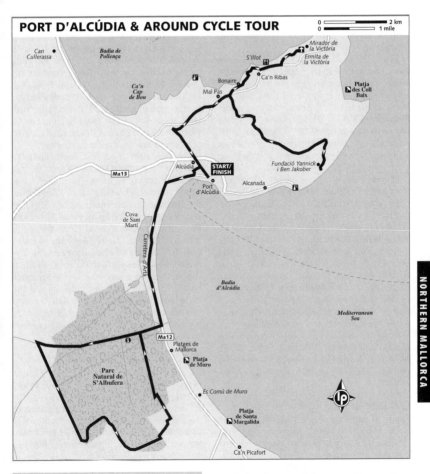

PORT D'ALCÚDIA & AROUND CYCLE TOUR

RIDE FACTS

Start/finish Port d'Alcúdia
Distance 32km (41km including detour)
Difficulty easy to moderate
Bike hybrid or mountain bike

signed left at the first roundabout you come to. Carretera d'Artà stretches rather uneventfully from here for 4.5km, before passing over a canal, at which point you should take an immediate right. A pitted road leads up to the **Parc Natural de S'Albufera's** information centre (see p148). From here, route 3 is the best option for cyclists, skirting the wetlands' edge and allowing leisurely pedalling. Despite the potholes, the peaceful surroundings and accompanying avian chorus make this a lovely ride, and there's plenty to keep a keen twitcher occupied.

Retrace your tracks to Port d'Alcúdia but follow the road (Carrer del Coral) round to the left instead of carrying along to the seafront. Continue until you hit a main road and take a left towards Alcúdia. After 2km you'll arrive at the **Plaça de Carles V** and one of the town's sets of turreted gates. Take a while to wander through the charming old town (see p142), or simply stock up on water or picnic fare.

From Plaça de Carles V head down the road leading to Carrer de la Creu (signed) and take the next available right. At the main road, turn left. After 2km you'll come to a small junction with Fundacio signed to the right; continue straight on.

Here, the road begins to undulate as it passes through upmarket **Mal Pas** and **Bonaire** where yachts bob calmly in the harbour, before climbing higher around the bay. You can pause at the beautifully sited but casual **Bar-Restaurante S'Illot** (☎ 971 546320; Camí vell de la Victòria s/n; mains €8.50-16.50, tapas €7-10; ◔ 11am-11pm), with a terrace overlooking the bay. It serves fish and tapas, as well as ice creams, and there's a great spot to picnic just next door.

If you've still got some energy left, follow the signs to the **Mirador de la Victòria**, the mountains rising to your right and a stunning view of the Badia de Pollença to your left.

You can take a well-earned break at the **Ermita de la Victòria**, where there's a snack bar and lodgings (see below). Once you've got your breath back, breeze all the way back down to Alcúdia or, if it's a Tuesday, consider a detour to the fascinating **Fundació Yannick i Ben Jakober** (p143), a left turn when you return to the junction at the Bodega del Sol restaurant. Otherwise follow the signs back to Port d'Alcúdia.

You can rent bikes at many of the car-hire places along Carretera d'Artà. At **Carpay** (☎ 971 891779; Avinguda de Pere Mas Reus 2) you pay €6 to €10 per day depending on bike type and number of days.

CAP DES PINAR

From Alcúdia and Port d'Alcúdia, a great chunk of land juts eastward into the deep blue, bristling with Aleppo pine woods at its eastern end as it rises to a series of precipitous cliffs. From Alcúdia go northeast through residential Mal Pas and Bonaire on a scenic route that stretches to Cap des Pinar. Unfortunately, the cape is military land and off limits but the rest is well worth it. After 1.5km of winding coast road east of Bonaire you reach the beach and bar-restaurant of S'Illot. Overlooking it all is the horrible hulk of the **Albergue la S'Illot** (☎ 971 545395; dm/full board €14.50/26.50; ◔ Mar-Nov), basic but good value if you don't mind bunking down in dorms.

our pick **Ermita de la Victòria** (☎ 971 549912; www .lavictoriahotel.com; Carretera Cap des Pinar; s/d €45/66) About 600m east of S'Illot, a side road winds up high to a magnificent viewpoint and this early 15th-century hermitage. The 12 renovated rooms have a crisp feel, all white walls and cream linen with timber window shutters and beams.

The massive stone walls and terracotta floors lend it Mediterranean grace and the position is perfect. The nearby **restaurant** (☎ 971 547173; ◔ Tue-Sun) is great for a simple paella while gazing out over the bay below. From here, it's about a 40-minute uphill walk to **Sa Talaia**, a 16th-century lookout tower with views to the north, east and south. Back on the main road, walk about 1.5km east from the junction to where the road is blocked. It's worth the trip to continue savouring the changing views.

Another option on this peninsula is to head for the **Platja des Coll Baix**. From Alcúdia it's about 8km to an open spot in the woods where you can leave your car or bike. Follow the directions for the Fundació Yannick i Ben Jakober (p143) and keep on for another 2km. From this spot, you could climb the south trail to Sa Talaia. Then follow the signs to Coll Baix, a fairly easy half-hour descent. The main trail will lead you to the rocks south of the beach, from where you have to scramble back it. A small flotilla of sailboats and the occasional tour boat can populate the bay, so early morning (sunrise!) is the best time to visit this lovely grey pebbly-sandy affair lapped by translucent waters.

PARC NATURAL DE S'ALBUFERA

As the southward sprawl of Port d'Alcúdia peters out into a shady seaside strip of hotels, apartments, supermarkets and eateries, the inland side of the Ma12 reveals a haven of natural beauty. The 688-hectare **Parc Natural de S'Albufera** (Map p134; ◔ 9am-7pm Apr-Sep, 9am-5pm Oct-Mar) is home to a bustling selection of bird life. A much greater area of wetland emerged more than 100,000 years ago. In the 19th century especially, attempts were made (with differing degrees of success) to dry out the mix of salt and fresh water to create cultivable land and combat malaria. The so-called Gran Canal at the heart of the park was designed to channel the water out to sea. The five-arched **Pont de Sa Roca** bridge was built over it in the late 19th century to ease travel between Santa Margalida and Alcúdia. Many of the *marjales* (parcels of arable land won from the wetlands) date to the same period.

The island government bought some of the land in 1985 and the park was born. Its name derives from an old Arab toponym, Albuhayra (lagoon). Around 400 plant species and 230 bird species (80% of the types of bird known in the Balearic Islands), some of them permanent residents and others migratory, have been catalogued here.

The **Centro de Recepción de Sa Roca** (☎ 971 892250; ⏰ 9am-4pm) is about 1km from the park entrance and can provide information on the park and its bird life. From here, you can walk or cycle about 12km of trails (there are four signposted paths). Some *aguaits* (timber bird-watching observatories – come inside and watch in silence) are better than others. You'll see lots of wading birds in action from the Bishop I and II *aguaits* on the north side of the Gran Canal. Holders of the Targeta Verda (p16) can use park bicycles and binoculars for free.

Facing the sea across from the park entrance is **Platja de Muro**, which stretches north to Port d'Alcúdia and south to Ca'n Picafort. A 3km stretch of it is backed by **Es Comú de Muro**, a thick tangle of Aleppo pines and other dune flora that gives the beach a wilder feel and is part of the Parc Natural.

Buses between Ca'n Picafort and Alcúdia stop by a small car park near the park entrance.

SOUTH OF ALCÚDIA

CA'N PICAFORT & AROUND

A smaller version of Port d'Alcúdia, Ca'n Picafort (7km further southeast around the bay) and its southern extension, **Son Bauló**, is a package-tour frontier town, somewhat raw and raggedy. But the beaches are pretty good and there are some interesting archaeological sites. There has been a settlement of some sort here since at least 1860.

Information

The **tourist office** (☎ 971 850310; Plaça de Gabriel Roca; ⏰ 9am-1pm & 5-7.30pm Mon-Fri Easter-Oct) is at the south end of Ca'n Picafort.

Sights & Activities

The bulk of the town is an uninspiring grid of streets backing on to **Platja de Santa Margalida**, a crowded shallow beach with turquoise water. The promenade behind it is jammed with eateries offering everything from chip butties to Jaegerschnitzel.

The best beach options lie beyond the centre. To the northwest (walk along the beach from the heart of Ca'n Picafort) the beach of **Ses Casetes dels Capellans** (signposted off the Ma12 at the roundabout where you enter Ca'n Picafort

from the north) is broad and backed by several beach restaurants and bars that exude a relaxed feel. Keep walking north about 1km and you are on the beach of Es Comú de Muro (left).

To the southwest, where the Son Bauló hotel and apartment belt ends, is **La Platja de Son Bauló** and, beyond the trickle of water from the Torrent de Son Bauló, the wilder **Platja de Son Real**. The latter is not kept as clean as the former, but it is worth walking along here for several reasons. This almost 5km stretch of coast, with snippets of sandy strands in among the rock points, is backed only by low dunes, scrub and bushland dense with Aleppo pines. Much of this area between the coast and the Ma12 highway, once private farmland, has been converted into the **Finca Pública de Son Real** (admission free; ⏰ 10am-7pm Apr-Sep, 10am-5pm Oct-Mar). Its main entrance is just south of the Km18 milestone on the Ma12, and the ramshackle buildings of a once proud *possessió* (now being renovated) host an information office for those who wish to walk the property's several trails. From the seaside, you can cross the fence at various points.

From the *possessió*, one trail leads through a largely abandoned fig plantation to the overgrown Talayotic ruins of **Es Figueral de Son Real**. This settlement dates at least to 1000 BC and consists of several buildings.

Greater visual impact comes from the **Necròpolis de Son Real**, on the sea about 10 minutes' walk southeast of Platja de Son Bauló. It appears to have been a Talayotic cemetery with 110 tombs (in which the remains of more than 300 people were found). The tombs have the shape of mini-*talayots* and date as far back as the 7th century BC. Some suggest this was a commoners' graveyard. Please don't walk on the tombs.

A few hundred metres further southeast, the **Illot dels Porros** also contains remains of an ancient necropolis. It's a fairly easy swim for the moderately fit.

Virtually in front of the islet is one of two obelisk-shaped aiming towers. Its twin is further up the hill within the Finca Pública de Son Real (for more on these see the boxed text, p150).

Sleeping & Eating

The waterfront of Ca'n Picafort is lined with ageing apartments and 1970s hotel blocks whose façades could often do with a lick of paint. They are much of a muchness and mostly work with package tour agencies.

Hostal El Cel (☎ 971 851394; hotelelcel@gmail.com; Passeig de Colom 79; d €45) A handy cheapie on the corner of Carrer de les Illes Canaries and one block back from the beach. The rooms are done in basic off-white and are bereft of all but the essentials. Most have balconies though and this place often has something going at short notice.

Casal Santa Eulàlia (☎ 971 852732; www.casal-santaeulalia.com; Carretera de Santa Margalida-Alcúdia Km6; s/d €195/220; ☾ dinner Mar-Oct; Ⓟ 🚫 🖳 🖳) If being 2km inland from Ca'n Picafort (take the Ma3140) doesn't bother you, this rural retreat is just what the doctor ordered. The huddle of stone houses dates to 1242 and has been renovated with classic rural taste. A Jacuzzi bubbles below ground in the former grain silo. The restaurant has a fine reputation. They sometimes set up a barbecue by one of the pools.

Bar Sa Ximada (☎ 971 852310; Carretera d'Alcúdia 29; menú del día €8, meals €20-25; ☾ Mon-Sat) This workaday bar restaurant specialises in meat (around €11 to €14 for big slabs) grilled on hot stones. The midday set meal is filling and simple, served with a 1.5L bottle of *tinto de verano* (red wine mixed with lemonade). It's on the way out of town towards Port d'Alcúdia.

The waterfront and Avinguda de Josep Trias are lined with eateries, bars and pubs (all largely indistinguishable from one another). If you don't feel like watching *Coronation Street* while scoffing Yorkshire pudding you'll have

---

TAKING AIM

From just south of Port d'Alcúdia to Colònia de Sant Pere, you will see obelisks on or near the waterfront. No, the ancient Egyptians weren't here. As WWII raged around the Mediterranean after the Spanish Civil War, the Spanish navy decided to set up a series of *torres de enfilación* (aiming towers) for submarines operating in this strategic bay. They were built in pairs around the bay and allowed sub commanders to get more precise firing bearings, using the then red-painted tips of these obelisks (those in Ca'n Picafort have been restored, painted in bright white with their blood-red tips). Each obelisk was built 200m from its twin, and each pair at a distance of 1240m from the next.

---

to head to the Ma12, where several locals' places are scattered.

Drinking & Entertainment
The bulk of the pubs and bars, and a couple of *discotecas* for revelling until dawn, are bunched together on and around Avinguda de Josep Trias.

Getting There & Away
BUS
Bus 390 runs from Palma to Ca'n Picafort (€4.55, one hour 10 minutes, seven Monday to Saturday, four Sunday and holidays) via Llubí and Santa Margalida and on to Son Serra.

The 352 bus is the main service between Ca'n Picafort and Port de Pollença (€2.20, one hour), via Port d'Alcúdia and Alcúdia. It runs as often as every 15 minutes in summer, but drops to 11 runs from November to April.

CAR & MOTORCYCLE
Ca'n Picafort is on the Ma12 at about the halfway point along the Badia d'Alcúdia. From Palma, take the Ma13 motorway to Inca, turn off for Muro and then Ca'n Picafort.

SON SERRA DE MARINA
This sprawling holiday residential development spreads 5km east along the coast from Son Bauló. Mallorquins and Germans alike flock to its southeast edge, for here starts the dune-backed **Platja de Sa Canova** (aka S'Arenal or Platja de Son Serra), a 2km stretch of virgin beach. Archaeology fans may notice the square-based **Talayot de Son Serra** at the entrance to the town from the Ma12 highway.

Where the beach meets the settlement is where most people gather, among them wind and kite-surfing enthusiasts. Most wander into the **El Sol Sunshine Bar** (☎ 971 854029; Carrer de Joan Frontera; ☾ daily; 🖳) at some point for breakfast, lunch, dinner or a cocktail. With its wicker chairs, internet point and laid-back feeling, it generates an almost Malibu vibe (only the accents are more like Munich). Friday is pizza day and Sunday's for brunch (10am to 3pm). Inquire about the **Apartamentos 2 Playas** (☎ 630 017858; www.lavila.org/playamonte; 🚫) upstairs. There are six, which can take up to four people each. Prices vary depending on number of people, days and season. In August, two people would pay €160 for two days.

Some buses on the Palma–Ca'n Picafort run continue to here.

GETTING AWAY FROM IT ALL

Northeast along the coastal Ma3331, 3km from Colònia de Sant Pere and past a couple of often Poseidon grass–covered beaches, is the somnolent holiday settlement of **Betlem**. Not much goes on here, although you'll find two snoozy restaurants. Betlem is the beginning point for some pleasant striding. Along the coast, a 3km 4WD trail hugs the Aleppo pine–fringed shoreline till it reaches a tiny protected bay called **Es Caló**, where a couple of sailboats occasionally find shelter and a handful of people stretch out on the stony strand and swim in the emerald waters. Behind you, dramatic limestone hills rise sharply, some barely clothed in swaying grass. The brown earth of the coast is fragile and the bent trees are testimony to the prevailing windy clime. **Cap Ferrutx**, the windy cape north of Es Caló, is a tougher nut to crack as there are no trails.

Another trail climbs south from the southern entry to Betlem into the hills to reach the 19th-century **Ermita de Betlem** (after about 50 minutes' exertion). Hermits still live a silent life of self-sufficiency and contemplation in this sublime spot. Those not of a mind to walk can approach by car from Artà (see p167). The narrow, snake-like Ma3333 meanders for about 5km through woodland and fields before taking off to reach the top of the ridge at around 7km. The views down over the sea are breathtaking from this crest. The road then drops 2km to the hermitage, which lies at the western edge of the **Parc Natural de la Península de Llevant** (p169). Those who have walked up from Betlem can continue east over the ridge deeper into the park. It takes about 1½ hours from Betlem to **S'Alquera Vella d'Avall**, from where other trails splinter out across the park.

COLÒNIA DE SANT PERE

Named after the patron saint of fishers (St Peter), this peaceful spot was actually founded in 1881 as an agricultural settlement. Little farming goes on nowadays and the huddle of houses has expanded beyond the central square and church to accommodate a small populace that seems to be on permanent vacation. In the centre of town on the shady Passeig del Mar, some splash about in the water on the sandy, protected **Platja de la Colònia de Sant Pere**. Nearby is the small marina and fishing port. About 2.5km west, after the residential area of **S'Estanyol** (aka S'Estany des Bisbc), **Platja de Sa Canova** (see opposite) starts. From S'Estanyol the only way to Sa Canova is on foot.

Sleeping & Eating

Hotel Rocamar (☎ 971 828503; www.hotelrocamar.net; Carrer de Sant Mateu 9; s/d €80/117; 🅿 🖳 🖳) This renovated hotel is a breath from the central square and beach. Creams, beiges and browns dominate the décor and the spacious, light rooms have parquet floors and pleasantly neutral, white furniture. From the roof terrace, where you can plonk into the Jacuzzi, you can see the deep blue sea.

Sa Xarxa (☎ 971 589251; Passeig del Mar s/n; meals €30-45; 🕙 Tue-Sun mid-Feb–mid-Jan) They'll do all sorts of things for you at 'the Net', including Atlantic sole and an array of meat options, but the reason to come is for the catch of the day done simply in a salty crust. This shady, German-owned spot is the last in line as you head east along the waterfront. Everything, from the mozzarella and tomato salad with the fabulous pesto, to the carpaccio with a hint of truffle oil, is done with a delicate touch.

Getting There & Away

BUS

The 481 bus (a taxi bus for a maximum of four people) runs between Artà and Colònia de Sant Pere (€1.80, 30 minutes, up to six times a day). You must call ☎ 650 233957 by 7pm the day before to book the service.

CAR & MOTORCYCLE

Off the Ma12 road between Artà and Port d'Alcúdia, 7km west of Artà, a side road proceeds 4km north to Colònia de Sant Pere.

The Interior

Until the 1960s, the bulk of Mallorca's wealth came from farming. From potatoes to pork sausages, carobs to figs, and olive oil to wine, Mallorca both fed itself and exported to mainland Spain and beyond. Many of these traditional activities continue, although much farmland lies semiabandoned. As rural family fortunes have declined, the phenomenon of rural tourism has appeared as a knight in white armour to save some of the villages and country manor houses that otherwise would have quietly rotted away.

The area covered in this chapter is divided into a corridor running from Palma to Sa Pobla and known as Es Raiguer, a flat zone that hugs the foothills of the Serra de Tramuntana. To the south and east stretch the broad plains of Es Pla (the Plain), occasionally punctuated by hills topped by a monastery, hermitage or castle. The towns often have few outstanding sights beyond Cyclopean-looking churches, but offer a time-stood-still view of Mallorca. You'll discover hidden cloisters, lordly houses, Arab wells, ancient windmills, and out-of-the-way villages with traditional eateries in centuries-old wine cellars. All over the plains, routes and junctions have for centuries been marked by crucifixes. These 'road signs' are often of a singular beauty.

Shoppers should look out for fine wines, leather in Inca and pearls in Manacor.

HIGHLIGHTS

- Go on a leather-buying spree and feast traditionally in a *celler* in **Inca** (p155)
- Hunt for pearls in the showrooms of **Manacor** (p162)
- Revel at the Festes de la Verema in the wine capital of **Binissalem** (p154)
- Get lost in the **villages** north of Inca (p157)
- Inspect Murano's competition at the **Gordiola glassworks** outside Algaida (p160)
- Take divine inspiration from the views at the **Santuari de Sant Salvador** (p164)
- See how the rural señors lorded over the land at the mansion-museum of **Els Calderers** (p162)

★ Inca
★ Binissalem

Algaida ★

Els Calderers
★

★ Manacor

Santuari de
★ Sant Salvador

ES RAIGUER

Although the Ma13 motorway is quicker, it is more interesting to follow the old route (Ma13a) out of central Palma through the 'burbs, capturing the change as you plough through the capital's conurbation to the countryside.

SANTA MARIA DEL CAMÍ & AROUND

Just beyond the expanding commuter belt the Ma13a widens to become the bar-lined Plaça dels Hostals as you roll into Santa Maria del Camí. On its southern flank at No 30 rises the 17th-century **Antic Monestir de Nuestra Señora de la Soledad**, aka Can Conrado. If the main doors happen to be swung open, you can peer into the magnificent front courtyard, while a glimpse of the rear gardens can be had around the corner at Carrer Llarg. That street leads to the original heart of the town, Plaça de la Vila, a quiet medieval square presided over by the 17th-century **Casa de la Vila** (Town Hall).

One of the island's biggest names in wine, **Bodegas Macià Batle** (☎ 971 140014; www

.maciabatle.com; Camí Coanegra s/n; 9am-7pm Mon-Fri mid-Jun–mid-Oct, 9am-6.30pm Mon-Fri, & 9.30am-1pm Sat mid-Oct–mid-Jun) is based just outside of central Santa Maria.

The town's big celebration is the **Festes de Santa Margalida**, held over almost three weeks in July with concerts, traditional dances and communal meals. The key day is the 20th.

Northeast of central Santa Maria is one of the island's most exquisite country-manor getaways, **Read's Hotel** (☎ 971 140261; www.readshotel.com; Ca'n Moragues; d from €417; P ⚔ 🖳 🐕). Set in immaculate gardens with thick palm trees,

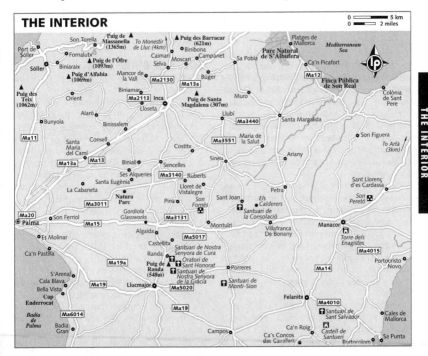

THE INTERIOR

this warm stone mansion offers 23 rooms. The better ones have their own terraces. There are indoor and outdoor pools and a spa. The main restaurant (meal €80), run by Marc Fosh and holder of a Michelin star, is one of the high points. From Plaça dels Hostals, follow the signs down country lanes for about 2km.

A couple of kilometres east of Santa Maria, **Consell** is another wine village that allows itself to be startled into life by its markets on Thursdays and Sundays.

The easiest way to get to stops along this route is by the regular Palma–Inca train. Santa Maria is 18 to 23 minutes from central Palma.

BINISSALEM

pop 6200 / 131m

Two more kilometres on from Consell and you enter the heart of the wine industry in this part of Mallorca, Binissalem (which like several towns in Es Raiguer has retained its Arabic name). Most of its buildings are made of a local white stone, and the central bulk of the **Església de Nostra Senyora de les Robines** is no exception.

From the mid-18th to the early 19th century, Binissalem's prosperity as a winemaking town was reflected in the building of several notable mansions. One that has been well preserved is Can Sabater, a country residence for the writer Llorenç Villalonga (see p37) and now the **Casa-Museu Llorenç Villalonga** (☎ 971 886014; www.cmvillalonga.org; Carrer de Bonaire 25; admission free; ⏲ 10am-2pm Mon-Sat & 4-8pm Tue & Thu). The furniture comes from his family and you can see how these manor houses worked, with a bread oven, 18th-century wine vats, a room set aside for the crushing of grapes underfoot, stables and so on. Summer concerts are held in the garden.

A weekly market is staged on Fridays, but much more important is the **Festes de la Verema** (aka Festa d'es Vermar), held on the last nine days of September to celebrate the yearly grape harvest with folk dancing, crafts markets, exhibitions and lots of local tipples. It culminates in a big public supper of *fideus de vermar,* a noodle dish with rabbit, snails and *sobrassada* (local sausage), among other things!

On the central square, sleep in the delightful **Scott's** (☎ 971 870100; www.scottshotel.com; Plaça de l'Església 12; s/d from €142/187; P ⛷ 🖵 🐾), a town house converted into a tasteful, country-style

comfort zone. Beautifully presented rooms and suites, all quite different, are siren songs to the weary, with cotton-percale sheets, goosedown pillows and Persian rugs. The flower-filled courtyards are a joy. They are planning to open a restaurant, but you can eat well at nearby **Singló** (☎ 971 870599; Plaça de l'Església 5; meals €20-30). Despite the cafeteria feel, it offers some enticing dishes, such as *porcella rostida* (roast suckling pig) or *bacallà a la mallorquina* (cod prepared with tomato and potato).

Binissalem is synonymous with wine. You can visit the big winery (launched in 1931), **José Luis Ferrer** (☎ 971 511050; www.vinosferrer.com; Carrer del Conquistador 103; guided tours €5.50; ⏲ tours 11am & 4.30pm Mon-Fri, 11am Sat, shop 9am-7pm Mon-Fri, 10am-2pm Sat), at the west end of the town, but you must call ahead. To step back in time, wander into **Ca'n Novell** (☎ 971 511310; Carrer de Bonaire 17; ⏲ 8am-1pm & 3-8pm Mon-Fri, 8.30am-2pm Sat), where locals fill their own bottles from huge, 18th-century vats. Made of olive wood and held together by sturdy rings of oak, these grand old barrels were a standard feature of cellars and mansions across much of this part of the island.

Binissalem is another eight minutes on from Santa Maria del Camí on the Palma–Inca train (€1.25).

SOUTH OF BINISSALEM

A 5km tootle south brings you to the town of **Biniali**.

ourpick **Sa Torre** (☎ 971 144011; www.sa-torre .com; Carrer de les Alqueries 70; d €134; P ⛷ 🐾), located about 1km west of town, is a wonderful haven that rests on the edge of the tiny hamlet Ses Alqueries (now home mostly to Palma commuters). This grand *finca* (manor house) has been in the same family since 1560 and offers five spacious, self-catering apartments. Some of the apartments look right onto a stand of almond trees, which are a treat to contemplate when they're in blossom. The former wine cellar, its high, dark vaults lined by 18th-century vats, is now home to a fine restaurant (meals €40; open Wednesday to Saturday).

Another 2.5km southwest, **Santa Eugènia** huddles up against something that can rarely be found in central Mallorca – a hill. It's worth passing through just to head up that hill (246m) for the views. At the other end of town, three windmills line a ridge that

---

WE DO IT OUR WAY

Andreu Villalonga's family has been making and selling wine in Binissalem under the label Ca'n Novell since at least 1932. Theirs is one of the few cellars left in Mallorca that sells *a granel* – straight from their giant, 18th-century timber vats into whatever container you bring along. Villalonga – no relation to the novelist, Llorenç (p37), who had his summer house a few doors down – is in the midst of the grape harvest in mid-September.

Is it looking like a good year? We have had to cut down part of the harvest that wasn't good, but the remainder is of excellent quality. The first harvest phase is done. We harvest in three lots, according to grape type, waiting for the right moment – in all it takes a few weeks.

Have things changed since your great-grandfather made wine? Enormously. You don't see anyone ploughing fields with mule and plough anymore! No-one knows how to make those timber vats we have. In the '30s, 50 to 60 houses made wine here. They made and sold it, but by March/April they were out. This was an agrarian society and families made a bit of everything. They didn't just live from wine.

Do you export? About 95% of what we make is for local consumption. In all Mallorca, only about 2000 hectares of grape are cultivated – which is very little.

Is it hard to live from this? It depends. In Mallorca there are many tiny wine-makers who will have trouble surviving… We're a middle-sized business and one of the only cellars to sell direct and *a granel*. We also bottle, but we are not in the Binissalem Denominación de Orígen (appellation). We don't want to be told what to do and how. We do what we want: make better wine, and cheaper!

Are you worried about climate change? It's a concern. Spain is becoming a desert. They are making wine in southern England. In some years the wine we make here may be more like that in Morocco or Algeria – higher in sugar and alcohol and with less acidity… If we don't change our ways and use of combustion engines, it's a worry, in the mid- to long term… Nowadays in Mallorca, we have an intermittent summer eight months of the year. There's hardly any winter. That's a fact.

---

could be the prow of the good ship Santa Eugènia.

ourpick **L'Escargot** (☎ 971 144535; Carrer Major 48; meals €30-35; ☽ dinner Wed-Mon), a delightful Gallic oasis in a two-storey house with a garden, is the other compelling region to visit the area. Indulge in various French cuts of beef, such as *onglet*, and follow with a tangy fruit crumble. The restaurant is just off the main road to Santa Maria del Camí, opposite a curio that could be left over from Arab days – an enormous *aljub* (cistern) that supplied the town with water until 1950. Markets are held here on Saturdays.

A couple of kilometres southwest of Santa Eugènia on the Ma3011 to Palma, kids will like **Natura Parc** (☎ 971 144078; www.mallorcaweb .net/naturaparc; Carretera de Sineu Km15.4; adult/child 3-12 yr/child under 3 yr €7/4.50/free; ☽ 10am-7pm), with everything from kangaroos to flamingos prancing about in relative freedom.

From Biniali, a 3.5km hop eastward brings you to the straggling rural centre of **Sencelles**, which you could probably skip, although it livens up a bit for the Wednesday market.

Those looking for a country stay should sneak out of Dodge down the Ma3140 and make for the hamlet of **Ruberts**, home to **Son Jordà** (☎ 971 872279; www.sonjorda.com; s/d €87/118; P ☒ ☒). Found just by the 18th-century parish church, it comprises three 16th-century houses with 21 rooms, some of them oozing rustic charm, others a little bare. It has tennis courts and a restaurant. The tiny hamlet takes visitors by surprise on 16 July with its colourful processions for the **Festa de la Verge del Carme**.

The 311 bus from Santa Maria del Camí runs to Sencelles via Santa Eugènia, but only three or four times a day (€1.05, 20 minutes).

INCA

pop 23,030 / elev 130m

Inca is the island's third-largest city – not the most attractive of places, but it's at the heart of the island's leather industry. Spanish shoemakers Camper and Farrutx started here.

Inca may have known Roman settlement and appears to have once had a mosque. It

THE INTERIOR

grew rapidly after 1229 and prospered as a centre for the manufacture of textiles, shoes, ceramics and wine. The city slumped in the 1970s but today seems to have largely recovered.

The first impression upon driving into town is one of heat and traffic. Although the tangle of the sprawling new town augurs nothing good, there are a few interesting points in the town centre. A stroll down Carrer Major to Plaça de Santa Maria Major, dominated by the **church** of the same name and lively cafés, is pleasant. You probably won't be able to get a look inside the nearby **Convent de Sant Francesc** (Carrer del Vent), but you can see the baroque **Claustre de Sant Domingo**, adjacent to the church off the like-named square.

A handful of noble's houses, easily recognised by their generous, semicircular stone entrance archways, is scattered about the city centre.

For extraordinary views, head east out of Inca for 2km and take the turn-off to the **Ermita de Santa Magdalena**. Then head south another 2.5km and continue up **Puig de Santa Magdalena**

MILES OF MILLS

The plains country is sprinkled with windmills, around 900 by one estimate – as many as 2500 by another. These were used mainly for pumping subterranean water for irrigation or grinding grain (the latter generally have conical roofs and/or a raised position). Some of the grain mills date to the 18th century, while most of the water mills evolved from an 1847 design. All had ceased functioning by the 1970s, but efforts to restore the mills have intensified since the '80s and some have been converted into holiday homes, restaurants and so on. Some water mills are even working again, restored largely for aesthetic reasons, although one idea is to have them generate some electricity.

(307m) to reach the *ermita* (chapel) – a privileged position from where your gaze will sweep across the plains to the Serra de Tramuntana and the Alcúdia and Pollença bays.

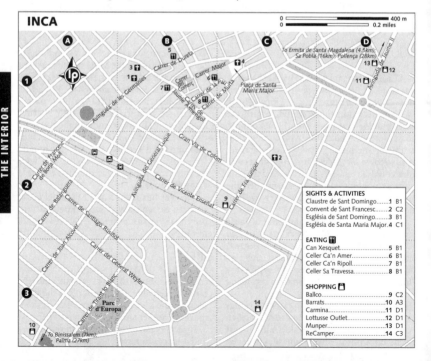

INCA

0 _____ 400 m
0 _____ 0.2 miles

To Ermita de Santa Magdalena (4.5km);
Sa Pobla (16km); Pollença (28km)

Plaça de Santa Maria Major

SIGHTS & ACTIVITIES		
Claustre de Sant Domingo	1	B1
Convent de Sant Francesc	2	C2
Església de Sant Domingo	3	B1
Església de Santa Maria Major	4	C1

EATING 🍴		
Can Xesquet	5	B1
Celler Ca'n Amer	6	B1
Celler Ca'n Ripoll	7	B1
Celler Sa Travessa	8	B1

SHOPPING 🛍		
Ballco	9	C2
Barrats	10	A3
Carmina	11	D1
Lottusse Outlet	12	D1
Munper	13	D1
ReCamper	14	C3

To Binissalem (7km);
Palma (27km)

THE INTERIOR

Festivals & Events

Markets are staged in Inca on Thursdays, Fridays and Sundays. The Thursday market is a major rural affair, and local leather is wheeled out in massive fashion. The third Thursday of November, **Dijous Bo** (Good Thursday; www.dijous-bo.com), is the town's biggest shindig, with processions, livestock competitions, sporting events, concerts and general good humour.

Eating

A peculiarity of Inca is its *cellers*, basement restaurants in some of central Inca's oldest buildings. As a rule, you'll find hearty Mallorcan cooking, to be washed down with local wines. The latter were once stored in the enormous 18th-century barrels that still line the *cellers*' walls.

ourpick **Celler Ca'n Ripoll** (☎ 971 500025; Carrer de Jaume Armengol 4; meals €20-25; ☉ Mon-Sat) This enormous, cathedral-like 18th-century cellar features a high beamed ceiling resting on a series of stone arches, and offers hearty meals with specialities like *sesos a la romana* (deep-fried brains).

Celler Sa Travessa (☎ 971 500049; Carrer de Murta 16; meals €20-25; ☉ Sat-Thu) In much the same category as Celler Ca'n Ripoll, house specialities here range from rabbit with onion to *llengua amb tàperes* (tongue with capers).

Celler Ca'n Amer (☎ 971 501261; Carrer de la Pau 139; meals €25-30; ☉ Mon-Sat) Typical Mallorcan cooking is the name of the game in this old house that seems out of place amid the more modern and impersonal buildings that surround it.

Can Xesquet (☎ 971 884040; Carrer de Dureta 6; meals €35-40; ☉ Tue-Sat, lunch only Sun) This is altogether a different kettle of fish, popular with business folk for its extensive *menú del día* (€15). The décor has a slightly stiff designer feel, with high-back chairs and modern art on the walls. In the kitchen they like to depart a little from the norms with dishes such as *solomillo* (sirloin) and fresh foie gras.

Shopping

Leather goods, particularly shoes, are Inca's shopping draw. Check out Gran Via de Colom, Avinguda de Jaume II and Avinguda del General Luque. Several places stand out:

Ballco (☎ 971 500810; www.ballco.com; Carrer de Vicente Enseñat 87)

Barrats (☎ 971 500803; www.barrats1890.com; Avinguda del General Luque 480)

> **IF IT'S NOT A QUELY, IT'S NOT WORTH EATING**
>
> Mallorquins are not that fussed about Inca's leather, but the biscuit manufacturer Quely is sacrosanct. The Domènech family started producing long-life biscuits for mariners in Inca in 1853. When the factory burned down in the early 1990s it was considered a tragedy by all Mallorquins – no Mallorquin child would be without his or her *quelis* at lunchtime. Schools organise visits to the rebuilt factory and there's even a Quely Club (www.quelyclub.com) for children.

Carmina (☎ 971 880938; www.carminashoemaker.com; Avinguda de Jaume II s/n)

Lottusse Outlet (☎ 971 507988; www.lottusse.com; Avinguda de Jaume II s/n)

Munper (☎ 971 881000; www.munper.com; Avinguda de Jaume II s/n)

ReCamper (☎ 902 364598; www.camper.com; Polígon Industrial s/n; ☉ 10am-8.30pm Mon-Sat) Camper's factory outlet.

Getting There & Away

If you're not driving down the Ma13 motorway from Palma, get the train along the same route, which runs frequently (€1.80, 35 to 40 minutes).

NORTH OF INCA

A scattering of towns and hamlets riding up into the foothills of the Serra de Tramuntana invites gentle touring. Three kilometres west of Inca is **Lloseta**, another shoe-making town. In early June it stages a fair in Plaça d'Espanya with local shoe manufacturers.

The town has no great appeal except as home to the tempting **Petit Hotel Cas Comte** (☎ 971 873077; www.hotelcascomte.com; Carrer del Comte d'Aiamans 11; s/d €107/127.50; 🅿 🍴 🖳 🛋), a pearl of a place in a fine stone mansion next to the central parish church; the spa facilities are a big draw. Have dinner at **Celler Ca'n Carrossa** (☎ 971 514023; Carrer Nou 28; meals €30; ☉ Tue-Sun, closed Oct-Dec), where you can sit inside by the exposed stone walls or opt for the garden. The best idea is the set tasting menu, which has all sorts of creative touches. Book ahead.

About 1.5km east of Lloseta on the road to Alaró, wine lovers can call in at the German-owned and prize-winning **Bodegas Castell Miquel** (☎ 971 510608; www.castellmiquel.com; ☉ 4-8pm Mon-Fri),

You can't miss the place – it looks like a little white castle. Besides wines like the 'Stairway to Heaven' shiraz, the German pharmaceutical professor who runs it has also developed a kind of red-wine pill, Resveroxan, that supposedly contributes to a longer and healthier life.

From Lloseta, the Ma2113 road straggles west through the hamlet of Biniamar. At a junction 2km further on, you can strike north for **Mancor de la Vall**, which has a pretty-enough centre but is most interesting for the 3km drive uphill to the **Ermita de Santa Lucia**, from where you can enjoy views to the south. About 2.5km east of Mancor, **Selva** is a sprawling place that also owes some of its wealth to the leather business. Two kilometres north, **Caimari** is known for olive oil. Visit the factory and shop of **Oli Caimari** (☎ 971 873577; www .aceites-olicaimari.com; ☽ 9am-8pm Mon-Sat, 10am-2pm Sun). The best time to visit is in November and December, when the oil is made. The Ma2130 road north of Caimari is a spectacular route leading to the **Monestir de Lluc** (p132).

A narrow lane northeast out of Caimari leads to the intriguing hamlet of **Binibona**. Hemmed in by three mountain peaks, it has become a much sought-out spot for those in search of tranquil but stylish rural getaways. Half a dozen places in and around it offer shelter: check their combined website (www .som7.com).

In the centre, **Hotel Can Furiós** (☎ 971 515751; www.can-furios.com; Camí Vell de Binibona 11; s/d €171/214; ⬚ ⬚ ⬚) is a renovated 16th-century stone mansion with a handful of rooms and suites. The hotel's restaurant (set menu only, €37) has made a name for itself with its carefully pieced-together Mediterranean cuisine.

Finca Ets Abellons (☎ 971 875069; www.albellons .com; s/d €123/171; ⬚ ⬚ ⬚ ⬚), 1km north of Binibona, is a stone farmhouse in the hills. The 12 rooms (half with own terrace) have terracotta floors, timber ceilings and graceful, rural antique furnishings.

ourpick **Es Castell** (☎ 971 875154; www.fincaescastell .com; Carrer de Binibona s/n; s/d €110/145; ⬚ ⬚ ⬚ ⬚) is a 14th-century farm estate, set out on a ledge by itself in the shadow of the mountains, that encompasses a muddle of sturdy stone houses and 300 hectares dominated by olive trees, and makes the perfect rural escape. It is run with flair and the rooms have an appealing rustic feel, with terracotta floors, timber furniture and marble-topped chests of drawers. The restaurant (meals €35)

serves copious meals of mostly their own farm products.

Three kilometres south of Binibona is Moscari, from where you branch east for 2.5km to **Campanet**, the most engaging of all these villages. Encrusted onto a sharp ridge, the town's central square, Plaça Major, is dominated by a gaunt Gothic church, but the surrounding cafés are busier than the ill-attended Mass. Just downhill, the **Posada de Biniatró** (☎ 971 509530; Carrer de Miquel 20; ☽ 10am-1pm & 7.30-9.30pm Tue-Fri, 7.30-9.30pm Sat) is a three-storey town house exhibiting works by a battery of island artists born from 1950 on. Almost 3km north of Campanet, set in a beautiful stretch of little-visited countryside, there's a small country chapel, the **Oratori de Sant Miquel**. Just beyond are the **Coves de Campanet** (☎ 971 516130; www .covesdecampanet.com; Camí de ses Coves s/n; adult/child over 10 yr €9.50/5; ☽ 10am-7pm Apr-Sep, 10am-6pm Oct-Mar). Scientists find these caves especially interesting as they are home to a local species of blind, flesh-eating beetle.

ourpick **Agroturisme Monnàber Vell** (☎ 971 516131; www.monnabervell.com; s/d €117/151; ☽ closed mid-Nov–Jan; ⬚ ⬚ ⬚ ⬚), a few hundred metres south of the Oratori de Sant Miquel, is found at the end of a track that winds through the fields and woods. The standard double rooms are comfortable if a trifle bland, but the suites have plenty of character. You enter through a grand, cobbled courtyard and proceed through the cool common areas to where people will be dining out back. The infinity pool makes you feel you are about to swim straight into the trees. For an extra €20, dinner is included.

The best way to get around this area is with your own transport.

SOUTH OF INCA

A brief loop immediately south of Inca has the town of Sineu as its main objective. Follow the Ma3440 southeast for 8km and you hit upon **Llubí**. It is especially worth the effort for the **Festa del Siurell** on the Saturday before the Tuesday of Carnaval. This singular bit of fun involves townsfolk dressing up as *siurells*, the traditional Mallorcan whistles (p37). That night, a big *siurell* is burned in effigy in Plaça de l'Església, which is dominated by the outsized parish church, the **Església de Sant Feliu**.

In the event you need to stay, **Hotel Ca'n Pericó** (☎ 971 857138; www.canperico.com; Carrer de la Farinera 7; s/d €55/80; ⬚ ⬚) is a family-run hotel with three pretty rooms about 50m downhill from the church. For hearty, straightforward local cooking, **Sa Tàperera** (☎ 971 522195; Carrer del Doctor Fleming 5-7; menú del día €7.50, meals €20; ☒ lunch & dinner Tue-Sat, lunch Sun) is a welcoming spot.

SINEU
pop 2740 / elev 151m
Seven kilometres south on the Ma3511, the dense, ochre mass of Sineu rises on the horizon, draped across a ridgeback. This is without a doubt one of the most engaging of Mallorca's inland rural towns, especially if you can make it to one of its busy livestock markets. At its heart is Sa Plaça, a busy square fronted by several bars and the crumbling sandstone, late-Gothic façade of the 16th-century **Església de Santa Maria**.

Less visible but in some respects more interesting is the 17th-century **Convent de la Concepció** (Carrer del Palau 17), a two-minute stroll southwest of Sa Plaça. Walk inside and to the right you'll see a *torno*, a small revolving door through which you can receive pastries made by the nuns in return for a few euros. Walk around the block and you'll notice great protruding buttresses holding up the thick walls on the other side of this building. This is where King Jaume II had his inland residence built, making Sineu the de facto capital of rural Mallorca, although its role as a palace didn't last long. It appears the palace was an adaptation of the prior Muslim *al-qasr* (castle), possibly dating to the 10th century.

North of Sa Plaça, the *ajuntament* (town hall) is housed in the 17th-century baroque **Convent dels Mínims** (Carrer de Sant Francesc). You can generally wander in any time to admire the somewhat neglected cloister. One block west, where Carrer del Vent meets Carrer dels Bous, is a beautiful example of a waymarking cross, the 1585 Renaissance **Creu dels Morts** (Cross of the Dead).

REGIONAL SPECIALITIES
Eels are big in the east, especially around Sa Pobla. Local produce still influences menus, so don't be startled by surprising recipes such as tongue with capers. The interior of Mallorca is serious wine country, with two DO (Denominación de Orígen) areas, Binissalem and Pla i Llevant (roughly the southeastern sector of the island).

Downhill on the southeast flank of the town is an open area known as **Plaça des Fossar**, where the town's big market days are held. Another 100m further east you encounter the whimsical, German-run **S'Estació Contemporary Art Museum** (☎ 971 520750; www.sineuestacio.com; Carrer de S'Estació 2; ☒ 9.30am-1.30pm & 4-7pm Mon-Fri, 9.30am-1pm Sat), where local and foreign-resident contemporary artists display work on three floors.

Sineu's weekly livestock market on Wednesdays is one of the few to have retained its true agricultural flavour, but the big one is the annual **Sa Fira**, a major produce market held on the first Sunday of May and dating to 1318. On the second Sunday in December, the **Fira de Sant Tomás** features the annual *matanza* (pig slaughter). This follows the year-long fattening of the pigs and is not for the faint-hearted.

ourpick **Hotel León de Sineu** (☎ 971 520211; www.hotel-leondesineu.com; Carrer dels Bous 129; s/d €95/120; P ☒ ☒), set in a 15th-century house that was long used as a wine cellar, maintains much of its traditional look and offers eight rooms of varying size and décor, much of which dates to the 18th and 19th centuries. The stone-vaulted restaurant offering meals made with local products has a solid reputation. Out back, the gardens fall away down several levels, stuffed with fountains, palms and huge sunflowers, leading to the pool.

Watch your step as you descend into **Celler Es Grop** (☎ 971 520187; Carrer Major; meals €20-25; ☒ Tue-Sun), a cheerful old whitewashed cellar with huge, old wine vats and a mix of local and standard Spanish dishes. Grilled fish and a handful of meat dishes are solid.

Trains on the Palma–Manacor line run here (from Palma €2.45, 50 minutes). The station is about 100m from Plaça des Fossar.

SA POBLA & MURO
Sa Pobla may be the end of the (railway) line from Palma, but it is no cultural desert. **Can Planes** (☎ 971 542389; www.ajsapobla.net; Carrer d'Antoni Maura 6; ☒ 10am-2pm & 4-8pm Tue-Sat, 10am-2pm Sun & holidays) houses two museums. On the ground floor is the **Museu d'Art Contemporani** (admission free), a rotating display of works by Mallorquin and foreign artists residing on the island. Much of the work runs from the 1970s to the 1990s. Upstairs, the **Museu de Sa Jugueta Antiga** (admission €4) is a touching collection of old toys. Remember *baldufes* (spinning tops)? Immense dollhouses, clunky fire engines, toy kitchen stoves and even a cardboard and plastic bullring with *toreros*

(bullfighters) and dead bulls (1960) are among the many curios. That's about it for this grid-street rural centre whose wealth was built on potato and other vegetable crops, which still bring in a pretty penny today with European exports (especially to the UK).

A lively **market** is held on Sundays. The **Festes de Sant Antoni Abat** (16 to 17 January), with blessings for work animals, processions, fireworks, folk music and dancing, is one of the big events of the year. The night of the 16th is the most lively time. The annual **Mallorca Jazz Festival** (www .jazzinmallorca.com) sees international acts playing on various nights of August in Plaça Major.

Antic Celler Ca'n Cotà (☎ 971 862377; Carrer de la Lluna 27; meals €30-35; ☺ lunch & dinner Mon, Wed, Fri & Sat, lunch only Tue & Thu) has been serving meals since 1846. Set in a modest house, it's cool and dark inside, but the temperature rises with a variety of tasty meat specialities, like the tender *tournedo de solomillo con foie y reducción de Pedro Ximènez* (a sirloin tournedo with *foie* in a sherry reduction).

Five kilometres south across the potato flats from Sa Pobla, Muro boasts an outsized parish church in the sandstone **Església de Sant Joan Baptista** (Plaça de la Constitució), a brooding Gothic creation reminiscent of Sineu's main church (p159). The fusty **Museu Etnològic** (☎ 971 860647; Carrer Major 15; adult/child €2.40/free; ☺ 10am-3pm & 5-7pm Thu, 10am-3pm Tue-Wed & Fri & Sat, 10am-2pm Sun) is housed in the 17th-century **Can Simó**. Inside are all sorts of traditional tools and household items, along with a dilapidated waterwheel in the garden. Check out the display of colourful, naïve *siurells* (see p37).

Sa Pobla is an hour by train from Palma (€2.65, 57 minutes) via Inca. The station, where buses also terminate, is about 1km southeast of central Plaça de la Constitució. Muro is on the same line.

PALMA TO MANACOR

From Palma's ring road, Via Cintura, the four-lane Ma15 winds out across the flat heartland of Es Pla to Manacor. Along the way are plenty of intriguing detours.

ALGAIDA

pop 3750 / elev 201m

Centred on a Gothic church, the **Església de Sant Pere i Sant Pau**, this quiet farming community kicks up its heels for the **Festes de Sant**

GIVING MURANO A RUN FOR ITS MONEY

It's believed the Phoenicians introduced glass-making to Mallorca in the 2nd century BC, although by the Middle Ages, the supreme European glass-makers were those of Murano, in Venice. The story goes that one such artisan, Domenico Barrovier, sought refuge in Mallorca and passed on his know-how. By the 17th century, Mallorcan glass was competing on European markets, but the industry declined in the following century. During this unlucky time, in 1719, the Gordiola family got involved in the business. After decades of difficulties, Gordiola's glass began to achieve recognition, and the family has almost single-handedly maintained the island's glass tradition to this day.

Honorat (16 January) and the **Festa de Sant Jaume** (25 July). On both occasions, *cossiers* dance for an appreciative local audience. The origins of the *cossiers* and their dances are disputed. A group of dancers (six men and one woman), accompanied by a devil, perform various pieces that end in defeat for the demon.

Algaida's main attraction lies 2.5km west on the Ma15. The **Gordiola glassworks** (☎ 971 665046; www.gordiola.com) is set in a roadside mock-Gothic palace, for which the Mallorquins seem to have a penchant. You can wander into the **factory area** (admission free; ☺ 9am-1.30pm & 3-6pm Mon-Sat, 9am-noon Sat) on the ground floor to observe glass-makers working and sweating. Upstairs, the **museum** (admission €2; ☺ 9am-7pm Mon-Sat, 9am-1.30pm Sun) has a curious collection of glass items from around the world. It hasn't been updated in a while, so nonexistent countries like Formosa and Czechoslovakia are represented.

The town is blessed with eateries, mostly on or near the highway. Head out of town about 1km along the Ma3131 towards Pina for the sprawling roadside restaurant of **Can Mateu** (☎ 971 665036; Carretera Vella de Manacor, Km21; meals €40; ☺ Wed-Mon, Mar-Jan); for centuries it was a pit stop for country folk heading to the City (ie Palma). Dig into some Mallorcan classics, like *frit Mallorquín* (fried lamb innards), *cargols* (snails) and *arros brut* (a local rice dish).

Various buses heading from Palma to the east coast stop here (€1.70, 20 to 25 minutes).

THE INTERIOR

The most regular service is the 490 Palma–Felanitx run (five to nine services daily).

SANTUARI DE NOSTRA SENYORA DE CURA

Southwest of Algaida rises the 548m hill of **Puig de Randa**, atop which stands this gracious monastery (☎ 971 660994; ✆ 10.30am-1.30pm & 2.30-6pm). As with most such monasteries, it was built partly for defence purposes, though one supposes that the monks enjoyed the heavenly views, too. Ramon Llull (p30) lived here as a hermit, praying in a cave (now closed to visitors). In the 16th century, the Estudi General (university) in Palma created the Col·legi de Gramàtica here, and for centuries thereafter live-in students grappled with the complexities of Latin grammar, rhetoric and other classical disciplines. Today, in the **Museu Ramon Llull** (donation requested), you can see all sorts of curios, from farm implements to old photos of the monastery.

The **Hospedería** (☎ 971 120260; s/d/ste €40/62/93; P ⌨) has 31 doubles and four junior suites that are simple but spick-and-span.

The trip up to the Santuari is part of the fun. Approaching from Algaida, those with a love of quirky detours can peel off to the left (east) about 2km south of the town and scoot 2.5km along a back lane to **Castellitx**, a handful of houses and a purportedly 13th-century chapel (usually closed). Back on the main road, you quickly arrive in the village of **Randa**, from where it's 5km to the Santuari. Along the way you can detour to see the completely restored Santuari de Nostra Senyora de la Gràcia (after 1.5km) and the **Oratori de Sant Honorat** (4km). You know you're almost at the top when you see the huge golf ball sitting on a metallic tee. (Actually, it's a communications centre.)

Down in Randa, a peaceful overnight option is the flower-surrounded, stone **Es Recó de Randa** (☎ 971 660997; www.esrecoderanda.com; Carrer de Sa Font 21; s/d €113/145; P ⌨ ⌨). The rooms have a classic feel with generous beds, exposed ceiling beams and terracotta floors. Dine with a view in the hotel restaurant, beloved of Palma diners with itchy feet.

MONTUÏRI

pop 2340 / elev 160m

From Randa, it's 8km northeast on the Ma5017 to Montuïri, sitting on a sharp ridge and known for its apricots. That very colour

infuses the place with a soft glow in the early morning. The sandstone **Església de Sant Bartomeu** dominates Plaça Major, through which runs Carrer Major, graced by the occasional mansion and bar.

On the eastern exit heading for Lloret de Vistalegre (the Ma3220) is the **Museu Arqueològic de Son Fornés** (☎ 971 644169; www.sonfornes.mallorca.museum; Carrer d'Emili Pou s/n; adult/student €3/1.80; ✆ 10am-2pm & 4-7pm Tue-Sun Mar-Oct, 10am-2pm Tue-Sun Nov-Feb). Housed in a cactus-fronted former mill, it explains the history of the Son Fornés *talayot* (watchtower), which was inhabited from around 900 BC to the 4th century AD. On show are artefacts dug up on the site. The *talayot* is one of the most important on the island and easy enough to visit. Head 2.5km northwest out of Montuïri on the Ma3200 towards Pina and you'll see it to the right (east) of the road. There are two main circular dwellings (in surprisingly good shape) and the remains of nine other structures.

The **Festa de Sant Bartomeu** (patron saint of the village) falls on 24 August. The main event is traditional dancing by the *cossiers* (both on the eve and the 24th). On Easter Sunday, locals celebrate **S'Encuentro**, in which a figure of Christ resurrected is met in a parade by one of the Virgin Mary, who does some excited hops to show her joy at the resurrection of her son. Monday is market day.

The 490 bus (see Algaida, opposite) is one of the most regular from Palma (€3.30, 40 minutes).

AROUND MONTUÏRI

Pina lies 5.5km northwest of the Son Fornés *talayot*. Stop for a look at **Sa Font**, one of the few reminders of the Arab presence on the island. This complex *qanawat* (well and water distribution structure) is difficult to date but was taken over by the Muslims' Christian successors after 1229. It lies 50m south of the **Església de Sants Cosme i Damià**, on the road to Lloret de Vistalegre.

Sant Joan, 5km northeast of Montuïri, is a typical rural backwater but vaguely interesting for a quick peek at the **Santuari de la Consolació**. A minor climb along the lines of Pollença's Calvari (p134) leads to this chapel, but the views are more limited here than is usually the case simply because it's not that high up. (No pain, no gain!)

About 4km southeast, on a pretty country back road (and well signposted), a stout rural

---

FINE POSSESSIONS

In rural Mallorca, the most powerful families owned grand farmsteads. Their Arab predecessors had been known as *alqueries*, but to the Christians who took over the island after 1229, they came to be called *possessions*, the equivalent of the southern French *mas* or Catalan *masia*. The oldest, dating to the 14th and even 13th centuries, had a marked defensive character, with watchtowers and forbidding walls that opened onto a *clastra* (courtyard). Over the following centuries these farmsteads became more complex. In the main building, the (often absentee) señors (lords) of the property would have their residence. In the surrounding outbuildings – *ses cases* (the houses) – would be located the dwelling of the *amo* (the main resident farmer and local boss), along with the *tafona* (olive press), *celler* (cellar), mill and other farm buildings. With the rapid decline in agriculture in Mallorca since the 1960s, the role of these estates has also lost significance. Some *possessions* are semiabandoned, but curiously the phenomenon that helped rob them of their purpose – tourism – might save them from destruction. A growing number are being converted into rural lodgings for tourists in search of an alternative to bucket-and-spade holidays. Three of these are Els Calderers (below), Ca N'Aí (p122) and Finca Son Brull (p137).

---

mansion has been converted into a period museum. **Els Calderers** (☎ 971 526069; www.todoesp .es/els-calderers; adult/child €8/4; ☒ 10am-6pm Apr-Sep, 10am-5pm Oct-Mar) was built around 1750. On the ground floor, around a leafy courtyard whose fountain gurgles contentedly away, are the main salons and guest rooms, along with the family chapel and wine cellar (every decent *finca* had one of each). You can sample a little house red. As a letter from 1895 (on display) notes, the Els Calderers wine was *muy flojito* (very average). This doesn't seem to have changed.

PETRA
pop 1910 / elev 120m

Pretty Petra's principal claim to fame is its favourite son, Juníper Serra, born here in 1713. A Franciscan missionary and one of the founders of what is now the US state of California, he could have had no inkling of his destiny as he grew up in this rural centre.

The **Museu Fra Juníper Serra** (☎ 971 561028; Carrer des Barracar Alt 6; ☒ by appointment only) contains mementos of his missionary life. Next door at No 4 is the house in which he was born. Walk to Carrer des Barracar Baix 2 and ring the bell. If you get lucky, you'll get admission to the house and museum. (If not, you won't.) All over the streets in this part of town are ceramic depictions of his eventful life.

Four kilometres southwest of Petra on a wooded hill stands the **Ermita de la Mare de Déu de Bonany**, where Juníper Serra gave his last sermon in Mallorca before heading for the New World. Climb up on foot or drive. Elements of the present church date to the 18th

century but the place was overhauled in 1925. The views over the plains are magnificent.

Wine lovers should make for **Bodegas Miquel Oliver** (☎ 971 561117; www.miqueloliver.com; Carrer de Sa Font 26; ☒ 8am-3pm Mon-Fri), one of the island's better wine-makers.

Spend a quiet night at **Hotel Sa Plaça** (☎ 971 561646; www.saplacapetra.com; Plaça de Ramón Llull 4; s/d €90/109; ☒ closed Nov; ☒ ☐), an 1840s stone town house, with just three rooms and a popular restaurant, overlooking a pleasing square with a fountain. For a no-nonsense, wintry Mallorcan feed (meat is the go here), wander into **Es Celler** (☎ 971 561056; Carrer de l'Hospital 26; meals €20; ☒ Tue-Sun).

Petra is one stop short of Manacor (nine minutes) on the Palma–Manacor train line and gets one service a day in both directions. From Palma the trip takes just under an hour and costs €3.20.

MANACOR
pop 31,260 / elev 128m

The island's second-largest city, Manacor lies at the end of the Ma15's asphalt rainbow, where you'll find a pot of pearls, one of the town's best-known exports. This industrial town, however, is no gem. *Mobles* (furniture) is the biggest business here, though some fine vineyards dot the immediately surrounding countryside.

The **tourist office** (☎ 971 847241; http://turisme.ma nacor.org; Plaça de Ramon Llull; ☒ 9am-2pm Mon, 9.30am-1.30pm Tue-Fri) is in the town centre.

The massive **Església de Nostra Senyora Verge dels Dolors** (Plaça del General Weyler; ☒ 8.30am-12.30pm & 5.30-8pm) was raised on the site of the town's former mosque and has a hybrid Gothic/neo-Gothic architecture. Just off the square, in the courtyard of an apartment block, is the dishevelled **Torre del Palau**, all that remains of a royal residence that Jaume II built in the 13th century. Another tidbit of history is the 14th-century **Torre de Ses Puntes** (☎ 971 844741; Plaça de Gabriel Fuster Historiador s/n; ☟ 6.30pm-8.30pm). Once part of the city's defences, it's now used for exhibitions.

A short walk north brings you to the baroque **Església de Sant Vicenç Ferrer** (under renovation), attached to a fetching **cloister** (Carrer de Muntaner) around which government offices are now housed.

Just outside Manacor, on the Ma4015 to Cales de Mallorca, is the **Torre dels Enagistes** (☎ 971 843065; www.manacor.org; ☟ 9.30am-2pm & 6-8.30pm Mon & Wed-Sat mid-Jun–mid-Sep, 10am-2pm & 5-7.30pm Mon & Wed-Sat, 10.30am-1.30pm Sun mid-Sep–mid-Jun), a fortified rural spread from the 14th century that today sits forlornly in a dusty void next to the road. It is home to the **Museu d'Història de Manacor**, a mingling of prehistoric, Bronze Age and early Christian artefacts. Among the displays are modest mosaics unearthed at the site of the 5th-century early-Christian basilica **Son Peretó**, which you can see through a fence 6km northeast of Manacor just off the Ma15 to Artà. It is the only such remaining site on the island.

ourpick Ca'n March (☎ 971 550002; Carrer de València 7; meals €25; ☟ Tue-Sun, closed evenings late Jul-late Sep; ☒ Ⓥ) is a good spot to tuck into serious Med-Mallorcan grub. Fish is the house's strong point, prepared with a minimum of fuss using salt from Es Trenc and island olive oil. Other dishes have an adventurous touch – you might find yourself served lamb in a date sauce, and Asian spices crop up. There's also a vegetarian set menu.

Most visitors come to Manacor for the manufactured pearls. Several companies make them, but **Majorica** is the best known. The company was founded by Eduard Heusch, a German, in 1902. It has a two-storey **showroom** (☎ 971 550900; www.majorica.com; ☟ 9am-8pm Mon-Fri, 9am-7pm Sat & Sun & holidays) on the edge of town on the road to Palma. Upstairs you can see a handful of people working on the creation of pearls, but the real factory is elsewhere and not open to visits. For the competition, check out **Orquidea** (☎ 971 644144; www.perlasorquidea.com; ☟ 9am-7pm Mon-Fri, 9am-1pm Sat & Sun), a two-minute walk closer to the centre of town.

Three DO Pla i Llevant winemakers have vineyards around Manacor. **Toni Gelabert** (☎ 971 552409; www.vinstonigelabert.com; Camí dels Horts de Llodrà Km1.3) does some superb whites. Take the Ma14 south out of Manacor; after 2km is a small sign on the right to the vineyard, another 1.5km down the lane. Don't turn up after about 6.30pm.

Manacor is a transport hub. The train from Palma runs once an hour (€3.70, one hour and six minutes). Various buses on cross-island routes call in too, terminating in front of the train station, a 10-minute walk from Plaça del General Weyler.

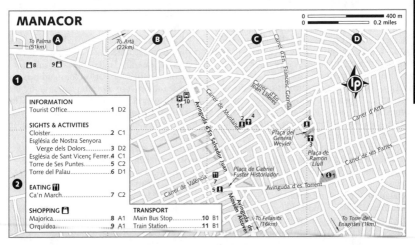

MANACOR

0 ──────── 400 m
0 ──────── 0.2 miles

INFORMATION	
Tourist Office.......................1	D2

SIGHTS & ACTIVITIES	
Cloister..............................2	C1
Església de Nostra Senyora Verge dels Dolors..............3	D2
Església de Sant Vicenç Ferrer.4	C1
Torre de Ses Puntes...............5	C2
Torre del Palau......................6	D1

EATING 🍴	
Ca'n March..........................7	C2

SHOPPING 🛍	
Majorica.............................8	A1
Orquidea.............................9	A1

TRANSPORT	
Main Bus Stop................10	B1
Train Station...................11	B1

THE INTERIOR

PALMA TO FELANITX

Some 20km southeast of Palma is **Llucmajor**, a farming town whose name stems from the Roman Lucus Maiorus, suggesting the area was once a great forest. The big event that has never been forgotten was the fratricidal battle between Mallorca's King Jaume III and Aragón's Pedro IV (see p27).

The town centres on Plaça d'Espanya, which is lined by half a dozen bars. A brisk walk from here offers the only sight of consequence, the **Centre Cultural Claustre Sant Bonaventura** (Carrer d'es Convent), an as-yet-unfinished modern exhibition space partly located in an 18th-century, sandstone cloister.

The Ma19 hurtles 13km southeast across the flatlands to **Campos**, the original 'sleepy rural town' that is unlikely to detain you. As you are propelled out the other side en route to **Santanyí** (see p190), you can't help notice that you're in serious windmill territory. An astonishing number have been restored in the several kilometres mostly south of the Ma19.

About 9km north of Campos, **Porreres** has a certain style. It has always been a quite prosperous farming town, living on the proceeds of local wheat, wine, fig, almond and carob crops. Of passing interest is the **Museu i Fons Artístic del Ajuntament** (☎ 971 166617; Carrer del Reverend Agustí Font; ☽ 11am-1pm Tue, Thu & Sat), a 19th-century house with temporary art exhibitions, two blocks from Plaça de l'Església and its hulking parish church. Sybarites will be more curious about the **Jaume Mesquida winery** (☎ 971 647106; www.jaumemesquida .com; Carrer de la Vileta 7; ☽ 8am-7pm Mon-Fri).

Four kilometres south of Porreres off the Campos road, the **Santuari de Monti-Sion** (☎ 971 120260), a former monastery, was first erected in the 14th century and is especially curious because of its pentagonal cloister. The views all around Es Pla are inspiring and the monks' cells have been modernised to rent out to guests. Since early 2006 the administrators have been waiting for permits, water and electricity to open their doors.

Not far before the turn-off to the Santuari, a sign points east to **Son Mercadal** (☎ 971 181307; www.son-mercadal.com; Camí de Son Pau; d €105; P ☒ ☒), a tastefully restored 19th-century country estate that makes a perfect rural halt. Surrounded by 7 hectares of land, Mercadal offers a homy atmosphere and plenty of tranquillity. Lone travellers can sometimes get a reduced rate. The eight doubles are tastefully equipped with 19th-century timber furniture and embroidered linen.

Felanitx, 13km northeast of Campos, has a reputation for ceramics, white wine and capers. It makes an interesting stop in its own right and because of a couple of startling hilltop monuments nearby.

Lording over the heart of the town is the baroque façade of the **Església de Sant Miquel** (Plaça de Sa Font de Santa Margalida) which got its present makeover in 1762. Above the Renaissance portal stands a relief of St Michael, sticking it to a discomfited-looking devil underfoot. Across the road and directly in front of the church, a flight of stone steps leads down to the Font, once the main town well. Carrer Major runs below the flank of the church, which in 1844 collapsed onto a passing Easter procession and left 400 dead. Behind the church is the town market; the best time to browse is Sunday morning.

After the fun of shopping, do some penance; Felanitx has its own version of Pollença's **Calvari** (p134). Head along Carrer des Call (off Carrer Major) and at its end you will see 113 steps rising up over a ridge. Fewer steps than Pollença, you may think, but the trail winds around in a long, steady, 15-minute climb that feels like murder on a hot Sunday afternoon. The stations of the cross mark the way to the 1852 chapel.

About 7km south of Felanitx, the proud walls of the **Castell de Santueri** turn a craggy peak into a defensive bastion. Take the Ma14 for 2km, then follow the signs to the left (east). The road winds 5km to the base of the castle's white walls. You can scramble up to the (closed) entrance, where the views extend southeast, far out to sea.

A badly defined walking path links the castle to the **Santuari de Sant Salvador**, a hilltop hermitage 5km southeast of Felanitx. It is easier instead to take the Ma4010 for Portocolom and peel off after less than 1km, heading south along the Ma4011 to reach the top of the hill (509m). The hermitage was originally built in 1348, the year of one of the most disastrous waves of plague in Europe. Perhaps here, far from ports and towns, the hermits were safe. It has undergone several refits since then. Aside from the church, there's not an awful lot to see but the views are heavenly. You can stay in simple rooms in a modern **annexe** (☎ 971 827282; d €30).

The 490 bus runs five to nine times daily from Palma to Felanitx (€3.90, 1¼ hours) via Montuïri and Porreres.

Eastern Mallorca

It's as though someone came in with a giant spoon and gouged out cove after rocky cove along Mallorca's east coast, creating some of the island's most iconic scenery in the form of scorching white sandy beaches, turquoise waters and dramatic beachside cliffs. Of course, such beauty is hard to keep a secret, and the coves here are some of the most popular tourist destinations on Mallorca. Package tourists, families, last-minute weekenders…they all want to experience a bit of island bliss.

We can't lie; there are some true monstrosities along the east coast. When Mallorca's tourism industry began growing in the 1950s and '60s the floodgates were swung wide open, permitting the overdevelopment that's transformed former fishing villages into endless strings of whitewashed apartment buildings, curry restaurants, 'authentic' Spanish eateries and souvenir shops.

Yet, contrary to the stereotype, not everything is geared toward mass tourism. All you need is a bit of curiosity and a decent map to hunt down the charms of this region – unspoilt coves, seaside towns that still retain their fishing-village air, ancient Stone Age ruins, pretty hilltop hamlets, fine rural hotels and excellent dining. Having your own car helps a great deal as you navigate Mallorca's farm roads and country lanes, but those armed with patience can make good use of the local bus system. If you have the time (and the leg strength), eastern Mallorca is a great place to explore by bike; several popular routes are indicated in this chapter.

HIGHLIGHTS

- Dig into Mallorca's ancient history at **Ses Païsses** (p167), one of the most important *talayotic* sites on the island
- Delve into the centre of the earth at the **Coves del Drac** (p177), a spectacular cave system
- Hike through the wooded hills of the **Parc Natural de la Península de Llevant** (p169) to reach gorgeous, unspoilt coves
- Soak up rays on Cala Ratjada's pretty **Platja de Cala Agulla** (p171)

Platja de Cala Agulla ★

★ Parc Natural de la
Ses Païsses ★   Península de Llevant

★ Coves del Drac

EASTERN MALLORCA

EASTERN MALLORCA

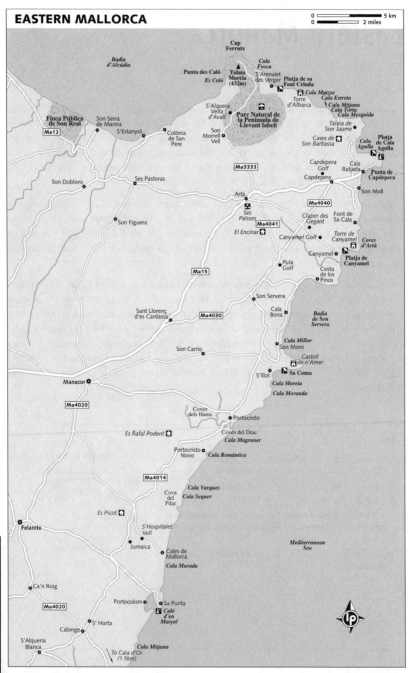

EASTERN MALLORCA

ARTÀ & AROUND

Boasting the poetic distinction of being the first place in Mallorca to see the morning sun, the island's northeastern corner is a refreshingly low-key area where rounded hills stubbled with green stretch out in every direction, and calm, pine-lined beaches (some accessible only by foot, horseback or boat) dot the coastline. Fascinating historic monuments, good hiking territory and one of the best beach resorts on the east coast all provide convincing excuses for a visit.

ARTÀ

pop 6730

The antithesis of the buzzing resort culture found just a few kilometres away, the quiet inland town of Artà beckons with its maze of narrow streets, appealing cafés and medieval architecture, which culminates in an impressive 14th-century hilltop fortress that dominates the town centre.

Information

Locutorio Artà (Carrer del Mestral 10; internet per hr €2; 11am-10pm) This call centre, ironically, won't give out a phone number. Opening hours are notoriously flexible.
Police station (☎ 971 829595; Plaça d'Espanya 1) Located in the *ajuntament* (town hall).
Post office (☎ 971 836127; Carrer de la Ciutat 12; 8.30am-2.30pm Mon-Fri, 9.30am-1pm Sat)
Tourist office (☎ 971 836981; Carrer de Costa i Llobera s/n; 10am-2pm Mon-Fri) Located in the old train station, it sometimes hosts art exhibits.

Sights

Begin on Carrer de la Ciutat, the prettiest street in town, which is lined with shops, restaurants and squares rimmed with cafés. Head uphill to reach the historic centre, which is basically a maze of pedestrian-friendly (though unkempt) streets lined with old, often neglected homes. At its heart is the shaded Plaça d'Espanya, home to the **ajuntament** (town hall) and the **Museu Regional d'Artà** (☎ 971 829778; Carrer d'Estel 4; 10.30am-1.30pm Tue-Fri, 11am-1pm Sat), where those interested in ancient and traditional Mallorcan culture will get a small thrill out of the mismatched curios on display.

Follow the signs uphill to Sant Salvador, but before you reach the famous sanctuary you'll pass the Gothic **Transfiguració del Senyor**

parish church. Here, a small **museum** (admission €2; 10am-2pm & 3-6pm) shows off religious art. The church, built atop the foundations of a Moorish mosque, was begun soon after the Christian reconquest, although the façade dates to a 16th-century renovation. Inside, highlights include a large rose window, an ornately carved wooden pulpit, and an altar painting depicting Christ on Mount Tabor.

From here, 180 steps lead up along the grand, cyprus-lined **Via Crucis** (Way of the Cross) toward the **Santuari de Sant Salvador**, a walled fortress built atop an earlier Moorish enclave and enclosing a small church. Far and away the most famous sight in town, this much-restored castle-like complex boasts all the elements of a medieval fortress, down to the stone turrets ringing the top. The views from here take in the entire town and pastoral scene surrounding it – fertile fields dotted with stone farmhouses and backed with the bald, bumpy peaks of the Serra de Llevant.

The walls were built in the 14th century to encompass the town itself and protect it from pirates or invaders. Now you'll find only walkways, a simple **cafeteria** (see p169) and an unremarkable salmon-coloured **church**, which was built in 1832 after the modest chapel that pre-dated it was purposely burnt to the ground following a cholera epidemic.

You can also reach Sant Salvador by a steep, curvy road (worth considering if the sun is really blazing), but most people find the walk pleasant exercise.

SES PAÏSSES

Just beyond Artà proper lie the remains of a 3000-year-old settlement, the largest and most important *talayotic* site on Mallorca's eastern flank. The looming stone gateway to **Ses Païsses** (☎ 619 070010; admission €1.30; 10am-1pm & 2.30-6.30pm Mon-Sat Apr-Oct, 9am-1pm & 2-5pm Mon-Sat Nov-Mar) is an impressive transition into

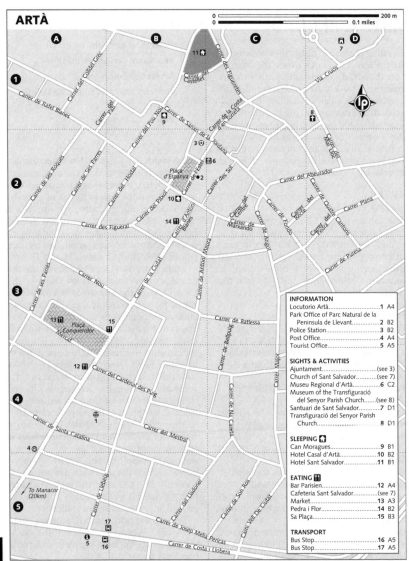

ARTÀ

INFORMATION	
Locutorio Artà	1 A4
Park Office of Parc Natural de la	
Peninsula de Llevant	2 B2
Police Station	3 B2
Post Office	4 A4
Tourist Office	5 A5

SIGHTS & ACTIVITIES	
Ajuntament	(see 3)
Church of Sant Salvador	(see 7)
Museu Regional d'Artà	6 C2
Museum of the Transfiguració	
del Senyor Parish Church	(see 8)
Santuari de Sant Salvador	7 D1
Transfiguració del Senyor Parish	
Church	8 D1

SLEEPING	
Can Moragues	9 B1
Hotel Casal d'Artà	10 B2
Hotel Sant Salvador	11 B1

EATING	
Bar Parisien	12 A4
Cafeteria Sant Salvador	(see 7)
Market	13 A3
Pedra i Flor	14 B2
Sa Plaça	15 B3

TRANSPORT	
Bus Stop	16 A5
Bus Stop	17 A5

the world of prehistoric Mallorca, a world that is still shrouded in mystery despite ongoing archaeological investigations. While we know little about their social or religious lives, we can easily glean that safety was an issue for these ancient peoples; they lived behind a double ring of stone walls. Today you can only see the base of these walls. Within them,

small stone houses whose foundations are still clearly visible were built in a circular pattern around a central *talayot*, or watchtower.

You could easily spend an hour or two wandering among the 13,500-sq-metre site, which is dotted with shady trees. To get the most out of your visit, buy the guidebook for sale at the site.

It's easy to get here from Artà. From the large roundabout east of the tourist office, follow the signs toward Ses Païsses; if you're walking or cycling, it's less than a kilometre from the main road.

HIKING & CYCLING
The tourist office gives out an excellent brochure called *Bike Tours* that includes a dozen routes through the area that you can complete on foot or by bike. Detailed maps, photos and route notes make this an excellent source for planning your own excursion.

Many cycling routes follow farm paths through the countryside. Particularly recommended are the Artà–Cala Ratjada route, which passes by Ses Païsses, and the route (about 7km) from Artà to the Ermita de Betlem hermitage (p151).

Festivals & Events
Don't miss the curious **Festa de Sant Antoni Abat**, held on 16 and 17 January, when every one gets in traditional costume and heads to the Santuari de Sant Salvador for dancing, music and a downright odd display of backwards-facing equestrians swinging long sticks around.

Sleeping
The sleeping options in Artà itself are few but fantastic.

Hotel Casal d'Artà (☎ 971 829163; www.casaldarta.de; Carrer de Rafel Blanes 19; s/d €46/86; 🅐) A wonderful old mansion in the heart of town, this charming hotel gives a glimpse of traditional living. Tall ceilings, tiled floors and antique wooden furniture all have a distinctly Mallorcan air.

Can Moragues (☎ 971 829509; www.canmoragues.com; Carrer del Pou Nou 12; s/d €86/125; 🅟 🅐 🅐) A cheery yellow country-house-turned-hotel, Can Moragues offers cosy, impeccably clean rooms that respect the house's original architecture, with touches like exposed stone walls and wood-beam ceilings.

ourpick Hotel Sant Salvador (☎ 971 829555; www.santsalvador.com; Carrer del Castellet 7; r €185-225; 🅟 🅐 🅐) The eight rooms of this luxurious boutique hotel echo the dignified character of this restored manor house, with canopied beds and antique furnishings. Surrounded by a lush garden, the hotel also runs a stylish bar and two classy restaurants. There's a steep price drop October through to April.

Eating & Drinking
The gastronomy in Artà is top rate, with a string of charming eateries (many with terraces or sidewalk seating) running along Carrer de la Ciutat and other finds scattered around town. On Tuesdays, a **market** sets up on Plaça Conqueridor.

Pedra i Flor (☎ 971 829536; Carrer d'Antoni Blanes 4; 🕙 10am-1pm & 5-8pm Mon-Fri, 5-8pm Sat) This delightful flower-shop-cum-café serves coffee, tea, wine and sandwiches on a few small sidewalk tables.

Cafeteria Sant Salvador (☎ 971 836136; Carrer Costa Sant Salvador; mains €6-12; 🕙 Tue-Sun) Up beside the Santuari, this simple cafeteria serves sandwiches and a few mixed plates (meat, veggies and salad served together) in the spacious dining room or breezy terrace. The best thing about it is the panoramic view over the town and countryside.

Sa Plaça (☎ 971 829352; Carrer de la Ciutat 18; mains €7-12) A simple but charming pizzeria just off the Plaça Conqueridor, this is a great spot for a quick lunch or pizza to go.

ourpick Bar Parisien (☎ 971 835440; Carrer de la Ciutat 18; mains €11-19) An appealing mix of old and new draws a sophisticated crowd to this stylish restaurant, famed for its fresh market cuisine, Moroccan specialities (served Sundays only) and exquisite desserts. Occasional concerts at night.

Getting There & Away
Nine bus lines service Artà, all of them coming and going from the bus stops flanking Carrer Costa i Llobera at the main entrance to town. Major lines include Bus 411 to Palma (€8.10, one hour 20 minutes, five daily Monday to Saturday, three on Sunday) via Manacor (€2.40, 25 minutes) and Bus 446 to Alcúdia (€4.80, 50 minutes, six daily Monday to Saturday) and Port de Pollença (€5.60, one hour).

PARC NATURAL DE LA PENÍNSULA DE LLEVANT
About 5km north of Artà begins the Parc Natural de la Península de Llevant, a mountainous park covering a good chunk of the Serra de Llevant mountain range, culminating in the **Cap de Ferrutx**.

This often windswept and rugged territory is popular with bird-watchers – cormorants and Audouin's gulls are common – and offers the hiker plenty of options in a fairly small space. A classic walk takes you through the heart of the park from **S'Alquera Vella d'Avall** (where you can park – take the Ma3333 north of Artà for the **Ermita de Betlem** and follow the signposted turn off right at Km4.7) to the coast and a little beach at **S'Arenalet des Verger**. Reckon on two hours' walking time. To reach the same point from the east along the coast, you could start at **Cala Estreta** (where it is also possible to park). This walk follows the coast to **Cala Matzoc**, on past the medieval watchtower **Torre d'Albarca** and west. It takes another hour to reach S'Arenalet des Verger. Beyond that, the coast becomes harder to negotiate.

The **park office** (☎ 971 836828; Carrer de l'Estel 2) in central Artà (virtually on Plaça d'Espanya) can help with itinerary maps. It also stages guided walks, generally in Catalan and Spanish only, Saturdays from 10am until noon.

CAPDEPERA
pop 11,074
Eight kilometres due east of Artà, this small, dusty village is at first glance a bit run-down, but if you stick around for a visit its charms shine through. Most people head straight to the top of the village, where the early 14th-century **Castell de Capdepera** (☎ 971 818746; adult/child €2/1.50; �},9am-7.30pm Apr-Oct, 9am-4.45pm Nov-Mar) stands guard. A walled complex built on the ruins of a Moorish fortress, the castle was constructed under the orders of Jaume II (son of the conquering Jaume I), who envisioned it as the boundary of a protected town.

The **church**, a simple stone affair, contains a valuable wooden crucifix dating to the 14th century but is otherwise fairly nondescript. The watchtower, called **Torre Miquel Nunis**, predates the rest of the castle and is probably of Moorish

construction. In the 1800s a taller, round tower was built inside the original rectangular one.

In the town below, you can grab a coffee or quick lunch at one of the quaint cafés lining the Plaça Orient. On Wednesdays, a small **fresh market** sets up here.

Things around here are generally calm and quiet, except during festivals like **Sant Bartomeu**, a week of exhibits, concerts, parades and fireworks (18 to 25 August). Other festivals include **Sant Antoni** (Saint Anthony's feast day; 17 January), which includes a traditional animal-blessing ceremony, the **mercat medieval** (medieval market; third weekend in May) and **L'Esperança** (Virgin of Hope's feast day; 18 December).

For accommodation in the area, **Cases de Son Barbassa** (☎ 971 565776; www.sonbarbassa.com; Camí de Son Barbassa, Capdepera; s/d €144/246; �}, Feb-Nov; Ⓟ ⌧ ☐ ☐) is a lovely rural estate with a 16th-century stone tower watching over it and is dotted with olive and almond trees. The hotel itself has 12 rooms, all individually decorated in a rustic chic style that preserves the original architectural elements of the house. The hotel is located just off the road to Cala Mesquida.

Bus 411 links Capdepera to Palma (€9.05, 1½ hours, up to five daily), via Artà (€1.10, 10 minutes) and Manacor (€3.30, 35 minutes). Bus 441 runs along the east coast, stopping at all the major resorts, including Porto Cristo (€2.75, 55 minutes, up to 10 daily) and Cala d'Or (€7.75, one hour 25 minutes).

CALA RATJADA
pop 5960
With its tight hub of a town centre, a handful of petite sandy beaches and a pretty promenade meandering along a rocky, wave-beaten

---

GETTING AWAY FROM IT ALL

Heading north from Cala Ratjada, you'll find a wonderfully undeveloped stretch of coastline specked with beaches. Long-time favourites of nudists, these out-of-the-way coves are no secret, but their lack of development has kept them calm and pristine.

Cala Mesquida, surrounded by sand dunes and a small housing development, is the most accessible, with free parking and regular bus service (Bus 471) from Cala Ratjada (25 minutes, up to 15 daily).

It requires more determination to access the undeveloped coves due west. **Cala Torta**, **Cala Mitjana** and the beachless **Cala Estreta** are all found at the end of a narrow road that ventures through the hills from Artà, yet a more interesting way to arrive is via the one-hour walking path from Cala Mesquida.

Further west, and following a 20-minute trek along the coast from Cala Estreta, **Cala Matzoc** comes into view. The spacious sandy beach backs onto a hill where the ruins of a *talayot* (watchtower) once used to guard the coast from pirates still stands.

coast, Cala Ratjada is easily the most photo-genic of the large eastern resorts. Still, the place is very popular with German tourists and is not immune to overcrowding, especially at the height of summer. To find a quiet spot to lay your towel you might choose to head to one of the coves just out of town.

The main drag, Carrer de l'Agulla, has several worthy shops, but it's marred by a string of tacky Chinese restaurants, cheapo souvenir shops and video games rooms. More-stylish shopping options are found along Carrer de Elionor Servera. Along the seafront, the **Passeig Marítim** (aka Avinguda América) provides the ideal spot for an evening stroll, while the sprawling **harbour** nearby is an endless chain of restaurants, bars and ice-cream parlours.

Information

MYM Informática (☎ 971 565636; Carrer de Nereides 32; internet per hr €2; ☼ 11am-11pm Mon-Sat, 5-11pm Sun) Check your email at this tidy spot.

Tourist office (☎ 971 563033; www.ajcapdepera.net; Carrer del Castellet 5; ☼ 9am-1.30pm & 3.30-6pm Tue-Fri, 9am-1.30pm Sat, 9am-3.30pm Mon) This small office off the Plaça dels Pins has a wealth of information about nearby attractions.

Sights & Activities

BEACHES & WATER SPORTS

Cala Ratjada's most accessible beach is the busy **Platja de Son Moll**, just in front of Passeig Marítim in the centre of town. Perpetually crowded with sunbaked tourists, it's one long carpet of sizzling flesh in the summer.

If you don't mind the walk, drive, bike or tourist-train ride, you're much better off heading either north or south of the resort to lovely and less-crowded beaches. North of town is the **Platja de Cala Agulla**, a calm bay bathed by turquoise waters and hemmed in by hills blanketed in pine trees. There's precious little development to be seen from the sand, but the beach itself is packed with umbrellas for rent. Just north of Cala Agulla is the quieter **Platja de ses Covasses**, where the lack of a wide beach keeps visitors at bay.

Just south of Cala Ratjada is **Font de Sa Cala**, a beach suburb accessible via the tourist train where the crystalline waters are perfect for **snorkelling**. The serene beach is surrounded by a harshly beautiful rocky coast.

Divers can get their scuba fix at **Mero Diving** (☎ 971 565467; www.mero-diving.com; Avinguda de Na

---

> **GOLF IN NORTHEASTERN MALLORCA**
>
> A handful of golf courses are within easy reach of Artà, Capdepera, Cala Ratjada and Cala Millor. Find well-maintained greens and great views at the following places:
>
> ■ **Capdepera Golf** (☎ 971 818500; www.golfcapdepera.com; Carretera Artá-Capdepera Km3.5; 18 holes €75; ☼ 8am-7pm)
> ■ **Canyamel Golf** (☎ 971 841313; www.canyamelgolf.com; Avinguda d'es Cap Vermell, Urbanización Canyamel; 18 holes €80; ☼ 8am-8pm)
> ■ **Pula Golf** (☎ 971 817034; www.pulagolf.com; Carretera Son Servera-Capdepera Km3; 18 holes €125; ☼ 8am-7pm)

Lliteres s/n; per dive from €29; ☼ 9am-6pm May-Oct) on Cala Lliteres, or at **Dive & Fun** (☎ 971 818036; www.mallorcadiving.de; Font de Sa Cala; per dive €46; ☼ 9am-6pm Apr-Nov), located in the Beach Club Hotel in Font de Sa Cala.

Illa Balear (☎ 971 810600; www.cruceroscreuers.com; adult/child return €22/11; ☼ 10am-4pm) runs cruises between Cala Ratjada and east-coast resorts like Cala Bona, Sa Coma and Porto Cristo.

WALKING & CYCLING

To beat the crowds, take the **walking trail** that leaves from the far northern end of Cala Agulla (aka Cala Nau) and head through the pines of a protected natural area toward the pristine **Cala Mesquida**, a beach backed with dunes. The round trip is 10km. Along the way, a smaller trail veers off to the right at the signpost for the 'torre', the **Talaia de Son Jaumell** watchtower. The trail (7km round trip from Cala Agulla) is marked with red dots, and the reward at the end is a spectacular panoramic view.

You can rent bicycles as well as in-line skates and mopeds at **JB Bicis** (☎ 971 565178; Carrer de Nereides s/n; bike rental per day €8; ☼ 9am-1pm & 3-7pm Mon-Fri, 9am-noon & 5-7pm Sat & Sun). Mountain bikes are the speciality at **M Bike** (☎ 639 417796; www.m-bike.com; Carrer de L'Agulla; bike rental per day €10-28; ☼ 9am-12.30pm & 4-6pm Mon-Fri, 9am-11am & 6pm (for returns only) Sat, 10am-11am & 5-6pm Sun).

The tourist office offers daily guided hikes or bike trips May through to October.

HORSEBACK RIDING

Stables where you can sign up for day trips and equestrian classes are popular in and

EASTERN MALLORCA

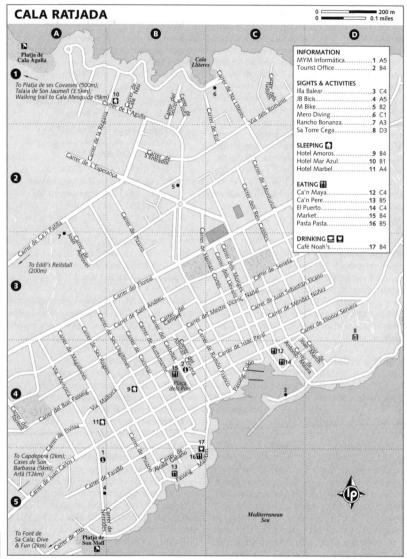

CALA RATJADA

INFORMATION	
MYM Informática	1 A5
Tourist Office	2 B4

SIGHTS & ACTIVITIES	
Illa Balear	3 C4
JB Bicis	4 A5
M Bike	5 B2
Mero Diving	6 C1
Rancho Bonanza	7 A3
Sa Torre Cega	8 D3

SLEEPING	
Hotel Amoros	9 B4
Hotel Mar Azul	10 B1
Hotel Marbel	11 A4

EATING	
Ca'n Maya	12 C4
Ca'n Pere	13 B5
El Puerto	14 C4
Market	15 B4
Pasta Pasta	16 B5

DRINKING	
Café Noah's	17 B4

around Cala Ratjada, and a selection of excellent coastal and wooded trails extend out from town. Check in with **Eddi's Reitstall** (☎ 630 150551; www.ne-goc.com/Eddies-Reitstall-Cala-Ratjada; Carretera Palma-Capdepera; rides per hr €15; ☒ 11am-1pm & 4-7pm Mon-Sat) or **Rancho Bonanza** (☎ 971 565664; www .ranchobonanza.com; Carrer de Ca'n Patilla s/n; rides per hr €15; ☒ 8am-8pm Mon-Sat, 8am-1pm Sun), who runs

four to five excursions daily with pony rides available for kids six years and under.

SA TORRE CEGA

On a hilltop outside town sits **Sa Torre Cega** (☎ 971 563033; www.fundbmarch.es), an estate named for the 15th-century 'blind tower' (ie windowless tower) that sits at its centre.

Owned by the Fundació Bartolomé March, the estate possesses a beautiful Mediterranean garden that's home to a collection of some 70 sculptures by such greats as Eduardo Chillida, Josep Maria Sert, Henry Moore, Auguste Rodin and others. Although at the time of writing it was closed for renovations, in the future visits will be organised through the tourist office.

Festivals & Events

Cala Ratjada's main festival, the **Festes del Carme**, celebrates the Verge del Carme, the holy patroness of fisherfolk. It is held 15 and 16 July and includes an elaborate maritime procession, fireworks, and a host of cultural events. A feast on 16 August honours the town's patron, **Sant Roc**, with more fireworks and concerts.

Sleeping

There are dozens of hotels and 'aparthotels' in and around Cala Ratjada. You can make last-minute online accommodation bookings at the local hotel association's site, www.firstsunmallorca.com.

Hotel Marbel (☎ 971 563895; www.hotelmarbel.com; Carrer de Magellanes; per person €33; ❤ May-Oct; ✖ 🖳 🖳) You won't get sea views at this intimate 20-room hotel a few blocks from Platja Son Moll, but you'll get bright, cheery rooms, friendly service and a great deal. It's especially popular with equestrians; the owners are horse lovers who happily recommend area stables.

Hotel Mar Azul (☎ 971 563200; www.hotelmarazul .net; Carrer de l'Agulla s/n; per person €39; ❤ May-Oct; ✖ 🖳 🖳) The Hotel 'Blue Sea' indeed offers stellar vistas of the glistening Mediterranean from its perch overlooking the sea. Its comfortably old-fashioned rooms, seaside terrace café and central location (2km from Cala Agulla and a 10-minute walk to the centre of Cala Ratjada) make it a good bet.

Hotel Amoros (☎ 971 563550; www.hotelamoros.com; Carrer de Ses Llegitimes 37; s/d €50/80; ❤ Feb-Nov; ✖ 🖳) This ochre-coloured, 75-room hotel a couple of blocks off the beach has a laid-back, family feel. Rooms are breezy with terraces, most of which overlook the pool.

Eating

Self-caterers can head to the Saturday **market** in the town centre, or to one of several **Spar** supermarkets. As in other resorts, these small and often overpriced stores offer the only easy way to stock up on provisions.

Pasta Pasta (☎ 971 818744; www.pastapasta.org; Avinguda América 3 (Passeig Marítim 3); mains €4-12; ❤ Mar-Oct) This stylish seaside villa, where tasty pizzas, pastas and salads are served with style, is perfect for families or groups.

El Puerto (☎ 971 565003; Carrer de Gabriel Roca 3; mains €9-18; ❤ Jan-Nov) At the far end of the harbour, you'll find a handful of seafood restaurants including this cosy spot, where tasty fish soup and *chipirones a la andaluza* (fried cuttlefish) share menu space with tapas and meat dishes.

Ca'n Maya (☎ 971 564035; Carrer d'Elionor Servera 80; mains €9-20; ❤ Tue-Sun Mar-Dec) Savour shellfish and seafood – such as grilled squid, grilled salmon and swordfish – on the rustic-feeling glassed-in terrace by the harbour.

Ca'n Pere (☎ 971 563005; Passeig Marítim s/n; mains €8-25; ❤ Apr-Oct) The outdoor dining room, built up on a rocky outcrop overlooking the sea, makes you feel like you're eating aboard a boat. The menu features everything from kid-friendly spaghetti to ostrich meat, but Pere's strength is seafood.

Drinking

A plethora of kitschy bars line the waterfront near the harbour; if loud music and big drinks are your style, then look no further.

ourpick Café Noah's (☎ 971 818125; www.cafenoahs .com; Avinguda América 2) A bohemian-vibed bar and café with a trailing list of cocktails. This hip nightspot draws a well-heeled crowd for drinks and live music. During mealtimes, you can also get a quick bite here.

Getting There & Away

Bus 411 links Palma de Mallorca and Cala Ratjada, via Artá, with up to five runs daily in each direction (€9.35 return, two hours). The same bus stops in Capdepera (10 minutes) and Manacor (20 minutes).

From the port, Cape Balear runs a daily hydrofoil to Ciutadella (see p210).

COVES D'ARTÀ & PLATJA DE CANYAMEL

Rivalling Porto Cristo's Coves del Drac (p177), yet under far less strain from tourism, are the majestic **Coves d'Artà** (☎ 971 841293; www.cuevas-dearta.com; Carretera de les Coves s/n; admission €9; ❤ 10am-6pm May-Oct, 10am-5pm Nov-Apr), a series of natural caves burrowed into the coast just 1km outside

EASTERN MALLORCA

of Canyamel. Although the dramatic lighting (sometimes in disco-lounge-like colours) may seem hokey, there's no doubting that this is a seriously beautiful work of nature.

The guided visits, which last 25 minutes to 40 minutes depending on the size of the group and are offered in English, German, Spanish and French, lead visitors through an unassuming fissure in the rock wall that buffers the coast. Soon you'll find yourself in a soaring vestibule, walking along a raised footpath past the 22-metre-tall 'Queen of Columns' and through several other rooms, including the 'Chamber of Purgatory' and 'Chamber of Hell'. The interesting stalactites and stalagmites are the stars of the show, although the management tries to add a little spice to the visit with light-and-sound features.

To get to the caves, follow the signs toward the Coves d'Artà from the Pm404 coastal highway that runs between Capdepera and Son Servera. The tourist boats run by **Barcas Coral** (☎ 971 563622; to Font de sa Cala/Cala Ratjada €10/12; ♥ Apr-Oct) make three 45-minute trips daily in high season between Cala Ratjada and the caves, stopping at Font de sa Cala on the way. A series of steep stone steps means that there is no disabled access.

After a visit to the caves, head just a few hundred metres south down the coast to the pleasant **Platja de Canyamel**, a busy but not overbuilt beach resort. Just 3km off the shore stands the famed **Torre de Canyamel** (☎ 971 841134; Carretera Artà-Canyamel; admission €3; ♥ 10am-5.30pm Tue-Sat), a defence tower of Muslim origin. A short drive away, on a little dirt path near Canyamel Golf, is an even older reminder of the past, the ancient settlement **Claper des Gegant** (♥ 10am-6pm), featuring a circular *talayot*, defensive walls and several rooms.

SON SERVERA & AROUND
pop 10,950

The inland agricultural village Son Servera may seem like little more than a quick blip on the highway to the coast, but it is worth a brief stop. Settled since ancient times (the countryside is scattered with megalithic monuments) and an agricultural village since the 13th century, Son Servera enjoys a privileged setting among woods, meadows and groves of almond and fig trees. This is prime cycling territory, and many popular routes trace the country roads branching out from town.

In town, you can't miss the unfinished **iglesia nueva** (new church), which was begun in 1905 but left partially built when the money ran out 25 years later. These days occasional concerts are held in the neogothic shell that would have been the church's choir stall and main nave. Also look out for the **Pont d'en Calet** aqueduct, on the Manacor road at the town entrance.

On Friday a **fresh market** sets up in town, and on the second Sunday of each month, a **flea market** is held on the Plaça de Sant Joan. Important festivals include **Sant Antoni** (17 January) and the holy week preceding Easter, when **Good Friday** sees an elaborate re-enactment of the taking down of Christ's body from the cross.

JAIME FERRIOL, OWNER OF MERO DIVING

Jaime Ferriol has been diving on Mallorca since 1969, when he opened Mero Diving (Spain's oldest dive shop) in the heart of Cala Ratjada. After nearly 40 years of diving in the cave-rich waters around Cala Ratjada, he says he 'wouldn't trade this place for anything'.

Why is Cala Ratjada a great place to dive? It's famous for its underwater caves, like La Catedral, Jaume I, Jaume II and Jaume III. The mouths of the caves are only 7m or 8m below the surface, but the caves extend up to 150m into the earth, so you need to be an experienced diver to explore them.

What is your favourite dive spot? I love a place we call the 'Big Cheese'. It's a rock so full of holes that it looks like a huge piece of Swiss cheese.

When is the best time to dive here? You can dive May through to the end of October, but the very best times are in September and October, when you'll see more marine life and when there aren't so many people.

What species can divers expect to see? We spot barracudas, tunas, dolphin fish and many other species.

EASTERN MALLORCA

Several rural hotels inhabit picturesque farmhouses nearby. Elegant **El Encinar** (☎ 971 183860; www.elencinardearta.com; PM-4041 Km3; r €90-170; Mar-Oct; P 🐾 🛱), off the highway that runs from Artà to Son Servera, is an 18th-century farmhouse that has been tastefully converted into an intimate 12-room hotel surrounded by lush gardens. Details such as the locally woven *roba de llengües* (striped cloth) textiles in the bedrooms, and the lounge with fireplace and library add a homy touch.

Overlooking the Pula golf course and run by the same owners, **Petit Hotel Cases de Pula** (☎ 971 567492; www.pulagolf.com; Finca Pula S/n; r €121-199; P 🐾 🛱) is a beautifully restored 16th-century estate. Ten immaculate rooms (most of them sprawling suites) offer indulgence and comfort in a luxuriously rustic setting.

Bus 414 links Son Servera with Palma (€7.85, two hours, twice daily Monday to Saturday) via Cala Millor, Porto Cristo and Manacor.

CALA MILLOR TO PORTOCOLOM

The coast stretching from Cala Millor to Portocolom is either loved or loathed, depending on who's talking. For the millions of tourists who descend every year on its sandy beaches and splash in its gentle waves, this place is paradise. But for those who mourn the loss of Mallorca's once-pristine coastline, the abundance of gleaming white hotels and sparkling turquoise swimming pools is nothing short of an abhorrence.

If you're looking for all-inclusive mega-resorts, look no further. Cala Millor, S'Illot and Cales de Mallorca have bargain-basement accommodation, all-you-can-eat buffets aplenty, and so many restaurants touting food 'just like mum makes' that you could feel as though you'd never left home.

If, however, you're seeking a quieter, more Mallorquin style of holiday, don't despair. This stretch of coastline is popular for a reason – it's undeniably beautiful. And the crowd-weary don't have to shy away. Stay in one of the cosy rural hotels and drive, cycle or hike to off-the-beaten-path beaches such as Cala Romàntica or Cala Varques, or dine in one of the farmhouse-style restaurants that hide just beyond the bustle.

CALA MILLOR & AROUND

Too bad you can't keep a place this pretty a secret. At twilight, when the sun turns the sky violet and the water a soft shade of aquamarine, you can almost imagine that the concrete jungle inland was just a mirage. Alas, by day it's all too obvious that tall apartments and hotels stretch as far as the eye can see, and a big KFC is one of the more prominent restaurants on the coast. The saving grace of Cala Millor (Best Cove, a dubious name) is that its nearly 2km-long beach is large enough to absorb masses of sun worshippers on all but the busiest summer days. Also, the seaside promenade running behind it is an enjoyable place for a stroll.

Get a map and brochures about local attractions at the **tourist office** (☎ 971 585864; www .visitcalamillor.com; Passeig Marítim s/n; 9am-5pm Mon-Fri, 9am-3pm Sat), a kiosk right on the promenade. Another, larger office is located in the town hall. Get online at **Cala Millor Cyber Centre** (☎ 971 587557; Avinguda d'en Joan Servera Camps 1; per hr €1.50; 10am-2pm & 4-9pm Mon-Sat).

To escape the crowds, set off for a challenging seaside **hike** to the **Castell de n'Amer**, which overlooks the sea.

South of Cala Millor, near-unbroken development continues south through the mushrooming resorts of **Son Moro**, **Sa Coma**, **S'Illot**, **Cala Moreia** and **Cala Moranda**. The only people likely to go to these sprawling examples of out-of-control urbanisation are those who have booked package holidays in these hotels.

Beyond the resort sprawl is the **Safari-Zoo** (☎ 971 810909; Carretera Portocristo-Son Servera Km5; adult/child €13/9; 9am-7pm Apr-Sep, 9am-5pm Oct-Mar), where you see wild animals from the comfort of your car. If anything, it's an interesting cool-day activity.

Just north of Cala Millor the construction boom gives one last sputter at the former fishing village of **Cala Bona**, a resort that's managed to hang on to at least a few of its fisherfolk. There is no natural beach here, although thanks to modern technology three small coves have been topped off with imported sand. Just beyond them stretches a lovely rocky coastline.

Bus lines 441, 446, 447 and others run up and down the east coast, linking Cala Millor with Cala Bona and resorts such as Cala d'Or (€6.85, 1¼ hours). Bus 412 heads to Palma (€8.20, 1½ hours, up to 15 daily). To get to the airport, book the **Ultramar Express** (☎ 902 102521; per person €18) airport transfer service.

PORTO CRISTO

pop 6620

Home to Mallorca's grandest caves, Porto Cristo is above all a day-trip destination and attracts thousands of would-be spelunkers to its vast underground caverns. It's true that as a resort it lacks some of the bang of glitzier destinations elsewhere on the coast, but what Porto Cristo is missing in glamour it makes up for in unassuming charm.

First established as the medieval fishing port of Manacor (although few historical constructions remain), it later became one of the

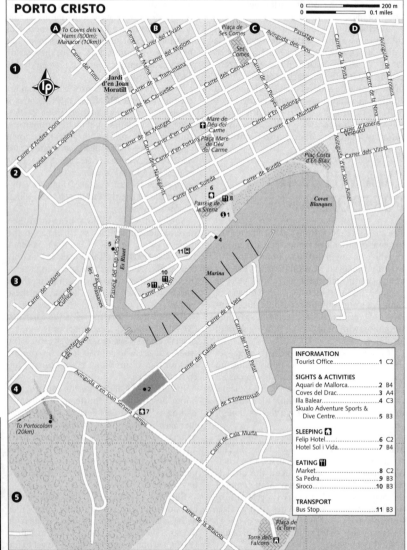

PORTO CRISTO

INFORMATION	
Tourist Office	1 C2

SIGHTS & ACTIVITIES	
Aquari de Mallorca	2 B4
Coves del Drac	3 A4
Illa Balear	4 C3
Skualo Adventure Sports & Dive Centre	5 B3

SLEEPING	
Felip Hotel	6 C2
Hotel Sol i Vida	7 B4

EATING	
Market	8 C2
Sa Pedra	9 B3
Siroco	10 B3

TRANSPORT	
Bus Stop	11 B3

EASTERN MALLORCA

island's first beach hot spots thanks to its calm natural harbour. The town's glory has faded, but its setting on a pristine harbour is as pretty as it ever was, and the fact that so many of its visitors bus out at the end of the day is just added appeal for those that like their seaside holiday on the quiet side.

The **tourist office** (☎ 971 815103; www.manacor .org; Carrer del Moll; ⏲ 9am-4pm Mon-Fri) sits at the end of a wharf. A sprawling **market** (⏲ 9am-2pm Sun) selling produce, artisan goods and the tacky souvenirs sold in resorts across the globe takes over the Passeig de la Sirena on Sunday mornings.

Sights & Activities

Most of the activity crowds alongside the **Passeig de la Sirena** and the **harbour**, where a small crowded **beach** provides the perfect place to observe the comings and goings of fishing boats and yachts in the **marina**. Beside the beach you'll find the **Coves Blanques**, a handful of small caves that were inhabited during the Talayotic period and were later used by fishers for shelter.

No-one comes to Porto Cristo without passing by one of the grand underground caves nearby. A 15-minute walk from the centre on the southern edge of town, the **Coves del Drac** (Dragon's Caves; ☎ 971 820753; www.cuevasdeldrach .com; Carretera de les Coves s/n; admission €9.50; ⏲ entry on the hr 10am-5pm mid-Mar–Oct, staggered entries 10.45am-4.30pm Nov–mid-Mar) attract a long stream of visitors who descend 25m underground to follow a guide through breathtakingly beautiful (and cleverly exploited) chambers, theatrically lit in bright colours and adorned with impressive stalactites and stalagmites. The hour-long tour delves into the most beautiful parts of the 2km-long limestone tunnel and also includes a visit to the subterranean lake where a classical music concert is held. Get here early, especially in summer, as the long lines can have you waiting for hours.

With a very similar style and only slightly less tourist appeal are the **Coves dels Hams** (Hams Caves; ☎ 971 820988; www.cuevas-hams.com; Carretera Manacor-Portocristo Km11; adult/child €12/free; ⏲ 10am-5pm Mar-Oct, 11am-4.30pm Nov-Apr), another underground labyrinth where you can walk around marvellous rock formations and hear an underground lakeside concert. For €4 more, you can also see a 15-minute digitally enhanced video about Jules Verne inside a cave auditorium.

Scarcely 150m from the Coves del Drac is the **Aquari de Mallorca** (Aquarium of Mallorca; ☎ 971 820871; Carrer del Gambí 7; adult/child €5/2.50; ⏲ 10.30am-6pm Apr-Oct, 11am-3pm Nov-Mar), a modern aquarium focused on Mediterranean marine life.

To swim with the fish, head to **Skualo Adventure Sports & Dive Centre** (☎ 971 822739; www .sportextreme.com; Passeig del Cap d'es Toll; per dive €35, plus equipment €16; ⏲ 9am-6pm Mon-Sat). Or take a cruise on a **glass-bottom cruise boat.** Several companies, including **Illa Balear** (☎ 971 810600; www .cruceroscreuers.com; adult/child up to €22/11; ⏲ 10am-4pm) tour the coast.

Festivals & Events

Porto Cristo goes all out with a bonfire and 'dance of the devils' for the eve of **Sant Antoni** (16 and 17 January), the traditional blessing of animals. Another party comes 16 July with the feast day of the patroness of fisherfolk, the **Verge del Carme**.

Sleeping

Hotel Sol i Vida (☎ 971 821074; Avinguda d'en Joan Servera Camps 11; s/d from €26/43; 🏊) The friendly roadside Hotel Sol i Vida sits between the aquarium and the Coves del Drac. Rooms are stark and services simple, but with a pool, bar-restaurant and tennis court this is a cheap and cheery place to stay.

Felip Hotel (☎ 971 820750; Carrer de Burdils 41; s/d from €70/110; 🌐 🖳 🏊) Since 1890 this once-stately hotel has dominated Porto Cristo. While no longer the grande dame it once was, the Felip still retains an old-world elegance. Rooms are on the small side but artfully placed mirrors make the most of the space. Dark wood, bronze lamps, marbled bathrooms and bullfight-themed art on the walls reveal its old-fashioned soul.

Eating

Running along the waterfront is a string of restaurants all serving essentially the same thing: a wonderful seaside view accompanied by an internationally flavoured menu of salads, rice dishes, grilled fish, and meats smothered in sauces.

Siroco (☎ 971 822444; Carrer del Verí s/n; mains €11-17; ⏲ May-Oct) For inventive seafood dishes and Mallorcan specialities, this waterfront restaurant is a great option.

Sa Pedra (☎ 971 820932; Carrer del Verí s/n; mains €12-25; ⏲ May-Oct) The varied menu at this upscale eatery includes everything from pasta to paella; there's a little something for everyone.

Getting There & Away

A dozen bus lines serve Porto Cristo, among them lines 412 and 414 to Palma (€7.20, 1½ hours, up to 11 daily) via Manacor and Vilafranca; lines 441, 442 and 443 connect to the east-coast resorts (varied prices, scores of buses); and line 445's once-daily trip north to Port de Pollença (€7.05, two hours 10 minutes) via Artà (€3.40, one hour).

SOUTH OF PORTO CRISTO

The coast running south of Porto Cristo is pocked with a series of beautiful, unspoilt coves, many of them signposted from the Ma4014 highway linking Porto Cristo and Portocolom. The largest and most developed of the bunch is **Cala Romàntica**, where a few hotels form one of the island's more serene resorts and a rough promenade has been hewn out of the rock face by the sea.

Beyond Cala Romàntica you can seek out coves and caves such as **Cala Varques** (known for the complex cave on the cliff above the cove), **Cala Sequer**, **Cova del Pilar** or **Cala Magraner** (see right). None has direct car access; plan on walking at least the last few minutes.

In this area, you could sleep at the fairy-tale **Es Rafal Podent** (☎ 971 183130; www.topfincas .com; Carretera Manacor-Cales de Mallorca Km6; r €85-154; [P] [X] [R]), a restored 15th-century manor house on an organic farm. The house has been divided into five romantic apartments, ideal for couples or families. You'll find it on a country lane 4km from Cala Romàntica.

Nearby, you can stay at the charming rural hotel **Es Picot** (☎ 667 735276; www.espicot.com; Camí de Sa Mola Km3; r €113; [P] [X] [R]), 5km from Cala Varques. Six simply decorated rooms with terraces and amazing views comprise this intimate hotel, whose restaurant featuring 'authentic Mallorcan cuisine' is a real treat. Free internet access for laptops from the terrace.

CALES DE MALLORCA & AROUND

A series of once-pristine beaches and coves was the *raison d'être* for the proliferation of unattractive mega-hotels that goes by the name of Cales de Mallorca. The prison-style architecture of a few of these 1970s monstrosities is undeserving of the surroundings – broad white-sand beaches walled by limestone cliffs and caressed by a calm sea. Unsurprisingly,

this area is popular with beach goers looking for easy access to sea, sun and sand.

When you just can't handle another day at the beach, there are other diversions. Just beyond the resort you'll find **Jumaica** (☎ 971 833979; Carretera Portocolom-Porto Cristo Km4.5; adult/child €6/3; [Y] 9am-7pm Apr-Sep, 10am-4.30pm Oct-Mar), a small tropical park complete with banana grove, where young'uns may get a kick out of the small animals and birds.

For a dose of history, seek out the prehistoric settlement of **S'Hospitalet Vell**, at Km1 of the Carretera de Cales de Mallorca. There's no visitors centre at this 2200-year-old *talayotic* site; just let yourself in and pull the gate closed behind you.

Cales de Mallorca offers no end of large hotels, many of which can be booked only through big travel agencies, but you don't have to veer far from the coast to discover places with infinitely more charm. Just 3km from Cala Murada sits serene **S'Aigo** (☎ 971 833050; www.fincasaigo.com; Carretera Portocolom-Portocristo Km2.4; r €230-345; [P] [R]), an ivy-smothered rural estate whose two self-catering stone houses sleep 12 people each. Ideal for groups and families, the rustic stone houses are set amid the shady Mallorcan countryside.

WALK: FOUR COVES

Just north of Cales de Mallorca the chaos of the resorts falls away and nature takes over. Over the 6km between Cales de Mallorca and Cala Romàntica, there's only pine-specked rocky coves, pitted cliff faces and the aquamarine of the Mediterranean. The walk begins at **Finca Can Roig**, a rural estate near Cales de Mallorca. To get there, take the Carretera Porto Cristo–Portocolom (Ma4014) and at Km6 turn east toward Cales de Mallorca. Continue 2.2km and veer left; after 200m you'll reach the entrance to Can Roig.

Leave your car here and strike out along the wide, rocky track that parallels the coast. After about 15 minutes, a slightly narrower path turns off to the right. Follow it alongside a small gully and through patches of trees to reach **Cala Bota**, a sheltered cove with a small sandy beach. A steep trail meanders around and above the cove, giving a bird's-eye view of its beauty.

From Cala Bota, backtrack on the trail you came in on, and turn right toward the next cove, **Cala Vigili**. The track brings you to a smaller trail that heads off right down to this narrow cove,

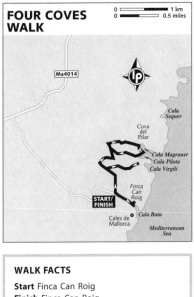

FOUR COVES WALK

WALK FACTS

Start Finca Can Roig

Finish Finca Can Roig

Distance 13km

Duration 2½ hours

where a small shelter houses a dinghy. (The walk down takes about 10 minutes.)

Return to the main trail and continue to your right. You'll pass a small trail on your right, but keep straight until you come upon a second path. Take it towards the third cove, **Cala Pilota**, backed by vertigo-inducing cliffs.

Head back to the main trail and walk just a couple of minutes before coming to a fork. Take the left-hand path, which rolls down to the final cove, **Cala Magraner**, the grandest of the bunch both in size and beauty. The trail is wide at first but stops in a clearing; another, narrower trail leads you the last few minutes. After splashing in the crystalline waters, exploring the small caves that dot the rock and keeping an eye out for the rock climbers that frequent this spot, turn back and walk the full length of the main trail back to Finca Can Roig.

PORTOCOLOM

pop 3813

A sleepy place as far as east-coast holiday resorts go, Portocolom cradles a natural harbour (one of the few on the island) and at-

tracts German, British and Spanish families in equal numbers. Fishing boats, sailing boats and the odd luxury yacht bob in the calm waters here, creating an idyllic view from the bars, restaurants, villas and hotels that line the horseshoe-shaped bay. Within reach of town are some fine beaches, such as the immaculate little cove of **Cala Marçal** and, on the northern end of town, **Cala s'Arenal**, the locals' preferred beach.

There's not much left of the old port town that was once a key part of the island's wine exports. The village itself is a mix of haphazardly built apartment buildings scattered among hardware stores and banks, and shady streets lined with big villas.

Get maps and brochures galore at the **tourist office** (☎ 971 826084; Avinguda de Cala Marçal 15; 9am-3pm Mon-Fri, 4-6pm Tue & Thu, 10am-1pm Sat). Next door, check your email at the **Eurocafe** (☎ 971825081; Avinguda de Cala Marçal 10; per hr €2; 11am-10pm).

Activities

Most of the activities here are focused on the Mediterranean. Scuba fans can head to **Bahia Azul Dive Center** (☎ 971 825280; www.bahia-azul.de; Ronda de Creuer Balear 78; per dive €39; 9.30am-6pm Mon-Sat, 9.30am-noon Sun Apr-Oct), the diving centre in the Hostal Bahia Azul that offers courses, try dives and equipment rental. To get out on the water, sign up for a day cruise with **Caribia Yacht Charters** (☎ 656 288179; www.caribia yachtcharters.com; Carrer del Llop 3, no 6; adult/child €95/67; 9am-1pm & 4-8pm Mon-Sat). You can also hire skippered yachts by the day (from €500) or week (from €2390), or rent a motorboat by the day (from €260 per day if you have a boating license). You could also take a **kayak** trip with **Mallorca Aquatica** (☎ 649 077313; Avinguda de Cala Marçal 14; 2hr tour €18; 10am-6pm May-Oct), which acts as a diving centre as well and offers dives from €40.

Walkers and cyclists have plenty of options nearby. South of town, starting from Cala Marçal, an 8km **walking trail** links a half-dozen coves, many of which are accessible only by foot or boat, eventually reaching Cala Ferrera. The tourist office can provide a map and route description for this and other excursions. Inland, many of the country lanes are signposted for cyclists and are also used by equestrians. You can rent a bike at **Moto Sprint** (☎ 971 824858; Avinguda de Cala Marçal; per day €9.50; 9am-1pm & 4-9pm Apr-Oct).

EASTERN MALLORCA

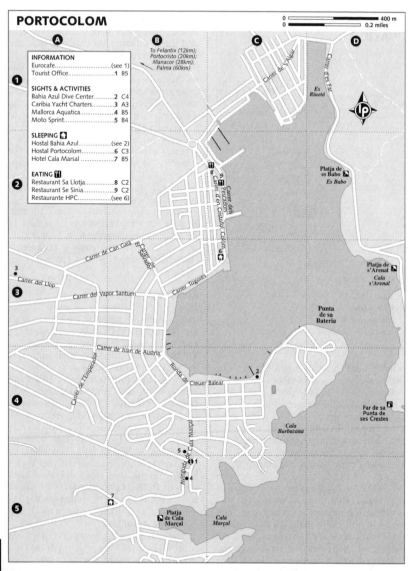

PORTOCOLOM

INFORMATION
Eurocafe.............................(see 1)
Tourist Office..........................1 B5

SIGHTS & ACTIVITIES
Bahia Azul Dive Center.........2 C4
Caribia Yacht Charters...........3 A3
Mallorca Aquatica..................4 B5
Moto Sprint............................5 B4

SLEEPING
Hostal Bahia Azul..................(see 2)
Hostal Portocolom...................6 C3
Hotel Cala Marsal 7 B5

EATING
Restaurant Sa Llotja...............8 C2
Restaurant Se Sinia................9 C2
Restaurante HPC...................(see 6)

Sleeping

There are no big hotels here, but the intimate guesthouses and unpretentious *hostales* are a great choice for independent travellers.

ourpick Hostal Portocolom (☎ 971 825323; www .hostalportocolom.com; Carrer d'en Cristòfol Colom 5; per person €35; 🛇) Situated right on the waterfront, this fabulous little *hostal* offers up squeaky-clean rooms with parquet floors and sunny décor. The restaurant downstairs is 'resort chic'.

Hostal Bahia Azul (☎ 971 825280; www.bahia-azul .de; Ronda del Creuer Balear 78; s/d €39/59; 🛇 Apr-Oct; 🛇 🛇) Run by a Mallorquin-German couple, this 15-room hotel offers breezy Mediterranean-themed rooms (ask for one with a sea view) and service geared towards divers and cyclists. Extras include a leave-one-take-one library, a sauna, and an intimate patio with sun lounges.

Hotel Cala Marsal (☎ 971 825225; www.hotelcala marsal.com; Platja de Cala Marçal; per person €45; ☼ May-Oct; ✖ ☐ ☎) On a breezy bluff overlooking Cala Marçal (ask for a sea view), this family-oriented hotel has comfortable but run-of-the-mill rooms with balconies, and extras such as tennis, squash and volleyball courts and bicycle rental for guests.

Eating

Restaurante HPC (☎ 971 825323; Carrer d'en Cristòfol Colom 5; mains €9-23) The stylish, high-ceilinged restaurant below the Hostal Portocolom offers a bit of everything, from homemade pizzas to paella, grilled grouper, Mallorcan suckling pig and duck magret.

Restaurant Se Sinia (☎ 971 824323; Carrer dels Pescadors s/n; mains €11-22; ☼ Tue-Sun Feb-Oct) With menus designed by artist Miquel Barceló and chairs marked with plaques bearing the name of famous people who have sat there, this classic maritime eatery is the most respected place in town. Fresh fish of all kinds and homemade desserts are the house specialities.

Restaurant Sa Llotja (☎ 971 825165; Carrer dels Pescadors s/n; mains €13-27; ☼ Tue-Sun Feb-Oct) A sleek eatery with a wonderful terrace overlooking the fishing boats moored in the harbour, Sa Llotja tempts with dishes like monkfish, lobster stew or herb-encrusted lamb.

Getting There & Away

Ten bus lines service Portocolom, including the coastal routes 441, 442 and 443 (varied prices, dozens daily). Up to seven buses link with Palma (€5.10, 1½ hours).

EASTERN MALLORCA

Southern Mallorca

The fortresslike geography that dominates the coast between the Badia de Palma (Bay of Palma) and the outskirts of Colònia de Sant Jordi has made this area one of the least-developed of the island. Much of the coast is buffered by tall, nearly impenetrable cliffs splashed with the sapphire blue waters of the Mediterranean. They may not be very accessible, but their untamed, raw beauty is hypnotising.

Beyond the cliffs are intimate coves and long beaches, true marvels of nature that wow with their beauty. Whether they're the hard-to-access coves enshrouded by fjord-like cliffs, or silky sweeps of sand backed by pines and junipers, these are some of Mallorca's best beaches. Still, the area's often unforgiving coastline, the existence of parks and natural areas, and the proliferation of working farms and rural estates has kept this part of the island blessedly intact – for now.

Change, however, may not be long in coming. If the countless cranes on the horizon are any indication, the already impressive number of macro-chalets and planned communities along the coastline is only going to grow. It only takes a glance at over-the-top resorts like Cala d'Or to see how quickly construction can transform the spirit of a place.

While these days much of the southern coast seems rather sleepy, this wasn't always the case. One of the first areas on the island to be settled, the south welcomed settlers from the first millennium BC onward, thanks to its calm bays, protective cliffs and variety of vegetation. A wealth of ancient sites, like Capocorb Vell, allow you to peek in on the area's past.

HIGHLIGHTS

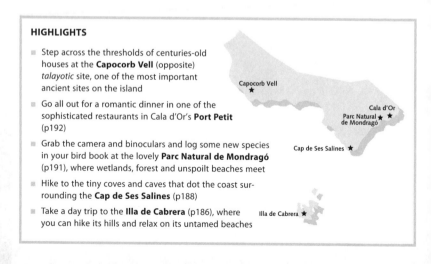

- Step across the thresholds of centuries-old houses at the **Capocorb Vell** (opposite) *talayotic* site, one of the most important ancient sites on the island

- Go all out for a romantic dinner in one of the sophisticated restaurants in Cala d'Or's **Port Petit** (p192)

- Grab the camera and binoculars and log some new species in your bird book at the lovely **Parc Natural de Mondragó** (p191), where wetlands, forest and unspoilt beaches meet

- Hike to the tiny coves and caves that dot the coast surrounding the **Cap de Ses Salines** (p188)

- Take a day trip to the **Illa de Cabrera** (p186), where you can hike its hills and relax on its untamed beaches

Capocorb Vell ★

Cala d'Or
Parc Natural ★ ★
de Mondragó

Cap de Ses Salines ★

Illa de Cabrera ★

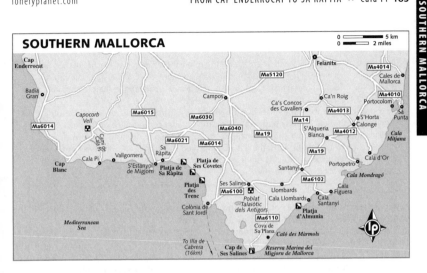

FROM CAP ENDERROCAT TO SA RÀPITA

The lonely stretch of coastline running along the island's southernmost flank is pristine and unspoilt, a refreshing sight squeezed between the high-rise hotels on the east coast and the high-speed activity of the Badia de Palma.

CALA PI

This modest resort has the reputation of catering to the retiree crowd, but the truth is that anyone seeking a low-key seaside holiday and a bit of solace can find it here. The beach is found at the end of a steep staircase so, retirees or not, whoever plans to swim and sunbathe should be in decent physical shape. There is no wheelchair, stroller or disabled access.

The beach itself, devoid of services of any kind, is only 50m wide but stretches more than 100m inland. It's flanked on either side by inhospitable, fjord-like cliffs that ensure

OUR TOP PICKS

- **Restaurant** La Caracola, Portopetro (p191)
- **Hotel** Hostal Restaurante Playa (p186)
- **Beach** Platja des Trenc (p187)
- **Resort** Portopetro (p191)

the inlet stays as still as bath water, making it a popular place for boats to anchor.

Away from the beach, there is not much going on. On the coast, a round 17th-century defence tower pays homage to the Mallorca of ages past, when pirate threats made towers like this, and the dozens of others that once lined the coast, a necessity. A web of streets lined with large chalets and the occasional restaurant stretches to the east, blending seamlessly with the urbanisation of Vallgornera (p184), a low-key place known for being home to the Balearics' longest cave.

The best places to stay in the area are rural hotels like **Sa Bassa Plana** (☎ 971 123003; www.sabas saplana.com; Carretera Cap Blanc Km25.4; r per person from €34; P 🕑 🛇). Set on a working farm, 90% of the food served is grown on the premises. The 10 double rooms and 12 suites (with kitchenette) are outfitted with antique furniture, evoking an old-world elegance. Half-board is available.

our pick **Restaurante Miquel** (☎ 971 123000; Torre de Cala Pi 13; mains €13-20; 🕑 Mar-Oct), a Mallorcan-style farmhouse with a huge patio, is warmly recommended, and has a fabulous fixed-price lunch (€15) with specialities like paella, mussels in marinara sauce or grouper with lemon sauce.

Bus 520 links Cala Pi and Palma once in the morning and once in the evening (€4.75, 1½ hours).

CAPOCORB VELL

At the sprawling prehistoric village of **Capocorb Vell** (☎ 971 180155; Carretera Arenal-Cap Blanc Km23; admission €2; 🕑 10am-5pm Fri-Wed), one of the larger and

---

GETTING AWAY FROM IT ALL

Take the Ma6014 highway south from S'Arenal to explore the lesser-known reaches of the southern coast. Continue down this prim two-lane highway and turn right at the sign pointing to 'Cap Blanc'. You'll soon come across a lighthouse and desolate-seeming military compound. Park beside the fence.

You can't reach the lighthouse, but a trail setting off from the fence leads you on a five-minute walk through scrubby bushes and over the pitted rocks to a sheer cliff. The views of the Mediterranean are nothing short of majestic. Breezy and sunny, this is a fabulous picnic spot, but be careful with kids or dogs; there is no fence and the drop is abrupt. Be sure to bring the camera; the ruddy-coloured cliffs running up the coast are begging to be photographed and there are often fishing birds nearby.

---

better-preserved ancient sites on the island, you can wander along maze-like pathways and beside rough stone structures that date to 1000 BC. The site, which includes 28 dwellings and five *talayots* (tower-like structures made with stone and, in the case of Capocorb Vell, no mortar) was probably used through Roman times.

The site sits at a bend in the highway and has ample parking. There are toilets and a modest bar where you can get drinks and snacks. You'll need a car or bike to get here; the site is 4km north of Cala Pi, 5km north of Cap Blanc, and 12km south of Llucmajor on the Ma6014 highway.

SA RÀPITA & AROUND

The rural Ma6014 highway parallels the coast for several kilometres, rolling past the gnarled olive trees of old Mallorcan estates and the crumbling rock walls that define their borders. This is a popular route for cyclists, so if you're driving take special care with hills and sharp curves.

Several even smaller highways veer off towards the coast. The Camí de Cala Pi sets off towards the urbanisation of **Vallgornera** (3km east of Cala Pi and accessible by road from the resort), where a half-dozen **caves** burrow their way through the rock underfoot. Some are truly impressive, with underground rivers and lakes or spectacular stalactites and stalagmites. The most famous cave here, **Cova des Pas de Vallgornera**, is also the Balearics' longest, at 6435m. Most caves can be visited but you should go with a guide or local expert, such as **Jose Antonio Encinas** (☎ 609 372888; www.inforber.com/mallorcaverde in Spanish), an avid hiker and spelunker who acts as a walking and caving guide in his spare time. A coastal trail linking Vallgornera and S'Enstanyol de

Migjorn (about 5km) leads past some of the caves.

Further east, turn left on the Ma6015 to reach sleepy Sa Ràpita, a seaside village whose rocky shoreline, harangued by waves, provides a scenic diversion from the rest of the shabby town. One glowing exception to this less-than-inspiring destination is the fabulous Restaurant Ca'n Pep (opposite).

Past Sa Ràpita, the Ma6030 highway steers inland and shoots up towards Campos. From the highway, you could turn right onto the potholed country roads that bounce their way east towards the ramshackle hamlet of **Ses Covetes**. A €5 parking fee (which includes a free post-beach shower) allows you to wander among a handful of informal bars and restaurants and down to the long and silky **Platja de Ses Covetes**. This unspoilt (although not uncrowded) beach forms part of the **Reserva Marina del Migjorn de Mallorca** (a protected marine reserve), and no buildings mar its backdrop of dunes and pines. If you walk east along the shorefront, you'll soon come upon Platja des Trenc (p187), which is similarly pristine.

Sleeping & Eating

This area is a popular lunch or picnic destination, yet few people make it their home base. There are no large hotels to speak of, but a growing number of farmhouses-turned-guesthouses make it possible to stay nearby.

Son Perdiu (☎ 971 100995; www.sonperdiu.com; Pm6014, Km32; house €295-545; 🗙 🗩) Families or groups looking for a bit of rest and relaxation will find it in spades at Son Perdiu, a lovely stone farmhouse that sleeps 14 and dates to 1805.

Can Canals (☎ 971 640757; www.cancanals.es; Carretera Campos-Sa Ràpita, Km7; s/d €65/110; 🕑 closed Jan; 🅿 🗩) A rustic restaurant (mains €16 to €25) and guesthouse near Ses Covetes where you can sample Mallorcan specialities like fried octopus, roasted lamb or the traditional vegetable stew, *tumbet*. The 12 well-appointed rooms are located inside the lovely farmhouse and are simply oozing with Mallorcan charm.

ourpick **Restaurant Ca'n Pep** (☎ 971 640102; Avinguda Miramar 30; mains €8-24; ☽ Tue-Sun Dec-Oct). One of many seafood eateries in Sa Ràpita, this local institution is rightfully famous for its seafood and rice dishes. The décor is predictably maritime and the menu has a helpful visual listing of all fish served, although some, like the local *cap roig* (red head) are so ugly that you may rather not know what you're eating!

Getting There & Away

Bus 515 runs to and from Palma (€4.55, one hour, up to five times daily).

COLÒNIA DE SANT JORDI & AROUND

More than any other resort area in Mallorca, the southeastern tip of the island celebrates its natural beauty. West of the family resort Colònia de Sant Jordi stretches the 7km of the unspoilt Platja des Trenc, while to the southeast a vast nature reserve protects a long swathe of rocky coastline softened by pristine beaches. Offshore sits the Balearics' only national park, the Parc Nacional Marítim-Terrestre de l'Arxipèlag de Cabrera (usually simplified to 'Illa de Cabrera'), while inland a smattering of preserved *talayotic* sites interrupt a serene, pastoral landscape.

COLÒNIA DE SANT JORDI
pop 2380

The biggest beach resort of the southern coast, Colònia de Sant Jordi has long been the summering spot of choice for Palma residents. A prim town whose well-laid-out streets form a chequerboard across the hilly landscape, the Colònia is a family-friendly place surrounded by some of the best and least-developed beaches on Mallorca.

The town itself is none too thrilling, but then again no-one is here to admire the architecture when there's such gorgeous scenery nearby. A supremely romantic boardwalk follows the rocky coast all the way around the Colònia. It's ideal for a hand-in-hand stroll or a leisurely bike ride.

The **tourist office** (☎ 971 656073; www.mallorcainfo .com; Carrer del Doctor Barraquer 5; ☽ 8am-2pm Mon-Fri), located inside the town civic centre on the eastern side of town, has stacks of information, including brochures that outline popular walking and cycling trails.

Activities

Colònia de Sant Jordi's main attractions are its wonderful beaches, both in town and beyond its borders. Best known is the Platja des Trenc (p187), a 20-minute walk from the northwestern end of town.

This is excellent cycling territory; myriad trails cut through the placid countryside near

---

JOAN CALDÉS, HOW TO RUN A CASA RURAL

In 1997, then 50-year-old Joan Caldés and his family turned the estate house on their family farm into a *casa rural*. In doing this they joined hundreds of others across the island who have tuned in to the growing number of travellers who, instead of holidaying in a busy resort, want a taste of the quiet countryside.

Why is rural tourism and agrotourism so popular now? Because on the coasts we've let people build too much and now all the hotels there seem the same. People want something different. They want to be in the countryside, relax, go at their own pace, get away from the crowds.

What's special about your casa rural? This house has been in the family forever, I don't even know when we got it. It's at least 200 years old and we haven't changed it much at all, we only added the modern touches necessary to make it a comfortable, inviting house.

Why did you decide to invest in rural tourism? Up until 10 years ago, a caretaker lived in this house and we lived off the farmland surrounding it. We still grow grain and vegetables, and we have sheep and goats, but these days it's very hard to live off the land. So we decided to open the house to travellers. People love being here in the country, but I've never had anyone ask to help with the farm work!

town. Rent bikes at **Team Double J** (☎ 971 655765; www.teamdoublej.com; Avinguda de la Primavera 9; per day from €10; ✆ 9.30am-1pm & 3-6pm Feb-Oct), where the team can also give you information on area routes.

Right in the middle of town, the concrete gives way to the fenced-in fields of the **Escola Hípica Reitschule** (☎ 971 655055; Avinguda de la Primavera 26; rides per hr €18; ✆ 4.30-7.30pm Mon-Sat), a ranch where anyone aged four and up can take one-hour horse-riding lessons.

Get on the water with a little help from **Boat Service** (☎ 659 980659; www.boatservice.es; Platja d'es Port; boat hire per hr from €10; ✆ 10am-7pm May-Oct), a friendly company near the tourist office that rents sail boats, pedal boats, and small motor boats. It also offers intensive sailing courses (five hours for adults, 10 hours for kids) for €120.

Sleeping

Although there are a few big hotels, most of what you'll find here is smaller in scale and geared towards families, cyclists or independent travellers.

Pensión es Turó (☎ 971 655057; hostalesturo@telefonica .net; Plaça es Dolç s/n; per person €21-33; ✆ May-Oct) It's definitely worth paying a bit extra for a room with a view at this homy *hostal* right on the water. The 15 rooms, which sit above the Restaurant Es Zuro (right), are pleasantly bright and breezy, with crisp white bed linens and tiled floors. But the real draw is the incredible location. Half-board available.

Hostal Restaurante Playa (☎ 971 655256; www .restauranteplaya.com; Carrer Major 25; s €29-36, d €48-60) Traditional Mallorcan fabrics, rustic wooden furniture and a cheerful Mediterranean air make this unfussy hotel by the water an excellent option. Downstairs a seaside restaurant serves island specialities.

Hostal Colonial (☎ 971 655278; Carrer de l'Enginier Gabriel Roca 9; per person €32, 2-/4-person apt €70/82; ✆ Mar-Nov) A fresh yellow-and-blue-décor marks the eight orderly rooms in this friendly, family-run hotel in the centre of town. It also has a famed gelateria (right), and bikes are available for guests.

S'Hort d'es Turó (☎ 971 649575; www.hortdesturo .com; Carretera Ses Salines-Colònia de Sant Jordi Km2.5; per person €52-71; ✆ Apr-Oct; ✖ ✆) Just beyond Colònia de Sant Jordi is a handful of excellent rural hotels and guesthouses, including this restored manor house, now home to five family-friendly apartments.

Aparthotel Isla de Cabrera (☎ 971 655000; www .hotelislacabrera.com; Avinguda del Marquès de Palmer s/n; 2-person apt incl breakfast & dinner €86-170; ✆ May-Oct; ✖ ✆ 🖳) The 78 one-bedroom apartments of this three-storey hotel a few blocks off the beach are sunny and spick-and-span, with a cheery Mediterranean décor, balconies, sofa beds and view of the pool area. The same company also runs the Hotel Isla de Cabrera (☎ 971 655000; Carrer del Roció s/n), where rooms have a similar style (doubles €115).

Eating & Drinking

Colònia de Sant Jordi's cafés and restaurants crowd mainly along the waterfront. By night all attention is on the Avingunda de Primavera, where nearly all the bars are located.

Restaurant Es Zuro (☎ 971 655057; Plaça es Dolç s/n; mains €8-14; ✆ May-Oct) Simple, no-frills fare like spaghetti, Spanish omelettes, and lamp chops are served on the huge seaside terrace. The food is homy and filling but it's the setting that's really amazing.

Marisol (☎ 971 655070; Carrer de l'Enginier Gabriel Roca; mains €7-19; ✆ Thu-Tue Feb-Oct) Enjoy Marisol's pastas and pizzas, fish and shellfish, rice dishes and stews at a table on the spacious covered terrace by the water.

Gelateria Colonial (☎ 971 655256; Carrer de l'Enginier Gabriel Roca 9) Ice cream–lovers from across Mallorca know this wonderful family-run gelateria in the heart of town. There's also a traditional Mallorcan restaurant (mains €15 to €23) serving fresh fish and vegetables grown in their garden. Upstairs is the Hostal Colonial (left).

Restaurante-Bar Pep Serra (☎ 971 655399; Carrer de l'Enginier Gabriel Roca 87; mains €15-25; ✆ May-Oct) Famous for its paella and seafood (it has its own fishing boat), this appealingly unsophisticated yet still pricey waterfront eatery has a few sidewalk tables and a laid-back air.

Getting There & Away

Bus 502 links the town to Palma (€5.45, up to eight times a day, 1¼ hours).

PARC NACIONAL MARÍTIM-TERRESTRE DE L'ARXIPÈLAG DE CABRERA

Nineteen uninhabited islands and islets make up the only national park in the Balearic Islands, the **Parc Nacional Marítim-Terrestre de l'Arxipèlag de Cabrera** (☎ 971 725010; Illa de Cabrera; ✆ 10.30am-3.30pm), an archipelago whose dry, hilly islands are known for their bird life, rich marine environment and abundant lizard populations. The **Illa de Cabrera** is the largest island of the archipelago and the only one you can visit, sits just 16km off the coast of Colònia de Sant Jordi and is accessible by boat from the resort. Other islands are used for wildlife research.

Although private boats can come to Cabrera if they've requested navigation and anchoring permits in advance from the park administration, nearly all visitors arrive on the organised cruises led by **Excursions a Cabrera** (☎ 971 649034; www.excursionsacabrera.com; Carrer de l'Explanada del Port; adult/child €31/15; ☒ 9.30am-4.30pm May-Oct). Only 200 people per day (300 in August) are allowed to visit this highly protected natural area, so reserve your place at least a day ahead. The one-hour trip leaves daily at 9.30am and returns by about 4.30pm.

After sailing past a few small islands swarming with birds, you'll be dropped off on Cabrera, where there's a tiny information office, public restrooms, a canteen and a covered eating area. Although Excursions a Cabrera offers a lunch for €7, you're better off bringing a picnic.

During the day you're pretty much on your own. Many people simply enjoy the wonderfully calm beaches, **Sa Plageta** and **S'Espalmador**. Even the Spanish royal family comes to these sandy shores to escape the crowds on the main island! You could also take one of the guided walks offered by rangers. The island's fragile ecosystem means that at times the park seems overprotected; there are few trails open to the public, and to walk most of them you'll either need to tag along with a guide or request permission from the park office.

On the cruise back to Colònia de Sant Jordi, the boat stops in **Sa Cova Blava**, a gorgeous cave with crystalline waters where passengers can take a dip.

At the time of writing, a new park visitors centre was under construction.

Sights & Activities

The best-known walking route heads up to a restored 14th-century **castle**, a fortress once used to keep pirates off the island. It was later converted into a prison for French soldiers, more than 5000 of whom died after being abandoned in 1809 towards the end of the Peninsular War. The 30-minute walk (guided walks are sometimes available) to the castle

meanders along the northern side of the island before taking you to the 80m-high bluff where the castle looms. There are great views over the bay.

Guides also sometimes lead the 20-minute walk to **Es Celler**, a farmhouse owned by the Feliu family, who owned the entire island in the early 20th century. It's now a small museum with history and culture exhibits. Nearby stands a monument to the French prisoners who died on Cabrera.

Other possible routes lead to the **N'Ensiola lighthouse** (four hours; permission required), the southern sierra of **Serra de Ses Figueres** (2½ hours, permission required), or the highest point of the island, the 172m **Picamosques** (three hours, permission required).

The island is a wonderful place for **scuba diving** or **snorkelling**. While you need special permission to dive here, you can snorkel off the beach. Or, in July and August, sign up for the guided snorkelling excursions offered by park rangers.

Wildlife

The Balearic lizard is the best-known species on Cabrera. This small lizard runs the roost on the archipelago, where it has few enemies and has been allowed to prosper and multiply.

This is prime territory for bird-watching: marine birds, birds of prey and migrating birds all call Cabrera home at least part of the year. Common species include the fisher eagle, the endangered Balearic shearwater, Audouin's gull, Cory's shearwater, shag, osprey, Eleonora's falcon and peregrine falcon, as well as 130 or so migrating birds.

PLATJA DES TRENC

ourpick **Platja des Trenc**, the largest undeveloped beach on Mallorca, runs 3km northwest from the southern edge of Colònia Sant Jordi. With long stretches of blindingly white sand and an idyllic setting among pine trees and rolling dunes, des Trenc proves just how pretty the Mallorcan coast was before development got out of hand.

Ironically, it's thanks to the out-of-control building sprees elsewhere on the island that this strip of sand has remained so pristine. Locals outraged by the concrete jungles of places like S'Arenal and Cales de Mallorca fought long and hard to save des Trenc from a similar fate, digging their heels in and eventually freezing the 1980s plan to convert this

SOUTHERN MALLORCA

TIME 'MARCHES' ON: THE STORY OF JOAN MARCH

The March family owns nearly 3% of Mallorcan territory, not to mention a hefty portion of the island's grandest manor houses, its weightiest art collections and its biggest bank. The family patriarch, Joan March Ordinas, was the world's seventh-richest person when he died in 1962, leaving his family extensive land holdings and a string of rumours about the questionable sources of his money. Revered and reviled in Mallorca, Joan March was an astute businessman who founded the successful Banca March and invested heavily in Mallorca.

These days the family runs ambitious cultural foundations that dabble in everything from art and archaeology to theatre and music. March's descendants still own more than 100 sq km of land on the island and no matter what their critics say, they've proven to be excellent stewards of it, preserving the vast majority as forest and farmland. The largest *possessió*, or estate, is Sa Vall (opposite), an unspoilt natural paradise near Ses Salines.

For more on the family and its cultural foundations, check out www.march.es and www .fundbmarch.es.

---

area into a sprawling golf and beach resort, even after some building permits had already been issued. Des Trenc is now considered a 'natural area of special interest'. Officially a nudist beach, it draws a mixed clothed and unclothed crowd.

While there are no buildings in sight, the beach here is no secret, so don't expect to be sunbathing alone. Sun loungers and umbrellas are for rent, and there's a bar where you can get food.

To reach the parking lot (per vehicle €6), take the signed turn-off west off Ma6040. The narrow, paved road passes mounds of yellowed salt at the Salines de Llevant salt fields then winds its way alongside fields sprinkled with wildflowers to reach the low-lying marsh area near the beach. Expect to walk a few hundred metres to des Trenc itself.

SES SALINES

Used as a source of salt since the days of the Romans, Ses Salines (the Salt Fields) is an unassuming agricultural centre whose main attractions lie beyond the village itself. Replete with walking and cycling trails, this is above all a rural area where nature reigns supreme. The fact that it is so beautifully unspoilt is thanks in large part to the March family (above), who own the island's largest *possessió* (rural estate), Sa Vall, covering 35 sq km of the municipality.

Just outside Ses Salines is the sprawling **Botanicactus** (☎ 971 649494; www.botanicactus .com; Carretera Ses Salines-Santanyí km1; adult/child €7/4; ⌚ 9am-7.30pm May-Aug, 9am-6pm Sep-Apr), which claims to be the largest botanical garden in Europe. Come to wander among its 1000-

plus species of Mediterranean, exotic and wetland plants.

One kilometre out of Ses Salines, heading towards Colònia de Sant Jordi, turn left at the sign for **Poblat Talaiòtic dels Antigors** to sample the area's ancient history. Past the town cemetery and down an unpaved road, the site appears on your left. There's no visitors' centre and only rusted and virtually illegible plaques, so use your imagination to see how these low stone walls would have once constituted a prehistoric settlement.

Follow the Ma6110 highway south of Llombards to reach the **Cap de Ses Salines**, a beautiful bluff with a lighthouse. There's not much here at the cape, but stretching out along either side of it are wonderfully unspoilt beaches protected by the Reserva Marina del Migjorn. The eastern beaches are hewn out of the coastal cliffs that run up towards exquisitely beautiful coves like **Caló des Màrmols**, beaches like the **Platja d'Almunia** and caves like **Cova de Sa Plana**. A rugged coastal path links them all in an 8km trail. The western beaches are covered in the following pages.

WALK: CAP DE SES SALINES TO COLÒNIA SANT JORDI

Pristine coastline can be hard to come by in Mallorca, but this walk has it in abundance. A coastal trail between **Cap de Ses Salines** and **Colònia de Sant Jordi**, it's a flat but rocky trek across battered coastal rock outcroppings and forgotten sandy beaches perfect for swimming. Be sure to take your bathing suit and plenty of water; there are no fresh water sources and very little shade along the way.

Ideally, you would leave one car at the trail-head and another at the walk's end in Colònia de Sant Jordi, although you could also plan to walk back, or take a taxi (☎ 971 655278; the 20-minute ride should cost about €20).

Leave your car on the shoulder of the road at Cap de Ses Salines, which is signposted from the main highway. From here, head towards the sea and turn right (west). You will see the Mediterranean glistening in a thousand shades of blue to your left, the Illa de Cabrera in the distance and the extensive **Sa Vall** estate, owned by the March family, bordering the walk on your right. This private estate is an endless expanse of scrubby Mediterranean vegetation and is home to two important wetland areas; it's an ideal bird-watching location. You can usually arrange a visit through the **ajuntament** (town hall; ☎ 971 649454).

After 30 minutes of a fairly flat walk over the pitted, ruddy-coloured calcareous rocks that populate the coast here (the same ones as those used in Palma's Catedral, p68), you'll come upon the first 'virgin' beach of the walk, **Platja des Cargol**, which is protected by a natural rock pier. In summer this place can get quite crowded on land and at sea; it's a popular spot to drop anchor.

Plants you'll see along the trail include wild asparagus and leafy *azucena de mar* (sea purslane), whose fragrant white flowers appear in July and August. Along the beaches, dried *poseidonia* (poseidon grass) leaves wash up from the sea floor. Most bathers turn their noses up at these unattractive brown invaders, but *poseidonia* (an endangered sea grass) plays a vital role in marine biodiversity, producing more oxygen and biomass than any other plant. You might also spot cormorants, one of the most common fishing birds.

Continue along the coast to reach other coves and beaches, like **Cala en Tugores** (one hour further on) **Platja de Ses Roquetes**, **Platja**

WALK FACTS

Start Cap de Ses Salines
Finish Colònia de Sant Jordi
Distance 9km
Duration three hours

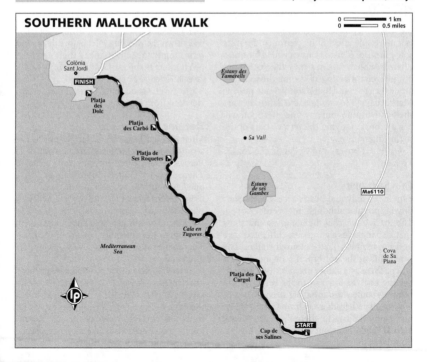

SOUTHERN MALLORCA WALK

des Carbó (after 2¼ hours) and finally **Platja des Dolc** (after three hours). The beaches, with their fine-as-flour sand and gentle waves the colour of turquoise, are truly breathtaking. It can get crowded here in summer but the idyllic setting amid juniper trees and squawking seagulls ensures that it always feels like an escape.

When you get to the town of Colònia de Sant Jordi, you've reached the end of the walk.

SANTANYÍ TO CALA D'OR

The resorts that creep up the island's eastern flank have grown into a more or less continuous stream of hotels, seafood restaurants and umbrella-packed beaches. The only exception to the sprawl in the busiest part of southern Mallorca is the Parc Natural de Mondragó, a bit of fresh air in the form of immaculate beaches rimmed with ruddy cliffs and junipers.

SANTANYÍ & AROUND

The busy inland town of Santanyí differs from most of the settlements nearby in that tourism is a mere side effect of its charm, and not its sole purpose. A historic town with a long and often troubled past, it's now the social and commercial meeting place for those living along the coast and in the countryside nearby. Market days (Wednesdays and Saturdays) are the busiest times, but any fine afternoon will see a crowd enjoying the terrace bars of the main square.

Up to six buses head to Palma (€5.55, 1½ hours).

Cala Santanyí

Santanyí's only real beach access, Cala Santanyí is popular although not overdeveloped. The spacious beach is the star in a scenic show that also includes a gorgeous, cliff-lined cove and impossibly cobalt-coloured waters. The beach sits at the bottom of a ravine of sorts where there is a sandy car park (walking or cycling back to town or to the resort centre requires some substantial leg strength).

A small path leads away from Cala Santanyí and along the coast, where the natural rock arch **El Pontàs** rises out of the surf. This is a popular spot to **snorkel**.

Cala Llombards

A petite cove defined by rough rock walls topped with pines, **Cala Llombards** is a truly beautiful place. A small informal beach-hut **bar** and rows of sun loungers shaded by palm-leaf umbrellas constitute the extent of human intervention. The main thing that's on offer is the soul-satisfying view – turquoise waters, a sandy beach and the reddish rocks of the cliffs that lead like a promenade towards the sea.

To reach Cala Llombards, follow the sign off the Ma6102 down a stone-walled road bordered by meadows of grazing sheep. Follow the rather circuitous route though a residential area to reach the beach.

CALA FIGUERA

If you could see Cala Figuera from the air, it would look like a snake with its jaws open wide, biting into the pine trees and low buildings of the resort. Although the town itself is rather dumpy and offers little in the way of entertainment, the romantic, restaurant-lined port is one of the prettiest on the east coast. A few yachts and pleasure cruisers line up beside the painted fishing boats, but Cala Figuera retains its air of old-world authenticity. Local fishers really still fish here, threading their way down the winding inlet before dawn and returning to the port to mend their nets.

You can rent bikes at **Bike Total** (☎ 971 645271; Carrer de Bernareggi 26; bicycles per day €9; ☺ 9-11am & 6-7pm). Several good trails (some of them steep) start out from here.

Sleeping

Most of Cala Figuera's lodging options are strung out along the pedestrian Carrer de la Verge del Carme that runs up from the port. There are no big hotels, but just about everyone has rooms or apartments for rent.

Hostal-Restaurant Ca'n Jordi (☎ 971 645035; www .osteria-hostal-canjordi.com; Carrer de la Verge del Carme 58; s/d €28/42) The simple, spacious rooms with balconies offer splendid views over the inlet. The owners also rent out a few apartments and villas.

Hotel Villa Sirena (☎ 971 645303; www.hotelvillasi rena.com; Carrer de la Verge del Carme 37 d €66, 2-/4-person apt €71/116; ☺ May-Oct; ☒) Perched on a bluff at the edge of the resort, this pleasant two-star hotel has enviable views of the sea. Rooms aren't fancy, but extras like a breezy seaside terrace make this a great choice.

Apartamentos Casa Marina (☎ 971 645178; www
.apartamentoscasamaria.com; Carrer de la Marina 26; 4-person
apt €75) Small yet inviting, and done up in a typically Mediterranean style, with simple wooden
furniture, bright linens and balconies, these
town-centre apartments are a great deal.

Eating

Most of the eateries are also dotted along the
town's main commercial strip.

Es Port (☎ 971 645140; Carrer de la Verge del Carme 88;
mains €8-17) The intoxicating aroma of pizzas
and calzones will draw you to this popular
family-friendly place.

Mistral Restaurante (☎ 971 645118; Carrer de la Verge
del Carme 42; mains €10-15) Choose between tasty,
typical tapas or more-elaborate dishes like
grilled sole fish with potatoes at this stylish
spot (on your right as you descend into the
port).

L'Arcada (☎ 971 645178; Carrer de la Verge del Carme 80;
mains €10-19) Although the pizzas here are popular, this cosy spot also does mean renditions of
typical Mallorcan dishes like *tumbet,* stuffed
eggplant and various seafood dishes.

Getting There & Away

Bus 502 makes the trip from Palma (€6, 1½
hours) via Colònia de Sant Jordi and Santanyí no more than three times a day, Monday
through Saturday.

PARC NATURAL DE MONDRAGÓ

A natural park encompassing beaches, dunes,
wetlands, coastal cliffs and inland agricultural
land, the 785-hectare **Parc Natural de Mondragó** is
a beautiful area for swimming or hiking. Most
people who head this way come to take a dip
in the lovely **Cala Mondragó**, one of the most
attractive coves on the east coast. Sheltered
by large rocky outcrops and fringed by pine
trees, it's formed by a string of three protected
sandy beaches (two with a bar each and one
with a restaurant) that are connected by rocky
footpaths.

Bird-watchers have a ball with the varied
species found in the area, which include falcons and turtledoves. There are myriad plant
species as well, including marine thistles,
houseleeks, violets and sea lilies. Taking one
of the **walking trails** that crisscross the park will
give you plenty of bird-watching opportunities. Get detailed route information at the
small **park office** (☎ 971 181022; ☼ 9am-4pm) by
the parking lot.

One of the best times to see the Cala
Mondragó is by night, when the sunbathers
abandon their posts and the beach is left
eerily quiet. Experience it yourself by staying at the **Hotel Playa Mondragó** (☎ 971 657752;
www.playamondrago.com; Cala Mondragó; per person from
€30; P ⯑ ⯑), a modest hotel barely 50m
back from one of the beaches. It's a tranquil
option, and the better rooms have balconies
and fine sea views. It also operates its own
restaurant downstairs, although there are a
couple of other informal beach restaurants
here as well.

Just 2km south of Portopetro, the beach
is accessible via a web of country roads and
bike paths. Bus 507 links Mondragó with Cala
d'Or (€1.25, 30 minutes, seven times daily
Monday through Friday) and a few other
seaside resorts.

PORTOPETRO

There's something in the air in Portopetro.
This intimate fishing port's slower pace and
laid-back style is immediately apparent as
you stroll its steep, shady streets and look out
over the protected natural inlet that originally
made this town such a hit with fishers.

Although the ballooning urban sprawl of
Cala d'Or (just to the north) means that the
two are nearly touching geographically, tame
Portopetro is worlds away from the excesses
of its neighbour. Centred on a boat-lined inlet
and surrounded by residential estates, Portopetro is really just a cluster of harbourside
bars and restaurants, with a couple of small
beaches nearby.

Sleeping & Eating

Restaurant Celler Ca'n Xina (☎ 971 658559; Passeig
del Port 52; mains €5-18; ☼ May-Oct) Serving delicious Mallorcan specialities like *trampó,*
paella, stuffed eggplant and the catch of the
day, this homy eatery boasts a shady terrace
by the port.

ourpick La Caracola (☎ 971 657013; Avinguda del Port
40; mains €6-12) In addition to the usual suspects
of paella and pasta, this enduringly popular
place has been pleasing diners with plates of
stuffed squid, homemade soups and *tumbet*
for 20 years. Not the flashiest place in town,
it's usually the most crowded, which is always
a good sign.

Varadero (☎ 971 657428; Passeig del Port 61; mains
€12-27; ☼ Mar-Nov; V) This chic new place has
caused a stir across the island with its frisky

international menu and postdinner chill-out lounge, when low music infuses the teak-furnished waterside terrace with a tropical feel. At lunch sample the creative salads and sandwiches (€4 to €14).

Blau PortoPetro (☎ 902 222070; www.blau-hotels .com; Avinguda des Far 12; per person from €55 ☯ Mar-Nov; Ⓟ 🍽 🖥 🎿) The only five-star hotel in the vicinity, the Blau made a real splash when it opened in 2005. A chic spa and hotel with all the amenities, this is no intimate boutique hotel, but its 300-plus rooms offer the ultimate in style and comfort.

Getting There & Away

Up to five buses a day head from Portopetro to Palma (€6, 1½ hours) and Cala d'Or (€1.25, 10 minutes).

CALA D'OR
pop 3690

Although the pretty cove beaches and calm, azure waters are still here, it's hard to imagine this flashy, overgrown resort as the quaint fishing village of its roots. These days, Cala d'Or (literally 'Cove of Gold') represents tour-

istic sprawl at its most untamed. There seems to be no rhyme or reason to its haphazardly laid-out streets, which are lined with high-rise hotels and strung out along a series of coves and small beaches. Each *cala* has its own main drag, where pubs, restaurants and souvenir shops flourish, making it very difficult to get a handle on the place.

The largest *calas* from west to east are **Cala Egos**, where there's a tiny, overcrowded beach; **Cala Llonga** (Port Petit), home to the marina; **Cala d'Or** (Cala Petita), with its tree-lined shores; **Cala Gran** (Big Cove), with the widest beach of the lot; **Cala Esmeralda**, considered the prettiest cove; and **Cala Ferrera**, a busy, long beach backed by hotels.

Cala d'Or's real claim to fame is its yacht marina, **Port Petit**, one of the most glamorous on Mallorca. It's thanks in large part to the fashionable yacht set that Cala d'Or is earning a reputation as a stylish, live-large kind of place. The upmarket restaurants around Cala Llonga are proof of the area's highbrow style.

Not everything here is ultra classy. Those who choose to base themselves in one of the

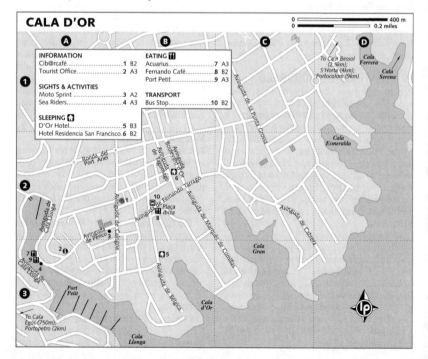

CALA D'OR

| 0 | 400 m |
| 0 | 0.2 miles |

INFORMATION
Cib@rcafé..............................1 B2
Tourist Office.........................2 A3

SIGHTS & ACTIVITIES
Moto Sprint 3 A2
Sea Riders...............................4 A3

SLEEPING 🏠
D'Or Hotel..............................5 B3
Hotel Residencia San Francisco.6 B2

EATING 🍴
Acuarius..................................7 A3
Fernando Café.........................8 B2
Port Petit................................9 A3

TRANSPORT
Bus Stop................................10 B2

To Ca'n Bessol (2.5km); S'Horta (4km); Portocolom (9km)

Cala Ferrera
Cala Serena
Cala Esmeralda
Cala Gran
Cala d'Or
Cala Llonga
Port Petit

To Cala Egos (750m); Portopetro (2km)

Ronda del Port Ariel
Avinguda de Cala Llonga
Avinguda de Fèrrico
Avinguda de Calonge
Avinguda de Cala Llonga
Avinguda de la Punta Grossa
Avinguda de Tàrrago
Avinguda de Marquès de Comillas
Avinguda de Cabrera
Avinguda Boulevard
Avinguda de Tagomago
Avinguda d'Or
Avinguda de Fernando Tàrrago
Plaça Ibiza
Avinguda de Bèlgica

countless cheap 'all-inclusive' hotels that fill Cala d'Or should be willing to share their holiday with thousands of other sun seekers (most from the UK) and should think about renting a car to escape the hordes.

Information

Get information at the **tourist office** (☎ 971 826084; Avinguda de Cala Llonga, s/n; ☷ 9am-2pm Mon-Fri, plus 4-6pm Tue & Thu, 10am-1pm Sat). Check email (and get coffee) at **Cib@rcafé** (☎ 971 060202; Avinguda de Calogne 20; per hr €4; ☷ 10am-8pm Mon-Sat Mar, Apr & Oct-Dec, 10am-10pm Mon-Sat May-Sep).

Activities

There is no shortage of companies offering boat trips up and down the coast. **Sea Riders** (☎ 615 998732; Cala Llonga; 35-min tours adult/child €21/16; ☷ 11.30am-3.30pm Apr-Jun & Sep-Oct, 11.30am-4.30pm Jul & Aug), in Cala Llonga, offers a kid-friendly boat ride as well as a faster 'adrenaline' ride.

Rent a bike and cycling equipment at **Moto Sprint** (☎ 971 650907; Carrer d'en Perico Pomar 5; bicycles per day €6-12, baby seats per day €1; ☷ 8am-1pm & 4.30-8pm). Or sign up for one of several activities (a kayak excursion, hike, cycling trip or quad outing) with **Xplore Mallorca** (☎ 971 659007; www.xploremal lorca.com; day trips €15-50; ☷ May-Oct).

Sleeping

Most hotels here cater almost exclusively to package tourists and may be impossible to book on the spot. There are, however, a few exceptions.

Hotel Residencia San Francisco (☎ 971 657072; antonia@viajestraveldor.com; Avinguda de Tagomago 18; s €21-43, d €24-48; ☷ May-Oct) An unassuming yet perfectly comfortable guesthouse on one of the main inland streets, San Francisco boasts prim rooms with balconies and modern bathrooms. Rooms overlooking the back patio are breezy and quiet.

D'Or Hotel (☎ 971 657249; www.hotelcalador.com; Avinguda de Bélgica 33; s/d €105/180; ☷ Apr-Oct; ☒ ☒) Built in 1932 and later used as a military barracks, the D'Or has returned to life as a 95-room hotel overlooking the rocky Cala d'Or. The tidy rooms have balconies and garden

or sea views, and there's a fine restaurant downstairs.

Ca'n Bessol (☎ 639 694910; www.canbessol.com; Carrer de la Sisena Volta 287; r €118-168; ☒ ☒) Just off the highway linking S'Horta with Cala Ferrera, on the outskirts of Cala d'Or, lies this sprawling family-run rural hotel, a fantastic alternative to the towers found closer to the resort. Four romantic rooms with antique furnishings overlook a lush garden and pool area.

Eating & Drinking

There are loads and loads of smoky bars and predictably bad pizzerias in Cala d'Or, but if you try a bit harder you can uncover the town's hidden jewels. The Port Petit is a great place to go for high-quality seafood and atmospheric dining.

Acuarius (☎ 971 659876; Port Petit 308; mains €4-27; ☷ Feb-Nov) A wide variety of salads, fresh fish dishes and a mean *frit Mallorquí* (Mallorcan-style fried lamb) are served on this spacious terrace overlooking the yacht port.

Fernando Café (☎ 971 657011; Plaça Ibiza 31; mains €6-15; ☷ May-Oct) Amid the cookie-cutter bars and restaurants, this sophisticated place is a real find. The food – pizza, pastas and fish dishes – isn't wildly different from standard resort fare, but the romantic atmosphere created by white tablecloths, candles and a garden setting make it special. After dinner enjoy the excellent coffees, teas and cocktails.

ourpick Port Petit (☎ 971 643039; Port Petit; lunch menú €19, mains €23-28, dinner menú €39-55) One of Mallorca's top tables, the high-end Port Petit offers innovative spins on classic Mallorcan seafood and produce, served on its sleek, covered upstairs terrace looking down over the yacht port.

Getting There & Away

Bus 501 heads to Portopetro (€1.25, 10 minutes, five times a day), then on to Palma (€6.80, 1 hour 20 minutes, up to six times a day). Bus 441 runs along the eastern coast, stopping at all the major resorts, before reaching Capdepera (€7.75, 85 minutes, up to 10 times a day).

Directory

CONTENTS

ACCOMMODATION

Outside the peak season of late June to early September, you can usually find a place in Palma and most key locations without booking. In the high season, booking becomes much more important. Many hotels take reservations by email and, whether by phone or email, many will ask for a credit card number.

Out of season (especially November to Easter) many places on the coast (except Palma) shut. Increasingly Palma is becoming a weekend short-break destination, which means that even in low season it can be an idea to at least call ahead.

Prices throughout this guidebook are generally high-season maximums, although we also often indicate where significant price falls occur in shoulder or low season. Prices

> **BOOK ACCOMMODATION ONLINE**
>
> For more accommodation reviews and recommendations by Lonely Planet authors, check out the online booking service at www.lonelyplanet.com. You'll find the true, insider lowdown on the best places to stay. Reviews are thorough and independent. Best of all, you can book online.

should always be taken as a guide only. We divide accommodation categories into budget (less than €60 for a double), midrange (€60 to €170) and top end (from €170 to the stars).

For some tips on villa searches, see p17.

Camping & Hostels

There are no official camping grounds on the island (the last of them closed in 2006), although it is possible to pitch a tent in a couple of spots (at the Monestir de Lluc, p132, and at the Hipocampo activities centre in Porto Cristo, p176). Free camping is feasible (technically you must be at least 50m from the seaside). Since most land in Mallorca is privately owned this often depends on getting permission. The Porto Cristo Hipocampo also offers youth hostel–style dorm accommodation. There are two other youth hostels: one in Platja de Palma, near the capital, and the other in Cap des Pinar (p148) in the north.

Hotels & Hostales

Officially, places to stay are classified into *hoteles* (hotels, one to five stars) and *hostales* (one to two and, very rarely, three stars).

A *hostal* (sometimes called a *pensión*) is basically a small private hotel, often a family business. The better ones can be bright and spotless with rooms boasting full en suite bathroom.

Hoteles cover the full range of quality from straightforward roadside places and bland but clean ones, through to charming boutique jobbies and super-luxury hotels.

Many places to stay of all types have a range of rooms at different prices. At the budget end, prices will vary according to whether the room has only a *lavabo* (washbasin), *ducha* (shower) or *baño completo* (full bathroom, that is, bath/shower, basin and loo). At the top end you may pay more for a room on the *exterior* (outside) of the building or with a *balcón* (balcony) and will often have the option of a suite. Seaside views frequently attract higher rates.

Checkout time is generally between 11am and noon.

The island's main hoteliers' association, the **Federación Hotelera de Mallorca** (www.mallorca hotelguide.com) runs a hotel-booking engine for the island. Check also the **Asociación Hotelera de Palma** (☎ 971 283625; www.visit-palma.com) for the capital. For hotels with character, narrow your search by looking at **Reis de Mallorca** (www.reisdemallorca.com).

Refugis

Simple hikers' huts *(refugis)*, mostly but not exclusively scattered about the Serra de Tramuntana, are a cheap alternative to hotels when hiking. Some are strategically placed on popular hiking routes. Many are run by the **Consell de Mallorca's environment department** (☎ 971 173700; www.conselldemallorca.net/mediambient /pedra), while others are run by the **Institut Balear de la Naturalesa** (Ibanat; ☎ 971 517070; ⏰ book 10am-2pm Mon-Fri). Dorm beds generally cost around €10 in each; some also have a couple of double rooms and meal service. Call ahead, as more often than not you'll find them closed if you just turn up.

Rural Properties

Numerous rural properties, mountain houses and traditional villas around the island operate as upmarket B&Bs. The **Associació Agroturisme Balear** (☎ 971 721508; www.agroturismo-balear.com) has more than 100 places on the books.

Many of the properties are historic and often stylish country estates offering outstanding facilities, including swimming pools, tennis courts, and organised activities and excursions. Double rooms (often sleeping three) cost about €60 to €200 per day. The local tourism authorities like to subdivide them into three categories: *agroturisme* (accommodation on working farms, where sometimes the income from the lodgings allows the farms to keep working), *turisme de interior* (mansions converted into boutique hotels in country towns) and *hotel rural* (usually a country estate converted into a luxury hotel).

Mallorca Farmhouses (☎ 0845 800 8080; www.mfh .co.uk) is a well-presented UK-based site with an extensive range of properties.

Other websites worth trawling:

Agroturismo Balear (☎ 971 717122; www.baleares .com/fincas)

Finca Mallorca (www.fincamallorca.de in German)

Finca Mallorca Hotel (www.finca-mallorca -hotel.de in German)

Fincas 4 You (www.fincas4you.com)

Guías Casas Rurales (www.guiascasasrurales.com in Spanish)

Las Islas Reisen (☎ 05069-34870 in Germany; www .las-islas-reisen.de)

Rustic Rent (☎ 971 768040; www.rusticrent.com)

Secret Places (www.secretplaces.com)

Top Rural (www.toprural.com)

Traum Ferienwohnungen (www.traum-ferienwoh nungen.de).

BUSINESS HOURS

Generally Mallorquins work Monday to Friday from about 9am to 1.30pm or 2pm and then again from 4.30pm or 5pm for another three hours. Shops and travel agencies are usually open similar hours on Saturday as well, although many skip the evening session.

Big supermarkets and department stores, such as the El Corte Inglés chain (two stores in Palma), open from about 9.30am to 9.30pm Monday to Saturday.

Many government offices don't bother opening in the afternoon, any day of the year. In summer, offices tend to go on to *horario intensivo*, from 7am to 2pm.

Museums all have their own opening hours: major ones tend to open for something like

---

GET THEE TO A MONASTERY!

For a more meditative retreat from the daily grind, you could opt for one of a handful of monasteries (technically hermitages, as their inmates were hermits and not monks) that offer rooms on the island. The most obvious choice is Monestir de Lluc (p132). No longer functioning as a hermitage but attractive for its spectacular location is the Santuari de la Mare de Déu des Puig (p135) outside Pollença. Others include the Santuari del Sant Salvador (p164), outside Felanitx, the Santuari de Monti-Sion (p164) in Porreres and the Santuari de Nostra Senyora de Cura (p161) outside Algaida.

PRACTICALITIES

■ Use the metric system for weights and measures.

■ Plugs have two round pins, so bring an international adaptor; the electric current is 220V, 50Hz.

■ If your Spanish is up to it, try the following newspapers: *El País* (or the free, constantly up-dated, downloadable version, *24 Horas*, on www.elpais.es), the country's leading (centre left) daily; *ABC*, for a right-wing view of life; and *Marca*, an all-sports (especially football) paper. The main local newspaper is the Spanish-language *Diario de Mallorca*. It gets competition from *Ultima Hora*. For Catalan, read the *Diari de Balears*. Many major newspapers from around Europe are available at newsstands in Palma and most tourist centres.

■ Tune into Radio Nacional de España's (RNE) Radio 1, with general interest and current af-fairs programmes; Radio 5, with sport and entertainment; and Radio 3 (Radio d'Espop), with admirably varied pop and rock music. The most popular commercial pop and rock stations are 40 Principales, Cadena 100 and Onda Cero. Local stations in Catalan include Radio Balear Palma, IB3 Ràdio, Ona Mallorca and Onda Melodía (easy listening). German listeners can tune into Insel Radio (95.8FM). Around the Magaluf area you can hear The English Hour from 8pm on Radio Càlvia at 107.4FM.

■ Switch on the box to watch Spain's state-run Televisión Española (TVE1 and La 2) or the inde-pendent commercial stations (Antena 3, Tele 5, Cuatro, La Sexta and Canal Plus). Local sta-tions with programmes in Catalan (and its Mallorcan variant) are TV Mallorca and IB3. Cable and satellite TV are widespread.

normal Spanish business hours (with or without the afternoon break) but some have their weekly closing day on Monday.

For bank and post office opening hours, respectively, see p200 and p201.

As a general rule restaurants open for lunch from about 1pm to 4pm and for dinner from 8pm (most locals wouldn't go out to eat before 9pm to 10pm) to midnight. At lunch and dinner you can generally linger quite a while after the kitchen closes (generally about 3.30pm and 11pm respectively). Some, but by no means all, places close one or two days a week. Some also shut for a few weeks' annual holiday.

Bars have a wider range of hours. Those that serve as cafés and snack bars can open from about 8am until the early evening. More nightlife-oriented bars may open in the early evening and generally close around 2am (3am on Fridays and Saturdays), although in some noise-sensitive areas of central Palma you'll find closing time is closer to 1am. Clubs gen-erally open from midnight, when they're dead, to 5am or 6am.

CHILDREN

As a rule Spaniards are very friendly to chil-dren. Any child whose hair is less than jet black will be dubbed *rubio/rubia* (blond/e). Spanish children stay up late and at fiestas it's common to see even tiny ones toddling around the streets at 2am or 3am.

Practicalities

Discounts are available for children (usually aged under 12) on public transport and for admission to sites. Those under four gener-ally go free.

You can hire car seats for infants and chil-dren from most car-rental firms, but book them in advance. You cannot rely on restau-rants having high chairs and few have nappy-changing facilities. In better hotels you can generally arrange for childcare. You could also check out the website **Canguroencasa** (www .canguroencasa.com in Spanish), where you can search for English-speaking babysitters *(canguros)*. You will also find ads at www.loquo.com (search under Baleares).

Sights & Activities

As well as the obvious attractions of beaches (and seaside activities), swimming pools and playgrounds, there are other good options.

Boat trips will nearly always work for kids. Consider the glass-bottomed boat tours of the kind that operate from **Sant'Elm** (p110).

Alternatively, try the ride to **Illa Sa Dragonera** (p110), or to Ciutadella in Menorca from **Cala Ratjada** (p210). Boat excursions are also organised to **Cabrera** island from Colònia de Sant Jordi (p186).

The natural wonders of Mallorca's caves will be a hit with most kids. First up come the **Coves del Drac** in Porto Cristo (p177), followed closely by the nearby **Coves dels Hams** (p177) and the **Coves d'Artà** (p173). Several other such caves dot the island.

Several watery fun parks are dotted about the island. **Aqualand** (p102; www.aqualand.es) has two branches. Near the Portals Nous highway exit, not far from Magaluf, there is also **Marineland** (p104; www.marineland.es), with performing dolphins and other sea critters. **Hidropark** (p145; www.hidropark.com), near Port d'Alcúdia, is another such park with rides, wave pool, foam races and more. Theme parks, like Magaluf's **Western Park** (www.western park.com) might also keep the wee ones content. Palma's **Aquarium** (p101) is also a big hit.

For more information, see Lonely Planet's *Travel with Children* or the websites www.travelwithyourkids.com and www.familytravelnetwork.com.

CLIMATE CHARTS

Mallorca enjoys a moderate Mediterranean climate, which does not imply moderation throughout the year. July and August can be torrid, with average daily highs hovering around the 30°C mark and frequently well above. Cyclers and hikers will certainly want to give the island a miss in high summer! Far more pleasant are spring and autumn (May and June and September to mid-October). If you are not wedded to a beach holiday, a low-season excursion to Mallorca is well worth considering. Palma makes a great short-break city destination at any time of year and although rainfall is more likely in winter, more often than not you'll encounter pleasant, sunny conditions.

CONSULATES IN MALLORCA

The bulk of foreign embassies in Spain are in the capital, Madrid. Some maintain consulates or honorary consulates in Palma de Mallorca. Among them are:

Austria (Map pp70-1; ☎ 971 728099; Carrer del Sindicat 69)

Germany (☎ 971 707737; Edificio Reina Constanza, Carrer de Porto Pi 8)

Ireland (Map pp70-1; ☎ 971 719244; Carrer de Sant Miquel 68a)

Italy (Map pp70-1; ☎ 971 724214; Passatge Joan XXIII 6)

Netherlands (Map pp70-1; ☎ 971 716493; Carrer de Sant Miguel 36)

Sweden (☎ 971 725492; Carrer de St Jaume 7)

Switzerland (☎ 971 768836; Camí de C'an Guillot 23, Establiments)

UK (Map pp70-1; ☎ 971 712445, emergency ☎ 91 308 52 01; Carrer del Convent dels Caputxins 4, Edifici B)

USA (☎ 971 403707; Edificio Reina Constanza, Carrer de Porto Pi 8).

Australian, Canadian and New Zealand citizens can, as Commonwealth citizens, approach the UK consulate on some matters. They may then be referred on to their respective embassies. French citizens should contact their consulate in Barcelona.

CUSTOMS

Duty-free allowances for travellers entering Spain from outside the EU include 2L of wine (or 1L of wine and 1L of spirits), and 200 cigarettes or 50 cigars or 250g of tobacco.

There are no duty-free allowances for travel between EU countries and there are no restrictions on the import of duty-paid items into Spain from other EU countries for personal use. You *can* buy VAT-free articles at airport shops when travelling between EU countries.

DANGERS & ANNOYANCES

Mallorca is safe. The main thing to be wary of is petty theft. Most visitors to Mallorca never feel remotely threatened, but that is no reason not to exercise the usual caution.

Scams

Theft is mostly a risk in the busier resort areas and Palma. You are at your most vulnerable when dragging around luggage to or from

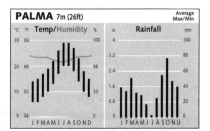

your hotel. Watch for pickpockets and bag snatchers.

Talented petty thieves generally work in groups and capitalise on distraction. More-imaginative strikes include having someone dropping a milk mixture onto the victim from a balcony. Immediately a concerned citizen comes up to help you brush off what you assume to be pigeon poo and, thus suitably occupied, you don't notice the contents of your pockets slipping away.

Watch out for an old classic: ladies offering flowers (the so-called *claveleras*, because they usually offer *claveles*, ie carnations) for good luck. We don't know how they do it, but if you get too involved in a friendly chat with these people, your pockets always wind up empty. They are regularly rounded up by the police but are soon back in the streets.

Carry valuables under your clothes if possible – not in a back pocket, daypack or anything easily snatched away. Don't leave baggage unattended. Ignore demands to see your passport unless they come from a uniformed police officer. Keep a firm grip on daypacks and bags at all times.

Always remove the radio and cassette player from your car and never leave any belongings visible in the car. Hire cars and foreign-plated cars are especially vulnerable. Anything left on the beach can disappear in a flash when your back is turned.

Report thefts to the national police. It is unlikely that you will recover your goods but you need to make this formal *denuncia* for insurance purposes. To avoid endless queues at the police station *(comisaría)*, you can make the report by phone (☎ 902 102112) in various languages or on the web at www .policia.es (click on 'Denuncias'). The following day go to the police station of your choice to pick up and sign the report, without queuing.

If your passport has gone, contact your embassy or consulate (see p197) for help in issuing a replacement.

Natural Dangers

The usual precautions should be taken when indulging in water sports, such as diving. In summer, waves of stingers (jellyfish) can appear on the island's beaches and there's not much you can do (despite talk of volunteers being employed to net the buggers). See p213.

DISCOUNT CARDS

At museums, never hesitate to ask if there are discounts for students, young people, children, families or the elderly.

Student & Youth Cards

An ISIC (International Student Identity Card; www.isic.org) may come in handy (there is also a teachers' version, ITIC), although about all it is officially good for is a discount on Avis car rental and Palma's city sightseeing bus.

You'll have more luck with a Euro<26 (www.euro26.org) card (known as Carnet Joven in Spain), which is useful for those under 26. For instance, Euro<26 card holders enjoy 10% or 20% off many ferries and discounts at some sights and attractions, cinemas, shops and more. You can find comprehensive lists on the respective websites.

FOOD

Mallorca offers plenty of temptations for the palate. A growing emphasis on attracting mid- to high-end visitors has also pushed the culinary barometer up since the early 1990s, and the island is dotted with charming, romantic and gourmand-friendly restaurants. For a whiff of what's cooking in Mallorca's kitchens, see p45.

In the course of this guidebook we provide a broad selection of eateries. We divide listings into budget (up to €20 for a full meal, including dessert and house wine), midrange (€20 to €50) and top end (€50 and up).

GAY & LESBIAN TRAVELLERS

Homosexuality is legal in Spain and the age of consent (with certain caveats) is 13 years old, as for heterosexuals. In 2005 the Socialist president of Spain, José Luis Rodríguez Zapatero, gave the conservative Catholic foundations of the country a shake with the legalisation of same-sex marriages. In Mallorca the bulk of the gay scene takes place in and around Palma (see p95).

Ben Amics (Map pp70-1; ☎ 971 715670; www.benam ics.com; Carrer del Conquistador 2; ☒ 9am-3pm) is the island's umbrella association for gays, lesbians and transsexuals. The local general information website **Entiendes Mallorca** (www .yuki.es) contains info on bars, saunas, clubs and more. You may be able to pick up the printed version *(Entiendes Mallorca)* in the tourist offices.

HOLIDAYS

The two main periods when Spaniards (and Mallorquins are no real exception) go on holiday are Semana Santa (the week leading up to Easter Sunday) and August. It just so happens that half of Europe descends on Mallorca about this time of year too! Accommodation can be hard to find and transport is put under strain.

There are 14 official holidays a year, to which most towns add at least one to mark their patron saint's day. Some places have several traditional feast days, not all of which are official holidays, but which are often a reason for partying. For a selection see pp20–22.

The main island-wide public holidays:

Cap d'Any (New Year's Day) 1 January
Epifania del Senyor (Epiphany) 6 January – in Palma a landing of the Three Wise Men (Reis Mags) is staged in the port, followed by a procession
Dia de les Illes Balears (Balearic Islands Day) 1 March
Dijous Santa (Good Thursday) March/April
Divendres Sant (Good Friday) March/April
Diumenge de Pasqua (Easter Sunday) March/April
Festa del Treball (Labour Day) 1 May
L'Assumpció (Feast of the Assumption) 15 August
Festa Nacional d'Espanya (Spanish National Day) 12 October
Tots Sants (All Saints) 1 November
Dia de la Constitució (Constitution Day) 6 December
L'Immaculada Concepció (Feast of the Immaculate Conception) 8 December
Nadal (Christmas) 25 December
Segona Festa de Nadal (Boxing Day) 26 December

INSURANCE

A travel-insurance policy to cover theft, loss and medical problems is a good idea. It may also cover you for cancellation or delays to your travel arrangements.

EU citizens are entitled to the full range of health-care services in public hospitals, but you will need to present your European Health Insurance Card (inquire at your national health service before leaving home). Private insurance is still a good idea, however.

Check that the policy covers ambulances or an emergency flight home. For details of car insurance, see p210.

Worldwide travel insurance is available at www.lonelyplanet.com/travel_services. You can buy, extend and claim online anytime – even if you're already on the road.

INTERNET ACCESS

Travelling with a portable computer is a great way to stay in touch with life back home. Make sure you have a universal AC adaptor and a two-pin plug adaptor for Europe. Most laptops are wi-fi enabled, meaning you can log onto hot spots. Some hotels offer this service and occasionally you'll find cafés, restaurants and even shops with hot spots. In many cases (such as at Palma's airport and most hotels) you must pay a fee.

There are some cybercafés in Palma and the main coastal resorts and towns. They typically charge about €1.50 to €3 per hour.

LEGAL MATTERS

If you're arrested you will be allotted the free services of a duty solicitor (abogado de oficio), who may speak only Spanish (and Mallorquin). You're also entitled to make a phone call. If you use this to contact your embassy or consulate, the staff will probably be able to do no more than refer you to a lawyer who speaks your language. If you end up in court, the authorities are obliged to provide a translator.

In theory you are supposed to have your national ID card or passport with you at all times. If asked for it by the police, you are supposed to be able to produce it on the spot. In practice it is rarely an issue and many people choose (understandably) to leave passports in hotel safes.

Drugs

Cannabis is legal in very small amounts for personal use. Public consumption of any drug is illegal.

Police

The Policía Local operates at a local level and deals with such issues as traffic infringements

---

LEGAL AGE

Travellers should note that they can be prosecuted under the law of their home country regarding age of consent, even when abroad.

- The right to vote: 18 years old
- Age of consent: 13 years old (heterosexual and homosexual but with restrictions involving minors with adults)
- Driving age: 18 years old

CLAMPING DOWN ON SMOKING, SORT OF

Spain is following the trend to banning smoking in public places…up to a point. National legislation bans smoking in public spaces larger than 100 sq metres. This means that most bars and restaurants can choose to adopt a no-smoking policy on their premises or not. The great majority in Mallorca, as elsewhere in Spain, have remained permissive in this regard. Bigger places, by law, should either be entirely nonsmoking or create properly separated areas for smokers (generally too expensive for most places to contemplate). Observation of the law seems uneven. Frequently in clubs that are clearly vastly bigger than 100 sq metres, punters can be seen puffing away quite undisturbed. Some hotels offer nonsmoking rooms. Restaurants, bars and hotels with a clear nonsmoking policy are indicated in this guide with the ⊠ symbol.

and minor crime. If your car is towed it's because these guys called the removal truck.

The Policía Nacional is the Spanish state police force, dealing with major crime and operating especially in the cities. The military-linked Guardia Civil (created in the 19th century to deal with banditry) is largely responsible for highway patrols, borders and security and often has a presence in more remote areas where there is no Policía Nacional station (*comisaría*). They also deal with major crime and terrorism and there is frequently an overlap (and occasional bickering) with the Policía Nacional.

MAPS
City Maps
The free maps handed out by tourist offices in Mallorca's towns are generally adequate. In Palma, however, you may want to purchase a more detailed commercial map. The standard tourist office hand-out is next to useless.

The more or less water-resistant *Palma de Mallorca* (by Splashguides) is a reasonable take on the city centre scaled at 1:5000. For the big picture (all the 'burbs), get Michelin's No 78 *Palma de Mallorca*, scaled at 1:10,000 but poor on the city centre. Surprisingly, if you get lucky and the tourist office at the airport gives you the free map produced by the department store El Corte Inglés, you will have a very good map for central Palma.

Island Maps
One of the better and clearer island maps is Freytag and Berndt's *Mallorca* (1:100,000, with a small map of central Palma). At the time of writing, however, it still had the old highway codes. Another one with no apparent brand name (but look for the compass logo at the bottom) is called *Mapa Mallorca* (in its Spanish edition) and is scaled at 1:130,000. It

does have the new highway codes and is of a more resistant paper.

Kompass produces a digital (CD) map of the island. Choose what you need (at a scale of up to 1:10,000) and print out! It is GPS compatible. Again, at the time of writing the road codes had not been updated.

Walking Maps
Walking maps need to be scaled at least at 1:25,000. Anything bigger is near useless.

Alpina Editorial produces three such maps to the Serra de Tramuntana range (*Mallorca Tramuntana Sud*, *Mallorca Tramuntana Central* and *Mallorca Tramuntana Nord*). These come with detailed walk descriptions in a solid booklet. The first two are in Catalan and Spanish with English and German summaries, while the third is in Catalan and German only.

The *Kompass Wanderbuch 942 Mallorca* (in German) by Wolfgang Heizmann, comes with detailed walking maps.

Walk! Mallorca (North & Mountains), by Charles Davis, is packed with walks, basic maps and GPS aid. You'll need to buy maps though.

Spain's Centro Nacional de Información Geográfica (CNIG, www.cnig.es) covers a good part of the island in 1:25,000 scale sheets.

Some map specialists in other countries, such as **Stanfords** (☎ 020-7836 1321; www.stanfords .co.uk; 12-14 Long Acre, London WC2E 9LP) in the UK, have a good range.

MONEY
As in 14 other EU nations (Austria, Belgium, Cyprus, Finland, France, Germany, Greece, Ireland, Italy, Luxembourg, Malta, the Netherlands, Portugal and Slovenia), the euro is Spain's currency. It is divided into 100 cents.

Coin denominations are one, two, five, 10, 20 and 50 cents, €1 and €2. The notes are €5, €10, €20, €50, €100, €200 and €500.

Exchange rates are given on the inside front cover of this book and a guide to costs can be found on p16.

Banks mostly open from about 8.30am to 2pm Monday to Friday. Some also open Thursday evening (about 4pm to 7pm) or Saturday morning (9am to 1pm).

Ask about commissions before changing money, especially in exchange bureaux (look for the sign *cambio*), which can charge outrageous amounts. The only advantage of these is they tend to open longer hours. You'll find some in central Palma and the main resorts.

ATMs
Many credit and debit cards can be used to withdraw money from *cajeros automáticos* (ATMs). Among the most widely usable cards are Visa, MasterCard, American Express, Cirrus, Maestro, Plus, Diners Club and JCB. Many banks do not offer an over-the-counter cash advance service on foreign cards. There is usually a charge (1.5% to 2%) on ATM cash withdrawals abroad.

Cash
There is little advantage in bringing foreign cash into Spain, which you can't replace if lost or stolen.

Credit & Debit Cards
You can use plastic to pay for most purchases. You'll often be asked to show your passport or some other identification when using cards in shops. Many institutions add 2.5% or more to all transactions (cash advance or purchases) on cards used abroad.

If your card is lost, stolen or swallowed by an ATM, you can telephone toll free to have an immediate stop put on its use. For MasterCard the number in Spain is ☎ 900 971231, for Visa it's ☎ 900 991124 and for Diners Club ☎ 901 101011.

AmEx is also widely accepted (although not as commonly as Visa or MasterCard). If you lose your AmEx card, call ☎ 900 994426.

Taxes & Refunds
In Spain, value-added tax (VAT) is known as IVA (*ee-ba; impuesto sobre el valor añadido*). On accommodation and restaurant prices,

it's 7% and is often included in quoted prices. On retail goods and car hire, IVA is 16%. To ask 'Is IVA included?', say '*¿Está incluido el IVA?*'.

Visitors are entitled to a refund of the 16% IVA on purchases costing more than €90.15 if they are taking them out of the EU within three months. Ask the shop for a cashback, tax-free (or similar) refund form showing the price and IVA paid for each item, and identifying the vendor and purchaser. Then present the refund form to the customs booth for IVA refunds at the airport, port or border from which you leave the EU.

For more information, see www.spain refund.com.

Tipping
The law requires menu prices to include a service charge; tipping is a matter of choice. Most people leave some small change if they're satisfied: 5% is normally fine and 10% generous. Porters will generally be happy with €1. Taxi drivers don't have to be tipped, but a little rounding up won't go amiss.

Travellers Cheques
Most people are perfectly happy to wander around Mallorca with plastic. The advantage of travellers cheques is that they can be replaced if lost or stolen and so it might not be a bad idea to carry some of your money in this form. Visa, AmEx and Travelex are widely accepted brands with (usually) efficient replacement policies. Take along your ID when you cash travellers cheques.

If you lose your AmEx cheques, call 24-hour freephone number ☎ 900 994426. For Visa cheques call ☎ 900 948973; for MasterCard cheques call ☎ 900 948971. It's vital to keep your initial receipt and a record of your cheque numbers and the ones you have used, separate from the cheques themselves.

POST
The Spanish postal system, **Correos** (☎ 902 197197; www.correos.es), is generally reliable, if a little slow at times. For opening hours, see entries throughout this guide. Many branch post offices open 8am to 2pm, Monday to Friday.

Postal Rates & Services
A postcard or letter weighing up to 20g costs €0.58 from Spain to other European countries,

and €0.78 to the rest of the world. The same would cost €2.82 and €3.02, respectively, for registered *(certificado)* mail. Sending such letters *urgente*, which means your mail may arrive two or three days sooner than usual, costs €2.95 and €2.85, respectively. Stamps for regular letters, including those being sent abroad, can also be bought at most tobacconists (look for the 'Tabacos' sign).

Sending & Receiving Mail

Delivery times for ordinary mail are up to a week to other Western European countries (although often as little as three days); to North America up to 10 days; and to Australia or New Zealand up to two weeks.

All Spanish addresses have five-digit postcodes – use them!

Lista de correos (poste restante) mail sent to you will be delivered to the town's main post office unless another is specified. Take your passport when you pick up mail. A typical *lista de correos* address looks like this:

Jenny JONES
Lista de Correos
07001 Palma de Mallorca
Spain

SHOPPING

Mallorca is known above all else for its leather products, especially shoes. Brands like Camper and Farrutx have become international beacons – their products are stylish, moderately priced and, especially in the case of Camper, easily found all over Spain. To really indulge your leather fantasies, head for the inland town of Inca, which is bursting with leather stores.

The other big item associated with Mallorca, and Manacor in particular, are cultivated pearls, especially of the Majorica brand. Majorica now makes them abroad but still operates a small factory in Manacor, as well as a shopping outlet there. Blown glass also has some history on the island. The best-known name is Gordiola, based near Algaida (and with a couple of stores in Palma).

Ceramic traditions in Mallorca were to a large degree imported from the mainland (especially from Catalonia and Valencia). Today you will find a smattering of workshops producing nice pieces around the island.

A classic Mallorcan item is the *siurell*, a white clay whistle in the form of a human figure or rural scene. Most are mass produced nowadays.

Foodies could look out for wines, or some of the local liqueurs, which include Palo (a mix of fortified wine, gentian, carob beans and caramelised sugar), *hierbas* (or *herbes*, a herbal liqueur) and *mesclat*. The latter is a potent mix of Palo and aniseed. Local cheeses and other food products, especially the giant *ensaïmades* (puff pastries) that all Spaniards seem to take home with them, are further options.

Urban sophisticates will find plenty of boutiques and department stores (especially the national chain, El Corte Inglés) in Palma.

Open-air markets take place in towns across the island and the tourist office can provide lists with the days they take place. They are best in the morning.

SOLO TRAVELLERS

About the only real practical disadvantage of travelling solo in Mallorca is the cost of accommodation. As a rule, single rooms (or doubles let as single rooms) cost around two-thirds of the price of a double.

TELEPHONE

The ubiquitous blue payphones are easy to use for international and domestic calls. They accept coins, *tarjetas telefónicas* (phonecards issued by the national phone company Telefónica) and, in some cases, credit cards. *Tarjetas telefónicas* come in €6 and €12 denominations and, like postage stamps, are sold at post offices and tobacconists.

Mobile Phones

Mallorquins, like other Spaniards, adore *teléfonos móviles* (mobile/cell phones) and shops on every high street sell phones with prepaid

---

TAKING YOUR MOBILE PHONE

If you plan to take your own mobile phone to Spain, check in advance with your mobile network provider that your phone is enabled for international roaming, which allows you to make and receive calls and messages abroad. Check on costs (which can be prohibitive) and whether or not you have to pay for voicemail (and how much). Remember to take an international adaptor for your plug and note the phone and serial numbers in case of loss. If your phone is unblocked, it will probably work out cheaper to buy a local SIM card and use that.

cards from around €80 for the most basic models.

Spain uses GSM 900/1800, which is compatible with the rest of Europe and Australia but not with the North American GSM 1900 or the totally different system used in Japan. If your phone is tri- or quadriband, you will probably be fine.

Phonecards
Cut-rate phonecards can be good value for international calls. They can be bought from *estancos* (tobacconists) and newsstands, especially in Palma and coastal resorts – compare rates if possible because some are better than others. *Locutorios* (call centres) that specialise in cut-rate overseas calls are another option.

Phone Codes
To call a Mallorcan number, dial the international access code (☎ 00 in most countries), followed by the code for Spain (☎ 34) and the full number (including the Mallorca area code, 971, which is an integral part of the number). For example, to call the number ☎ 971 455683 in Palma, you need to dial the international access code followed by ☎ 34 971 455683. Note, a handful of numbers in Palma start with 871 and not 971.

The access code for international calls from Spain is 00. To make an international call dial the access code, wait for a new dialling tone, then dial the country code, area code and number you want.

You can dial an operator in your own country for free to make reverse-charge calls – pick up the number before you leave home. You can usually get an English-speaking Spanish international operator on ☎ 1008 (for calls within Europe) or ☎ 1005 (rest of the world).

For international directory inquiries dial ☎ 11825. Be warned: a call to this number costs €2!

Within Spain, you must always dial the full area code with the number. All numbers have nine digits and most begin with 9. Dial ☎ 1009 to speak to a domestic operator, including for a domestic reverse-charge (collect) call *(llamada por cobro revertido)*. For national directory inquiries, dial ☎ 11818.

Mobile phone numbers start with 6. Numbers starting with 900 are national toll-free numbers, while those starting 901 to 905 come with varying conditions. A common one is

902, which is a national standard rate number. In a similar category are numbers starting with 803, 806 and 807.

TIME
Mallorca (like mainland Spain) has the same time as most of the rest of Western Europe: GMT/UTC plus one hour during winter and GMT/UTC plus two hours during the daylight-saving period, which runs from the last Sunday in March to the last Sunday in October.

The UK, Ireland, Portugal and the Canary Islands, a part of Spain out in the Atlantic Ocean, are one hour behind mainland Spain and Mallorca.

Although the 24-hour clock is used in most official situations, you'll find people generally use the 12-hour clock in everyday conversation.

TOURIST INFORMATION
Local Tourist Offices
Palma and many other centres have an *oficina de turismo* or *oficina de información turística* for local information. In Palma you will find two. Addresses and details are provided throughout the guide. The **Consell de Mallorca tourist office** (☎ 971 712216; www.infomallorca.net; Plaça de la Reina 2; ☺ 9am-8pm Mon-Fri, 9am-2pm Sat) in Palma covers the whole island.

Tourist Offices Abroad
Information on Mallorca is available from the following international branches of the Spanish national tourist board, Turespaña (www .spain.info or www.tourspain.es):

Austria (☎ 0151 29580; viena@tourspain.es; Walfischgasse 8, 1010-1 Vienna)
Canada (☎ 416-961 3131; www.tourspain.toronto.on .ca; 2 Bloor St W, Suite 3042, Toronto M4W 3E2)
France (☎ 01 45 03 82 50; www.espagne.infotourisme .com; 43 rue Decamps, 75784 Paris)
Germany (☎ 030-882 6543; berlin@tourspain.es; Kurfürstendamm 63, 10707 Berlin) Branches in Düsseldorf, Frankfurt am Main and Munich.
Netherlands (☎ 070-346 59 00; www.spaansverkeers bureau.nl; Laan van Meerdervoor 8a, 2517 The Hague)
Portugal (☎ 21-354 1992; lisboa@tourspain.es; Avenida Sidónio Pais 28 3° Dto, 1050-215 Lisbon)
UK (☎ 020-7486 8077; www.tourspain.co.uk; PO Box 4009, 2nd fl, 79 New Cavendish St, London W1A 6NB)
USA (☎ 212-265 8822; www.okspain.org; 666 Fifth Ave, 35th fl, New York, NY 10103) Branches in Chicago, Los Angeles and Miami

There are also offices in Belgium, Italy, Poland, Switzerland, the Scandinavian countries, Argentina, Brazil, Mexico, China, Japan and Singapore.

TOURS

Several companies offer interesting tours heading to Mallorca. **Headwater** (☎ 08700 662650 in UK; www.headwater.com) offers enticing one-week walking and cycling tours, staying in boutique hotels and indulging in good local food. **Naturetrek** (☎ 01962 733051 in UK; www.naturetrek.co.uk) has a one-week bird-watching holiday to Mallorca, as does **Heatherlea** (www.heatherlea.co.uk). Horse lovers might like to choose from the two horse-riding holidays offered by **Unicorn Trails** (☎ in UK 01762 600606; www.unicorntrails.com). **Balearic Discovery** (☎ in UK 08702 432272, in Mallorca 971 875395; www.balearicdiscovery.com) does tailor-made trips to Mallorca. Cobble together your own itinerary with their help. They also have a set activities trip where you can choose activities from sea kayaking to horse riding. **Mallorca Wandern** (www.mallorca-wandern.de) proposes group hiking tours in Mallorca, while **Bitou** (www.bitou.de) can organise bike tours. **Mallorca Muntanya** (www.mallorcamuntanya.com) also organises a range of hiking tours at all levels. Another good place to look for hiking and biking tours is **Vuelta** (http://vuelta.de). **Bikesport.de** (www.bikesport.de) has plenty of links to other bike tour agents. **Compact Tours** (www.compact-tours.de) offers a one-week trip that includes tours of old Palma and excursions to various points around the island. For winery tours try **Mallorca Wine Tour** (www.majorcawinetour.com).

TRAVELLERS WITH DISABILITIES

Mallorca is not overly disabled-friendly but some things are slowly changing. Disabled access to some museums, official buildings and hotels represents something of a sea change in local thinking, although it remains a minority phenomenon. You need to be circumspect about hotels advertising themselves as disabled-friendly, as this can mean as little as wide doors to rooms and bathrooms or other token efforts. Palma city buses are equipped for wheelchair access, as are some of those that travel around the island. Some taxi companies run adapted taxis – they must be booked in advance.

Organisations

Associació Balear de Persones amb Discapacitat Física (Asprom; Map pp66-7; ☎ 971 289052; www.asprom.net; Carrer de Pasqual Ribot 6) The island's disabled persons' organisation but is more of a lobby than a source of practical holiday information.

Disability Now (☎ 020 7619 7323; www.disabilitynow.org.uk) Has a limited list of disabled-friendly accommodation in Spain.

Desperado's Hire Shop (☎ 971 681558; www.mobilitymallorca.com; Sant Miquel de Liria 5, Torrenova) Based in the Palmanova area (p104) and hires out mobility scooters for the disabled.

Easyrider Mobility Hire (☎ 971 545057; www.easyridermobilityhire.com) An Alcúdia-based outfit also hiring mobility scooters.

Mobility Scooters (☎ 971 132538; www.mobilityscootersmallorca.com) Delivers mobility scooters for hire to customers around the island.

VISAS

Spain is one of 16 member countries of the Schengen Convention, an agreement whereby 14 EU member countries plus Iceland and Norway have abolished checks at internal borders. As of 2007 the EU is made up of 27 countries. For detailed information on the EU, see http://europa.eu.int.

EU, Norwegian and Icelandic nationals need no visa, regardless of the length or purpose of their visit to Spain. If they stay beyond 90 days they are required to register with the police (although many do not). Legal residents of one Schengen country (regardless of their nationality) do not require a visa for another Schengen country.

Nationals of many other countries, including Australia, Canada, Israel, Japan, New Zealand, Switzerland and the USA, do not need a visa for tourist visits of up to 90 days in Spain. If you wish to work or study in Mallorca, you may need a specific visa, so contact a Spanish consulate before travel. If you are a citizen of a country not mentioned in this section, check with a Spanish consulate whether you need a visa.

The standard tourist visa issued by Spanish consulates is the Schengen visa, valid for up to 90 days. A Schengen visa issued by one Schengen country is generally valid for travel in all other Schengen countries. These visas are not renewable.

Extensions & Residence

Nationals of EU countries, Iceland, Norway and Switzerland can enter and leave Spain at will and do *not* need to apply for a *tarjeta de residencia* (residence card). They instead have to be registered on an EU foreigners' register (for which they receive a piece of paper). This piece of EU legislation was supposed to make life easier for EU citizens, although it seems to have failed in that regard. It also means that you must carry your own national ID card or passport around (eg to show when making purchases with credit cards).

People of other nationalities who want to stay in Spain longer than 90 days are supposed to get a residence card. This can be a drawn-out process and starts with an appropriate visa issued by a Spanish consulate in your country of residence.

Photocopies

All important documents (passport data page and visa page, credit cards, travel insurance policy, air/bus/train tickets, driving licence etc) should be photocopied before you leave home. Leave one copy with someone at home and keep another with you, separate from the originals.

WOMEN TRAVELLERS

Travelling in Mallorca is largely as easy as travelling anywhere else in the Western world. Still, you may still occasionally find yourself the object of staring, catcalls and unnecessary comments. Simply ignoring them is sufficient, but learn the word for 'help' *(socorro)* in case you need to draw other people's attention. Remember that eye-to-eye contact and flirting is part of daily Spanish life and need not be offensive.

By and large, Spanish women have a highly developed sense of style and put considerable effort into looking their best. While topless bathing and skimpy clothes are in fashion on the island's coastal resorts, people tend to dress more modestly in the towns and inland.

WORK

Nationals of EU countries, Switzerland, Norway and Iceland may freely work in Spain, and hence, Mallorca. If you are offered a contract, your employer will normally steer you through any bureaucracy.

Virtually everyone else is supposed to obtain, from a Spanish consulate in their country of residence, a work permit and, if they plan to stay more than 90 days, a residence visa. These procedures are well nigh impossible unless you have a job contract lined up beforehand.

You can start a job search on the web, for instance at **Think Spain** (www.thinkspain.com). Translating and interpreting could be an option if you are fluent both in Spanish and a language in demand. Teaching English and some other languages is another option if you are qualified. Language schools are listed under 'Academias de Idiomas' in the Yellow Pages. Be aware that many are cowboy outfits that pay poorly.

Many bars (especially of the UK and Irish persuasion), restaurants and other businesses (such as car hire) are run by foreigners and look for temporary stuff in summer. Check any local press in foreign languages (see p65), which carries ads for waiters, nannies, chefs, babysitters, cleaners and the like.

It is possible to stumble upon work as crew on yachts and cruisers. Check out the situation in the port of Palma de Mallorca. A good place to put out feelers is Hogan's (p94).

Transport

GETTING THERE & AWAY

Most visitors to Mallorca fly into Palma's international airport. It is possible to arrive by ferry from various points along the Spanish coast (Alicante, Barcelona, Dénia and Valencia). The neighbouring islands of Ibiza and Menorca are also linked to Mallorca by air and ferry. Flights, tours and rail tickets can be booked online at www.lonelyplanet.com/travel_services.

ENTERING THE COUNTRY
Passport

Citizens of most of the 27 EU member states and Switzerland can travel to Spain with their national identity card. Citizens of countries that don't issue ID cards, such as the UK, need a full passport.

If applying for a visa (see p204), check that your passport's expiry date is at least six months away. Non-EU citizens must fill out a landing card.

By law you are supposed to have your passport or ID card with you at all times.

AIR
Airport & Airlines

Sant Joan airport (☎ 902 404704; www.aena.es) is 8km east of Palma de Mallorca. In summer especially, masses of charter and regular flights form an air bridge to Palma from around Europe. Low-cost airlines figure among them.

From the UK, EasyJet and Ryanair can get you there for as little as £30 one way (plus taxes), depending on how far in advance you book, while German budget airlines like Air Berlin shuttle in passengers from all over Germany.

The Sant Joan aerodrome came into commercial use in 1935 and by 1962 was registering a million passengers a year. In 2006 it absorbed 22.4 million passengers. The arrivals hall is on the ground floor of the main terminal building, where you will find a tourist information office, money exchange offices, car hire, tour operators and hotel booking stands. Departures are on the 2nd floor. For buses and taxis between the airport and Palma, see p99.

Airlines serving Palma include:

Aer Lingus (EI; ☎ in Ireland 0818 365000, in Spain 902 502737; www.aerlingus.com) Flies from Dublin.

Air Berlin (AB; ☎ in Germany 01805 737800, in Spain 902 320737; www.airberlin.com) German budget airline with direct flights from cities all over Germany, Austria and mainland Spain, as well as Amsterdam, Basel, Copenhagen, Helsinki, Lisbon, London (Stansted), Milan, Moscow, Rome and Zürich.

Air Europa (UX; ☎ in Spain 902 401501; www.aireuropa.com) Flies to Palma from Paris, Rome, Milan and all over Spain.

BMI (BD; ☎ in UK 0870 607 0555; www.flybmi.com) Flights from London (Heathrow) and other UK airports. Also from Amsterdam, Dublin, Düsseldorf, Frankfurt, Gothenburg, Hamburg, Oslo and Stockholm.

British Airways (BA; ☎ in UK 08708 509850, in Spain 902 111333; www.britishairways.com) Flights from London.

Brussels Airlines (SN; ☎ in Spain 807 220003, in Belgium 0902 51600; www.brusselsairlines.com) Flights from Brussels.

Condor (DE; ☎ 01805 707404; www6.condor.com) Flights from various German cities.

Darwin (0D; ☎ in Switzerland 0848 177177; www.darwinairline.com) Seasonal flights from Bern and London (City).

EasyJet (U2; ☎ in UK 0905 821 0905, in Germany 09001 100161, in Spain 902 299992, in Switzerland 0900 000195; www.easyjet.com) Flies from various London and other UK airports. Also direct flights from Basel and Geneva (Switzerland), Berlin and Dortmund (Germany) and Madrid.

Excel Airways (XL; ☎ in UK 0870 169 0169) Flights from several UK destinations.

Finnair (AY; ☎ in Spain 902 178178; www.finnair.com) Flights from Finland.

Germanwings (4U; ☎ in Germany 09001 919100, in Spain 916 259704; www.germanwings.com) Flies from Cologne, Dortmund, Hamburg and Stuttgart.

Iberia (IB; ☎ in Spain 902 400500; www.iberia.es) With its subsidiary Air Nostrum, flies from many mainland Spanish cities.

Jet2 (LS; ☎ in UK 0871 226 1737; www.jet2.com) Flights from Belfast, Blackpool, Leeds, Manchester and Newcastle.

Jetair (JAF; ☎ in Belgium 070 220000; www.jetairfly .com) Flights from Belgium.

Lagunair (N7; ☎ in Spain 902 340300; www.lagunair .com) Small Spanish airline with flights to Palma from León, Salamanca and Valladolid.

Lauda Air (OS; ☎ 0820 320321; www.laudaair.com) Flights from Austrian airports.

LTU (LT; ☎ 02119 418456; www.ltu.com) Flights from various German cities, including Cologne, Düsseldorf, Frankfurt and Munich.

Lufthansa (LH; ☎ in Germany 01805 838426, in Spain 902 220101; www.lufthansa.com) Flights from main German centres.

Martinair (MP; ☎ in Netherlands 020 601 1767; www .martinair.nl) Flights from Amsterdam.

Monarch (ZB; ☎ in UK 0870 040 5040, in Spain 800 099260; www.flymonarch.com) Scheduled and charter flights from London (Luton), Birmingham and Manchester.

MyAir (8I; ☎ in Italy 899 500060; www.myair.com) Flights from Rome and Milan.

Niki (HG; ☎ in Austria 08207 37800, in Germany 01805 737800, in Spain 902 320737; www.flyniki.com) Flights from various Austrian and German cities.

Ryanair (FR; ☎ in UK 0906 270 5656, in Germany 09001 160500, in Italy 899 678910, in Spain 807 220032; www .ryanair.com) Flies from London (Stansted) and Liverpool, Frankfurt (Hahn) and Düsseldorf (Weeze) in Germany and Pisa (Italy).

Spanair (JK; ☎ in Spain 902 131415; www.spanair.com) Flights from most mainland Spanish centres and a handful of European cities.

Sterling Airlines (NB; ☎ in Denmark 7010 8484, ☎ in Spain 917 496643; www.sterling.dk) Flights from Copenhagen, Stockholm, Helsinki and other Scandinavian airports.

Swiss (LX; ☎ in Switzerland 0848 700700, in Spain 901 116712; www.swiss.com) Swiss sometimes has surprisingly good deals from Zürich.

Thomson Fly (TOM; ☎ in UK 0870 1900737; www.tho msonfly.com) Flights from many UK cities.

Transavia (HV; ☎ in Netherlands 0900 0737, in Spain 902 114478; www.transavia.com) Low-cost flights from Amsterdam.

TUIfly.com (X3; ☎ in Germany 09001 099595, in Spain 902 020069; www.tuifly.com) Flights from all over Germany.

Vueling (VLG; ☎ in Spain 902 333933; www.vueling .com) Budget airline with flights from Barcelona and Madrid.

T R A N S P O R T

CLIMATE CHANGE & TRAVEL

Climate change is a threat to the ecosystems that humans rely upon, and air travel is the fastest-growing contributor to the problem. Lonely Planet regards travel, overall, as a global benefit, but believes we all have a responsibility to limit our personal impact on global warming.

Flying & Climate Change

Pretty much every form of motorised travel generates CO_2 (the main cause of human-induced climate change) but planes are the worst offenders, not just because of the distances they allow us to travel, but because they release greenhouse gases high into the atmosphere. Two people taking a return flight between Europe and the US will contribute as much to climate change as an average household's gas and electricity consumption over a year.

Carbon Offset Schemes

Climatecare.org and other websites use 'carbon calculators' that allow travellers to offset the level of greenhouse gases they are responsible for with financial contributions to sustainable travel schemes that reduce global warming.

Lonely Planet, together with Rough Guides and other concerned partners in the travel industry, supports the carbon offset scheme run by climatecare.org. Lonely Planet offsets all of its staff and author travel.

For more information check out our website: www.lonelyplanet.com.

Tickets

Full-time students and those under 26 sometimes have access to discounted fares. Other cheap deals include the discounted tickets released to travel agents and specialist discount agencies. Low-cost carriers sell direct to travellers and the internet is often the easiest way of locating and booking reasonably priced seats. There is also no shortage of online agents, including:

- www.cheaptickets.com
- www.ebookers.com
- www.expedia.com
- www.flightline.co.uk
- www.flynow.com
- www.openjet.com
- www.opodo.com
- www.planesimple.co.uk
- www.skyscanner.net
- www.travelocity.co.uk
- www.tripadvisor.com.

Australia & New Zealand

There are no direct flights from Australia or New Zealand to Spain. If you plan to visit Mallorca as part of a wider European tour, book a low-cost flight on the web from wherever you choose to land in Europe.

STA Travel (☎ 1300 733 035; www.statravel.com.au) and **Flight Centre** (☎ 133 133; www.flightcentre.com.au) are major dealers in cheap airfares in Australia. For online bookings try www.travel.com.au.

Both **Flight Centre** (☎ 0800 243 544; www.flightcentre.co.nz) and **STA Travel** (☎ 0508 782 872; www.statravel.co.nz) have branches throughout New Zealand. The site www.travel.co.nz is recommended for online bookings.

Germany

Recommended agencies:
Expedia (www.expedia.de)
Just Travel (☎ 08974 73330; www.justtravel.de)
Lastminute (☎ 01805 284366; www.lastminute.de)
STA Travel (☎ 01805 456422; www.statravel.de) For travellers under the age of 26.

Italy

CTS Viaggi (www.cts.it) specialises in student and youth travel.

Rest of Spain & Portugal

From mainland Spain, scheduled flights to Palma are operated by Iberia (Air Nostrum), Air Europa, Spanair and a couple of low-cost

airlines. Inter-island flights to/from Ibiza and Menorca are operated by Iberia (Air Nostrum), Air Berlin and Spanair. These take less than 30 minutes and can easily cost €100 a pop.

A nationwide travel agency is **Halcón Viajes** (☎ 807 7227222; www.halconviajes.com). A good cut-price travel agent in Madrid and Barcelona is **Viajes Zeppelin** (www.viajeszeppelin.com).

From Lisbon you have to connect in Madrid, Barcelona or Valencia for Palma. **Tagus** (☎ 707 225454; www.viagenstagus.pt; Rua Camilo Castelo Branco 20) is a reputable travel agency with branches all over Portugal.

UK & Ireland

Discount air travel is big business in London. Advertisements for travel agencies appear in the travel pages of the weekend broadsheet newspapers, *Time Out,* the *Evening Standard* and in the free online magazine *TNT* (www.tntmagazine.com).

Good agencies for charter flights from the UK to Spain include **Avro** (☎ 0870 4582841; www.avro.co.uk), **JMC** (ww5.thomascook.com) and **Thomson** (☎ 0870 1650079; www.thoms on.co.uk).

From Ireland, check out offers from Aer Lingus.

USA & Canada

There are no direct flights from North America to Mallorca. You will connect in Madrid or another European hub.

San Francisco is the ticket consolidator (discount travel agent) capital of the USA, although good deals can be found in Los Angeles, New York and other big US cities.

The following agencies are recommended for online bookings:

- www.itn.net
- www.lowestfare.com
- www.orbitz.com
- www.sta.com (for travellers under the age of 26).

SEA

Spain's main ferry company, **Acciona Trasmediterránea** (☎ 902 454645; www.trasmediterranea.es), runs services between Barcelona and Valencia (on the mainland) and Palma de Mallorca. Services also connect Palma with Ibiza and Maó (Menorca). Tickets can be purchased from any travel agency or online. The company adds on a cheeky extra ticket fee of €11 per person and €13 per vehicle on all tickets (this fee is not included in the prices quoted below). All services transport vehicles.

From Barcelona there are two daily services from about Easter to late October. A high-speed catamaran leaves at 4pm (€75 for standard seat, €157.50 for small car; four hours), while an overnight ferry leaves at 11pm (€46.50 for standard seat, €131.50 for small car; 7¼ hours). The return trips from Palma are at 10am or 11.30am (catamaran) and 1pm (ferry). On the ferries you can opt for various cabins if you need more comfort or some shuteye. On some days in the peak July and August period, a fast ferry from Barcelona is added at 7am (return 8.30pm). Between late October and March, only the overnight ferry continues to run (daily at 11pm). The return trip leaves Palma at 1pm (except Sundays, when it leaves at 11.30pm).

From Valencia the situation is similar and prices are the same. From about Easter to late October, a slowish catamaran leaves at 4pm (six hours) and an overnight ferry at 11pm (7½ hours), Monday to Saturday. Only the catamaran runs on Sundays. From late July to the end of August, a faster catamaran replaces the 4pm boat and leaves at 7.45pm (4¼ hours). The return catamaran trip from Palma leaves at 7.30am, while the ferry departs at 11.45am (seven hours) or midnight (eight hours). The faster catamaran leaves at 7.15am.

A daily fast ferry links Alicante and Palma via Ibiza in August, leaving Alicante at 3.15pm (€84 per person, €175 per small vehicle; 7½ hours). The return trip leaves Palma at 7am (7¾ hours).

Between the Balearic Islands there are also various services. Acciona Trasmediterránea runs two fast ferries or catamarans a day between Palma and Ibiza City from Easter to the end of October (€49.50 for standard seat, €96 for small car; 2¼ hours; generally leaving Ibiza at 7am and 7.45pm, and Palma at 7.30am and 8.45pm). On some Sundays there's also a slow ferry at 7pm (€35.50 for standard seat, €96 for

small car; 3½ hours). Curiously, the service drops to once a day in August (presumably people are so hot and flat out on the beaches that they can't be bothered island-hopping!). From November to March, the slow Sunday ferry continues to run as normal.

From about Easter to mid-November, a weekly ferry runs from Maó to Palma (€35.50 for standard seat, €96 for small car; 5½ hours), leaving at 5.30pm on Sundays and returning from Palma at 8am.

The inter-island ticket booking fee is €6 per person and €9 per vehicle.

Baleària (☎ 902 160180; www.balearia.com) operates ferries to Palma from Barcelona, Valencia and Dénia (via Ibiza). From mid-June to the end of September, a high-speed ferry runs direct from Barcelona to Palma at 4.30pm (10.30am from Palma). Another runs to Alcúdia (northeast Mallorca) from Barcelona (5¾ hours) via Ciutadella (3¾ hours) in Menorca (it then leaves Alcúdia at 8am). A ferry leaves Barcelona at 11pm (seven hours) and returns at 12.30pm. The Barcelona–Alcúdia service also runs in the first half of May. The slower ferry service remains in place in the second half of May and October.

From Dénia (connecting bus from Valencia), two daily ferries (one a fast ferry) head to Palma (five to 8¾ hours) via Ibiza City from March to October. The fast ferry leaves Dénia at 5pm and the ferry at 8.30pm. The other way, departures are at 8am and 9.30am respectively. In the peak July and August period, Balearia puts on an extra fast ferry on this route, leaving Dénia at 8am and Palma at 5pm.

A standard ferry also runs from Valencia to Palma via Ibiza six or seven days a week from mid-May to October at 10.30pm (eight hours). It leaves Palma at 11.15am. One fast ferry (two hours) and one conventional boat (four hours) link Palma to Ibiza from mid-March to October. Up to two other fast ferries are added to this run in July and August.

From the mainland you pay €59 to €98 for a seat, depending on the crossing. The fares between Palma de Mallorca and Ibiza range from €53 to €68.

Iscomar (☎ 902 119128; www.iscomar.com) has a ferry service from Barcelona to Palma (€34 per person, €99 per small car; 7½ hours; daily in summer). A similar service operates from Valencia (€34 per person, €99 per small car; nine hours; six days a week in summer). One

TRANSPORT

or two daily ferries shuttle between Ciutadella on Menorca and Port d'Alcúdia on Mallorca (€40 per person, €61 per small car one way; 2½ hours) between mid-March and mid-December.

Cape Balear (☎ 902 100444; www.capebalear.es) operates two fast ferries daily to Ciutadella (Menorca) from Cala Ratjada (Mallorca) in summer for €80 one way (bizarrely, it costs €50 return if you do a same-day return trip!). The crossing takes 45 minutes.

You can compare prices and look for deals at **Direct Ferries** (www.directferries.es).

GETTING AROUND

CAR & MOTORCYCLE

Although you can get about much of the island by bus and train, having your own vehicle allows you greater freedom. Mallorca, especially on the west and north coasts, and along narrow country roads in the centre of the island, is ideal for motorcycle touring.

Bring Your Own Vehicle

Always carry proof of ownership of a private vehicle. Third-party motor insurance is required throughout Europe.

Every vehicle should display a nationality plate of its country of registration. It is compulsory in Spain to have a warning triangle (to be used in case of breakdown) and a reflective jacket. Recommended accessories are a first-aid kit, spare-bulb kit and fire extinguisher.

Driving Licence

All EU member state driving licences are recognised throughout Europe. Those with a non-EU licence are supposed to obtain a 12-month International Driver's Permit (IDP) to accompany their national licence, although you will find that national licences from countries like Australia, Canada, New Zealand and the USA are often accepted.

Fuel & Spare Parts

Petrol (*gasolina*) prices vary between service stations (*gasolineras*). Lead free (*sin plomo*; 95 octane) costs an average €1.08/L. A 98-octane variant costs €1.19/L. Diesel (*gasóleo*) comes in at €0.96/L.

You can pay with major credit cards at most service stations.

Most vehicle makes can be dealt with by local mechanics, but more popular brands include Seat, Volkswagen, Renault and Fiat.

Hire

About 30 vehicle-hire agencies are based in Palma and plenty of them operate around the island. To rent a car you have to have a licence, be aged 21 or over and, for the major companies at least, have a credit or debit card. See p99 for specific suggestions.

Insurance

Third-party motor insurance is a minimum requirement in Spain. Ask your insurer for a European Accident Statement form, which can simplify matters in the event of an accident. A European breakdown assistance policy such as the AA Five Star Service or RAC Eurocover Motoring Assistance is a good investment.

Road Rules

Drive on the right. In built-up areas the speed limit is 50km/h, which rises to 100km/h on major roads and up to 120km/h on the four-lane highways leading out of Palma.

Motorcyclists must use headlights at all times and wear a crash helmet if riding a bike of 125cc or more.

Vehicles in traffic circles (roundabouts) have the right of way.

The blood-alcohol limit is 0.05%. Breath tests are becoming more common and if found to be over the limit you can be judged, fined and deprived of your licence within 24 hours. Fines range up to around €600 for serious offences. Non-resident foreigners will be required to pay up on the spot (at 30% off the full fine).

Taxi

You can get around the island by taxi and, depending on how many of you there are and what kind of luggage you have, it can sometimes be handy. Prices are posted at central points in many towns. Rates go up at weekends, on holidays and from 9pm to 6am. About the most expensive trip you can do is from the airport to Cala Ratjada (€86, or €97 for the night rate).

BICYCLE

Although the going in the mountainous areas can be tough, much of the island is reasonably flat and can be easily discovered by bike. You can take your own or hire one on the spot. The tourist authorities publish a booklet called *Cicloturismo* (Cycling Tourism), which you can also see on the web (www.illesbalears.es, click on 'Sport Tourism'). It suggests routes across the island. Signposts have been put up across much of rural Mallorca indicating cycling routes (usually secondary roads between towns and villages). In the northeast, you can get on to a network of so-called Ecovies (Ecoroutes, see p137). We have also suggested some cycling routes on p100 and p146. See p58 for more information.

Hire

Cycle-hire places are scattered around the main resorts of the island, including Palma. Details of bike-hire places appear in the course of this guide. If you wish to start touring from Palma, see p100.

Purchase

The cost of purchasing a bike is much like anywhere else in Europe. You'll find bike shops in Palma and some other centres but resale is not necessarily easy, so unless you want to transport your acquisition back home, you should probably favour hire. If you want to buy secondhand, check out **Loquo** (www .loquo.com), which has a section for the sale of bicycles, before you leave home.

BUS

The island is roughly divided into five zones radiating from Palma. Bus line numbers in the 100s cover the southwest, the 200s the west (as far as Sóller), the 300s the northeast and much of the centre, the 400s a wedge of the centre and east coast and the 500s the south. These services are run by a phalanx of small bus companies, but you can get route and timetable information for all by contacting **Transport de les Illes Balears** (☎ 971 177777; http://tib .caib.es).

Most of the island is accessible by bus from Palma. All buses depart from (or near) the **bus station** (Map pp70-1; Carrer d'Eusebi Estada). Not all lines are especially frequent, however, and services

slow to a trickle on weekends. Frequency to many coastal areas drops from November to April and some lines are cut altogether (such as those between Ca'n Picafort and Sa Calobra or Sóller).

Getting around the Serra de Tramuntana by bus, while possible, isn't always easy. Bus 200 from Palma runs to Estellencs via Banyalbufar for example, while bus 210 runs to Valldemossa and then, less frequently, on to Deià and Sóller. Nothing makes the connection between Estellencs and Valldemossa and all but the Palma–Valldemossa run are infrequent.

Similarly, while you can reach just about any central-plains or east-coast town from Palma (sometimes with a change on the way), getting about between them can be more frustrating. Sometimes you have to get a train and connect to a local bus. More-out-of-the-way places can also be tedious to reach.

Fares are not especially onerous. One-way fares from Palma include Cala Ratjada (€9.35), Ca'n Picafort (€4.55), Port de Pollença (€5.25) and Port d'Andratx (€3.80).

LOCAL TRANSPORT

Palma is the only centre with its own local transport system (see p99). Buses are the main way around, although a new metro line (of more interest to commuters in the 'burbs than to visitors) runs from the centre to the university.

It is quite possible to get around Palma (especially the partly pedestrianised old centre) by bicycle, although cycling lanes are limited (the main one runs along the shoreline).

Palma is well endowed with taxis, with several stands around the city centre. Elsewhere on the island, you may not necessarily find them waiting when you need them, but generally they are fairly easy to order by phone.

TRAIN

Two train lines run from Plaça d'Espanya in Palma de Mallorca. One heads north to Sóller and is a panoramic excursion (p99). The other heads inland to Inca, where the line splits to serve Sa Pobla and Manacor (p98).

Health

CONTENTS

TRAVEL HEALTH WEBSITES

It's usually a good idea to consult your government's travel health website before departure, if one is available.

- Australia: www.smartraveller.gov.au
- Canada: www.hc-sc.gc.ca/english/index .html
- UK: www.doh.gov.uk
- United States: www.cdc.gov/travel

Travel health depends on your pre-departure preparations, your daily health care while travelling and how you handle any medical problem that does develop. Mallorca does not present any particular health dangers.

BEFORE YOU GO

Planning before departure, particularly for pre-existing illnesses, will save trouble later. See your dentist before a long trip, carry a spare pair of contact lenses and/or glasses, and take your optical prescription with you. Bring medications in their original, clearly labelled, containers. A signed and dated letter from your physician describing your medical conditions and medications, including generic names, is also a good idea. If carrying syringes or needles, be sure to have a physician's letter documenting their medical necessity.

INSURANCE

If you're an EU citizen, a European Health Insurance Card (EHIC), available from health centres or, in the UK, post offices, covers you for most medical care. It will not cover you for non-emergencies or emergency repatriation. Citizens from other countries should find out if there is a reciprocal arrangement for free medical care between their country and Spain. If you do need health insurance, consider a policy that cov-ers you for the worst possible scenario, such as an accident requiring an emergency flight home. Find out in advance if your insurance plan will make payments directly to providers or reimburse you later for overseas health expenditures. The former option is preferable, as it doesn't require you to pay out of pocket in a foreign country.

RECOMMENDED VACCINATIONS

No jabs are necessary for Mallorca but the WHO recommends that all travellers be covered for diphtheria, tetanus, measles, mumps, rubella and polio, regardless of their destination. Since most vaccines don't produce immunity until at least two weeks after they're given, visit a physician at least six weeks before departure.

INTERNET RESOURCES

www.ageconcern.org.uk Advice on travel for the elderly.
www.fitfortravel.scot.nhs.uk General travel advice for the layperson.
www.mariestopes.org.uk Information on women's health and contraception.
www.mdtravelhealth.com Travel health recommen-dations for every country; updated daily.
www.who.int/ith The WHO's publication *International Travel and Health* is revised annually and is available on this website.

FURTHER READING

Lonely Planet's *Travel with Children* in-cludes advice on travel health for younger children. Other recommended references are

Traveller's Health by Dr Richard Dawood (Oxford University Press) and *The Traveller's Good Health Guide* by Ted Lankester (Sheldon Press).

IN MALLORCA

AVAILABILITY & COST OF HEALTH CARE

If you need an ambulance call ☎ 061. For emergency treatment go straight to the *urgencias* (casualty) section of the nearest hospital. The island's main hospital is Palma's Hospital Son Dureta (see p68), but other important ones are based in Inca and Manacor. At the main coastal tourist resorts you will generally find clinics with English- and German-speaking staff. Most main beaches also have a Red Cross station (where you can go if stung by jellyfish, for instance).

Good health care is readily available, and *farmacias* (pharmacies) offer valuable advice and sell over-the-counter medication. In Spain a system of *farmacias de guardia* (duty pharmacies) operates so that each district has one open all the time. When a pharmacy is closed it posts the name of the nearest open one on the door. The standard of dental care is usually good.

TRAVELLER'S DIARRHOEA

If you develop diarrhoea, be sure to drink plenty of fluids, preferably an oral rehydration solution (eg Dioralyte). A few loose stools don't require treatment, but if you start having more than four or five stools a day, you should start taking an antibiotic (usually a quinolone drug) and an antidiarrhoeal agent (such as Loperamide). If diarrhoea is bloody, persists for more than 72 hours or is accompanied by fever, shaking, chills or severe abdominal pain you should seek medical attention.

ENVIRONMENTAL HAZARDS
Heat Exhaustion & Heat Stroke

Heat exhaustion occurs following excessive fluid loss with inadequate replacement of fluids and salts. Symptoms include headache, dizziness and tiredness. Dehydration is already happening by the time you feel thirsty – aim to drink sufficient water to produce pale, diluted urine. To treat heat exhaustion, replace lost fluids by drinking water and/or fruit juice, and cool the body with cold water and

fans. Treat salt loss with salty fluids such as soup or Bovril, or add a little more table salt to foods than usual.

Heat stroke is much more serious, resulting in irrational and hyperactive behaviour and eventually loss of consciousness and death. Rapid cooling by spraying the body with water and fanning is ideal. Emergency fluid and electrolyte replacement by intravenous drip is recommended.

Insect Bites & Stings

Bees and wasps only cause real problems to those with a severe allergy (anaphylaxis). If you have a severe allergy to bee or wasp stings, carry an 'epipen' or similar adrenaline injection.

In forested areas watch out for the hairy reddish-brown caterpillars of the pine processionary moth. They live in silvery nests up in the pine trees and, come spring, they leave the nest to march in long lines (hence the name). Touching the caterpillars' hairs sets off a severely irritating allergic skin reaction.

Some Spanish centipedes have a very nasty but nonfatal sting. The ones to watch out for are those with clearly defined segments, which may be patterned with, for instance, black and yellow stripes.

In summer, waves of stingers (jellyfish) can appear on the island's beaches and there's not much you can do about them (despite talk of volunteers being employed to net the buggers). Keep an eye out for them and if you see they're numerous, you'd best forget about swimming. There are two basic types of stinger, the *Rhizostoma pulmo* and *Pelagia noctiluca*. Traditionally the best method for casing the pain is to rub vinegar in, although Epsom salts are better for the *Pelagia noctiluca*. A bag of ice also soothes the pain. If none of these options are available, rub in salt water. Fresh water is not a good idea, as it can stimulate the sting. Head to a Red Cross stand (they are usually present on the main beaches) if you are stung. While the pain usually goes within a few days, marks from stings can still be visible weeks after.

Mosquitoes can cause irritation and infected bites. Use a DEET-based insect repellent.

Sandflies are found on many Mallorcan beaches. They usually cause only a nasty itchy bite but can carry a rare skin disorder called cutaneous leishmaniasis,

HEALTH

214 IN MALLORCA ·· Travelling with Children

Scorpions are found in Spain and their sting can be distressingly painful, but are not considered fatal.

Water

Tap water is generally safe to drink in Mallorca but rarely tastes very good, which is why most locals buy bottled mineral water, most it from sources in the Serra de Tramuntana. If you are in any doubt about whether water can be drunk (for example from public fountains), ask *¿Es potable el agua (de grifo)?* (Is the (tap) water drinkable?). Do not drink water from rivers or lakes as it may contain bacteria or viruses that can cause diarrhoea or vomiting.

TRAVELLING WITH CHILDREN

Make sure your children are up to date with routine vaccinations, and discuss possible travel vaccines well before departure as some vaccines are not suitable for children under one year of age.

WOMEN'S HEALTH

Travelling during pregnancy is usually possible but always seek a medical checkup before planning your trip. The most risky times for travel are during the first 12 weeks of pregnancy and after 30 weeks.

SEXUAL HEALTH

Emergency contraception is most effective if taken within 24 hours after unprotected sex. The website of the **International Planned Parent Federation** (www.ippf.org) can advise about the availability of contraception in different countries.

When buying condoms look for a European CE mark, which means they have been rigorously tested, and keep them in a cool dry place or they may crack and perish.

Language

Mallorca is a bilingual island, at least on paper. Since receiving its autonomy statute at the beginning of the 1980s, the use of the islanders' native Catalan *(català)* has recovered its official status alongside Spanish, or Castilian *(castellano)* as it is more precisely known. The reversal of Francoist policy, which largely eliminated minority languages from public life and schools, has not been as radical, however, as in Catalonia on the mainland.

Catalan, or its local dialect, *mallorquí*, can be read in newspapers, heard on the radio and TV and is largely the vehicle of education, at least at primary level. That said, it would be pushing a point to say that it had again become the primary language of Mallorca or the rest of the Balearic Islands. Those who left school before the 1980s were largely schooled in Spanish and often have a poor command of written Catalan. Today, despite the broad schooling in Catalan, some locals choose to speak Spanish (Castilian) anyway. The majority of migrants and seasonal workers from other parts of Spain and the bulk of resident foreigners show little inclination to learn Catalan – for many, Spanish alone is challenge enough. The reasoning is simple: if Spanish is an official language and everyone in Mallorca speaks it perfectly, why should I learn Catalan?

It has to be said too that the Mallorquins themselves are not always helpful in this regard. Frequently they find it easier to speak Spanish with non-Mallorquins, especially where the latter are clearly struggling. At the same time, the official line is that newcomers should make the effort to learn Catalan to integrate better. It's a tricky one, and it gets trickier. Pressure from the Catalan capital, Barcelona, to standardise the teaching of Catalan across Catalan-speaking territories (in this case to the detriment of the Mallorquí variant) has raised considerable hackles among islanders who have no more intention of speaking standard Catalan than the Scots have of affecting a southeast English accent.

Overall, Spanish remains the lingua franca, especially between Mallorquins and other Spaniards or foreigners. You'll often hear and read Catalan, and locals will be pleasantly surprised to hear you trying your hand at it (whichever variant), but just making the effort with Spanish will please most. In the tourist areas and especially along the coast, many locals have some command of English and/or German.

We've included a few phrases in (standard) Catalan in the boxed text on p221 for those who want to have a go (and win instant friends!).

SPANISH

For a more comprehensive guide to the Spanish language, pick up a copy of Lonely Planet's handy pocket-sized *Spanish Phrasebook* and *Fast Talk Spanish*.

PRONUNCIATION
Vowels

a	as in 'father'
e	as in 'met'
i	as in 'marine'
o	as in 'or' (with no 'r' sound)
u	as in 'rule'; **u** is 'silent' after **q** and in the combinations **gue** and **gui**, unless it's marked with a diaeresis (eg *argüir*), in which case it's pronounced as English 'w'

Consonants

While the consonants **ch**, **ll** and **ñ** are generally considered distinct letters, **ch** and **ll** are now often listed alphabetically under **c** and **l** respectively. The letter **ñ** is still treated as a separate letter and comes after **n** in dictionaries.

c	as 'k' before **a**, **o** and **u**; as 'th' when followed by **e** or **i**
ch	as in 'choose'
d	as in 'dog' when initial or preceded by l or n; elsewhere as the 'th' in 'then'
g	as in 'go' when initial or before **a**, **o** and **u**; elsewhere much softer. Before **e** or **i** it's a harsh, breathy sound, similar to the 'ch' in Scottish *loch* (**kh** in our guides to pronunciation).
h	always silent
j	as the 'ch' in the Scottish *loch* (**kh** in our guides to pronunciation)
ll	similar to the 'y' in 'yellow'
ñ	as the 'ni' in 'onion'
x	as the 'x' in 'taxi' when between two vowels; as the 's' in 'sound' before a consonant
z	'th' as in 'thin'

Word Stress

Stress is indicated by italics in the pronunciation guides included with all the words and phrases in this language guide. In general, words ending in vowels or the letters n or s have stress on the next-to-last syllable, while those with other endings have stress on the last syllable. Thus *vaca* (cow) and *caballos* (horses) both carry stress on the next-to-last syllable, while *ciudad* (city) and *infeliz* (unhappy) are both stressed on the last syllable.

Written accents indicate a stressed syllable, and will almost always appear in words that don't follow the rules above, eg *sótano* (basement), *porción* (portion).

GENDER & PLURALS

In Spanish, nouns are either masculine or feminine, and there are rules to help determine gender (there are of course some exceptions). Feminine nouns generally end with -**a** or with the groups -**ción**, -**sión** or -**dad**. Other endings typically signify a masculine noun. Endings for adjectives also change to agree with the gender of the noun they modify (masculine/feminine – **o**/-**a**). Where both masculine and feminine forms are included in this language guide, they are separated by a slash, with the masculine form appearing first, for example *perdido/a*.

If a noun or adjective ends in a vowel, the plural is formed by adding **s** to the end. If it ends in a consonant, the plural is formed by adding **es** to the end.

ACCOMMODATION

I'm looking for ...	*Estoy buscando ...*	e·stoy boos·kan·do ...
Where is ...?	*¿Dónde hay ...?*	don·de ai ...
a hotel	*un hotel*	oon o·tel
a boarding house	*una pensión/ residencial/ un hospedaje*	oo·na pen·syon/ re·see·den·syal/ oon os·pe·da·khe
a youth hostel	*un albergue juvenil*	oon al·ber·ge khoo·ve·neel

MAKING A RESERVATION

To ...	*A ...*
From ...	*De ...*
Date	*Fecha*
I'd like to book ...	*Quisiera reservar ...* (see 'Accommodation' for bed and room options)
in the name of ...	*en nombre de ...*
for the nights of ...	*para las noches del ...*
credit card ...	*tarjeta de crédito ...*
number	*número*
expiry date	*fecha de vencimiento*
Please confirm ...	*Puede confirmar ...*
availability	*la disponibilidad*
price	*el precio*

I'd like a ... room.	*Quisiera una habitación ...*	kee·sye·ra oo·na a·bee·ta·syon ...
double	*doble*	do·ble
single	*individual*	een·dee·vee·dwal
twin	*con dos camas*	kon dos ka·mas
How much is it per ...?	*¿Cuánto cuesta por ...?*	kwan·to kwes·ta por ...
night	*noche*	no·che
person	*persona*	per·so·na
week	*semana*	se·ma·na

May I see the room?

¿Puedo ver la habitación?	pwe·do ver la a·bee·ta·syon

I don't like it.
No me gusta.   no me *goos*·ta
It's fine. I'll take it.
Vale. La cojo.   va·le la *ko*·kho
Does it include breakfast?
¿Incluye el desayuno?   een·*kloo*·ye el de·sa·*yoo*·no
I'm leaving now.
Me voy ahora.   me voy a·o·ra

full board	pensión completa	pen·*syon* kom·*ple*·ta
private/shared bathroom	baño privado/ compartido	*ba*·nyo pree·*va*·do/ kom·par·*tee*·do
too expensive	demasiado caro	de·ma·*sya*·do *ka*·ro
cheaper	más económico	mas e·ko·*no*·mee·ko
discount	descuento	des·*kwen*·to

CONVERSATION & ESSENTIALS

When talking to people familiar to you or younger than you, it's usual to use the informal form of 'you', *tú*, rather than the polite form *Usted*. The polite form is always given in this guide; where options are given, the form is indicated by the abbreviations 'pol' and 'inf'.

Hello.	Hola.	o·la
Good morning.	Buenos días.	*bwe*·nos dee·as
Good afternoon.	Buenas tardes.	*bwe*·nas *tar*·des
Good evening/ night.	Buenas noches.	*bwe*·nas *no*·ches
Goodbye.	Adiós.	a·*dyos*
Bye/See you soon.	Hasta luego.	*as*·ta *lwe*·go
Yes.	Sí.	see
No.	No.	no
Please.	Por favor.	por fa·*vor*
Thank you.	Gracias.	*gra*·thyas
Many thanks.	Muchas gracias.	*moo*·chas *gra*·thyas
You're welcome.	De nada.	de *na*·da
Pardon me.	Perdón/ Discúlpeme.	per·*don* dees·*kool*·pe·me

(before requesting information, for example)

| Sorry. | Lo siento. | lo see·*en*·to |

(when apologising)

| Excuse me. | Permiso. | per·*mee*·so |

(when asking permission to pass, for example)

How are things?
¿Qué tal?   ke tal
What's your name?
¿Cómo se llama Usted?   *ko*·mo se *ya*·ma oo·ste (pol)
¿Cómo te llamas?   *ko*·mo te *ya*·mas (inf)
My name is ...
Me llamo ...   me *ya*·mo ...

It's a pleasure to meet you.
Mucho gusto.   *moo*·cho *goos*·to
Where are you from?
¿De dónde es/eres?   de *don*·de es/e·res (pol/inf)
I'm from ...
Soy de ...   soy de ...
Where are you staying?
¿Dónde está alojado?   *don*·de es·ta a·lo·*kha*·do (pol)
¿Dónde estás alojado?   *don*·de es·tas a·lo·*kha*·do (inf)
May I take a photo?
¿Puedo hacer una foto? *pwe*·do a·*sair* oo·na *fo*·to

DIRECTIONS

How do I get to ...?
¿Cómo puedo llegar a ...? *ko*·mo *pwe*·do lye·*gar* a ...
Is it far?
¿Está lejos?   es·ta *le*·khos
Go straight ahead.
Siga/Vaya derecho.   *see*·ga/va·ya de·*re*·cho
Turn left.
Gire a la izquierda.   *khee*·re a la ees·*kyer*·da
Turn right.
Gire a la derecha.   *khee*·re a la de·*re*·cha
I'm lost.
Me he perdido.   me he per·*dee*·do
Can you show me (on the map)?
¿Me lo podría indicar   me lo po·*dree*·a een·dee·*kar*
(en el mapa)?   (en el *ma*·pa)

here	aquí	a·*kee*
there	allí	a·*yee*
traffic lights	semáforos	se·*ma*·fo·ros
north	norte	*nor*·te
south	sur	soor
east	este	*es*·te
west	oeste	o·*es*·te

HEALTH

I'm sick.
Estoy enfermo/a.   es·*toy* en·*fer*·mo/a

EMERGENCIES

Help!	¡Socorro!	so·ko·ro
Fire!	¡Incendio!	een·sen·dyo
Go away!	¡Vete!/¡Fuera!	ve·te/fwe·ra

Call ...!

¡Llame a ...!		ya·me a
an ambulance		
una ambulancia		oo·na am·boo·lan·sya
a doctor		
un médico		oon me·dee·ko
the police		
la policía		la po·lee·see·a

It's an emergency.

Es una emergencia.   es oo·na e·mer·khen·sya

Could you help me, please?

¿Me puede ayudar,   me pwe·de a·yoo·dar
por favor?   por fa·vor

I'm lost.

Me he perdido.   me e per·dee·do

Where are the toilets?

¿Dónde están los baños? don·de es·tan los ba·nyos

I need a doctor (who speaks English).

Necesito un médico   ne·se·see·to oon me·dee·ko
(que habla inglés).   (ke a·bla een·gles)

Where's the hospital?

¿Dónde está el hospital? don·de es·ta el os·pee·tal

I'm pregnant.

Estoy embarazada.   es·toy em·ba·ra·sa·da

I'm ...	Soy ...	soy ...
asthmatic	asmático/a	as·ma·tee·ko/a
diabetic	diabético/a	dya·be·tee·ko/a
epileptic	epiléptico/a	e·pee·lep·tee·ko/a

I'm allergic	Soy alérgico/a	soy a·ler·khee·ko/a
to ...	a ...	a ...
antibiotics	los antibióticos	los an·tee·byo·tee·kos
nuts	las nueces	las nwe·se
peanuts	los cacahuetes	los ka·ka·we·tes
penicillin	la penicilina	la pe·nee·see·lee·na

I have ...	Tengo ...	ten·go ...
diarrhoea	diarrea	dya·re·a
a fever	fiebre	fee·eb·ray
a headache	un dolor de	oon do·lor de
	cabeza	ka·be·sa
nausea	náusea	now·se·a

LANGUAGE DIFFICULTIES

Do you speak (English)?

¿Habla/Hablas (inglés)? a·bla/a·blas (een·gles) (pol/inf)

Does anyone here speak English?

¿Hay alguien que   ai al·gyen ke
hable inglés?   a·ble een·gles

I (don't) understand.

Yo (no) entiendo.   yo (no) en·tyen·do

How do you say ...?

¿Cómo se dice ...?   ko·mo se dee·se ...

What does ... mean?

¿Qué quiere decir ...? ke kye·re de·seer ...

Could you	¿Puede ..., por	pwe·de ... por
please ...?	favor?	fa·vor
repeat that	repetirlo	re·pe·teer·lo
speak more	hablar más	a·blar mas
slowly	despacio	des·pa·syo
write it down	escribirlo	es·kree·beer·lo

NUMBERS

1	uno	oo·no
2	dos	dos
3	tres	tres
4	cuatro	kwa·tro
5	cinco	seen·ko
6	seis	says
7	siete	sye·te
8	ocho	o·cho
9	nueve	nwe·ve
10	diez	dyes
11	once	on·se
12	doce	do·se
13	trece	tre·se
14	catorce	ka·tor·se
15	quince	keen·se
16	dieciséis	dye·see·says
17	diecisiete	dye·see·sye·te
18	dieciocho	dye·see·o·cho
19	diecinueve	dye·see·nwe·ve
20	veinte	vayn·te
21	veintiuno	vayn·tee·oo·no
22	veintidós	vayn·tee·dohs
30	treinta	trayn·ta
31	treinta y uno	trayn·ta ee oo·no
32	treinta y dos	trayn·ta ee dos
40	cuarenta	kwa·ren·ta
50	cincuenta	seen·kwen·ta
60	sesenta	se·sen·ta
70	setenta	se·ten·ta
80	ochenta	o·chen·ta
90	noventa	no·ven·ta
100	cien	syen
101	ciento uno	syen·to oo·no

200	doscientos	do·syen·tos
1000	mil	meel
5000	cinco mil	seen·ko meel

SHOPPING & SERVICES

I'd like to buy ...
Quisiera comprar ...   kee·sye·ra kom·prar ...
I'm just looking.
Sólo estoy mirando.   so·lo es·toy mee·ran·do
May I look at it?
¿Puedo mirar(lo/la)?   pwe·do mee·rar·(lo/la)
How much is it?
¿Cuánto cuesta?   kwan·to kwes·ta
That's too expensive for me.
Es demasiado caro   es de·ma·sya·do ka·ro
para mí.   pa·ra mee
Could you lower the price?
¿Podría bajar un poco   po·dree·a ba·khar oon po·ko
el precio?   el pre·syo
I don't like it.
No me gusta.   no me goos·ta
I'll take it.
Lo llevo.   lo ye·vo

I'm looking for the ...	Estoy buscando ...	es·toy boos·kan·do
ATM	el cajero automático	el ka·khe·ro ow·to·ma·tee·ko
bank	el banco	el ban·ko
bookstore	la librería	la lee·bre·ree·a
chemist/ pharmacy	la farmacia	la far·ma·sya
embassy	la embajada	la em·ba·kha·da
laundry	la lavandería	la la·van·de·ree·a
market	el mercado	el mer·ka·do
post office	los correos	los ko·re·os
supermarket	el supermercado	el soo·per·mer·ka·do
tourist office	la oficina de turismo	la o·fee·see·na de too·rees·mo

Do you accept ...?	¿Aceptan ...?	a·sep·tan ...
credit cards	tarjetas de crédito	tar·khe·tas de kre·dee·to
travellers cheques	cheques de viajero	che·kes de vya·khe·ro

less	menos	me·nos
more	más	mas
large	grande	gran·de
small	pequeño/a	pe·ke·nyo/a

What time does it open/close?
¿A qué hora abre/cierra?   a ke o·ra a·bre/sye·ra

I want to change some money/travellers cheques.
Quiero cambiar dinero/   kye·ro kam·byar dee·ne·ro/
cheques de viajero.   che·kes de vya·khe·ro
What is the exchange rate?
¿Cuál es el tipo de   kwal es el tee·po de
cambio?   kam·byo
I want to call ...
Quiero llamar a ...   kye·ro lya·mar a ...

airmail	correo aéreo	ko·re·o a·e·re·o
letter	carta	kar·ta
registered mail	correo certificado	ko·re·o ser·tee·fee·ka·do
stamps	sellos	se·lyos

TIME & DATES

What time is it?	¿Qué hora es?	ke o·ra es
It's one o'clock.	Es la una.	es la oo·na
It's two o'clock.	Son las dos.	son las dos
midnight	medianoche	me·dya·no·che
noon	mediodía	me·dyo·dee·a
half past two	dos y media	dos ee me·dya
now	ahora	a·o·ra
today	hoy	oy
tonight	esta noche	es·ta no·che
tomorrow	mañana	ma·nya·na

Monday	lunes	loo·nes
Tuesday	martes	mar·tes
Wednesday	miércoles	myer·ko·les
Thursday	jueves	khwe·ves
Friday	viernes	vyer·nes
Saturday	sábado	sa·ba·do
Sunday	domingo	do·meen·go

January	enero	e·ne·ro
February	febrero	fe·bre·ro
March	marzo	mar·so
April	abril	a·breel
May	mayo	ma·yo
June	junio	khoo·nyo
July	julio	khoo·lyo
August	agosto	a·gos·to
September	septiembre	sep·tyem·bre
October	octubre	ok·too·bre
November	noviembre	no·vyem·bre
December	diciembre	dee·syem·bre

TRANSPORT
Public Transport

What time does ... leave/arrive?	¿A qué hora sale/llega ...?	a ke o·ra sa·le/ye·ga ...?
the bus	el autobus	el ow·to·boos
the plane	el avión	el a·vyon
the ship	el barco	el bar·ko
the train	el tren	el tren

the bus station	la estación de autobuses	la es·ta·*syon* de ow·to·*boo*·ses
the bus stop	la parada de autobuses	la pa·*ra*·da de ow·to·*boo*·ses
the left luggage room	la consigna	la kon·*seeg*·na
the pier/jetty	el embarcdero	el em·bar·ka·*de*·ro
taxi	taxi	tak·see
the ticket office	la taquilla	la ta·*kee*·lya
the train station	la estación de tren	la es·ta·*syon* de tren

The ... is delayed.
El ... está retrasado.   el ... es·*ta* re·tra·*sa*·do
I'd like a ticket to ...
Quiero un billete a ...   kye·ro oon bee·*lye*·te a ...
Is this taxi free?
¿Está libre este taxi?   e·sta·*lee*·bre *es*·te *tak*·see
What's the fare to ...?
¿Cuánto cuesta hasta ...?   kwan·to *kwes*·ta *a*·sta ...
Please put the meter on.
Por favor, ponga el taxímetro.   por fa·*vor* pon·ga el tak·*see*·me·tro

a ... ticket	un billete de ...	oon bee·*lye*·te de ...
one-way	ida	ee·da
return	ida y vuelta	ee·da ee vwel·ta
1st class	primera clase	pree·*me*·ra *kla*·se
2nd class	segunda clase	se·*goon*·da *kla*·se
student	estudiante	es·too·*dyan*·te

Private Transport

I'd like to hire a/an ...	Quisiera alquilar ...	kee·*sye*·ra al·kee·*lar* ...
4WD	un todoterreno	oon to·do·te·*re*·no
car	un coche	oon un *ko*·che
motorbike	una moto	*oo*·na mo·to
bicycle	una bicicleta	*oo*·na bee·see·*kle*·ta

Is this the road to ...?
¿Se va a ... por esta carretera?   se va a ... por es·ta ka·re·te·ra
Where's a petrol station?
¿Dónde hay una gasolinera?   *don*·de ai oo·na ga·so·lee·*ne*·ra
Please fill it up.
Lleno, por favor.   ye·no por fa·*vor*
I'd like (20) litres.
Quiero (veinte) litros.   kye·ro (vayn·te) *lee*·tros
diesel
diesel   *dee*·sel
petrol/gas
gasolina   ga·so·*lee*·na

(How long) Can I park here?
¿(Por cuánto tiempo) Puedo aparcar aquí?   (por *kwan*·to *tyem*·po) pwe·do a·par·*kar* a·*kee*
Where do I pay?
¿Dónde se paga?   *don*·de se *pa*·ga
I need a mechanic.
Necesito un mecánico.   ne·se·*see*·to oon me·*ka*·nee·ko
The car has broken down (in ...).
El coche se ha averiado (en ...).   el *ko*·che se a a·ve·*rya*·do (en ...)
The motorbike won't start.
No arranca la moto.   no a·*ran*·ka la *mo*·to
I have a flat tyre.
Tengo un pinchazo.   ten·go oon peen·*cha*·so
I've run out of petrol.
Me he quedado sin gasolina.   me e ke·*da*·do seen ga·so·*lee*·na
I've had an accident.
He tenido un accidente.   e te·*nee*·do oon ak·see·*den*·te

TRAVEL WITH CHILDREN

Do you have ...?
¿Hay ...?   ai ...
  a car baby seat
  un asiento de seguridad para bebés   oon a·*syen*·to de se·goo·ree·*da* pa·ra be·*bes*
  a child-minding service
  un servicio de cuidado de niños   oon ser·*vee*·syo de kwee·*da*·do de *nee*·nyos
  a children's menu
  un menú infantil   oon me·*noo* een·fan·*teel*
  (disposable) diapers/nappies
  pañales (de usar y tirar)   pa·*nya*·les (de oo·*sar* ee tee·*rar*)
  an (English-speaking) babysitter
  un canguro (de habla inglesa)   oon kan·*goo*·ro (de *a*·bla een·*gle*·sa)
  infant formula (milk powder)
  leche en polvo   le·che en *pol*·vo
  a highchair
  una trona   oo·na *tro*·na

CATALAN

Good morning.	*Bon dia.*
Good afternoon.	*Bona tarda.*
Good evening/ night.	*Bona nit.*
Goodbye.	*Adéu.*
Bye/See you soon.	*Fins aviat.*
Please.	*Sisplau, per favor.*
Thank you.	*Gracies.*
You're welcome.	*De res.*
Pardon me.	*Perdó.*
I'm sorry.	*Ho sento.*
What's your name?	*Com et dius?* (inf)
My name is ...	*Em dic ... ...*
It's a pleasure to meet you.	*Molt de plaer.*
Where are you from?	*D'on ets?* (inf)
I'm from ...	*Soc de ...*
I'd like a ...	*Voldria ...*
I don't like it.	*No m'agrada.*
It's fine. I'll take it.	*Está bé. L'agafo.*
I'm leaving now.	*M'en vaig ara.*
How do I get to ...?	*¿Com puc arribar a ...?*
Is it far?	*¿Está lluny?*
I'm sick.	*Estic malalt/a.*

Do you speak (English)?	*Parla/Parlas (anglès)?* (pol/inf)
I (don't) understand.	*Jo (no) entenc.*
How do you say ...?	*Com es diu ...?*
What does ... mean?	*Qué vol dir ...?*

Monday	*dilluns*
Tuesday	*dimarts*
Wednesday	*dimecres*
Thursday	*dijous*
Friday	*divendres*
Saturday	*dissabte*
Sunday	*diumenge*

Signs

Entrada	Entrance
Sortida	Exit
Obert	Open
Tancat	Closed
Informació	Information
Prohibit	Prohibited
Serveis	Toilets
Senyors/Homes	Men
Senyoras/Dones	Women

Also available from Lonely Planet:
Spanish Phrasebook and *Fast Talk Spanish*

Glossary

Most of the following terms are in Castilian Spanish, which is fully understood around the island. A handful of specialised terms in Catalan (C) also appear. No distinction has been made for any Mallorcan dialect variations.

agroturisme (C) – rural tourism
ajuntament (C) – city or town hall
alquería – Muslim-era farmstead
avenida – avenue
avinguda (C) – see *avenida*

baño completo – full bathroom with toilet, shower and/or bath
bodega – cellar (especially wine cellar)
bomberos – fire brigade

cala – cove
call (C) – Jewish quarter in Palma, Inca and some other Mallorcan towns
cambio – change; also currency exchange
caña – small glass of beer
canguro – babysitter
capilla – chapel
carrer (C) – street
carretera – highway
carta – menu
casa rural – village or country house or farmstead with rooms to let
castell (C) – castle
castellano – Castilian; used in preference to '*Español*' to describe the national language
català – Catalan language; a native of Catalonia. The Mallorcan dialect is Mallorquin
celler – (C) wine cellars turned into restaurants
cervecería – beer bar
comisaría – police station
conquistador – conqueror
converso – Jew who converted to Christianity in medieval Spain
correos – post office
cortado – short black coffee with a little milk
costa – coast
cuenta – bill, cheque

ducha – shower

ensaïmada (C) – Mallorcan pastry
entrada – entrance, ticket

ermita – small hermitage or country chapel
església (C) – see *iglesia*
estació (C) – see *estación*
estación – station
estanco – tobacconist shop

farmacia – pharmacy
faro – lighthouse
fiesta – festival, public holiday or party
finca (C) – farmhouse accommodation
flamenco – flamingo or Flemish; also means flamenco music and dance

gasolina – petrol
guardia civil – military police

habitaciones libres – literally 'rooms available'
hostal (C) – see *pensión*

iglesia – church
IVA – 'impuesto sobre el valor añadido', or value-added tax

lavabo – washbasin
librería – bookshop
lista de correos – poste restante
locutorio – telephone centre

marisquería – seafood eatery
menú del día (C) – menu of the day
mercat (C) – market
mirador – lookout point
Modernisme – the Catalan version of the Art Nouveau architectural and artistic style
mojito – popular Cuban rum-based mixed drink
monestir (C) – monastery
museo – museum
museu (C) – see *museo*

objetos perdidos – lost-and-found
oficina de turismo – tourist office; also 'oficina de información turística'

Páginas Amarillas – the Yellow Pages
palacio – palace, grand mansion or noble house
palau (C) – see *palacio*
pensión – small family-run hotel
plaça (C) – see *plaza*
platja (C) – see *playa*
playa – beach
plaza – square

port (C) – see *puerto*
possessió (C) – typical Mallorcan farmhouse
PP – Partido Popular (People's Party)
preservativo – condom
puente – bridge
puerto – port
puig (C) – mountain peak

rambla – avenue or riverbed
refugis (C) – hikers' huts
retablo – altarpiece
retaule (C) – see *retablo*

santuari (C) – shrine or sanctuary, hermitage
según precio del mercado – on menus, 'according to market price' (often written 'spm')

Semana Santa – Holy Week
serra (C) – mountain range
servicios – toilets
s/n – sin número (without number), in addresses

tafona (C) – traditional oil press found on most Mallorcan farms
talayot (C) – ancient watchtower
tarjeta de crédito – credit card
tarjeta de residencia – residence card
tarjeta telefónica – phonecard
terraza – terrace; pavement café
torre – tower
turismo – tourism and saloon car

urgencia – emergency

The Authors

DAMIEN SIMONIS

Coordinating Author, Palma & the
Badia de Palma, Western Mallorca,
The Interior, Northern Mallorca

Damien has been travelling to the Balearic Islands regularly since the mid-1990s. Undeterred by images of mass tourism (red-roasted holiday-makers sipping beer from giant tumblers from 11am and high-rise horrors), he discovered quickly that Mallorca was an extraordinarily beautiful micro-world. Few places offer so much in so little space: glittering seas and hidden coves, high cliffs and rugged mountains, urban sophistication and pretty villages, hearty food and fine wine. It's a combination that keeps luring him across the water from Barcelona. Apart from this guide, Damien has written LP's *Barcelona, Barcelona Encounter, Madrid, Canary Islands* and *Catalunya & the Costa Brava*. He also wrote much of their original *Spain* guide, which he continues to coordinate.

SARAH ANDREWS

Eastern Mallorca, Southern Mallorca

Slow country drives, seaside hikes, fresh seafood and off-the-beaten-track cove beaches just happen to be a few of Sarah's favourite things, so she felt right at home exploring eastern and southern Mallorca for this guide. She also wrote the Environment, Activities and Food & Drink chapters, and she contributed to the Palma & the Badia de Palma chapter.

Though she hails from North Carolina, Sarah has lived in Barcelona, Spain since 2000. From her office near the Mediterranean, she writes articles and the occasional guidebook about her adopted country and, in her spare time, debates the subtle differences between Catalan and Mallorquín.

CONTRIBUTING AUTHOR

Sally Schafer wrote the cycle tours in the Palma & the Badia de Palma and Northern Mallorca chapters. She was once the Commissioning Editor for Spain and Portugal titles in LP's London office. A cycle-commuter at home, Sally's time in Mallorca was an overdue insight into a wonderful two-wheeled world. She returned home intent on buying some padded cycling shorts.

Behind the Scenes

THIS BOOK

This first edition of *Mallorca* was researched and written by Damien Simonis and Sarah Andrews, with Sally Schafer contributing the cycling tours in the Northern Mallorca and Palma & the Bay of Palma chapters. Damien coordinated the book, which was commissioned out of Lonely Planet's London office and produced by the following:

Commissioning Editor Sally Schafer & Korina Miller
Coordinating Editor Kirsten Rawlings
Coordinating Cartographer Joanne Luke
Coordinating Layout Designer Jacqueline McLeod
Managing Editor Melanie Dankel
Managing Cartographer Adrian Persoglia
Managing Layout Designer Adam McCrow
Assisting Editors Lauren Hunt, Kim Hutchins, Ali Lemer, Erin Richards
Assisting Cartographers Barb Benson, Tadhgh Knaggs
Cover Designer Jane Hart
Project Manager Rachel Imeson
Language Content Coordinator Quentin Frayne
Talk2Us Coordinator Trent Paton

Thanks to Liz Abbott, Dave Burnett, Sin Choo, James Hardy, Laura Jane, Lisa Knights, John Mazzocchi, Cameron Neales, Naomi Parker, Malisa Plesa, Wibowo Rusli, Laura Stansfeld, Celia Wood

THANKS
DAMIEN SIMONIS

Thanks above all to Roberto Fortea and Verónica García. With Carlos García, Felipe Amorós and assorted friends, they opened doors, shared drinks and talked about their island. Miquel Àngel Part had key clues on bars. Antonio Bauzá and Alessandra Natale, Verónica Carretero, Bartomeu (Tolo) Alcover and Nati Barbosa all provided company and tips. Javier Terrasa of Arca, Andreu Villalonga and James Hiscock were generous with their time. *Moltes gràcies a tothom*!

Hillary Barrows and chopper champ Jill Downey were fine flatmates and my brother Desmond patient company in some trying moments.

Thanks to Anna Skidmore of Foment del Turisme, co-author Sarah Andrews and London chiefs Sally Schafer and Korina Miller. Also to the friendly Escape bar crew.

Finally, this is for Janique, who shared some privileged Mallorca moments.

SARAH ANDREWS

Mallorquins are a proud bunch and, much to my good fortune, are more than happy to talk about their island. Countless people shared their love and knowledge of all things Mallorcan and helped me along the way with ideas, suggestions and in-

---

THE LONELY PLANET STORY

Fresh from an epic journey across Europe, Asia and Australia in 1972, Tony and Maureen Wheeler sat at their kitchen table stapling together notes. The first Lonely Planet guidebook, Across Asia on the Cheap, was born.

Travellers snapped up the guides. Inspired by their success, the Wheelers began publishing books to Southeast Asia, India and beyond. Demand was prodigious, and the Wheelers expanded the business rapidly to keep up. Over the years, Lonely Planet extended its coverage to every country and into the virtual world via lonelyplanet.com and the Thorn Tree message board.

As Lonely Planet became a globally loved brand, Tony and Maureen received several offers for the company. But it wasn't until 2007 that they found a partner whom they trusted to remain true to the company's principles of travelling widely, treading lightly and giving sustainably. In October of that year, BBC Worldwide acquired a 75% share in the company, pledging to uphold Lonely Planet's commitment to independent travel, trustworthy advice and editorial independence.

Today, Lonely Planet has offices in Melbourne, London and Oakland, with over 500 staff members and 300 authors. Tony and Maureen are still actively involved with Lonely Planet. They're travelling more often than ever, and they're devoting their spare time to charitable projects. And the company is still driven by the philosophy of Across Asia on the Cheap: 'All you've got to do is decide to go and the hardest part is over. So go!'

terviews. I hope I'm not leaving anyone out when I thank Paco Mateu, Nicole Fraysse, Lluc Pujol Capó, Marc Vila, Pep Lluís Gradaille Tortella, Bartolomeu Frau i Oliver, Catalina Masuti, Jose Antonio Encinas, Amparo Vilar, Jaime Ferriol, Joan Caldés, Rich Strutt, and Anna Skidmore. Also, a huge thanks to Sally Schafer, Korina Miller, my co-author Damien and the whole LP gang. And finally, as always, *un gran abrazo* for the one who keeps me sane on and off the road, my husband, Miquel.

SALLY SCHAFER

Thanks to co-authors Damien and Sarah, to Korina and Cliff for their help, and to Chris, without whom I would never have tried the 'technical' single-track. Also thanks to Anna Skidmore from Foment del Turisme (Mallorca Tourism Board)

OUR READERS

Many thanks to the travelers who used the last edition and wrote to us with helpful hints, useful advice and interesting anecdotes:

A Palmer Acheson, Salvatore Acocella, Janet Adams, Lisa Adams, Shlomi Agmon, Andrea Amatori, Cesar Amin, Ruth Anderson, Richard & Rachel Antell, Janice Au **B** Linda Bak, Chrys Baldwin, Stefania Baraldini, Sean Barbour, Hayley Bennett, Niek Bergboer, Emily Berquist, Kristan Bills, Liz Bissett, Fredrika Björk, John Black, Rebecca Blakeway-Long, Sophia Blijdenstein, Viktor Blomqvist, William Blyth, Gina Bolotinsky, Tirza Bont, Ansgar Borbe, Carl Borda, Gerhard Bort, Tom Bottomley, Wendy Breen, Sara Brewer, Lincoln Brody, Helen Brotherton, Chris Brown, Ian Brown, Margo Buckles, Marjon Buis, Paul Butler, Victoria Buyukbalik **C** Michele Campbell, Ernesto Manuel Cantone, Daniela Carbone, Bonnie Carpenter, Elle Carrington, Ron Cassar, Elfreda Castonguay, Vivienne Cavagnoli, Celine Cayol, David Cervenjak, Dan Chavez, Ciprian Chelba, Susan Chisholm, Calvin Chu, Ans Compaijen, Shirley Connuck, Rachel Cotter, Tony Cotterill, Nathalie Coulembier, Laura Cucchi De Alessandri, Andrew Curran **D** Mike Dean, Ewoud Dekker, J Demolina, Steffen Deus, Chelsey Dipasquale-Hunton, Omar Do Nascimento, Baile Doite, Paul Dolinsky **E** Lauren Edwards, Paul Erskine, Carmen Espinosa **F** Ann Farris, Paul Fayle, Eva Fearn, Manuel Fernández, Deryn Fletcher, Niki Florin, Martina Forstner, James Franklyn, Catarina Frazão, Kathy Fredriksson, Rachel Freeman, Russ Fretwell, Heidi Frith, Mechthild Fuchs, Sean Fuller **G** Eric Gagnon, Peter Galloway, Antonio Garcia, Ronan Gawronski, Diana Gelhausen, Kate Gerry, Giovanna Giannelli, Anne Gibbins, Lady Gilwen, John Goldrick, Víctor Hugo Gonzalez Rodriguez, Malby Goodman, Beth Gorman, Richard Gould, Michael Grande, D E Gray, Anna Greve, Lawrence Gundabuka, Susil Gupta **H** Bella H, Barry Hall, Hanna Hallsten, Bree Hancock, Barbara Hauck, Sonja Hauser, Joanne Hedge, Kate Henderson, Per Høegh Henriksen, Ian Hodkinson, Mariette Hoeberichts, Rick Hogan, Anja Hoh, Tina Hostettler, Michiel Humblet, Marco Hurmall, Eileen Hutchinson **I** Blanche Iberg, Fabio Iori, Nicole Irsara, Kathleen Irvine **J** Danielle Jackson, L Jackson, Caroline Johansson, Wayne Johnson, James Johnston, Brian Jones, Janne Jorgensen, Julie Joyce **K** Dimitris Kaliakoudas, Zvi Kam, Kosta Karapas, Lorna Keeler, Jennifer Kelly, Gail Kepler, Roni & Ayala Klaus, Jessie Knapp, Beth Kohn, Maartje Koopman, Lauren Kurlander, Jill Kurman **L** Yesul Lee, Kevin Lahey, Andrea Lange, Jan Lauran, Eugene Lee, Xabier Legarreta, Erik Lehtinen, Johanne Leroux, Pat Lightfoot, Karine Ligneau, Lily Loring, Robert Loughnan **M** Julian MacLaren, Catharina Magnusson, Carolyn Maile, Maurice Margaix, Manuel Marino, Stefano Martorana, Wilma Masters, Ann Matthews, Simon Matthews, Kristine McCaffrey, Luke McCarthy, Meridyth McIntosh, John McLeod, Cheryl-Lynn McKinnon, John Mead, Duncan Melville, Gerald Meral, Sarah Miller, Stephanie Milner, Henrik Mitsch, Dr Fabian Mohr, Laura Moreno, Christian Most, Jane Mundy **N** Serhat Narsap, Randy Navo, David Negev, James Nicholson, Martin Nowacki, Marie Nyblom **O** Jenny O'Brien, Peter & Thérèse O'Neill, Maria & Fernando Ogayar, Ronald Ortman **P** M P, Vicky Page, Lucas Palmer, Anne-Marie Pambrun, Bala Pandion, Mirella Parsonage, Lisa Pash, Muriel Pasini, Ron Pasquini, Yaron Pedhazur, Steve Perkins, Alex Perry, Andrea Peskova, Steve Peters, Jan Pettersson, Joey Peverelli, Lukas Cheah Phin, Stefan Pichel, Chris Pitto, Bonn Poland, Jeremy Pollack, Beth Potter, Carolyn Pugsley **R** Sean Rahui, Frederieke Rasenberg, Kelly Rendek, Sharon Richards, Matthew Rideout, Anton Rijsdijk, James Riser, Julie Roberts, Gian Marco Roccia, Christophe Rosseel, Angelo Rossini, Marco Roth, Dakota Rubin, Jay Ruchamkin, Jon Rud **S** Jorge S, Carolina Salenius, Luis Samaniego, Michi Sanches, Andrea Santini, Mikael Schilling, Volker Schmidt-Wellenburg, Elke Schramm,

Patrick Schwizer, Patrick Sclater, Brian Scott, Jeanne Scown, Randy Selig, Linda Sevä, Joyce Sharman, Genevieve Shaw, Katie Jo Slaughter, Caroline Spiers, Clare Staines, Charlie Steel, Deborah Stein, Ivan Stockley, Andrea Strane, Laura Street, Marta Sueiras, Kirsi Suomi, Mait Svanstrom, Julia Swanson, Judy Szende **T** Kirk Talbott, David Taylor, Ilmar Tehnas, Bertil Teutelink, Martin Thom, Christopher Thompson, Stephanie Thorne, Stephen Tomlinson, Lynn Treanor, Peter Tyler **U** Reg Urquhart **V** Jeff Vaneerdewegh, Willem Van Lammeren, Mike Verbeeck, Benedicte Viola, Hans Visser, Frits Visser, Ebba Von Krogh, Michel Vranken, Sini Väisänen **W** Jessica & Henry Wadsworth, Nathan Walker, Rosemary Wallace, Dave Wallace, Anna Ward, Alan Waterman, Penelope Webb, Joshua Weiland, Gerald F Weingarth, Amy Welch, Kenny Wheeler, Scott Whitsett, Geraldine Whyte, Glen Wilchek, Ed Wilde, Pauline Wilkinson, Nick Williams, Jennifer Wilson, Rob & Ali Wilton, Helga Winster, Jerry Wirngarth, Jason Wojcechowskyj, Judy Wood, Andrew Wraight, Michael Wright **Y** Andrew Yale, Jenny Yeo, Jabi Zabala, Yadira Zayas **Z** Serena Zimmermann, Anke Zylmann

ACKNOWLEDGMENTS

Many thanks to the following for the use of their content:

Globe on title page ©Mountain High Maps 1993 Digital Wisdom, Inc.

Internal photographs p11 (#1) AA World Travel Library / Alamy; p12 (#1) Bartomeu Amengual / Alamy; p6 (#5), p11 #4 imagebroker / Alamy; p9 (#3), p8 (#5) LOOK Die Bildagentur der Fotografen GmbH / Alamy; p10 (#2) Rough Guides / Alamy; p7 (#2) Hans Strand / Corbis; p9 (#2) islandphoto.com; p11 (#2) Photolibrary; p10 (#3) SIME / Schmid Reinhard. All other photographs by Lonely Planet Images, and by Jon Davison p5.

All images are the copyright of the photographers unless otherwise indicated. Many of the images in this guide are available for licensing from Lonely Planet Images: www.lonelyplanetimages.com.

BEHIND THE SCENES

Index

INDEX

GreenDex

GOING GREEN

It's not surprising that in Mallorca, a small island with an ever-expanding tourism infrastructure, sustainability is on many people's minds. While not many places bill themselves as 'green', there are still plenty of options for supporting sustainability. The following restaurants, sights, accommodation, tours and shops have been selected by Lonely Planet authors as standing out for being 'green'. Some use only local produce, sell locally made goods or serve organic meals. Others provide sustainable options like cycling or eco-friendly accommodation. Though not officially accredited, we believe they demonstrate a commitment to sustainable tourism.

For more tips about travelling sustainably in Mallorca, turn to p16. You can also help us continue to develop our sustainable-travel content; if you think we've omitted someone who should be listed here or disagree with our choices, contact us at www.lonelyplanet.com/contact and set us straight for next time. For more information about sustainable tourism and Lonely Planet, see www.lonelyplanet.com/responsibletravel.

| 12am | 1am | 2am | 3am | 4am | 5am | 6am | 7am | 8am | 9am | 10am | 11am | 12pm |

ARCTIC OCEAN

International Date Line

Mon / Sun

CHUKCHI SEA

Queen Elizabeth Is *(Can)*

Ellesmere Is *(Can)*

BEAUFORT SEA

Banks Is *(Can)*

Victoria Is *(Can)*

BAFFIN BAY

9am Greenland *(Denmark)*

11am

GREENLAND SEA

NORWEGIAN SEA

Russia

Alaska *(US)*

3am

4am

5am

Baffin Is *(Can)*

Iceland

NORTH SEA

BERING SEA

GULF OF ALASKA

2am

HUDSON BAY

Canada

6am

LABRADOR SEA

8am

8.30am

United Kingdom

Ireland

NORTH ATLANTIC OCEAN

1am Midway Is *(US)*

NORTH PACIFIC OCEAN

United States

Bermuda *(UK)*

Azores *(Port)*

Portugal

Spain

Hawaii *(US)*

Mexico

GULF OF MEXICO

The Bahamas

Cuba

Haiti

Eastern Caribbean Islands

CARIBBEAN SEA

Morocco

Canary Is *(Sp)*

Mauritania

Mali

Cape Verde

12pm

Senegal

Burkina Faso

Guinea

Liberia

Ghana

GULF OF GUINEA

Guatemala

Nicaragua

Panama

Venezuela

Guyana

Colombia

Suriname

Galapagos Is *(Ecuador)*

EQUATOR

Kiribati

Ecuador

8am

Ascension *(UK)*

Samoa

2.30am

Peru

7am

Brazil

9am

Tonga

12am

Cook Is *(NZ)*

Tahiti

French Polynesia *(Fr)*

2am

Bolivia

SOUTH ATLANTIC OCEAN

1am

Pitcairn Is *(UK)*

3.30am

Easter Is *(Chile)*

Paraguay

Uruguay

New Zealand

12.45am

Chatham Is *(NZ)*

SOUTH PACIFIC OCEAN

Chile

Argentina

Tristan da Cunha *(UK)*

Gough Is *(UK)*

Falkland Is *(UK)*

South Georgia & South Sandwich Is *(UK)*

Bouvet Is *(Norway)*

| 12am | 1am | 2am | 3am | 4am | 5am | 6am | 7am | 8am | 9am | 10am | 11am | 12pm |

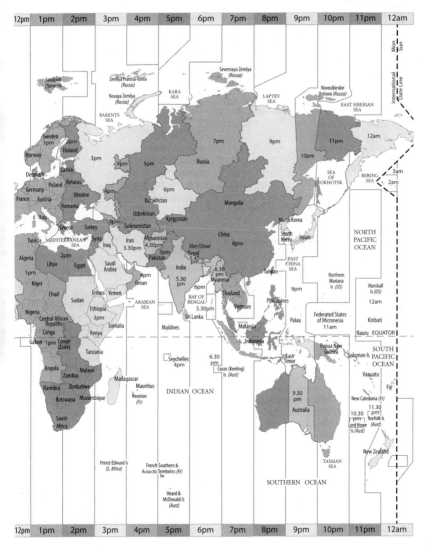

12pm | 1pm | 2pm | 3pm | 4pm | 5pm | 6pm | 7pm | 8pm | 9pm | 10pm | 11pm | 12am

Mon
Sun
International Date Line

Svalbard (Norway)

Zemlya Frantsa-Iosifa (Russia)

Novaya Zemlya (Russia)

KARA SEA

Severnaya Zemlya (Russia)

LAPTEV SEA

Novosibirskie Ostrovo (Russia)

EAST SIBERIAN SEA

BARENTS SEA

Sweden 1pm

Norway

Denmark

Germany

France

Austria

Italy

Finland 2pm

3pm

Latvia

Poland

Ukraine

Belarus

4pm

Romania

Greece

Turkey

Tunisia MEDITERRANEAN SEA

Algeria 2pm

Libya

Niger 1pm

Chad

Nigeria

Central African Republic

Congo

Gabon 1pm

Congo (Zaire)

Angola

Namibia

Botswana

South Africa

Zambia

Zimbabwe

Malawi

Mozambique

Madagascar

Mauritius

Reunion (Fr)

5pm

Kazakhstan

Uzbekistan

Turkmenistan

Kyrgyzstan

4pm

Syria

Iraq

Iran 3.30pm

Afghanistan 4.30pm

Pakistan 5pm

Nepal 5.45pm

India 5.30pm

Oman

Saudi Arabia

Egypt

Sudan

Eritrea Yemen

Ethiopia 3pm

Somalia

Kenya

Tanzania

ARABIAN SEA

Maldives

Seychelles 4pm

6.30pm Cocos (Keeling) Is (Aust)

INDIAN OCEAN

Russia 7pm

6pm

9pm

Mongolia

China 8pm

Tibet (China)

Myanmar 6.30pm

BAY OF BENGAL 5.30pm

Sri Lanka

Thailand

Vietnam

Malaysia

Indonesia

East Timor

10pm

11pm

12am

SEA OF OKHOTSK

BERING SEA 3am 2am

North Korea

South Korea

Japan

EAST CHINA SEA

Taiwan

Philippines

Palau

Papua New Guinea

NORTH PACIFIC OCEAN

Northern Mariana Is (US)

9pm

Federated States of Micronesia 11am

Solomon Is

Marshall Is (US)

12am

Kiribati

Nauru EQUATOR

SOUTH PACIFIC OCEAN

Vanuatu

New Caledonia (Fr)

Fiji

11.30 pm

10.30 pm Norfolk Is (Aust)

Lord Howe Is (Aust)

Australia 9.30 pm

New Zealand

TASMAN SEA

Prince Edward Is (S. Africa)

French Southern & Antarctic Territories (Fr)

Heard & McDonald Is (Aust)

SOUTHERN OCEAN

12pm | 1pm | 2pm | 3pm | 4pm | 5pm | 6pm | 7pm | 8pm | 9pm | 10pm | 11pm | 12am

MAP LEGEND
ROUTES

Freeway	Mall/Steps
Primary	Walking Tour
Secondary	Walking Tour Detour
Tertiary	Walking Trail
Lane	Track
One-Way Street	

TRANSPORT

Ferry	Tram
Rail	

HYDROGRAPHY

River, Creek	Water
Mangrove	

AREA FEATURES

Area of Interest	Land
Beach, Desert	Mall
Building	Market
Forest	Park

POPULATION

CAPITAL (STATE)	Small City
Large City	Town, Village
Medium City	

SYMBOLS

Sights/Activities
- Beach
- Castle, Fortress
- Christian
- Monument
- Museum, Gallery
- Point of Interest
- Ruin

Eating
- Eating

Drinking
- Drinking

Entertainment
- Entertainment

Shopping
- Shopping

Sleeping
- Sleeping

Transport
- Airport, Airfield
- Bus Station
- Parking Area
- Petrol Station
- Taxi Rank

Information
- Bank, ATM
- Embassy/Consulate
- Hospital, Medical
- Information
- Internet Facilities
- Police Station
- Post Office, GPO
- Telephone

Geographic
- Lighthouse
- Lookout
- Mountain, Volcano
- National Park

LONELY PLANET OFFICES

Australia
Head Office
Locked Bag 1, Footscray, Victoria 3011
☎ 03 8379 8000, fax 03 8379 8111
www.lonelyplanet.com/contact

USA
150 Linden St, Oakland, CA 94607
☎ 510 893 8555, toll free 800 275 8555
fax 510 893 8572
info@lonelyplanet.com

UK
2nd floor, 186 City Rd,
London ECV1 2NT
☎ 020 7106 2100, fax 020 7106 2101
go@lonelyplanet.co.uk

Published by Lonely Planet Publications Pty Ltd
ABN 36 005 607 983

© Lonely Planet Publications Pty Ltd 2008

© photographers as indicated 2008

Cover photograph: Artà village, Santuari de Sant Salvador/Fantuz Olimpio/SIME 4Corners Images. Many of the images in this guide are available for licensing from Lonely Planet Images: www.lonely planetimages.com.

Printed through Colorcraft Ltd, Hong Kong.
Printed in China.